IMPACTS OF
RACISM
ON WHITE
AMERICANS

IMPACTS OF
RACISM
ON WHITE
AMERICANS

Second Edition

Edited by
BENJAMIN P. BOWSER
RAYMOND G. HUNT

SAGE Publications
International Educational and Professional Publisher
Thousand Oaks   London   New Delhi

For information address:

SAGE Publications, Inc.
2455 Teller Road
Thousand Oaks, California 91320
E-mail: order@sagepub.com

SAGE Publications Ltd.
6 Bonhill Street
London EC2A 4PU
United Kingdom

SAGE Publications India Pvt. Ltd.
M-32 Market
Greater Kailash I
New Delhi 110 048 India

Printed in the United States of America

Library of Congress Cataloging-in-Publication Data

Main entry under title:
Impacts of racism on white Americans / Benjamin P. Bowser,
    Raymond G. Hunt, editors. — 2nd ed.
      p. cm.
    Includes bibliographical references and index.
    ISBN 0-8039-4993-6 (cloth). — ISBN 0-8039-4994-4 (pbk.)
    1. Racism—United States—Congresses. 2. Whites—United States—
    Attitudes—Congresses. 3. Afro-Americans—Civil rights—
    Congresses. 4. Race awareness—United States—Congresses.
    5. United States—Race relations—Congresses. I. Bowser, Benjamin
    P. II. Hunt, Raymond George, 1928-
    E184.A1I445 1996
    305.8'00973—dc20   95-41797

This book is printed on acid-free paper.

96 97 98 99 10 9 8 7 6 5 4 3 2 1

Sage Production Editor: Astrid Virding

*To the time when the myth of racial superiority
and inferiority no longer defines one to the other.*

Contents

Preface

At the start of the twentieth-century, Americans called racial issues "the colored problem." By mid-century, it had become "the Negro problem." More recently, it has been labeled "the black problem" or "the race problem." All are misnomers. Racial prejudice, discrimination and conflict are America's problem. From the nation's beginning, black-white relations have been the chief domestic problem of the United States. There have been Constitutional Amendments to address racial concerns; slave revolts and urban riots punctuate our racial history; and we even fought a bloody civil war over race.

Yet the terms "colored problem," "Negro problem" and "black problem" are revealing. Their clear implication is that the issue resides solely with African Americans, as if it were they who caused it and only they who endured the pain of the nation's racist heritage. To be sure, the heaviest burden of racial prejudice and discrimination has been bourn by black citizens. But they alone are not racism's only victims. Seldom recognized in popular thinking, even largely ignored by social science research, the cost of racism for white Americans is significant. That is the singular theme of this volume.

This second edition of *Impacts of Racism on White Americans*, then, addresses a critical and all-too-often ignored issue. Building on the earlier edition, it faces the issue head-on at all three levels of analysis—the individual, situational and institutional.

At the micro-level of individuals, several chapters discuss the effects of racism on whites personally. Using diverse, though complementary approaches, these chapters agree on several points that deserve initial emphasis here. First, racism is not immutable. It is not necessary baggage of the human condition. Some white Americans do not suffer from the malady; and others can relieve themselves of the burden under optimal conditions.

Second, racism does not exist in a personal vacuum. Observers often describe individual racism as if it operated in isolation from the rest of a person's personality. This view, we shall learn from these pages, is invalid. White racial attitudes are not one dimensional, nor are they completely separate from other attitudes and values. Often these other features of our personalities conflict with racism. Herein lies more potential for personal change in this domain that many assume.

Third, racism does not exist in a social vacuum. As this volume amply demonstrates, racism is caught from an infected society. It is taught, supported and advanced by many aspects of our society and culture. This obvious point has a not-so-obvious implication for white Americans.

Since the 1960s, people are understandably defensive about being tagged "racists." Even national politicians who blatantly play "the race card" feel the need to insist that they are not racist. Self-deceiving as this defense may be, it represents a strong, initial barrier to personal change. However, when we view racism in its social context, this defense can be allayed. Once seen as the social air we breathe, individual racism need not be regarded as a character defect about which we must be guilty and defensive. Guilt is not a helpful tool for change in this emotionally-charged domain.

In speaking of the social context of racism, however, we need to make one important qualification. The authors of this book direct their attention solely to the subject of American racism. This does not imply that racism is an American monopoly. It is, unfortunately, a worldwide phenomenon, though each area has its own distinctive style. As these pages describe, the American form shares with other nations particular aspects of English racism. Yet our unique national history of slavery and racial segregation also strongly shapes it.

At the meso-situational level of face-to-face contact, there is also an impact of racism upon whites. Since most white Americans have had either no or minimal social contact with black Americans, interracial social interaction is generally awkward at best. One immediate result of this lack of interracial contact is an ever-widening divergence of views between black and white Americans. Only occasionally, as with the differential reactions to the sensational O.J. Simpson murder trial, does this sharp divergence receive mass media attention.

Think also of these situational effects in national terms. One large part of the American population is uncomfortable with and unskilled at interacting with another large part of the population. These pages spell out the implications of this strained situation, especially for the work place.

Several chapters focus on the macro-level effects of racism on institutions and the society. And their conclusions may be the most surprising to readers. Quite apart from egalitarian values, many whites suffer from racism in self-interested economic terms. One recurrent point is that racism acts to obscure social class issues in American thought and action. This myopia is precisely the opposite of that suffered by Latin America. There class issues mask racism. This international contrast underscores the fact that both class and race issues are important. One does not reduce to the other. And, as these chapters illustrate, the combination of race and class is a complex interaction that involves much more than the simple addition of their separate effects.

Let me assure readers new to this type of macro-analysis that such contentions about the economic functions of racism do not require any form of a conspiracy theory. That is, the founding fathers need not have foreseen how their acceptance of slavery would serve to obscure class issues in the future. Nor must today's global business executives fully understand how domestic racism aids their efforts to restrain labor costs and transfer manufacturing overseas for cheaper labor. The point is that racism serves these functions, whether planned or not, and thereby is structurally reinforced.

Conspiracy theories typically oversimplify social life and fail to understand its complexity. Worse, such theories assume an unrealistic ability of human beings to foresee the future, to plan particular outcomes in complex social settings. Hence, conspiracy theories give the presumed plotters far too much credit. So social scientists give them little credence. And the macro-level contentions of this volume do not require them.

One last preliminary question deserves attention. While it considers people of color generally at appropriate points, this book centers on African Americans. A reader might well ask, then, why does this volume focus so heavily on this one group? The answer lies in the uniqueness of the black position in the United States.

The legacy of two centuries of slavery and another century of enforced segregation, joined with racist ideology, makes black-white relations the most difficult intergroup issue of all. This is not to imply that other groups, including white ethnicities, have not suffered from prejudice and discrimination in American history. But it is to say the African American situation is not only quantitatively but often qualitatively different from that of others. Blacks in the United States have experienced a special type of marginality. And anti-black discrimination alone reflects the confluence of race, slavery, and segregation.

Black American marginality uniquely combines a long history of being simultaneously an integral part and on the outside of the society. They are neither immigrants nor aliens. They perceive themselves and are perceived, even by white racists as "belonging" to American society. Recent comparisons of the white ethnic experience with this singular situation miss the point. European immigrants and blacks faced opposite problems. The new Europeans were seen as not "American" enough; the dominant pressure on them was to give up their strange and threatening ways and to assimilate. Blacks have been Americans of a lower caste; the dominant pressure on them was to "stay in their place" and not to attempt assimilation into the privileged caste.

This uniqueness is best reflected today in two social patterns—racial residential segregation and black-white intermarriage rates. African Americans are the most residentially segregated group by far in the urban United States. And such massive housing segregation makes discrimination in other areas—politics, education, jobs, and public services—easier and more likely. Moreover, black-white intermarriage rates are by far the lowest of any two major groups in the nation. Indeed, international surveys show Americans disapprove of black-white marriages far more than any other sampled country. Note, too, that this disapproval does not cover all interracial marriage; Asian-white marriage rates are far higher and rapidly increasing.

Black-white relations, then, are the shoal upon which American democracy has long floundered. All Americans feel its effects, though this has been far from apparent for many white Americans. Hopefully, this second edition of *Impacts of Racism on White Americans* will help redress this vital point.

—Thomas F. Pettigrew
Research Professor of Social Psychology
University of California, Santa Cruz

Introduction to the Second Edition

BENJAMIN P. BOWSER
RAYMOND G. HUNT

In the Introduction to the first edition of *Impacts of Racism on White Americans* (Bowser & Hunt, 1981), we wrote that racism was an expression of "institutionalized patterns of white power and social control" that were rooted in the "very structures of society." We also argued that racism in the United States is a "white problem" because "racist attitudes, behavior, and social structures have direct and indirect impacts on whites." People of color, of course, are involved and play important roles other than "hapless victim" in racist systems; but the principal burden of permanent change in the foundations of racism in the United States necessarily rests on European Americans and not only because they are the majority population, but also, and more importantly, because they hold the power necessary for change.

It is not people of color who operate or control the major institutions of American life: not governments, not corporations, not financial markets, not the media. Nor does what people of color think or feel become "public opinion." Their views do not shape the actions of the major institutions, nor can people of color create and maintain stereotypes about themselves as either model or deficient minorities.

The struggles of racially distinct peoples in the United States have been primarily for physical and cultural survival: to protest and to insist on fairness and relief from stigma and discriminatory treatment. This is a reactive role: Even in the rare moments when protest and militancy win concessions, the power actually to make desired changes lies not among people of color but elsewhere. As a necessity, their cries for change must be supported by some combination of a predominantly white Congress, white Supreme Court justices, the white media, white labor, a white business community, and white public opinion. Change must begin with those who control and have the power to affect this nation's institutions and belief systems, that is, with white Americans. Nowhere else does the leverage exist for long-term and enlightened social progress.

Consider this: What if by some miracle most individuals in the particularly problematic American racial groups—African, Puerto Rican, and Native Americans—woke up one morning and found themselves possessed of strong Protestant work ethics, intact families, high IQs, an abhorrence for illegal drug use and sales, clean neighborhoods, and speaking standard English? What are the chances of any of them being able to step right into the American dream without an equally miraculous transformation in the views, attitudes, behavioral dispositions, and institutional practices of powerful or influential sectors of white America?

Without white sponsorship, assistance, or patronage would ghetto schools suddenly offer quality educations; would people of color, solely on their qualifications, suddenly get jobs that previously went to Whites in fire departments, in high-paying unions and trades, and in the suburbs? Without change or assistance from Whites, would fear of black youth disappear; would banks, insurance companies, businesses locating plants, factories, and offices, food stores, home builders, illegal drug distributors, and police no longer either avoid or target black and other racial communities?

No miraculous transformation of African, Puerto Rican, and Native Americans (aside, perhaps, from bleaching) would eliminate or even materially reduce racially unequal outcomes. Only with the support of Whites who influence and control American institutions and actions would the "miracle" result in other than racially conditioned outcomes.

The fact is, however, that we do not need any sort of miraculous transformation of African, Puerto Rican, and Native Americans in order to find out whose problem race is and who has the power to change it. The experiences and reception of those people of color who do achieve qualities and qualifications comparable to the ones specified for our miracle already answer our questions about their reception.

During times of scarcity we know, of course, that people of color, regardless of their qualifications, are an economic and social threat to many Whites (Huckfedt & Kohfeld, 1989; Woodward, 1966). But during the 1960s, a period of economic growth and the civil rights movement, should there not have been a substantial movement by African Americans and other people of color into middle-class statuses? To be sure, some did move, but not many (Landry, 1987). In any case, the option of responding to minority aspirations for upward mobility with affirmative action, or anti-affirmative action, plainly is in the hands of white decision makers (in the U.S. Congress, state legislatures, governor's offices, and corporate executive suites), and the majority white public.

The race problem and the power to change it—enlightened or otherwise—belongs primarily to Whites and not simply because they are the numerical majority of the nation's population and voters. It is a matter of Whites having the statuses and associated power to maintain and advance their perceived interests. Whenever and wherever people of color have been a majority or near-majority of the population, whether it has been in states, cities, or regions, Whites still have maintained control, one way or another—the higher the proportion of Blacks in Southern states and regions, for example, the more intense were Jim Crow segregation codes (Woodward, 1966) and the frequency of lynchings (Corzine et al., 1988; Ziglar, 1988). Now, the higher the proportion of Blacks in cities, the higher are the rates of urban economic disinvestment and white flight (Goldsmith & Blakely, 1992).

Why have Whites insisted on holding power, both historically and in the present? The answer to this question is nuanced, but its essential element is not hard to find. With a "race problem," the subordination of whole classes of people based on color is justified and competition is reduced. If the "race problem" disappeared tomorrow, however, with people of color still a significant portion of the U.S. population, approximately one in five Whites would have real competition from a minority person with whom they did not have to compete before. The odds of white people being displaced from good jobs, housing, educational achievement, recognition, privilege, and income would be higher. And all Whites would face the long-term prospect of their children having more competition where more would fail to attain what their white parents have come to believe is "their" future wealth, power, and privilege. Other Americans, who up to now were counted out, would attain their share of the American dream.

We believe now, as we did in 1981, that this book is one of the books that must be read by anyone meaning to pick up the burden and face squarely the problem of racism in the United States. Yet when it first appeared in 1981, *Impacts of Racism on White Americans* received a few favorable reviews but was mostly ignored by reviewers. Some believed the book was 10 years too late, that it might have been "hot" at the beginning of the Nixon years in the 1970s, but in 1981 was exercising a theme that wasn't any longer topical.

Poor timing (and maybe weariness of yet another book on racism) may explain the book's modest early sales. But instead of tailing off after a couple of years (as is commonly the way with books), sales of *Impacts* increased, and—until recently—it continued to sell well. Thus, the book has had, and still has, readers. Furthermore, after a decade and a half it remains the only collection of writings focused expressly on Whites' motives for racism and on the ways racism has affected them.

So, why a new edition? One obvious reason is simply to assure currency. Inevitable developments in the literature, practice, and circumstances of white racism have occurred since 1981. Reactions against racial progress that were at first conditioned by economic recession in the 1970s, for instance, have turned out to have reflected the beginnings of a major transition in the U.S. economy. The basis of economic stratification in the United States has been shifting from its historic foundation in a domestic and national economy to grounding in the circumstances of an international economy with foreign spheres of trade and investment within which the United States is a (over-priced) part.

A declining need for working-class black labor was apparent in the 1960s. Now, in the 1990s, with downsizing, merging, subcontracting, and temporary services, a declining need for white labor has also became apparent. A booming, labor-intensive, and high-paying domestic American economy may be a thing of the past.

During the past two decades, the cost of living in the United States has risen something like 77%. Incomes, however, have risen much more slowly— now it takes two wage earners (or multiple jobs) to earn in real income what one earner (in one job) did in the recent past. Perhaps even more important for the longer term is change in the structures of opportunity in the United States and the access to technology and the information it controls about those structures. Lower-income people generally are at risk of further mar-ginalization in American society. And, in any case, economic transitions in the United States and the world surely will affect Whites' attitudes toward themselves and toward other races at the same time that they affect the socioeconomic statuses of minority people.

Meanwhile, instructive advancements in scholarly work on white identity and the social construction of race have emerged since 1980. Robert Terry

(1970) and David Wellman (1977) introduced the idea of white identity in the 1970s; but in the time since 1980, not only has there been new writing and theory on the topic, there has been significant social psychological and historical research as well. A historic and contemporary picture of Whites is being drawn that reveals heterogeneity, conscience, class consciousness, levels of self- and racial awareness, fear of losing "white" privilege, and more awareness of the plight of Blacks than we had ever thought. White identity and consciousness are intimately related to whether or not a person is racist, antiracist, or somewhere in between. White identity is historic, but it is also a fluid, living identity that is continuously being constructed and reconstructed.

A related development in research since 1980 has been the attention given to exploring the role of perceived self-interest in white racial attitudes. This important work implies that a particular sense of one's own racial superiority is *not* a necessary condition for opposing advancements for people of color. Instead, it may be sufficient to hold specific self-interested and/or just strong general beliefs that it is not groups but individuals, regardless of race, who must work for and thus earn advancement.

Viewing these developments, and others we will mention below, has led us to believe that the need for this second edition of *Impacts* may very well be greater today than it was for the first edition in 1981. This is not only because of deteriorating race relations, but because the American nation seems to be approaching a crossroad. One route leads to an inclusive and multicultural sense of the meaning of being an American—something (multicultural) America has always been, in fact. The other road leads to a police state: racial and political fascism where drugs and the media are primary tools of control, where Blacks and other people of color are the first victims, and the majority of declassed Whites are the next.

As we have said, reactions against racial progress that were conditioned at first by economic recession in the 1970s have turned out to be instead the beginning of a major transition in the U.S. economy and society. The time will come again when the American nation will have to face and respond to the grievances of African Americans and other people of color as it did for African Americans in the 1960s, 1920s, and 1870s.

If the problem of race in the United States is as we have outlined it—a complex set of issues centered around the maintenance of white identity, power, and privilege—and if it is as pressing a problem as we have said it is, should there not be many more books and articles that explore the issues involved and how they might be addressed? Surprisingly, there are not.

The Literature on Whites
and Racism to 1980

In the first edition of *Impacts* in 1981, we summarized the relatively small body of work by scholars who had up until then focused on racism and white Americans. Reviews of the literature showed that virtually the entire written record on race during this century had focused exclusively on various aspects of the experience of African Americans and other people of color (Ashmore, 1976; Harding, Prohansky, Kutner, & Chein, 1969). There were surveys of white attitudes and opinions, but they were used primarily to contrast the extent of differences, of inequalities, and of conflict between the races.

Writings on the experiences of African, Puerto Rican, Native, and other non-European Americans is important and necessary; but the pre-1980 literature had the curious quality of revealing almost nothing about the motivations of Whites and, while showing its effect on African Americans and others, did little to reveal countereffects of racism on white Americans.

In large part, the reason for this limited focus on who it is who is affected by racism has to do with how race relations have been defined. For most of the first half of this century, students of race relations tended to believe that racial bias and hatred grew out of personal ignorance and could be corrected through education and information about the people who suffered from bias and hatred.

A second reason for focusing on racism's objects grew out of the social action and reform bias of the social science scholars who addressed matters of race relations (Westie, 1964). This bias led to a much heavier focus on the "social problem" of race than on developing theories that might point to other more promising approaches to the subject, such as focusing on Whites. It now seems odd that important work on discrimination and prejudice against Blacks concentrated almost exclusively on Blacks rather than on those who act out the discrimination and prejudice (Bullock, 1966; Campbell, 1971; Ehrlich, 1973; Harding et al., 1969; Hoult, 1975; Katz, 1976; Pascal, 1972; Pettigrew, 1975; Schumann & Hatchett, 1974; Simpson & Yinger, 1959).

Yet another reason for a historically narrow focus on racism's outcomes is what Blalock (1967) called "theoretical particularism": a tendency to emphasize one-factor explanations of racial phenomena that can then be translated into simple practical solutions. However, attitudes were studied so narrowly that they were devoid of their social structural and social class contexts; there was the consistent bias of taking white behaviors and attitudes as normative and therefore not subjects for study in their own right; and, finally, there was (and is) an emphasis on description rather than analysis (Kinloch, 1974). (It is not certain, of course, that a more theory-driven approach to the study of race would have led to critical studies of white motives and the effect of racism on Whites. Conceivably it might only have overintellectualized the race problem, which is a continuing scholarly risk.)

Despite the biases and omissions, increasingly more sophisticated social scientific formulations were being applied in studies of the race problem during the period following World War II. Major advances came as scholars began using a social systems theoretical framework (Comer, 1972; Gelfand & Lee, 1973; Kinloch, 1974; Knowles & Prewitt, 1969; Pettigrew, 1975; Rothbart, 1976; Van den Berghe, 1967; Wilson, 1973). This approach outlined the interdependencies and interconnectedness among institutions and the behaviors of different groups of actors in a social system; and it offered a theoretical potential for seeing how white attitudes and behaviors shape institutional practices that negatively or positively effect people of color.

By the early 1970s, researchers had begun to note the lack of attention to Whites and of possible negative effects of racism on Whites as well as on others (Ashmore, 1976; Katz, 1976; Pettigrew, 1975; Van den Berghe, 1972). They all restated Saenger's (1965) earlier point that "no objective research has been undertaken on the effects of social prejudice on those who harbor it" (p. 23), and also Weston's (1972) observation that "Whites have been neglected as a subject for study" (p. xiv).

We suspect that many researchers had a general awareness of the asystematic treatment of Whites that was prevalent in pre-1980 studies of the race problem. But it was very difficult to make the transition from a topical focus on African Americans and others to a more inclusive and dynamic model. Several writers did manage to offer some ideas on the effects of racism on white Americans. Simpson and Yinger (1965), for example, listed initial benefits of prejudice and discrimination for Whites: (a) economic advantages for middle- and upper-class Whites, who could get cheaper labor from minorities than they could from other Whites; (b) sexual advantages from exploiting impoverished minority women—a practice that became a virtual institution in the South; (c) higher status and prestige from advantaged majority membership that would not exist if the minority bottom were not there; and (d) predictable and advantaged day-to-day interactions with members of lesser groups.

Simpson and Yinger (1965) also offered ideas about the costs of prejudice and discrimination for Whites: (a) personality distortion arising from tensions inherent in the "moral ambivalence" of maintaining superiority over others; (b) economic waste stemming from the costs of inefficient use of labor, wasted human resources, and lack of real competition; (c) the political debilitation of a racially divided society; (d) anxiety from false status that encourages one to support demagoguery; and (e) distorted international relations.

In retrospect, Simpson and Yinger's list is quite remarkable because it anticipated much later work on Whites and racism. For example, Weston (1972) subsequently connected the practice of domestic racism to the general belief that the United States was destined to rule over lesser races in Latin America, the Caribbean, and southeast Asia. In effect, racism served to justify U.S. overseas imperialism; but it also gave pause to any notions about adding nonwhite colonies for fear that more people of color would have to be granted citizenship and the right to vote. Other similar observations about the effect of racist practices on other seeming non-race-related behaviors of Whites were made by Shepard (1970), Downs (1970), Wilson, (1973), Kinloch, (1974), and Eisinger (1976).

A few early empirical studies dealing explicitly with the effects of racism on Whites appeared during the 1970s. Reynolds (1973) and Szymanski (1976) followed up Gary Becker's (1971) hypothesis that there were economic costs to racial discrimination, and both concluded that Whites did not gain from economic discrimination against non-Whites. Riedsel (1978) showed that racial discrimination helped to define sexual discrimination in the labor market; and other empirical work highlighted the link between racism and mental health. Pettigrew (1973), for instance, argued (from inferences based on the social psychological literature) that nonracists are mentally healthier than racists, a thesis that followed up on Saenger's (1965) argument that prejudice leads to a "coarsening of the emotions" on the part of the prejudiced person.

Levin (1975) argued that racial prejudice was not simply a flaw in the American character, but was intrinsic to the normative order of American society. Racial prejudice, it was suggested, persists because it is functional for both Whites and people of color. The best evidence for this view was drawn from historical work on American slavery. Lacy (1972) and Noel (1972) each provided examples of historic arguments that racism is intrinsic to the normative order.

Finally, two works that went straight to the mark were Terry's *For Whites Only* (1970) and Wellman's *Portraits of White Racism* (1977). Terry's book was one of the first to explore what it means to be "white" and suggested that there was a close connection between white identity and racism. Wellman provided an in-depth analysis of the lives of five Whites—a teenager, a longshoreman, a middle-aged suburban woman, a businessman, and a city financial director—and he used these cases to examine the way in which white identity, personal and social interests, and racial attitudes intersect.

Literature on Whites
and Racism Since 1980

The 1981 edition of *Impacts of Racism on White Americans* was the first, and to date the only, anthology of original writings that addressed the two essential questions: What motivates white racism, and what effects does racism have on Whites? Four of the book's 12 chapters were written by authors who earlier had attempted to address these questions (Terry, Chesler, Pettigrew, and Reich). Their and others' findings are summarized in Chapter 11 of this edition. In addition, this edition of *Impacts* presents new developments, advancements, and contributions to questions about white motives for and the effects of racism on Whites. (Two very helpful sources for bibliographic materials on these and related subjects are the Weinberg bibliography [1990] and *Sage Race Relations Abstracts* [1980-present].)

In the matter of white attitudes toward Blacks, survey research alerted us to a reversal: Attitudes had steadily improved from 1963 to 1972, but then began to reverse their trend (Condran, 1979; Cummings, 1980). Lipset's idea of working-class authoritarianism was one factor cited as an explanation of the reversal (Grabb, 1980); another explanation is a growing trend toward general conservatism in the United States that may or may not be connected to racial attitudes (Chin, 1985; Sniderman, Piazza, & Tetlock, 1991). Although not expressly demonstrated by the surveys (see Steeh & Schumann, 1992), a possible implication of the survey data (and a real cause for concern) is that white youth have more negative attitudes toward Blacks than did their parents.

Other research has shown a rising white ambivalence primarily toward Blacks that was paralleled by white avoidance of Blacks in general social distance (Tuch, 1988) and in racially mixed neighborhoods and schools (Farley & Frey, 1994; Wilson, 1979). In addition to deteriorating public opinion toward Blacks and white avoidance of Blacks, the election of Ronald Reagan as President and the emergence of a new and aggressive political Right with an express purpose to roll back the gains of the black movement since 1960 (Edgar, 1981), put a racially antagonistic agenda into national play. William Ryan (1981), who critiqued this trend toward reaffirming racial inequality, pointed out that, despite gains made since the 1960s, the black working class still was the worst off, and he argued that there was need of antiracist action within the white working class.

At the same time, Smith (1981) affirmed Herbert Blumer's thesis that white racial tolerance is conditioned by perceived group position: The lower a group's perceived position in racial stratification, the less tolerant were white attitudes toward others. Associated with this relationship between intolerance and perceived position is a common white unwillingness to accept minority "dominance" even when it occurs via democratic means: as when at-large elections are used to displace local black majorities (Herring & Forbes, 1994).

Manifestations of similar phenomena were observed in George Bush's first election campaign (Powledge, 1991); in the attempt by the former neo-Nazi and Ku Klux Klansman, David Duke, to become governor of Louisiana in 1990 (Ellison, 1991; Rose, 1992); in Jesse Helm's campaign for reelection in 1992 (McCorkle, 1991); in Tom Bradley's mayoral backing in Los Angeles (Sonenshein, 1993); and in Harold Washington's 1983 mayoral election in Chicago, where European ethnic voters united and became "white" to oppose Washington (Pinderhughes, 1987). Each of these cases showed that appeals to race result in increased white unity and resistance to Blacks, with liberal voters the only exception to the rule. Together, these examples call into question any notion of general racial pluralism in American politics (Pinderhughes, 1987).

Kluegel and Smith's (1982) important study of Whites' beliefs about black advancement showed that the media play a central role in white perceptions of black statuses: that they (Blacks) may have been seriously discriminated against in the past, but now have few structural barriers to opportunity and have achieved their present gains by reverse discrimination. Whites were found to generalize about opportunity structures from their own experiences, and if they believed that personal opportunities come from personal motivation, they were less likely to perceive structural barriers for Blacks.

Kluegel and Smith (1983) followed up their 1982 study by analyzing perceptions of affirmative action by affluent Whites. They found that affirmative action was often perceived as increasing competition. Affirmative action was opposed more out of self-interest and a sense that affirmative action clearly violates egalitarian principles than because of racial hostility. These findings were supported by Kinder (1986), but critiques by others pointed out a failure to distinguish the content of traditional scales of prejudice from "symbolic racism"—racism in perception only (Sniderman & Tetlock, 1986).

Meanwhile, Schumann, Stech, and Bobo (1985), Kluegel (1990), and Bobo and Kluegel (1993) each affirmed that white opposition to the implementation of any redress of racial inequality was not so much due to "prejudice as a separate and self-contained psychological state" as it was to a reflection of self-interest: that is, threats to power and control. Another team of investigators was able to demonstrate the related hypothesis: "White racial attitudes are made up of how black-white differences are perceived (perceptions) and accounted for (explanations) and how the deprived status of Blacks in the society is responded to (prescriptions)" (Apostle et al., 1983, p. 18).

The widespread white belief is that structural barriers to black mobility no longer exist; but studies of white-black mobility continue to show that inequities based largely on race still are being sustained (Jaynes & Williams, 1989; Oliver & Glick, 1982; Wolpin, 1992). Black gains have not only stopped, but—in selected instances—have reversed. What accounts for this growing deterioration in black participation in the economy?

An important factor is that—although the stock market continues to show record high transactions and profitability—between 1969 and 1976, 22.3 million jobs disappeared due to plant closings—30% of all manufacturing jobs in the United States (Bluestone, 1983). These jobs did not migrate to the sun belt, because 11% of all manufacturing jobs in the sun belt were also lost. They either disappeared through modernization or were moved overseas. Since 1969, corporate decision makers shifted capital away from industries with strong and, in many cases, racially integrated unions, where profits were not as high as desired, and from urban communities where insufficient economic concessions were granted. The consequence of these developments has been not only increasing relative black economic inequality, but also a greater concentration of wealth and income in the hands of the richest 5% of Americans (Danziger, Gottschalk, & Smolensky, 1989).

A dynamic line of investigation that has opened in the past decade has looked critically at the social construction of gender (Frankenberg, 1993) and race. Jeffrey Prager (1987) argues that Blacks have served as a lightning rod for American self-examination and consequently stand not on the outside but at the center of American culture and politics. When the role and place of Blacks is not at the forefront of attention, he maintains, self-examination of the meaning of being an American is not going on. Whites have benefited immeasurably from the presence of Blacks. Race in the United States is not a benign social construct.

There has been extensive background work done on the historical origins and intent of the white-black racial distinction in the past decade (see Allen, 1994; Bolton, 1994; Cecil-Fronsman, 1992; Sobel, 1987). What has emerged is clear evidence that race as we know it today was not somehow an innately given phenomenon. It is and has been a construct, originally conceived and advanced by the 17th-century American colonial planter class to address the major problems of that period, namely, intermarriages, uprisings, and rebellions by groups of European indentured servants and Africans who labored and were exploited together.

Common work and common low regard from colonial planters and employers meant that African slaves and European indentured servants had much in common. Laws were passed, however, intentionally to lower the status of Africans and raise the status of the European poor. The term *white*—and later *American*—was used to designate European unity across class and nationality as opposed to others, for example, "Indians" and "Blacks."

That today we still use, as an essential part of our American social identities, colonial historic constructions established to forge "white unity" has enormous implications. It implies that the very ways in which we see and relate to one another are such as to affirm white racial separation and superiority, as well as everyday taken-for-granted racism (see the sensitive research on white identity by Helms, 1990, and the work of Essed, 1990, 1991, and of McIntosh, 1995).

In a parallel development, racial sensitivity training has been transformed into white identity counseling. The fact that most Whites never have had to think about what it is and means to be white plays into historic racist conditioning that must be addressed in individual and group counseling before particular issues of race relations can be addressed effectively (Njeri, 1989). And Reynolds (1992) has suggested that one way to resolve the racist social construction of race is simply to do away with the concept—a prospect, however, most unlikely of achievement.

On this note, we leave this summary review of literature on racism and white Americans and turn to a quick preview of the contents of the remaining chapters of this second edition of *Impacts of Racism on White Americans*.

About Each Chapter

In Chapter 1, "Racism and White Racial Identity: Merging Realities," James M. Jones teams up with Robert T. Carter to up-date the definition of the three levels of racism Jones (1981) presented in the first edition of *Impacts* by reviewing new theory and research on white identity and describing the psychological stages one goes through to achieve an authentically nonracist white identity. From this new perspective, Jones and Carter then provide explanations of the variations in white expressions of and resistance to individual, institutional, and cultural forms of racism.

In Chapter 2, "White Identity and Counseling White Allies About Racism," Lillian Roybal Rose presents her work on white identity counseling, which provides a striking parallel to that of Jones and Carter, and reaffirms from practice what they have presented based on theory and empirical evidence. Roybal Rose shows us how one can effectively challenge Whites to advance from a lower to a higher level of white racial identity.

In the third chapter, "The Political Economy of White Racism in the United States," Louis V. Kushnick shows how institutional practices are essential to maintaining racism and that by obscuring real class differences, racism is used to exploit white Americans as well. He extends evidence presented in the first edition of *Impacts* by outlining the international importance of domestic racism. Domestic racism, he argues, frees U.S. capital to disinvest from the United States and use labor in other places of the world, all the while Americans believe their job losses and declining standard of living are due to affirmative action, illegal immigrants, and other issues where racial stereotyping can be used to obscure real institutional practices.

In Chapter 4, "Race and Egalitarian Democracy: The Distributional Consequences of Racial Conflict," Patrick L. Mason provides a successive approximation economic argument that complements Kushnick's thesis. White labors' income gains from racism (excluding Blacks and others from unions), he suggests, are trivial compared to the strategic loss of their collective bargaining advantage. Ironically, he shows that wages are highest where unions are racially integrated. But where wages are highest, profits are lowest, thereby providing a strong incentive for capital to move jobs where unions have failed to organize because of race.

Gerald Horne, in Chapter 5, "Race for the Globe: U.S. Foreign Policy and Racial Interests," provides a history of the conflicting race and class interests in U.S. foreign policy since the nation's founding. Traditionally, the "national interests" of the United States have been defined to be in the interests of white elites. These, Horne points out, have often at least potentially conflicted with interests of the majority of Whites and people of color. But racism has played an important role in obscuring these conflicts.

In Chapter 6, Walter W. Stafford returns to direct attention to the use of culture to generate racially oppressive outcomes. In "If We Live in a 'Post' Era, Is There a Post-Racism?" he argues that cultural racism has been indispensable in maintaining a pretense of "white" racial unity and superiority—which is precisely what the colonial forefathers intended for it to do. Neo-conservative and many "post thinkers," he argues, intend to continue the pretense of "white" racial unity into the next century, regardless of the multicultural historic and future character of the nation. They do so, Stafford says, because they cannot imagine a world where Europeans and European Americans are peers and co-contributors with non-Europeans in a world community; but the key to unlocking their imaginations lies in this nation's antiracist and multicultural communities.

Chapter 7 deals with the timely subject of "The Managing Diversity Movement: Origins, Status, and Challenges." In it, Octave Baker describes the development of business training efforts designed to help staff manage cultural and racial diversity. It is ironic that, while conservatives are seeking to curtail government efforts at redressing racial inequalities and many intellectuals are complicit in social and cultural "reforms" that would abet continuing cultural racism, the business community has found reasons to embrace diversity. Sympathy for affirmative action is not what moves them, as Baker shows. Rather, it is a practical matter: Their long-term survival and profitability in the United States depends upon better utilization of women and minorities and having access to diverse markets.

In Chapter 8, "The Impact of Racism on Whites in Corporate America," John P. Fernandez provides testimony from white and minority workers alike that shows diverging perceptions and insights about the negative effects of racism on the workplace. Based on his research and years of training experience, he suggests a course of action to address these issues, especially white males' unwillingness to accept the reality of workplace competition with people of color.

Robert W. Terry shows in Chapter 9 how he addresses the distorting effects of white racism on European Americans' values. "Diversity: Curse or Blessing for the Elimination of White Racism?" describes how he uses metaphors in his training as a means of getting beyond both the perceptual distortions and emotional defenses that are inevitably engaged when race is the topic. He shows that European Americans can look at and address the distorting effects of racism on their senses of self and perceptions of people and things, if they are given appropriate support and direction.

Chapter 10, "White Men's Roles in Multicultural Coalitions," is about one of the most difficult of all antiracism topics: how to make progress with white men. James E. Crowfoot and Mark A. Chesler provide a virtual primer on the problems that white men have working with women and people of color because of the interrelated biases of racism and sexism. The authors also provide suggestions on how white men can address these difficulties. But why would any white men want to do this? Crowfoot and Chesler's answer is that racism oppresses white men, too, and their personal growth and long-term security are dependent upon learning to work in a nonexploitative way with others.

Chapter 11 is a reprint of the concluding chapter of the first edition of *Impacts of Racism on White Americans*. It summarizes the major ideas, insights, and findings of the contributors to that volume (a number of whom are also contributors to this second edition). We reprint the chapter in this second edition because it still expresses the essentials of our thinking that this second edition of *Impacts* builds upon, extends, and updates.

Finally, in the last chapter, we offer an extension of the recommendations for future directions that were stated in the first edition, along with a perspective, some insights, and an outline of findings from the contents of this edition. The chapter and the book ends with an assessment of the critical nature of the present moment in history, not only for dealing with racism, but for deciding the future course of the American nation.

1

Racism and
White Racial Identity

Merging Realities

JAMES M. JONES
ROBERT T. CARTER

The Concept of Racism

As a concept, racism is relatively new, surfacing in popular parlance only during the late 1960s. As a fact of life, it is as old as this country and older. What is racism? Who is a racist? And what does white racial identity have to do with racism? These simple questions tend for some to lead to simple answers, some of which may be correct; but simplicity does not facilitate our understanding of racism and white racial identity.

The complexity of the concept of racism was acknowledged formally by the first author more than two decades ago (Jones, 1972), when he presented a three-part definition of *racism*—individual, institutional, and cultural. Each type of racism operates in some form in most Americans' psychic structure. Most white Americans learn through socialization and social-psychological development the relative and superior status of Whites vis-à-vis people of color. Most Americans are taught that European and American cultures, institutions, and lifestyles are superior to those of all other groups. The extent of awareness of individual, institutional, or cultural racism varies with people's racial identity. However, each type of racism is related to at least five or six racial identity statuses. The relationship between racial identity and racism is the following: Individual white racial identity is defined as a person's psychological orientation to race and is an important aspect of the person's identity. Each person's view of self as a racial being influences his or her perceptions, feelings, attitudes, and behaviors toward members of other racial groups. Racial identity permits analysis of multiple psychological and social expressions as aspects of racism. The definitions of the types of racism will follow and then the theoretical model of white racial identity statuses will be described. Next is a discussion of the mechanisms and processes that maintain each type of racism.

Individual Racism. The individual racist is

> one who considers that Black people (or people of color) as a group are inferior to Whites because of physical (genotypical and phenotypical) traits. [She or] he further believes that these physical traits are determinants of (inferior) social behavior and moral or intellectual qualities, and ultimately presumes that this inferiority is a legitimate basis for inferior social treatment of black people (or people of color) in American society. (Jones, 1972, p. 118)

The reader should note that individual racists' deeply held views regarding race are characterized by gross generalizations based on inaccurate assumptions about the connection between physical-biological traits and social-psychological characteristics that can be easily attributed to others, and are essential to maintaining their sense of self.

Institutional Racism. Institutional racism consists of "those established laws, customs, and practices which systematically reflect and produce racial inequalities in American society . . . whether or not the individuals maintaining those practices have racist intentions" (Jones, 1972, p. 131). The clearest indication of institutional racism is disparity in the circumstances of Whites and people of color, which continues from the past into the present.

Cultural Racism. Cultural racism is

> the belief in the inferiority of the implements, handicrafts, agriculture, economics, music, art, religious beliefs, traditions, language and story of

African (Hispanic, Asian, and Indian) peoples; . . . [and the belief that] Black (and other non-White) Americans *have no* distinctive implements, handicrafts, agriculture, economics, music, art, religious beliefs, traditions, language or story apart from those of mainstream white America. (Jones, 1972, p. 148)

Said another way, cultural racism is the conscious or subconscious conviction that white Euro-American cultural patterns and practices as reflected in economics, music, art, religious tenets, and so forth, are superior to those of other visible racial/ethnic groups (i.e., Native, Asian, Hispanic, and black Americans).

‣ These three levels of racism can be combined into one definition where a more powerful group can subordinate a less powerful group: *"Racism results from the transformation of race prejudice and/or ethnocentrism through the exercise of power against a racial group defined as inferior, by individuals and institutions with the intentional or unintentional support of the entire (race or) culture"* (Jones, 1972, p. 172).

Thus, racism is a complex social and psychological concept that justifies and produces systematically unequal outcomes for people of different races. The concept of racism used here emphasizes ideological and personal attitudes of racial superiority (individual racism), institutional power as a means of implementing ideological biases (institutional racism), and the broad-based cultural support of an ideology based on one racial group's worldview (cultural racism). White racial identity as a psychological model contends that each form of racism is embedded in each white person's ego structure and as such reflects variations in how and to what extent each white person is conscious of the various forms of racism. We will use this general classification in describing the current realities of racism. First, we will present the various ways individual Whites may manifest the various types of racism in their psychological makeup.

Helms's White Racial Identity Theory

Prior to the development of white racial identity theory, the only constructs available to understand and analyze Whites' racial responses were prejudice or individual racism. However, prejudice alone only explains how and perhaps why Whites harbor negative feelings toward Blacks and other people of color. Analyses of prejudice only reveal how individuals of any race feel about others, not about themselves. Also, the focus of prejudice analysis tends to be on the victims rather than the perpetrators. With respect to Whites' prejudicial attitudes toward people of color, little is known about how Whites think, feel, and behave with respect to their own whiteness. Also, analyses that use only prejudice or individual racism, with no psychological orientation to race for Whites, can be used to determine whether individuals are racist or not with little room for variation in Whites' racial beliefs or their expression. White racial identity theory allows for an understanding of various psychological expressions or resolutions regarding a person's own racial group membership and provides insight into how a person's own view of a racial self influences in turn views of other racial groups. Understanding a person's racial worldview from the perspective of racial identity theory also reveals how a person participates in and understands individual, institutional, and cultural racism. Having a knowledge of racial identity can serve to deepen our understanding of the mechanism used to maintain racism in all its forms.

White racial identity theory was initially introduced by Helms in 1984. White identity was proposed as a type of culture shock for Whites. In fact, the names of the statuses (formerly "stages") were adapted from culture shock models. Helms (1994) describes racial identity as ego statuses that mature in a sequential manner. However, all statuses may be present in a person's ego structure. Usually, one status has more influence on a person's racial worldview. The lower, less mature, and externally defined racial identity ego statuses are Contact, Disintegration, and Reintegration. The higher level statuses—characterized by mature, complex, and internally defined racial identity perspectives—are Pseudo-Independence, Immersion-Emersion, and Autonomy (Carter, 1995; Helms, 1990, 1992, 1994). The latter levels are characterized by the formation of a nonracist white racial identity.

Every white person in the United States is socialized with implicit and explicit racial messages about him- or herself and members of visible racial/ethnic groups (i.e., American Indians and Hispanic, Asian, and black Americans). Accepting these messages results in racism becoming an integral component of each white person's ego or personality. Alternately, evolving a nonracist white identity begins with individuals accepting their "whiteness" and recognizing the ways in which they participate in and benefit from individual, institutional, and cultural racism.

Is every white person in the United States racist? Not necessarily. Is every white person exposed to social, institutional, and cultural message that promote racism? Yes. What matters for a person's racial identity is how he or she interprets the messages received about racial groups. What his or her family teaches, denies, avoids, or confronts about race and how the issues are addressed in his or her community and peer group will determine where each person begins in the process of developing a mature racial identity. In a way similar to how people's knowledge and sophistication about their gender matures, depending on their willingness to learn and grow, their racial identity also matures from an externally defined identity to an internally and personally meaningful identity. It is currently unclear what specific events or experiences move a person from one status to another in racial identity development. It seems to be related to personal values, experiences, and individual resolve. Perhaps strong social movements and general shifts in societal values can also facilitate movement. By using the Helms perspective it is possible to distinguish among European Americans according to subtle divisions in their individual belief systems.

Racist White Identities

Contact. Contact begins when a person encounters the *idea* (images or stereotypes) or fact (real people) of Blacks and other visibly distinct racial groups. Attitudes about Blacks and people of color are externally derived and held in simple, unexamined ways. Such attitudes are usually accompanied by a lack of awareness of his or her whiteness. This level of racial identity might be thought of as the color-blind status, where the existence of race and racism are denied but the person's behavior and attitudes are guided by racist principles that have never been questioned. The person is only slightly aware of race and racial issues and is not aware of his or her own acts of individual racism or how she or he benefits from systemic racism (institutional and cultural). In the Contact status, European Americans have limited interracial social or occupational interactions. Most interactions operate from an essentially color-blind racial perspective where color is ignored and stereotypes are more salient.

Disintegration. Awareness that Blacks and people of color are not treated the same as Whites leads to inner conflict and to the second racial identity ego status, Disintegration. As a result of an awareness of the norms associated with racial inequality, "the person comes to realize that they are caught between two racial groups. And that to maintain their position among Whites depends on how well they can split their personality" (Helms, 1990, p. 57). This awareness of difference, again, is not complex or differentiated. Most information about race for self and others is taken from other people and is not the result of personal exploration. Nevertheless, intense confusion mingled with feelings of guilt, helplessness, shame, and anxiety is experienced. To reduce these feelings, the choices are (a) to avoid or limit contact with Blacks altogether; (b) to convince Whites that Blacks are not inferior, they just need some help overcoming social obstacles; or (c) to conclude that racism simply does not exist or, if it does, Whites today have little to do with it. The predominant expressions and experiences regarding race are confusion and conflict. Thus, the person still holds essentially racist views of people of color and participates in and benefits from institutional and cultural racism. Racial stereotypes are still the primary source of knowledge about self as White and other as person of color. Given the depth of belief in Whites' superiority and visible racial/ethnic group people's inferiority, the most likely choice is that racism does not exist or it is a remnant of the past. The potential now exists to move to the next level.

Reintegration. Helms describes the third status, following the Disintegration experience, as a mechanism for people to regain their psychological equilibrium and sense of group belonging, as well as a way to affirm Whites' superior social position relative to others as justified based on merit—they earned it. Here, also, a person relies more on social information and less on self-exploration of the complexities of race. It is comforting just to rely on the teachings of institutions, community, and family. It should be noted that this level of racial identity may be active and conscious or passive and subconscious.

Race-related inequalities are seen as being due to the inferiority or lack of effort of members of other racial groups. People come to believe that negative racial stereotypes were correct to begin with. Reaffirmation of "whiteness" around denial of unjust inequities leads more often to unconscious and covert expressions of racism, to fear about race, and to anger (Helms, 1990). It may take some powerful event, with either Blacks or Whites, for a person to question and begin to abandon this type of white racial identity. The multicultural movement may produce experiences that may trigger for many Whites an examination of long-held beliefs about race.

In these first three levels of white racial identity, where racism is reinforced, the qualitative differences are important. A person in the Contact status is racist without knowing it and thinks that the sociopolitical system and the nation's institutions treat all its citizens the same with regard to race. Such a person would be expected to be characterized by low levels of self-reported prejudice. Yet he or she would be likely to hold positive stereotypes of Whites and negative stereotypes of people of color, particularly Blacks. People characterized by the Disintegration status are aware that whiteness does matter but are confused by the contradictions in their awareness because they have not changed their fundamental beliefs about themselves and what it means to be white. Therefore, they might expect exaggerated and conflicting stereotypes of Blacks, people of color, and Whites. People in Reintegration are in denial of the basis of their racial advantages and must now work at maintaining the myth of white racial superiority and their identification with it. Therefore, they are likely to hold more prejudiced attitudes and perceptions of people of color.

Toward a Nonracist
White Racial Identity

Pseudo-Independence. This is the point where people begin to look inward and see race in more complex terms. This involves a reexamination of ideas and knowledge about race. Individuals begin to question the prevailing assumptions about the inferiority of people of color relative to Whites. They also begin to understand that Whites have responsibility for racism. Consequently, individuals become uncomfortable with their racist behaviors and start to alter their outlook. The Pseudo-Independent status is primarily intellectual, however, and is characterized by a sense of marginality and emotional distance. Individuals are not as strongly identified with Whites and are not openly or emotionally accepting of Blacks or people of color. They have not yet come to terms with individual, institutional, or cultural racism. Thus, stereotypes still predominate in their view of people of color, although some aspects of this view are questioned and examined. It is not until the next identity status that a person's racial perspective becomes complex enough to incorporate emotional as well as structural information about the mechanism of racism.

Immersion-Emersion. At this level, individuals come fully to terms with race. Myths and misinformation about people of color and Whites are recognized for what they are. The unpleasant and uncomfortable histories and perspectives of peoples who have been oppressed by Whites can be comprehended and understood, as well as the present consequences of long-term racial inequities. An emotional and cognitive integration of information and experiences is fueled by questions about race and racism at many personal and interpersonal levels: For instance, How can I feel proud of my race without being racist? Such questions lead to a path of learning and soul searching. Other Whites are sought out and become the source and locus for answers to the Immersion questions. The complex and automatic mechanisms of stereotyping are examined and conscious effort is used to restructure cognitive processing of racial information. During Immersion, individuals may read about others who have had similar identity journeys. They may form white consciousness raising groups; become active in working against racism by changing Whites' behaviors rather than focusing on the victims for solutions to their victimization. Changing Blacks or fighting for people of color is no longer their goal; they are more focused on changing Whites. Research has shown positive relationships with racial self-esteem, learning about racism, and other aspects of identity (e.g., ethnicity, religion). In addition, this level was found to be associated with coping strategies such as assuming responsibility and positive problem solving (Corbett, Helms, & Regan, 1992; Helms, in press).

* *Autonomy.* This final status is entered when the new meaning of whiteness is internalized and race is an accepted and valued part of an individual's personality—yet it does not require superiority relative to others. Because race is no longer a psychological threat, a person characterized by the Autonomy status has a more complex and sophisticated racial worldview and finds it possible to abandon cultural, institutional, and personal racism.
* Helms suggests that the person at this level of white racial identity development is open to new information about race and, consequently, is able to operate more effectively across races. He or she is better able to benefit from racial exchanges and sharing among members of various races and cultures.

White Racial Identity and Research

White identity theory has received empirical scrutiny, as is true of theories of black racial identity. Table 1.1 summarizes the research that has been conducted on Helms's white racial identity theory. People in the Contact status have low anxiety about race: They ignore race as an important aspect of identity and feel comfortable with Blacks, suggesting that people at this stage of development may be responding to something other than the person's blackness. They support both organization-wide and management interventions to promote equality in the workplace (Block, Roberson, & Neuger, 1995; Carter, 1990; Clancy & Parker, 1988; McCaine, 1986). People who are characterized by high levels of Disintegration and Reintegration attitudes tend to be less mature in interpersonal relationships: They prefer white helpers, endorse racism, do not support workplace equity, and are invested in traditional white American mainstream worldviews (Helms,

TABLE 1.1 Summary of White Racial Identity Research Findings

Status	General Theme	Emotional	Psychological	Social
Contact	Unaware of race	Discomfort with unfamiliar	• Low anxiety • Poor self-image • Dependent • Immature interpersonally	• Cross racial comfort • Euro-American cultural values • Endorses efforts to promote equity
Disintegration	Conflict/ confusion	Anger, guilt	• Immature interpersonally	• Prefers white counselor • Confused by Blacks • Euro-American values • Negative view of workplace race relations
Reintegration	Idealizes whiteness Devalues other races	Fear, anger	• High anxiety • Immature • Anti-black, pro-white	• Holds racists views • Euro-American values • Negative view of workplace race relations
Pseudo-Independent	Cognitive understanding of racial difference	Defensive	• Lacks affect • Mature interpersonally	• Prefers white counselor • Interracial dating OK • Comfortable cross-racially • Shift in work and cultural values • Mixed views of workplace race relations
Autonomy	• Nonracist • Accepts race as positive part of self and others	• Calm, secure • Self-confident	• Mature interpersonally • Self-actualized • Inner directed	• Supports racial integration • Balanced view of races • Shift in work and cultural values • Positive racial view of workplace

SOURCE: Studies summarized above: Block et al. (1985); Carter (1987, 1990); Carter & Helms (1990, 1992); Clancy & Parker (1988); Helms (1990); Helms & Carter (1991); McCaine (1986); Pope-Davis & Ottavi (1992); Ottavi, Pope-Davis, & Dings (1994); Taub & McEwen (1992); Tokar & Swanson (1992).

1990; Ottavi, Pope-Davis, & Dings, 1994; Pope-Davis & Ottavi, 1992, 1994; Taub & McEwen, 1992; Tokar & Swanson, 1991).

Pseudo-Independent attitudes were found in studies (e.g., Helms & Carter, 1991) to be predictive of preference for white counselors, acceptance of interracial marriage and dating, lack of affect, but a capacity for mature interpersonal relationships. But for people in this status there were mixed findings regarding workplace equity. The research suggests that people with Pseudo-Independent status attitudes also show more acceptance of Blacks with less emotional investment in racial issues and less preference for Whites when help is sought. Autonomy attitudes were related to support of racial integration, no preference for white counselors, a secure sense of self and others, support for workplace equity, and no rigid investment in traditional work and cultural values. In the Autonomy status there is less emphasis on white-only relationships, and individuals are secure in their relationships. At this level, individuals also develop a stronger self-concept. For these Whites, the investment in American culture has shifted. The shift in values suggests the person is more flexible and can view the world, self, and others from a less rigid and individualistic perspective, which characterizes lower racial identity statuses (see Carter, 1995).

The theory of white racial identity and the empirical evidence summarized in Table 1.1 suggest a strong relationship between the various racial identity ego statuses and prejudice as reflected in the maintenance of stereotypes of people of color and Whites. In addition, the presence of each type of racism in the ego statuses of white racial identity are supported by the empirical findings. But questions remain: How are these psychological processes maintained? What factors moderate or explain fixation at one status or movement to another? It appears that stereotypes and in-group and out-group preferences are operating in some way at each level of white racial identity below Autonomy. How do these social-psychological mechanisms work? That is, can stereotypes be altered or modified? How does a person operate against societal pressures to view a group of people in a certain way? The research and models in social psychology that have examined the formation, content, and mechanism of information processing as it pertains to prejudice, group preference, and stereotypes can shed some light on these questions. Therefore, the next section of this chapter will review the relevant literature in social psychology. The review will be organized according to each type of racism: individual, institutional, and cultural.

Racism's Changing Reality

INDIVIDUAL RACISM

Individual racism, particularly Whites' bias toward Blacks and other people of color, has been addressed through studies of prejudice. This type of racism is associated with the first three white racial identity statuses—Contact, Disintegration, and Reintegration. Of central concern for prejudice are the mechanisms that trigger and maintain racially based expectations, group comparisons, and the formation of specific attitudes. Much of the research literature in psychology has focused on race prejudice as an example of cognitive processing where there is bias nurtured by emotional and evaluative disregard by Whites for Blacks and people of color. One cognitive mechanism of prejudice is the use of stereotypes. Jones (1992) describes a stereotype as a preformed picture of the world and people—usually not based in reality—that is held in a person's consciousness and is derived from sociocultural norms. Such stereotypes operate to guide behavior, because the individual holds the view in his or her head as real, even though the picture may deviate from reality. "Stereotypes, then, define an expectancy that precedes and shapes experience. When the stereotypes are negative, a target of stereotypes is prejudged and his or her interactions are affected not by actual qualities or behavior but by pictures of 'someone else' in the perceiver's head" (Jones, 1992, p. 204). Jones's perspective on stereotypes has been supported by other social psychologists (e.g., Hamilton, Stroessner, & Driscoll, 1994), who point out that stereotypes as individual expectations about the majority of one's own and other racial groups are essentially held as personal schema of group characteristics and behavior. This view holds that the process of forming and applying stereotypes is automatic, regardless of whether or not the schemas are correct (Macrae, Milne, & Bodenhausen, 1994).

The long history of literature on racial stereotyping has shown that a shift has occurred from the extremely negative stereotypes of the mid-1930s (Katz & Braly, 1933) to somewhat more positive attitudes found in numerous more recent studies (e.g., Dovidio & Gaertner, 1986; Karlins, Coffman, & Walters, 1969). Although Whites' stereotypes of Blacks have become less negative, they are no less prevalent. For example, Dovidio and Gaertner (1986) found that overtly negative adjectives such as *lazy* and *superstitious* assigned solely to Blacks in 1933 had decreased by 1982 and overlapped with negative stereotypes of Whites as *stubborn* and *materialistic*. Dovidio and Gaertner also found that at least 10% of their sample still characterized Blacks as lazy, ignorant, aggressive, and materialistic. Though Whites were seen as materialistic (65% of Whites vs. 19% of Blacks), they were not seen as aggressive (10% of Whites vs. 19% of Blacks). In addition, Whites were seen as intelligent, alert, efficient, and scientifically minded whereas Blacks were not.

Also, empirical studies have tended to show that the content of stereotypes of groups other than one's own are less favorable than the content associated with one's own group (e.g., Huddy & Virtanen, 1995; Maass, Milesi, Zabbini, & Stahlberg, 1995; Noel, Wann, & Branscombe, 1995; Wilder, 1986). This is known as in-group/out-group bias and will be discussed latter in the chapter.

Another line of analysis suggests that stereotyping is a cognitive consequence of basic information processing tendencies that produce "errors" as a result of correlational illusions (Hamilton & Gifford, 1976). This view sees stereotypical judgments as resulting not from a motive to rationalize negative judgments, but as the consequence of a bias inherent in information process-ing. This line of research has concerned itself primarily with white attitudes about other racial groups or out-group attitudes. It does not consider how, as a consequence of racism or unsophisticated racial identity status, Whites come to see themselves as favored individuals or members of a favored racial group. It is not until the white person begins a search for internally oriented identities beginning with Pseudo-Independence that he or she begins to reject the externally imposed perceptions of Whites and other racial groups.

The classic studies by LaPierre (1934), Kutner, Wilkins, and Yarrow (1952), and DeFleur and Westie (1958) show considerable disparity between attitudes expressed toward racial groups and actual behavior toward indi-viduals from these groups. These studies show that in spite of negative attitudes expressed about black or Chinese people, in certain circumstances expressively prejudiced proprietors of public facilities in fact served or offered accommodations to black and Chinese people. The recent research literature on the attitude-behavior relationship suggests that offering accommodations may not reflect Whites' true feelings (e.g., Devine, 1989; Devine, Monteith, Zuwerink, & Elliot, 1991; Dovidio, Evans, & Tyler, 1986; Katz & Hass, 1988; Kinder & Sears, 1981; Sears, 1988; Sears & Kosterman, 1991). What may actually be occurring is that people at low levels of racial identity development (Contact, Disintegration, Reintegration, and Pseudo-Independence) may be responding in socially desirable ways and may be reactive in some situations in that they do not report their true attitudes and racial feelings. According to this line of research, it is possible to find strongly contrasting differences in professed nonprejudiced behaviors and attitudes and individuals' true racial group biases.

The data on stereotyping and on the relationships of attitudes to behaviors show a common theme. Over the years, attitude survey data suggest that the norm for racial attitudes has shifted from a sanctioned negative expression to an obligatory color-blind, suppressed, neutral, or positive expression. This shift is specifically associated with Whites' attitudes toward Blacks. This shift can be understood to imply a change in norms associated with both racial attitudes and behaviors. It is clear that things have changed, but there remains a core of bias that is difficult to eradicate. Some recent research suggests that inhibited racial stereotypes actually produce a rebound effect in which the suppressed stereotype comes to be held with more strength and power (Macrae, Bodenhausen, Milne, & Jetten, 1994).

Work by Devine (1989) and Devine et al. (1991) supports the idea that connections exist between racial identity statuses and social cognition. Devine and her colleagues explored differences in what respondents "would-should" feel in a number of interactions and what they actually would do.

Devine et al. (1991) studied how automatic processes affected the way prejudice toward Blacks and gays was expressed. They used a measure of modern or subtle racism and grouped respondents into three prejudice groups (high, medium, and low).

Devine was testing the influence of internal versus external standards of group perception and self-assessment and how these may be discrepant, as well as the notion that people are capable of controlling their personal biases, even when the bias is negative. The would-should discrepancies were larger for medium-prejudice respondents than for the other two groups. Low-prejudice people were uncomfortable with their cognitive dissonance and at the same time were self-critical. High-prejudice respondents also felt discomfort but were not self-critical. Such persons thought that there were good aspects about their would-should discrepancies. The study also found that the views of high-prejudice people were more likely to be derived from their perceptions of societal views, and that they felt strongly that they should follow these standards. This was not true for low- or medium-prejudice people. Low-prejudice people did not feel compelled to follow social standards while they adhered to personal standards. When the racial elements of a situation were explicit, a low-prejudice person would reject the stereotype and use his or her personal beliefs. These individuals operated in a fashion described by the Immersion-Emersion and Autonomy statuses of racial identity.

High-prejudice respondents in Devine et al.'s (1991) study resemble people characterized by the Reintegration status of racial identity. They do not feel the need to hide or mask their true feelings about race, and they derive satisfaction from their racism. They are also less likely to review the accuracy of their views when they receive new information. The moderately prejudiced respondents would be characterized by Contact and Disintegration statuses. They try to avoid behaving in racist ways, but there is a large difference between their behavior and their conscious intent. Discomfort and guilt arising from these gross inconsistencies may drive them toward greater racial identity maturity. Jones (1992) summarizes Devine's work this way: "Devine urges that although people may genuinely reject race-prejudicial ideology, nevertheless, they may respond automatically in prejudicial ways because of pre-adult socialization to stereotypical beliefs" (Jones, 1992, p. 212).

There are two research findings that show that even minimal or subtle negativity can be magnified into more profound racial antipathies through the operation of normal cognitive-motivational processes. The first is the phenomenon of illusory correlation, which has an effect on stereotypic judgments. The second is the effect of the social categorization of groups on the perception and preferences of in-group members.

Illusory Correlation. According to Acorn, Hamilton, and Sherman (1988), illusory correlation is a cognitive bias that affects information processing. It leads individuals to believe that correlation is causation, or that things that are only associated with one another are directly related. This phenomenon was extrapolated to the general literature on stereotyping by Hamilton and Gifford (1976), who found that subjects tended to overattribute infrequent traits to numerically smaller (minority) groups. As a result, the minority group was seen as more negative when the negative traits were less frequent, but more positive when the positive traits were less frequent. Hamilton and Gifford argue that if there is a belief that negative behaviors, traits, and attitudes are less frequently observed in a person's larger group, and visible racial/ethnic groups are by definition less numerous, then there will be a natural tendency to infer an illusory correlation between the members of the visible racial/ethnic group and the negative traits, behaviors, and attitudes.

McArthur and Friedman (1980) suggest a limitation on the illusory correlation phenomenon. They note that infrequency was the only basis for association in the Hamilton and Gifford study. In reality, there are prior associative linkages that follow from demographic characteristics. That is, stereotypes have already been formed with regard to people who are Hispanic, black, white, and so on. McArthur and Friedman compared the infrequency and prior associative connection and found that the prior connection has more influence on the evaluations than does the frequency. When infrequency and prior association with the demographic group are in the same direction, the results replicate Hamilton and Gifford's. However, when prior association of positive traits with a particular group is obtained, the association of those infrequent traits with an infrequently occurring group still produces a positive illusory correlation. McArthur and Friedman (1980) conclude that "Hamilton and Gifford's findings provide . . . a cognitive mechanism for the *formation* of stereotypes about unknown minority groups . . . [McArthur and Friedman's findings] . . . on the other hand, provide a cognitive mechanism for the perpetuation of existing stereotypes" (p. 623).

It is also possible to explain the findings of the study in terms of white racial identity status theory. Because people whose own racial self-knowledge is more complex would be less likely to operate on apparent relationships, they would be more inclined to question the tendencies reported above. The illusory correlation process and the importance of particular perceptions such as positive stereotypes for one's own group help explain how individual racism is formed and maintained. The common assumption about affirmative action, that a person of color is less qualified, illustrates this point.

An Example: White Reactions to Affirmative Action

One of the unanticipated consequences of affirmative action was the introduction of the notion that visible racial/ethnic group persons are less skilled in (or less qualified for) their positions and hence possess less desirable attributes. The illusory correlation phenomenon implies a tendency to overpredict the association between negative traits and visible racial/ethnic group status. In fact, that is one of the most common complaints of visible racial/ethnic group persons in many settings. It is assumed that they came into the work or school setting with substandard qualifications (Steele, 1990).

Much of the literature on racial attitudes reflects substantial ignorance about how people of other groups feel, think, prioritize goals, and so on. Historically, there has been—and there continues to be—an association between negative social and personal traits and membership in certain racial groups. Against this backdrop, it is important to note the operation of illusory correlational phenomena that clearly exacerbate the tendency to portray members of some racial groups in a negative manner. The majority group's members whose racial attitudes are shaped by illusory correlation may be unaware of their bias and may not intend to show any bias, particularly if most of the group's members are socialized to ignore their own race and racial identity as a significant aspect of their identity and social mobility. However, the combination of negative assertions about visible racial/ethnic group members with low racial identity status development and positive assertions about Whites as a group creates complex cognitive dynamics that lead almost inexorably to bias in interracial relations. Continued racial antipathies are due as much to such misperceptions as they are to simple racial animosity.

When racial conflict arises it is often due to the influences of generalized cognitive and affective processes operating at a group level. Social identity draws on individual processes that automatically employ the learned social comparisons and evaluations as reflected in the various levels of white racial identity. As Jones (1992) points out,

> social identity is linked to in- and outgroup distinctions, that outgroup memberships are undifferentiated in their social characteristics relative to in-group members, and the relative lack of complexity with which outgroup members are perceived leads to more extreme judgments of them. Since race is a heavily evaluated social category, it would be expected that social identity processes would increase the use of category-based judgments in interpersonal interactions. (p. 216)

INSTITUTIONAL RACISM

Institutional racism is a complex process with psycho-social conse-quences that will be addressed in more detail by Louis V. Kushnick (Chapter 3, this volume), Patrick L. Mason (Chapter 4, this volume), and Walter W. Stafford (Chapter 6, this volume). In this section, we will touch only briefly on some aspects of institutional racism. White identity theory has direct implications for how institutional racism is perpetuated and the difficulty we face in addressing it. Individuals' racial identity statuses combine to create group-level coalitions dominated by one primary racial identity status. Institutions can therefore be characterized by the various racial identity status coalitions. An institution can be color-blind, confused, or prefer Whites through standards that passively imply that Whites have the preferred qualifications. An institution can be Pseudo-Independent by bringing in people of color and ignoring their difference. Institutions can be Autonomous by valuing and integrating racial difference into organizational practice. Thus, what is seen as equal and equitable from an organization's or institu-tion's perspective is influenced by its members' and leaders' levels of racial identity.

Equality is a notion that appears regularly in popular conversation but rarely in actual fact. This is because so many Whites are characterized by less mature racial identity statuses and believe either that equality exists across racial groups or that the current system is justified, in part because of the prevalence of negative stereotypes held about visible racial/ethnic group people. Equity, on the other hand, exists when two people have equal input and their outcomes are also equal. Equality focuses on equal outcomes for individuals and proportional equity for groups. This point is illustrated in "equal opportunity" advertising where job opening announcements close with the standard "Equal Opportunity Employer," or "Affirmative Action Employer," or both. In an equity system, equal opportunity means simply that all applicants have an equal opportunity to obtain outcomes commensu-rate with their inputs. It does not mean preference based on race without consideration of qualifications. Equality of opportunity is meant to ensure that the equity system works properly. If a group in this society has a history of formal exclusion and disadvantage, then it will occupy lesser positions in all institutional structures, because inputs (knowledge and resources) needed to work the reward or outcome structure (such as education, credentials, experience, formal training, informal associations, etc.) have been less readily available to members of the group. If two runners have equal speed but one of them starts 50 yards ahead of the other in a 100-yard dash, there is no way the second runner can catch up. However, if a person professes a color-blind or confused racial perspective, then he or she is not likely to see differential group experiences as important. Such a person will argue that the runner starting behind in the race must not have prepared properly or did not hear the starting gun. Those who are avowed (Reintegration) or modern (Pseudo-Independent) racists would distort information that indicates such inequity.

Contemporary institutional leaders are caught on the horns of a dilemma. If they attempt to redress historical group disadvantage, they may disadvantage some individuals even though their group has enjoyed considerable advantage historically. If they disregard racial group membership and treat all persons "equally," they will perpetuate and exacerbate historical disadvantage for visible racial/ethnic groups.

In general, institutional racism is perpetuated when an institution does not acknowledge the history of racial discrimination in the United States and, further, does not employ some method of taking discrimination into account as it assesses individuals it wishes to employ or otherwise offer its services or opportunities. The foundation of institutional racism is cultural racism, which also promotes and maintains individual racism and unexamined racial identity statuses.

CULTURAL RACISM

Cultural racism is defined as presenting one's own racial group's cultural preferences and values as superior to those of other groups. European Americans have retained many cultural elements from their European heritage, and they have promulgated the notion that Euro-American philosophy, beauty, music, art, religions, and values are superior to those of 84% of the rest of the world's population.

Western society has had a tendency to categorize human groups according to simple visible traits and to infer mental, behavioral, and sociocultural capacities and tendencies from these traits. Also, it is important to note that the evaluation of others' capacities and their presumed correlates places those attributed to Western people and societies squarely at the top and all others in varying degrees of subordinate status. This tendency is apparent from the stereotyping literature where it is shown that Whites are seen by other Whites in almost exclusively positive terms.

As long as the only standards of cultural acceptability continue to be those models of European heritage and upper-class white Americans, visible racial/ethnic groups will always be seen as inferior unless they adopt the cultural ways thought to be better. Black Americans as a group cannot claim parity, even relative parity, as long as their legacy is an African past and their adaptational reality is viewed as the lower-class, urban ghetto. The popular notion of "cultural deprivation" as a description of black and Hispanic children attests to a wholesale disregard of Latino and black life and culture (Carter & Goodwin, 1994). Individual Blacks and Hispanics can escape only through semipermeable societal membranes that Du Bois (1903/ 1969) referred to as "the Veil," but in doing so they must distance themselves from Blacks (or Hispanics) as a group, both psychologically and cultur- ally, in order to be a "credit to their race" (see Helms, 1990, on black racial identity).

There are many ways in which cultural bias operates. One is that standards for acceptable performance are established in accordance with those tenden- cies, skills, or attributes of one group, and all other groups are measured against these. Poorer performance is viewed as indicative of lesser capacity. The IQ controversy is an excellent example. Operationally co-opting the discussion, Jensen (1969) defined intelligence as what IQ tests measure. Any deficiency in test scores is *pro tanto* a deficiency in intelligence. In his comparisons, Whites are portrayed as superior to Blacks. Also, Jensen (1995) has stated, "We [Jensen & Johnson, 1994] have found that, with large samples, that Blacks and Whites differ in head size and that head size is significantly correlated with IQ" (p. 42). Lastly, the authors of *The Bell Curve* (Murry & Hernstein, 1994) have echoed the same theme, using intelligence tests to argue that Whites are superior to Blacks and other people of color. They argue further that social policy and resources should not be used to redress racial inequities. Ideas of inherent racial inferiority of people of color seem to resurface every decade and are widely spread by means of media and news reports, regardless of the chorus of voices and empirical research that challenge and reject such claims.

It is possible to construct tests in which the content will favor one group over another (see, e.g., Helms, 1992; Williams, 1975). Whether we use IQ scores, speech, graduate record examination, dress, values, religion, or whatever, access to opportunities in this society is highly correlated less with an objective measure of merit than with a subjective measure of cultural attitude and orientation.

Linville and Jones (1980) argued that in-group members have more complex cognitive schemata of themselves than they do of out-group mem- bers. The result is that appraisals of out-group members will be more extreme; they will be seen as less diverse and as having a greater proportion of negative traits (Schruijer, Blanz, Mummendey, et al., 1994; Wann & Dolan, 1994) than will appraisals of in-groups, and that new information will have relatively less influence on appraisals for in-group than for out-group members. There are several mechanisms that maintain in-group bias. Among them are language; selective memory; and the size, power, and status of the group.

The cumulative effect of various cognitive (stereotyping, in-group bias, social power) and psychological (racial identity) processes is to enhance opportunities and cultural preferences for Whites and to truncate opportunities and devalue the cultures of visible racial/ethnic people. People in the United States who come from cultures other than European or American, regardless of the period of first contact with the United States, are characterized by personalities, habits, worldviews, languages, and customs considered deviant in this white Anglo-Saxon Protestant dominated culture.

Cultural racism combines with institutional power to reward individuals and groups in direct proportion to their relinquishment of these "deviant" attributes. Cultural racism is maintained by individuals whose racial identity status is low, thus promoting common societal notions of Whites and other racial groups. These attitudes and lifestyles are transmitted to children through socialization and reinforced by society's institutions, which reinforce and promote the dominant group's cultural patterns. The cycle or circle is therefore complete. Individual, institutional, and cultural racist practices intentionally and unintentionally define the fundamental problem of racism in this society—cultural insularity and culture-specific preference promote social and psychological (externally defined racial identity statuses) mechanisms that sustain racism in all its forms.

Power, Perception, and Racism

The processes associated with maintenance of white power and status are described by McIntosh's (1995) notion of white privilege and Helms's (1990) white racial identity theory. Keep in mind that cultural racism is embedded in the socialization, personalities, and institutions of the United States. Therefore, Whites (and people of color) are racially indoctrinated to believe that their customs, communication styles, and values are superior to those of other groups. They are also taught to deny in various ways any alternative view of their race. Whites learn that race is not salient (Contact status); or, if it is, they are taught to be guilt ridden, confused, and paternal (Disintegration); or they come to think that they have earned preference and privilege (Reintegration); or they think about racial injustice with no clear understanding of its full impact on themselves or others (Pseudo-Independence); or some come to achieve an unusual grasp of their whiteness and its meaning for self and others and are finally able to reject oppression and superiority (Immersion and Autonomy).

McIntosh (1995) points out that Whites are taught about racism as something that puts others at a disadvantage, not as something that harms Whites: "I think whites are carefully taught not to recognize white privilege" (p. 77). McIntosh goes on to say,

> I've come to see [white privilege] as an invisible package of unearned assets which I can count on cashing in on each day, but about which I was meant to remain oblivious. In fact, white privilege is like an invisible weightless knapsack of special provisions, assurances, tools, maps, guides, code books, passports, visas, clothes, compass, emergency gear, and blank checks. (p. 78)

She goes on to note that writing about white privilege has been difficult, in part because,

> My schooling gave me no training in seeing myself as an oppressor, as an unfriendly, unfairly advantaged person, or as a participant in a damaged culture. I was taught to see myself as an individual whose moral state depended on her individual moral will. At school we were not taught about slavery in any depth; we were not taught to see slave holders as damaged people; slaves were seen as the only group at risk for being dehumanized . . . whites are taught to think of their lives as morally neutral, normative and average, and also ideal, so that when we work to benefit others, this is seen as work which will allow them to be more like us. (p. 78)

McIntosh lists 43 specific unearned "privileges" that she can count on every day because of her *skin color.*

Yet she admits that, even after writing the list, her racial socialization was such that she could not recall the privileges and would often forget them even after they were written down.

> Having white privilege has turned out to be an elusive and fugitive subject. The pressure to forget is great, partly because it is unsettling to have to give up an unearned meritocracy. If these things are true, that is, it is not such a free country. One's life is not what one makes it, many doors open for me through no virtue of my own. These perceptions mean also that my moral condition is not what I had been led to believe. The appearance of being a good citizen rather than a trouble maker comes in large part from having all sorts of doors open automatically because of color. (p. 79)

McIntosh (1995) contends that Whites are not really privileged; that, in fact, they have "conferred dominance." They have been sanctioned to dominate others in order to have opportunity and power in the society. White cultural racism is maintained by holding on to the unacknowledged white preference or conferred dominance, and psychologically the preference is understood in various ways depending on the person's racial identity ego status.

The systemic nature of racism in all its forms is apparent, starting with the premise of individual racism. We have added institutional power exacerbated by historical white preference and immature racial identity ego statuses. In a democracy it is majority rule, we are told. Under these terms, visible racial/ethnic groups will lose when their best interests are in direct conflict with the majority's, unless for some reason their interests match the long-term best interests of the majority closely enough for the majority to "compromise" and give up something to the visible racial/ethnic groups. The white majority may compromise when visible racial/ethnic groups have enough in common with segments of the majority group that they can become members of a majority coalition (see Crowfoot & Chesler, Chapter 10, this volume). However, populism has been very difficult to maintain based on racial cooperation. Rather, it is imperative that Whites begin to accept the meaning and significance of their race and its power in the United States. Only then will this society reject the search for exemplars of a cultural ethos as if *civilization* and *Western civilization* were equivalent. It is the arrogance of cultural superiority that underlies the capacity to deny the humanity of other people in one era and to grant humanity only as a condition of cultural assimilation in another.

Conclusion

Historically, individual, institutional, and cultural racism have been represented as the abject denial of the rights of citizenship and humanity to visible racial/ethnic group people and a corresponding limitation, by design or default, of opportunities for their full participation in U.S. society. Over the years this blatant racism has been transformed from conspicuous oppression and enslavement into a subtle and complex systematic white preference or conferred dominance. The reality of racism is merged with each white person's racial identity status. Externally defined immature, unsophisticated statuses (Contact, Disintegration, Reintegration, Pseudo-Independence) are more prevalent and socially and culturally reinforced than nonracist, internally defined, complex, sophisticated and mature white racial identity statuses. Whites are socialized to believe that race pertains only to people of color and particularly to black people. They come to think and feel that racial disadvantage and advantage as manifested in historical traditions only harm or affect people of color. Whites are less aware of how, through their psychological orientation to their own racial group, the knowledge, information, stereotypes, in-group biases, institutional practices, procedures, and cultural preferences are shaped and maintained by their race and racism.

The essence of our position can be summarized as follows:

1. Race and racism have historically been a conspicuous part of the American sociopolitical system and an integral aspect of Whites' (and people of color's) personalities (racial identity ego status) and, as a result, people of color—and black people in particular—find themselves structurally hampered by institutional and cultural racism in contemporary society.

2. It is necessary to have systems that address or ameliorate the effects of past discrimination and racism (e.g., affirmative action). Such systems will, however conceived and implemented, have both negative and positive consequences. Negative consequences may include (a) attempts to stigmatize and attach demeaning attributes to presumed beneficiaries of such activities; and (b) displacement of people who, according to their race and group preference, are displaced from opportunities to which their background and racial norms suggest they are entitled. The positive consequences of such systems include interracial contact, which seems to lessen interracial animosity in certain appropriate contexts. There is a need for Whites to have opportunities to evolve positive, nonracist racial identity ego statuses, and for opportunities for visible racial/ethnic groups people to contribute their competence in situations that would not be accessible to them without such conscious efforts to value members of all racial groups.

3. The basis for achieving racial harmony and acceptance in our society does not mean ignoring race or looking past it. Quite the contrary: Racial acceptance involves the crucial step of rendering the notion of racial difference as a desirable value. All members of each racial group should possess such a mature self-concept. Then race can be a valued aspect of a person's identity and social life. It is also necessary to develop the means to implement racial consciousness in selection and evaluation activities such that we work to counter cognitive processes that automatically lead to individuals favoring their own group.

All Americans who participate in mainstream society can find a minority condition with which to identify, and most can claim an ethnic or racial heritage that informs dimensions of their personalities and socialization. How do we capitalize on these differences as strengths, given the domination of mainstream and traditional values and orientations that command so much attention? Interpersonal animosity, cognitive bias, and in-group preference notwithstanding, it seems to us that this utilization of our human resources is the most critical issue for the next century. It is vital that Whites as well as visible racial/ethnic group people claim race as a positive aspect of their identities. This is an important precondition for promoting a climate in which a person can be expected to have evolved a mature, internally defined level of racial identity and as such recognize and reject individual, institutional, and cultural racism. In this way, all racial groups can be valued contributors to American life.

2

White Identity and Counseling
White Allies About Racism

LILLIAN ROYBAL ROSE

The few insights I offer here about counseling white Americans on the complex problem of racism are drawn from many hundreds of workshops on cross-cultural communication that I have conducted throughout the United States, as well as from my experience of being a Mexican American who was raised in a politically active household in post-World War II East Los Angeles.

Our home was the hub of organizing activity for local and grassroots politics. The people involved in this movement were from diverse racial and ethnic groups in the community, including many from the dominant white culture. I experienced the "high" and sense of community that is an integral part of social movements; but I also witnessed people, even though united for a common cause, repeatedly slip into patterns of conflict, dissent, and in-fighting. I became perplexed with this phenomenon and sought to find frameworks and models with which to understand it better.

In the this chapter I present a synthesis of my understanding of these dynamics, with particular attention to the interlocking roles of Whites and People of Color in our society.

Method

Although white people in my workshops approach the issue of racism from differing and even opposing points of view, most seem to share varying degrees of discomfort, confusion, anger, and frustration regarding issues of race. Some are deeply aware of the injustice and inequities in our society. Others do not see these at all. Some have allied themselves publicly to the struggles for civil rights. Others are angry with and resistant to current social changes. Still, many have acted conscientiously in their personal, daily lives when encountering social oppression against others. There are Whites who want to help, yet feel inadequate and apologetic. Some try to sympathize, and are rebuffed; to lend a hand, and are accused of condescending; or to give from a "privileged" position, and patronize. Others do not seem to know what all the fuss is about. They may feel used, abused, ignored, invalidated, and slighted.

In my experience it serves no purpose to blame or shame Whites about racism—this only exploits the confusion and does not produce positive results. Rather, my approach is to help both Whites (nontargets of racism) and People of Color (targets of racism) move from positions of guilt and shame, or from rage and blame, to more "workable" frames of reference— toward the building of alliances.

To begin this effort, I teach people how to shift frames of reference, to see the world from another's point of view, and not to stay stuck in traditional belief patterns that have proven unworkable. A useful illustration of shifting one's frame of reference is seen in the work of William Perry (1968), who interviewed Harvard male undergraduates across their 4 years at the college. He asked a single standard question: "Why don't you start with whatever stands out for you about the year?" Based on their responses, Perry constructed a scheme that traced the intellectual development in his students of what psychologists today would call "vernacular epistemology." His scheme describes intellectual growth as movement through a sequence of intellectual positions from which people view the world of knowledge, truth, and value.

Pictured as a continuum, Perry's four main positions are Dualism, Multiplicity, Contextual Relativism, and Committed Relativism. Dualists he defined as absolutists, because they assumed a single right answer to every question, saw the world in terms of black and white, and distrusted people and situations that implied things were otherwise. In the next position, Multiplicity, gray areas in understanding appeared. Students at this point considered truth to be personal, privately held, and up to the individual. All opinions and views were equally valid. In the third position, Contextual Relativism, students decided that some views were "better than others," and that truth is "contextual." That is, its meaning depends on "the context in which it is embedded" and on "the perspective from which it is viewed." In the fourth position, Committed Relativism, students understood that "truth" depends on its context, yet at the core of that understanding rests a willingness, capacity, and courage to live a personal code of values and standards. This position permits a clear comprehension of conflicting views, without the moral paralysis that inhibits one from holding strong beliefs. (One can see, e.g., why in a given context a person might steal, and yet one might still believe that theft is wrong.) In this position, one learns to live with ambiguity and still embrace one's own view. One can hold a paradox without being paralyzed. Understanding and action are possible.

I qualify the limitations in Perry's study: His model is linear, so people may get the impression that there is a beginning and an end rather than a continual shifting in consciousness; he studied only white males, thereby reflecting that bias in the study; he did not take into consideration imbalances of power like institutionalized oppressions of class, race, gender, and so on; nor did he consider the role of emotions such as fear. But I believe the progressions Perry identifies are nonetheless valuable because he gives language to the process of intellectual movement; and because I have seen parallel progressions among more diverse groups as people experience shifts in their awareness and understanding on racial and other social issues.

In the years since Perry did his work, these positions have often been applied to developmental models of intercultural sensitivity by scholars like Milton J. Bennett (1986). There are striking similarities as well in the work of James A. Banks (1988). Dualism in Bennett's scheme applies to a group of ethnocentric stages characterized by denial and defense against cultural difference. Banks similarly describes a stage of ethnic captivity and psychological isolation in which members of stigmatized ethnic groups absorb the negative "myths" that are institutionalized in the society. In this stage, ethnic absolutists of the dominant culture (i.e., the nontarget group) cleave to a separatist ideology. They are often regarded as racists and bigots by cultural relativists.

Farther along the stages or positions of learning, both Bennett's and Banks's typologies equate the positions of Perry's multiplicity and relativism with a series of ethno-relative states, beginning in acceptance and ending with the global integration of an individual's racial view. People in this last position tend to maintain a broadened human identity that is "marginal" to any particular culture, while knowing and appreciating their ethnic "family home." In other words, they identify themselves as a part of the diversity (i.e., perceiving themselves as a *valid participant in* rather than as an *observer of* diversity); they embrace difference, yet understand the common human bond.

I stress the importance of each of us understanding our own cultural frame of reference. Becoming an ally of others, transferring understanding to the terms of another person's situation, demands a strong personal base. The creative models of ethnic and cultural learning developed by Perry, Bennett, and Banks are useful because they crystalize the notion of movement among referential frames. They provide a map people can visualize. The steps from racist to ally become, from that moment, identifiable and understandable positions on a scheme.

The Family Mirror

I have come to my conclusion about the necessity of claiming one's ethnic base by considering how white people behave without it. For those who don't feel settled in their ethnic foundation there is a tendency, in interactions with People of Color, to act out of guilt, pity, anger, or indifference, and their counterparts sense it. For example, if you see yourself as only "lending a hand" in the fight against racism, you are on the fringe, perhaps feeling sorry for someone. Inherent in that view is condescension. If you feel guilty, this can eventually lead to anger, and your behavior then becomes reactive and resentful. If you see yourself as having nothing to do with racism, there is a level of detachment and numbness that inevitably leads to a loss of intimacy.

To bring these points home, I frequently draw an analogy with the family. Family analogies are useful for two reasons. First, my audiences are usually racially and culturally diverse. Where historical, political, or literary examples may miss the mark for one group or another, almost everyone has experience of the family. Second, the child's experience in the family is often the site of first exposure to racial prejudice and social oppression.

I remind my audience of a common household scenario, the overworked father or mother who has "no time left over" to spend with the children. To make up for guilt, the standard remedy is to bring one's children a symbolic gift. The strategy usually fails. The children know the difference between a parent and a stereo, for instance. The stereo does not fill their need for love and attention. Gratitude, which might assuage the parent's guilt, is not forthcoming. Inevitably, as the cycle of guilt, bribery, and disregard continues, both sides start feeling cheated. The parent, who seeks understanding and forgive-ness but receives only indifference, feels taken advantage of. Usually it is the parent who explodes: "After everything I've given you! You don't appreciate how hard I work to provide for you!"

My audience gets the analogy right away. The members understand that I am describing a relationship of imbalanced power and that it permeates exchanges across all ages and oppressions. White people see themselves reflected in it. So, too, do People of Color, who have had to be successful at surviving. We have had to learn, often with a painful brilliance, that where the genuine article is not available, one can still persuade the holders of the goods—the scholarship, the grant, the job, the promotion. And where these goods are bestowed out of guilt, or wrested away through manipulation or intimidation, there is no trust, no respect, no real liking, on either side. The recipient feels no accomplishment. The "giver" feels used.

In this situation, the outcome for Whites is predictable. Unlike the analo-gous "parent," they can, and do, quit the struggle against racism. In my workshops I hear the familiar phrases: "Well, I used to help out in the struggle, but not anymore. Nobody appreciates it anyway. I'm sick of being the bad guy." I point out that these phrases are forms of emotional extortion. They actually mean, "I'll do what's just, so long as you behave." To avoid the misunderstanding that comes from these often entrenched patterns, I suggest that the group as a whole shift its frame of reference to operate from a paradigm that gives more equal footing, that is, a more workable assump-tion.

A philosophical basis for this approach is found in the work of the late Erica Sherover-Marcuse, Ph.D. In her 1986 book, *Emancipation and Con-sciousness,* she says,

> A dialectical perspective towards emancipatory consciousness understands that as a result of their life experience under an oppressive social system, even people who are engaged in movements for radical social change will have inevitably introjected or internalized various aspects of these condi-tions. It recognizes that an oppressive system also binds its victims to it, that there comes to be a certain "adherence," on the part of the oppressed themselves, to the prevailing order of unfreedom. Accordingly . . . in order to undo this adherence, individuals must engage in a deliberate and system-atic attempt to transform their own consciousness in an emancipatory direc-tion. (p. 5)

Sherover-Marcuse goes on to point out that this "unlearning" process that both Whites and People of Color must go through does not simply "happen."

It is the product of a sustained effort, the "deliberate undoing" of an oppressive social order.

I then ask people to shift to a "workable" frame of reference that begins with an article of faith—that all of us are born intelligent, good, loving, curious, and with a zest for life, and that through introspection, emotional healing, and personal commitment, whether we are in a target or a nontarget group we can confront social oppression in ourselves and our surroundings, and so make our immediate world a more equitable and creative place to live (Jackins, 1978). Having made this shift, we then proceed to explore information that can help clarify commonly held misconceptions and confusion about racism.

Defining Oppression

Oppression: unjust or cruel exercise of authority or power; something that oppresses esp. in being an unjust or excessive exercise of power. (*Webster's,* 1990)

Many of the questions that come up in my workshops have to do with the meaning of oppression. By definition, *oppression* is an abuse of power. But oppression breaks predominantly into two types: institutionalized and noninstitutionalized. Institutionalized oppression is a belief or attitude that is woven into the fabric of the dominant society. In institutionalized oppression the laws, policies, practices, and traditions of a society reflect the beliefs and attitudes of the dominant group. Jim Crow laws, de facto segregation, unequal job opportunities, and discriminatory school policies are all examples of institutionalized racism. In noninstitutionalized oppression, the abuse of power is perpetrated by people whose source of power is not their membership in a group but rather some circumstance or coincidence that gives them power unrelated to their group, such as being a boss, a landlord, or an administrator, or having a weapon. Noninstitutionalized oppression is an incident isolated from, or at least not reflecting, the policies (written or unwritten) of the dominant society.

With this understanding, when I speak of racism, I mean *institutionalized oppression,* which I define in this way: It is not an individual act against an individual. And it contains three components: *(a) the oppression is in the national consciousness*—it is an attitude or belief shared by the dominant group in a society; *(b) that attitude or belief is reinforced through the institutions of society* (i.e., the church, the government, the family, and the schools create policies that reflect the attitude); and *(c) it is maintained through an imbalance of social and economic power.*

Recognizing Oppression

To help recognize oppression, once again I depict the dynamics of racism in terms of the dynamics of the family. I begin by taking Whites in my workshops back to childhood and to my basic premise, the article of faith—that all human beings are born intelligent, good, loving, curious, and with a zest for life. Whites, in reviewing their early lives, find forms of oppression, analogous to the oppression of racism, by which they have been victimized themselves and to which they responded by forming protective patterns of behavior. By way of illustration, I start with my own experience. I tell them the story of my husband's socks.

In the first years of my marriage in the early 1970s, I felt comfortable staying home, managing the household, and caring for our two children, while my husband went to work outside the home. It was, after all, a familiar family pattern. These gender roles were assumed for people of our generation and they were tightly woven into the institutions of our society. After my younger child was in first grade I decided to go back to work part-time. Before many months went by it was clear to me that, in addition to working 3 days a week, I also continued to cook and clean and care for my family's needs. I had not traded responsibilities; I had simply added on. I began to resent this, but I didn't know how to reverse it. My virtue, my sense of self-worth, were woven into the state of my laundry. This went beyond healthy domestic pride. I would stack up all the T-shirts that were white, arrange all the colored shirts, and fold them neatly into people's bureaus. Socks were the focal point of my obsession. I would make sure that every one was paired, then line them up artistically in drawers.

After 2 years of this, the laundry was no longer laundry. It had turned into a symbol of my oppression. Finally, I mustered up the courage to tell my husband: "I will no longer do your laundry." I expected resistance, but there was none. My husband said, "Okay." He'd simply assumed it was important to me—after all, I had done it relentlessly all these years.

After weeks of his doing his own laundry, I was present one day when he came into the bedroom lugging a basket of jumbled-looking clothes. I watched while he opened his dresser drawers. Into one, he stuffed his underwear; into another, he rammed his T-shirts; into the third, he dumped his socks. They were not sorted. They were not folded. They were stuffed! I watched this from the bed and began to laugh—the sort of laughter that keeps people from crying. I thought of all the late nights I had spent folding and sorting, because I believed I should do so, long after the work made any sense.

I tell this story because it represents my personal index for the tenaciousness of habits trained into us as children. Once upon a time, our willingness to please saved us from parental disapproval. Later on, this adaptation becomes a handicap. As adults we persist in it, largely because we still believe it validates our worth. We continue it, even when it does not apply to present circumstances. I don't need to tell my audiences who taught me to fold socks, or to conform to gender expectations. Like any learned defense against parental or social disapproval, we can lug it right along with us into adulthood, even when those who induced it no longer hold real power over our lives.

I follow such stories by suggesting that people in my audience broaden their focus to apply examples of the family to other institutional frames of reference, and now to start looking at patterns of behavior, also originating from survival, that manifest in other oppressed groups. I say to them: "If you locate the mistreatment in your own lives, you won't become confused, you won't wonder why, you will remember analogous experiences. You will have a landmark, an index for oppression. You will remember having folded the socks."

Internalized Oppression

Among people who are targets of oppression, internalized oppression is grounded in a belief that the worst news we've heard about ourselves is true. It is taking to heart the misinformation, identifying with the message, then directing it against ourselves or others like us. Where there is an imbalance of social or economic power, we tend to turn our fear and rage inward, against ourselves and against members of our own group (Lipsky, 1987).

We direct it against ourselves through the abuse of alcohol or drugs or through other self-destructive behavior. In directing it against one's own group, women may believe even on a subliminal level, for example, that women are less intelligent than men and may not trust the competence of women professionals. Or People of Color may believe that their own group is lazy and deserves the stereotypes and mistreatment of the dominant society. Internalized oppression plays out in all groups that are targets of institutionalized mistreatment. As Sherover-Marcuse (n.d.) states, *"Internalized oppression is always an involuntary reaction to the experience of oppression on the part of the target group.* To blame the target group in any way for having internalized the consequences of its oppression is itself an act of oppression" (p. 2).

Occasionally the word *racism* is misused to describe the phenomenon of internalized racism. In an expression of *intraracial* prejudice (sometimes referred to as "colorism"), for instance, we are seeing the interaction of two individuals who are both oppressed by the broader inequities that underlie institutionalized racism. We are not seeing racism—we are seeing its effects. A light-skinned Latino, for example, may feel superior to a darker sister or brother; or the darker person may see him- or herself as inferior by comparison, and resent it. This is not racism. It is internalized racism—the result of racism.

It is true that some groups of People of Color stereotype and denigrate other groups based on race and skin color. These conflicts are racial acts and can be demeaning, disgusting, brutalizing, fearful, dehumanizing experiences. But as we broaden the lens to understand the larger society, we understand that the *real* power, the institutional power (with its larger implications), is not held by either party. In that regard, though terrible, this is not an act of institutionalized racism, but rather an aspect of internalized racism.

In making this distinction I do not absolve People of Color of responsibility for any behavior that is degrading to others based on race. But I believe that the distinction is important because people will often dismiss or minimize institutionalized oppression because, seeing oppressive behavior, they say, "There's racism in all groups."

Subtle forms of internalized oppression can also infiltrate other areas of life experience. Students, for example, after getting a low grade on a test, and having internalized the idea that they are not really smart, may look for someone whose grade is lower. We seek people to look better than, in order to feel better, in order to divert criticism from ourselves. These are the patterns we learned very early to keep from being called "bad" or "dumb." They were useful strategies for sustaining one's self-esteem. But the situations in which they first served us no longer exist. As adults, we have options: We can continue to sharpen our defenses, or we can acknowledge their obsolescence, grieve out the pain from the original injuries, and come up with creative alternatives.

Another example of internalized oppression occurs in the academic world—in a system that dehumanizes and demeans certain of its members—in its fierce competition; in the fear that shared ideas will be co-opted or stolen; in the comparative clout of advanced degrees awarded by more and less well-respected institutions; in the brutalizing relationships among colleagues of varying ranks across the system. It shows itself in the behavior among all ranks in the educational process: in the high school teacher, for instance, who performs from an inferiorizing conviction that her position is somehow lower than a university professor's. Buying into this misinformation, she plays out her conflict daily in the way she treats her students and views herself. Academics continue to engage in internecine, brutalizing behavior sanctioned and veiled by centuries of academic tradition. The book *Strangers in Paradise: Academics From the Working Class* (Ryan & Sackrey, 1984) is a useful contribution to a growing body of literature on academic classism.

Some form of internalized oppression can be identified in all segments of society and professions. If each of us attempts to understand how internalized oppression expresses itself in our own context, we will be less confused when we see it elsewhere.

In my workshops, I suggest that each person find a "landmark," a personal experience with internalized oppression, a memory that can be easily called up when feeling confused by other people's behavior. The best way to understand something in others is to see it in ourselves. One of my personal landmarks is the tale of the laundry. That night spent laughing (to keep from crying) over socks, remains a vivid reminder of my own internalized sexism. It is just a pattern, it makes no sense, but to be an effective ally, one has to get a feel for the confusion to understand it in others, not to take offense or to judge, but to come up with creative new and appropriate responses, and move on.

Restimulation

We carry internalized oppression around with us. It is an omnipresent, tenacious force that keeps us on the defensive, ready to jump into protective behavior at the slightest suggestion of remembered pain. The process that unlocks a buried pattern is called "restimulation." The sensation is like a relapse into an old illness.

To illustrate the reaction induced by restimulation, I often tell the story of my first job interview. I had graduated from college, bought a new suit, and compiled my résumé. We were in the middle of my answer to a hypothetical question—what would I do in a typical given situation?—when very abruptly the man who was interviewing me leaned across the desk and said, "Has anyone told you that you are a lovely lady?" By this time in my life, I knew enough about sexual harassment to know that this man was completely out of line. But I said, "Oh, thank you!" Even today, I tell people, I still have the gnawing fear that I may have even batted my eyelashes. Like a lot of female children in my generation, I had learned that smiling and saying thank you and batting one's eyelashes were all ways of surviving as a female. And so,

I did it. I became restimulated and then acted out the pattern of behavior that I had developed in order to survive.

I "knew" that this man was demeaning me and manipulating power in the workplace. Intellectually and emotionally, I was aware that he had violated my rights, yet restimulation prevented me from acting creatively. Instead, I fell back on defenses. It is worth noting here that I might have attacked him and still been acting out of restimulation, if that had been a pattern that had gotten me results when I was a child.

KILLING THE GOAT

When we are restimulated, patterns of internalized oppression cause us to "dramatize our feelings of rage, fear, indignation, frustration, and powerlessness at each other . . . often those closest to us" (Lipsky, 1987, p. 5). To convey the behavior of internalized oppression that is triggered by restimulation, I sometimes tell a story about two men and a goat. One man owns a goat. The other one doesn't. The man without the goat wants a goat, feels he deserves a goat, and is always upset with his neighbor for owning one. A Fairy Godmother appears to him one day and asks, "Why are you so angry?" The man says, "Look at him! Flaunting his goat all over town! It's disgusting." The Fairy Godmother says, "Don't worry! I'm here to grant you a wish. Just tell me what you want, and you will have it." The man thinks this over. Finally he says, "You mean you'll kill his goat?"

Before the parable of the goat becomes a mere fairy tale, I try in my workshops to link it to an event out of my own life. My purpose is to provide an illustration and to encourage people to apply what they are learning to their lives. I like to pick stories not directly related to racial issues, because they help to drive home the truth that oppression is universal.

My husband tells a boyhood story about a swing he and his friends made with a rope tied to a tree limb, which overhung a swamp. On the other side of the water the bank was shoaled. They could swing out, but if they swung too far, they would hit the bank. They decided to remove part of the shoal and began to dig it out by hand, but that proved hopelessly time-consuming. Fortunately, there was a bulldozer on a construction site a few blocks away. They took it in the middle of the night and dug out the shoal. Upon returning it, they encountered a security guard. He caught the boys, took their names, and notified the police.

Needless to say, my husband tells this story laughing—boys will be boys, and so on—a warm, humorous memory. At the end, where the point of my story comes in, he tells about the policeman who came to his house the next day, pretending to be furious, and how his father played along, to scare the boys. In fact, they got off without serious penalty.

In terms of the workshop audience, the story I am telling is not really about my husband—it is about me. It concerns my reaction when I first heard the bulldozer story and began to compare his childhood in white suburban Minnesota to mine as a Latino child in East Los Angeles. I describe for the audience my escalating anger. I was furious that the cop had merely "slapped his wrist." I repeat what I couldn't help saying at the time: "If you had been a Mexican kid growing up in East L.A. you'd still be in the slammer for what you did! If there were justice, you would have gone to jail." Because of restimulation I became confused and my first reaction was to "kill his goat." It did not occur to me that I was casting my anger in the wrong direction. It was racism I should be angry at, not what happened (or didn't happen) to those boys. I only grasped much later that what they experienced is what ought to happen to anyone: that the law can teach lessons and also be forgiving; that doing hard time for a harmless prank is never right. That's the kind of compassionate treatment I want for the rest of the world.

Concerning my husband's childhood, I still catch myself drawing comparisons: categorizing his experience as the experience of a white male, invalidating his treatment as a privilege, feeling angry that his childhood was so "easy," even though I know that it was not. Even though my irrational anger has become a signal I have learned to recognize as restimulation, I still continue to heal from these emotions, to try to overcome the confusion rather than be engulfed by it over and over.

Increasingly, as we come to see that restimulation from an old hurt is delusional, that it can transform fairness into "killing someone's goat," and as we discharge emotions and heal from the old wound, we can stop the old response.

Some Myths About Oppression

THE MYTH OF REVERSE RACISM

Occasionally, I meet white people in a workshop who have been painfully mistreated by a person of color. I tell them I am sorry it happened to them, I agree that it must have been horrible, the incident may even have occurred because they were white, and yet what we are discussing is not "racism in reverse." They may have been personally violated, but they are not the victims of an institutionalized policy. That is, People of Color *as a group* do not create and implement policy that determines where white people live, the quality of their education, the promotions in their jobs, and so on.

Whites *as Whites* are not at the continual mercy of a systematic racial oppression that demeans their humanity and dilutes their rights with policies that ignore and disenfranchise them (white people may experience this as targets of oppressions other than racism, e.g., sexism or classism, but this is different). In my workshops I never minimize the horror of the emotional, psychological, or physical injury of a victim of an unjust or violent act, nor do I align myself in any way with those who would use this distinction to justify mistreatment of people from the dominant culture.

However, I believe that it is important to understand the difference, because people often confuse noninstitutional mistreatment with institutionalized oppression; they have never thought about the "institutional" aspect in the definition of an oppression like racism. It is not uncommon for some white people, for example, to challenge as "unfair" the policies that are implemented to alleviate *institutionalized* oppressions on the grounds that they have "experienced racism" too.

I am not suggesting that People of Color cannot be oppressive. In my workshops I list eight common institutionalized oppressions, into some of which everyone must fall. I include the oppressions of adultism, classism, racism, sexism, heterosexism, anti-Semitism, ableism, and ageism. I use myself as an example, checking off in each case whether I am a target or a nontarget of that oppression. This tally defines me as a target in half the cases and as a nontarget in the others. On those oppressions where I am a nontarget, by virtue of being a nontarget, I hold the institutionalized power.

For example, I point out that around the oppression of ableism (the oppression of the disabled, including hidden disabilities such as speech, hearing, learning, etc.) in our society, I am a nontarget. This means that I might go for weeks without noticing if the curb I just stepped off was wheelchair accessible. I have, very simply, failed to see life from that perspective. It is not my intention to discriminate against disabled people. Nonetheless, the inability of the nontarget group to "see" the problem continues to have an inadvertent impact on the lives of the target group.

THE MYTH THAT OPPRESSION
BUILDS CHARACTER

Oppression is a powerful phenomenon, partly because breaking patterned responses is such hard work. Defense mechanisms spring up to convince the most discerning person that oppression has value, that it "taught us something," or "made us strong." I often hear people say, "Yeah, my father kicked me around a lot, but it made me strong, it built character." Giving credit to the oppression or the mistreatment keeps us in denial of the pain of the experience, thus impeding our healing. The tendency then is to reenact the mistreatment, to pass it on, instead of coming up with a new, effective, supportive, creative response. I ask the people in my audience to entertain the premise that they were always strong, that they always had character, and that they managed to hold onto it in spite of mistreatment and oppression, not because of them.

Similar confusion often surrounds physical illness. In Bill Moyers's (1993) book *Healing and the Mind,* he interviews Rachel Naomi Remen, who says:

> There is nothing romantic about illness. . . . Illness is brutal, cruel, lonely, terrifying. You have to understand that anything positive that emerges out of a real illness experience is not a function or characteristic of the nature of illness but of human nature. People have the natural capacity to affirm and embrace life in the most difficult of circumstances, and to help each other despite their circumstances. (p. 320)

THE MYTH OF EXPERIENCE

I begin exploring the myth of experience by asking workshop participants how they believe a typical white person becomes prejudiced against a black person. The most common reply is, "experience," that is, the white person has a bad experience with a black person, and therefore begins to distrust all black people.

Sherover-Marcuse made a "survey" in one of her workshops that sheds light on the myth of experience. She began by stating that an incident never creates the "ism," that the "ism," the social oppression, is a prejudice spread from nontarget to nontarget. A white man in the audience raised his hand. "I just can't buy that," he said. "My father was a minister. I was raised to believe all people were equal in the eyes of God. I really had no prejudice at all, until I moved to a poor, racially mixed neighborhood. The first week, my hubcaps were stolen. The next week, my stereo was stolen. Two days later, my tires were slashed. After a number of these incidents, you'd better believe I'm becoming prejudiced."

Sherover-Marcuse then asked how many people had had a one-to-one negative experience with a person of color? Fifteen or 20 people out of about 100 raised their hands. "All right. Am I to assume, then, that you were not prejudiced before? This incident occurred, and then you became prejudiced?"

The answers came back: "Yes, of course." Sherover-Marcuse posed another question: "How many people here have had a negative experience with a white person?" Most people in the room raised their hands. She asked, "Am I to assume, then, that you are prejudiced against white people?" The replies were almost uniform: "I never thought of them as white people. I just thought of them as jerks." The implication of the "survey" should be clear. If the theory of "experience" is valid, if prejudice arises directly from specific incidents, it should be applicable to every group. But, of course, it is not.

Then Sherover-Marcuse returned to her first assertion, that prejudice, which is the rationalization for systematic racism, is a message passed among nontargets. At this point she turned to the son of the minister and said, "Bet your parents would have loved it if you had brought home a black girl." The man's eyes darted. "That's where you learned racism," she said, "Right *there*."

These stereotypes are further reinforced throughout the system of the dominant culture via television, movies, textbooks, history classes, curriculum, tracking, and more. Once this message has been instilled, the first time a person of color's actions conform to the stereotype, the white person feels justified in rejecting that person's group. "I knew he would do that. They're all that way," the conclusion goes.

THE MYTH OF THE
MORE OPPRESSIVE CULTURE

The dynamics of every oppression would have us believe that certain cultures are more oppressive than others. For example, I have heard People of Color define European and American cultures as the *most* oppressive, while romanticizing their own. I have heard white American groups define cultures such as Middle Eastern cultures or Hispanic cultures as *most* oppressive to women, and so on. The result of this is that people often either become defensive of their culture and rigidly dualistic in that defense, or they may feel shamed, becoming apologetic and overcompensating. People of Color, buying into the myth that their culture is oppressive, believe on some level that in order to avoid mistreatment, they must become less "cultural." They then begin the slow and painful process of alienation and self-exile from their group. Calling oppressive behavior "culture," therefore, is not a workable frame of reference.

Oppression has a lot to do with society, but nothing whatever to do with culture. If an action devalues human life, it is not culture. It is oppression. Agreed, oppression comes in many forms. Sexism among Latinos, for example, may look different from sexism among Whites, but it is still sexism.

For instance, I hear people say that, as part of their culture, Mexican women defer to males. The suggestion is that they do not mind this "aspect of their culture," even to the extent of physical abuse. This notion is based on the fact that frequently the women do not leave their oppressive situations. However, it is finally becoming common knowledge that many battered white women are in precisely the same situation. But in their case it is called "syndrome" or "pathology." When referring to the dominant group, oppression is called what it is. When referring to nondominant groups, it's called "culture." When a white male treats women with disrespect, it's called sexism. When a man of color does so, it's called culture.

When I suggest that no group is more oppressive than any other, I am really asking people to shift perspectives. Of course we could go on calling oppression "culture," but how does that help us? What is the usefulness in identifying as ethnic, forces that devalue us and other human beings? Do we really need to hold on to oppression in order to maintain cultural authenticity? Culture doesn't tell men to batter women. Oppression does that. I should be able to stand with 100% of my cultural integrity intact and still refuse to be a victim of oppression. All women should be able to unite against sexism and still not abandon their group. Similarly, all men should be able to fight sexism and not feel less "manly." I believe that the function of culture is to make us whole and to inspire.

THE MYTHICAL HIERARCHY OF OPPRESSIONS

Part of the effect of oppression, when we are stuck in the pain of it, is to rank our pain above that of others. The worse the experience, the logic goes, the more valid or heroic the survivor. For People of Color, this aspect of internalized oppression plays out as we assess each other's authenticity in our group—who's "more Latino" than whom, who's "more Black" than whom. Accepting the premise that we can rank each other's validity as authentic members of our group, we then must become "super-Latino" or "super-Black," and so on. Or, we leave our group because on some level, depending on our personal experience, we feel like we cannot measure up. In either case, we must invest in pretense, in an image with no substance; and then we have to protect that image (always fearful that someone will blow our cover) by keeping each other at bay. Under these circumstances, our relationships can never be real, lasting, or intimate.

Some white participants in my workshops express their belief in the myth of the hierarchy of oppression in two predominant ways. One approach is to minimize everybody's pain and dismiss the specific circumstances of racism. They may say things like, "Life's been hard on all of us," thereby misunderstanding the difference in experience and, ultimately, minimizing their own experience. Sometimes this will lead them into what I call the "what about me" syndrome, because they feel the pain of their experience but the myth gives them no arena in which to express it. So they in turn minimize everybody's pain and feel angry and reactive when People of Color "complain" about racism.

The second way to reinforce the mythical hierarchy of oppression is to romanticize the painful experience of racism and to minimize the pain of their own experience as individuals or as members of other oppressed groups. Those who take this path end by feeling embarrassed to complain about or even acknowledge the depth of their own injuries. For example, when I was a counselor at a school with predominantly Mexican migrant children, idealistic young white teachers would seek me out to let me know that they were the "good Whites." In the course of our conversations we would inevitably get to their backgrounds and where they had done their student teaching. Many had done it at a white, affluent local high school. They would seem apologetic and start to minimize the concerns of the white students at that school. They would say things like, "The only pressing problem those kids had was the color of the car they were going to buy that year." They would try to assure me that they were happier being at our school, where the problems were "real." I wanted to say to them, "Don't do that. If you can't see the pain in the eyes of white children, you will always condescend to brown children."

I employ other methods to uncover the pain of oppression. One of these is to engage the workshop participants in an experiential exercise. First, I ask them to stand and clear the floor. Then we divide the room down the middle. We reserve one side for those who feel themselves to be targets of an oppression, and we reserve the other side for those who see themselves as nontargets. Then I ask people to disclose, by their location in the room, whether they are the targets or the nontargets of each oppression I name. Like a caller at a square dance I will say, for example, "Men on my right, women on my left," to delineate the oppression of sexism. Then I call out, "White people on my right, People of Color on my left," to delineate the oppression of racism. The composition of the room visibly shifts. I go on this way, calling out 20 forms of oppression commonly experienced in America. The room goes into motion each time I call. (In this setting, I stress that people should not disclose more than is comfortable for them, i.e., not reveal information about themselves that they are unwilling to have known outside the workshop.)

The constant shifting, as people cross and recross the room, illustrates the various power imbalances everyone experiences. People see themselves, and they see each other. I ask them to make eye contact, to make a human connection.

The oppressions, as manifested specifically in society, are endless. The exercise confirms two things: No one is always a target, nor always a nontarget; and no one feels good in either category. We have all been objects of oppression; we have all been its victims and its perpetrators. I ask people in my workshops to shift their frame of reference and to accept, as a workable premise, that the pain derived from any one oppression is as valid as the pain of any other. How can I, for example, as a person of color, claim that my pain is greater than the pain of someone who is physically disabled? How does one grade pain? I don't think suffering can be graded. In *Man's Search for Meaning,* Viktor E. Frankl (1959) writes,

> a man's suffering is similar to the behavior of gas. If a certain quantity of gas is pumped into an empty chamber, it will fill the chamber completely and evenly, no matter how big the chamber. Thus suffering completely fills the human soul and conscious mind, no matter whether the suffering is great or little. Therefore the "size" of human suffering is absolutely relative. (p. 64)

Moreover, attempting to rank suffering leads to thinking that colludes with internalized oppression. It encourages us to invest in the pretense of an authenticity based on such questions as, "Who is poorer than whom?" It contains the potential to set oppression's victims against each other as well as against the nontargets.

Exercises like these help Whites and People of Color to see that the patient exploration of one's own background can provide the crucial bridge to becoming an ally, because it opens ground that must be claimed for any honest cross-cultural communication to take place. It leads Whites to locate the sites of their own oppression, to see that both target and nontarget are dehumanized by oppression, to understand that oppression is universal, and to see that, on the receiving end, pain is not black or white or brown, or any other color. It is pain.

The Path to Alliance

White people tell me, as they shift frames of reference and come to an awareness about oppression, that the process is emotional, and for the first time they understand emotionally as well as cognitively the loss to them because of racism. They see that they were misinformed by people they loved and trusted, and so they feel betrayed; they belong to a group that has had dominance for generations, and so they feel guilt. If white people only confront these issues on a cognitive basis, they will wind up as hostages to political correctness. They will be careful about what they say, but their actions will be rigid and self-conscious. When the process is emotional as well as cognitive, the state of being an ally becomes a matter of reclaiming one's own humanity. Then there is no fear, because there is no image to tear down, no posture to correct. The movement to a global, ethnic point of view requires tremendous grieving. I encourage white people not to shrink from the emotional content of this process.

For People of Color, an encounter with a white person who knows what is right but has not processed it emotionally can be frustrating and exhausting. Every word, every signal breeds confusion. Whites busily guarding a politically correct posture are impossible to reach on a human level, because they have an image to protect.

When People of Color invalidate Whites, impugning their pain or rejecting their views as "privileged," it is usually a response to despair, to the hopelessness marginalized people feel when faced with a lack of the social access that white people enjoy simply by not being "colored." There are choices to be made in these transactions. White people can be miffed, condescending, obsequious, or defensive—they may dismiss a whole race, if they so choose; or they can back off from reactive behavior, remember who they are and what they believe in, locate a landmark, shift their frame of reference, and come up with a new, creative, human response.

As People of Color, we will have to heal from the experience of racism in order to embody what we want for the world. If we want justice, we must be just. If we want fairness, we must be fair. And if we want real and lasting change, we must be willing to touch others from the core of our humanity and our integrity, which means we must be real and without pretense.

Returning to William Perry's Committed Relativism, where people are willing to live a personal code of values and standards, I tell white people in my workshops that I expect them, as allies with power in the oppression of racism, to act justly and not dominate, regardless of the fact that we may never love them. For my part, I say to white people that I will always see their humanness even if they never understand about racism. Neither party can shrink from their commitment.

The Importance of Pride

Collective pride, which is a form of nourishing, group self-love, is an emotional experience that many white people find elusive. I want to be clear about what I mean by *pride*—for, even as I write, there is an increase in various forms of supremacy, or separatist or nationalist groups using the idea of "pride" as a framework for their philosophy based on hate. When I talk about pride, I am using the word in its purest sense, like love in its purest sense. The paradox, that we can only love someone else to the extent that we love ourselves, applies to "pride" as well. I am not talking about false pride, the pride that says, "I am something and you are nothing." I am talking about the pride that says, "To the extent that I love and appreciate myself, I can love and appreciate you." In collective pride we say, "To the extent that I can love and appreciate my group's difference, I can love and appreciate yours."

Again and again I see that collective pride is veiled for many Whites. In its place, they often feel a collective shame. Or they feel detached. Whites easily identify themselves as individuals, but not as members of a group. They may take a healthy pride in their personal strengths and accomplishments but, when it comes to recognizing a collective supportive cultural or ethnic foundation, they seem to be standing in quicksand to the waist.

In an essay for *Clinical Psychology Review,* Hope Landrine (1992) explains why Whites—and especially white males—have difficulty feeling collective pride. She identifies two schools of thought concerning the way people identify with "self." These are the "referential self," which is egocentric and Western in origin, and the "indexical self," which is sociocentric. Simply put, the referential self focuses on the "rugged individualist," whereas the indexical self focuses on "membership in community." Landrine points out that the concept and experience of the referential self is limited to a few Western cultures (and may be pronounced in the United States) as well as to white, male, middle-class Americans. The indexical self-experience applies to Asian Americans, African Americans, Native Americans, Hispanic Americans, and most white American women (Landrine, 1992).

It is important to note here that one perspective is not better than the other—both the indexical self (collectivism) and the referential self (individualism) have benefits as well as costs. However, I believe that those who seek to understand another group's collective experience, but cannot make the shift into an understanding of collective pride in their own group, operate from an irresolute position in any cross-cultural exchange.

In my workshops I often use a verbal exercise to help people explore this territory. The audience is usually racially diverse. I select from among them a white person whom I encourage to acknowledge and appreciate the freedoms Whites enjoy and take for granted, the rights that are as unquestioned as the air they breathe. I say that what matters is how each of us thinks and acts in our daily lives. What counts is the ability to shift our frames of reference, and to be able to understand and communicate from a place of personal integrity and intimacy. Then I ask the person to articulate racial pride—to say, "I am proud to be white." The first reaction is very often laughter. "I can't say that," they answer. Or they state their pride in a shallow way.

By the third or fourth exchange, the response hasn't changed much. Some say, "Don't be ridiculous. I can't relate to this." Others display discomfort, embarrassment, or denial. I ask them to think of their ancestors, in isolation from anything that is wrong with society. I urge them to remember the essence of their grandparents—their hard work, their wisdom, their kindness, their survival, their family devotion. I reiterate the paradox: that one can only love someone else to the extent that one loves oneself; one can only recognize and appreciate another person's difference to the extent that one can recognize and appreciate one's own. It is in the interest of real communication across the races that white people go back and claim their frame of reference, a collective appreciation of their group. This exercise does not usually have a fairy tale ending. Where there exists no frame of reference for a concept, it can't be conjured from thin air. On the other hand, their discomfort carries a weight they can't dismiss.

The loss brought about by racism affects the target and nontarget groups in different ways. The loss to the target group is usually evident—emotional, psychological, and physical injury, as well as unequal opportunity in all realms of society. But the loss to the nontarget group is usually masked. Landrine (1992) goes on to say that Westerners (particularly white males) "may pay psychological 'costs' " for this individualist concept of the self, and quotes from authors Shweder and Bourne (1982) that among these costs is the "lack of a meaningful orientation to the past. We come from nowhere, the product of random genetic accident. . . . Cut adrift from any larger whole the self has become the measure of all things" (Landrine 1992, p. 405, citing Shweder & Bourne, 1982, p. 132). "Community, nation, family, roles, and relationships are all secondary to the self" (Landrine, 1992, citing Sampson, 1989, p. 915). *"Each of these larger social units is presumed to exist in order to meet the self's needs, and will be rejected if it fails to do so"* (Landrine, 1992, p. 405, citing Sampson, 1989).

Using the language of my workshops, it appears that for Whites there is a loss of collective pride—not as a posture, but in its purer sense, as a connecting form of love. For Whites who are oblivious to their own essence, the appreciation of others will be postured and lacking substance, and therefore devoid of peerness, which is required for genuine human connection. Collective pride is not an end in itself; it is a means to an end—authentic human connections and intimacy across differences.

The concept of collective pride is much more evident to People of Color. As we heal from institutionalized racism, we usually understand early in the process the need to hold on to our identities and have pride in our own group. Even as we sort through our rage and despair and have to come to terms with our internalized misinformation in order to reach a state of healthy pride, there remains for most of us a general awareness that pride and identification with our group are central to our being and central to our healing.

The white person who understands collective pride on a deep personal level is usually our best ally. For example, when I was a counselor for students in a school whose population was one-third Mexican migrant students, we fought feverishly to improve bilingual services and to install a multicultural curriculum. As I reflect on my relationship with a white teacher who was one of our most ardent supporters, I believe it was no coincidence that he was also the president of the local chapter of the Sons of Norway.

I say in my workshops, "If you don't know pride, in your gut, then our pride will always threaten you. It will always feel as though People of Color are something because you are nothing, that we are colorful because you are bland, and that anything we gain is at your expense."

In areas where we are nontargets of oppression we must learn to love who we are, not just individually but collectively as well. The freedom to respond creatively cannot be achieved from a purely intellectual position. We must venture in, uncovering our personal essence and honoring our connection to our group. For example, we can denounce the socialization of males that perpetuates sexism and we can reject sexist behavior, but I believe that in order for men to be true peers and allies to women they must love the essence of their maleness. Without the emotional ground claimed through this process, their behavior will be based on a foundation of shame, guilt, anger, or detachment. No matter how well meant, their actions will be contaminated by condescension and patronage. No effective change can come from that.

The Loss

Throughout the text of this chapter I have made reference to the loss to nontargets of oppression. I have suggested that we work from a premise that whatever we do to fight oppression, it must be in each of our best interests.

The loss to all nontargets on any oppression is twofold: the lost capacity to assess a situation and act creatively and appropriately, and the loss of meaning among fellow human beings—the loss of intimacy, the loss of genuine human connections.

One of the best examples I have of this loss came out of a conference of women police officers (which was also attended by men). A white female police officer told a story about the way sexism played out in the police department where she worked. In the story she recounted, another white female officer had become the object of sexual harassment in her department. She reported the incident and the offending male officer was suspended. When the officer returned from his suspension, he launched a retaliatory campaign against her. It escalated for months. She found soiled sanitary napkins in her locker. She found used condoms in her desk. She found her reports deleted from her computer. This was a concerted effort, not the work of a single man. A "code of silence" was in effect. She continued to file complaints, but no one would break the code or "inform" on the offenders. One day, while working in the field, she was assaulted. When she ran to her car to call for a backup, she found her radio equipment had been jammed. As a result, she was wounded. She never learned who had jammed her radio. She resigned from the police force a few months later. There were many males on the force who had taken no active part in her harassment, but not one policeman crossed over to her defense.

By the time of the conference, this incident was 2 years old. The woman who told the story about her co-worker began physically shaking. She turned to the audience, pointed her finger, and said, "If one male, just one, had spoken up, it would have made all the difference in the world."

At this point, I turned to the audience and asked, "Are there any men here who were there at the time?"

At the back of the room, one white male raised his hand, very inconspicuously. His integrity wouldn't let him keep quiet; but I believe he was praying I wouldn't see him. I asked him to stand and I asked, "What were you feeling while all this was going on?" He put his hands in his pockets and replied in an academic tone, "I felt that it was highly unprofessional." I said, "Yes. But what were you *feeling* while all this was going on?" He thought about it. He said, "Well, I guess I felt somewhat confused."

Already, he was shifting his frame of reference to a more human point of view. I said, "Okay, just keep talking about it. What were you feeling?"

He said, "Well, I guess I felt scared." Scared, of what? He said, "Well, scared that if I stood up, if I said something, the attack would fall on me."

Gradually, he made small shifts in his frame of reference—he spoke more softly. His hands were shaking. He was, if you will, moving along Perry's continuum, beginning to see from a different place, and announcing every shift in his body language and in the things he said. Finally, he said, "I guess I felt sad."

I asked, "What did you lose?" This man was at least 6'3," a large white soldier of the law, standing with his hands stuffed into his pockets. Little by little his chin began quivering. His eyes were beginning to fill with tears. I had expected him to be defensive, to give excuses, or to remain detached and academic. To see him choosing to do otherwise was deeply affecting for the people in the room. I never learned his name, but I will love this man forever. He said, and I quote, "I lost the ability to be soft, I lost the ability to be kind, and I lost the ability to be just."

It is always in this intuitive, systemic shift that a person arrives at the right place to oppose oppression. It is Perry's (1968) "committed relativism," where one understands that "truth" depends on its context, yet at the core of that understanding rests a willingness and capacity to express a personal code of values and standards.

In the case of our story, I watched a policeman arrive at the right place to combat sexism. In another context, he might have been a she, might have been grappling with racism, classism, adultism, or one of a dozen versions of oppression. Because the policeman saw his own loss he began acting for himself—not for "women," not for that "poor ex-police officer," not for his own self-image. He saw what he had been missing. I would call it his humanity. He saw that the loss was also to himself.

3

The Political Economy of White Racism in the United States

LOUIS KUSHNICK

The plight of the white working class throughout the world today is directly traceable to Negro slavery in America, on which modern commerce and industry was founded, and which persisted to threaten free labor until it was partially overthrown in 1863. The resulting color caste founded and retained by capitalism was adopted, forwarded and approved by white labor, and resulted in subordination of colored labor to white profits the world over. Thus the majority of the world's laborers, by the insistence of white labor, became the basis of a system of industry which ruined democracy and showed its perfect fruit in World War and Depression

Du Bois, *Black Reconstruction in America*
(1966, p. 30)

AUTHOR'S NOTE: This chapter was made possible by generous financial support from the Faculty of Arts, University of Manchester; the University of Manchester Fund for Staff Travel in the Humanities and Social Sciences; and from the Small Grants Scheme in the Social Sciences of the Nuffield Foundation. I would like to thank Benjamin P. Bowser for his editing and scholarship; A. Sivanandan and my colleagues at the Institute of Race Relations for their support and for their model of committed scholarship; and Simon Katznellenbogen and Patricia Kushnick for their encouragement, support, and suggestions. The errors are, of course, mine.

In the 14 years since the first edition of *Impacts of Racism on White Americans,* there has been a massive increase in racial polarization in the United States, Britain, and the rest of Europe, both East and West. There has been an increase in racial violence in these areas and increasing scholarly recognition of the centrality of racism in the organization of modern Western societies (Cornacchia & Nelson, 1992; Horton, 1991; Stanfield, 1991). The successful playing of the race card in election after election has been accompanied by a rightward shift of mainstream political parties and a narrowing of the parameters of legitimate political discourse in the United States and Western Europe (Kushnick, 1995; Marable, 1993). This rightward shift in political and governmental action led to an increase in popular racism—the racism of common sense. Politicians then used this increase as a justification for further racist state actions, which in turn exacerbated popular racism . . . This growth of racism has accompanied, and made politically possible, greater class inequality and a restructuring of the political economies of the advanced capitalist countries at the expense of the working classes. All these events were anticipated in the first edition chapter (Kushnick, 1981), and developments in the decade and a half that have passed since 1981 have validated that analysis.

Another tendency that has appeared in the intervening years is an intellectual/ideological distancing of mainstream policy commentators from the analysis that sees the class implications and functions of racism in a global capitalist system. It is the argument of this chapter that the events of the 1980s and 1990s in the United States, Britain, and Europe have validated the analysis of the first edition and made it more necessary than ever for the relationship between racism and capitalism to be put on the political agenda. The dynamic, described by Du Bois in the introductory quotation, is as central and valid today as it was when he first wrote it.

The fundamental argument is not only that racism has blighted the lives of tens and hundreds of millions of people of color all over the world. It has also functioned worldwide to maintain class-stratified societies (Du Bois, 1966, p. 30). However, this racist system has been contested terrain for its entire history. Whites and people of color as both individuals and groups have resisted the imposition of the racist ideology and the racialized organization of society (Aptheker, 1992). It is important to study that resistance and to understand the conditions within which Whites opted for a more inclusive definition of "us" as opposed to the racially exclusive basis of identification that has been the dominant mode for most of the period under review.

In this chapter I will look at the development of racism during the development of capitalism, paying particular attention to the roles of slavery and imperialism. I will outline the institutionalization of racism in the early 20th century and its implications for different races in the metropole, and I will develop this theme in the context of the growth of working-class consciousness and organization. Finally, I will look at the contemporary position of the working class, the crisis in the capitalist system and its impact on workers in the metropole, and the resistance to that racism and the construction of alternative visions and practices.

Slavery, Early Capitalism, and the Origins of Racism

Plantation economies based on slavery in the New World provided for the development of manufacturing in the center of the world system, particularly in Britain. The triangular trade was a stimulus for British manufacturers and for economic development in the British settler colonies in North America. Africans were bought with British manufactured goods. Those who survived the middle passage in British ships had to be clothed and fed by British firms, and the crops they produced on the plantations provided both the raw materials for industry and the capital for investment in new plant and equipment in the South and New England (Bailey, 1990; Williams, 1967). The importance of the slave trade can be gauged by the following quote from a Liverpudlian authority writing in 1797:

> This great annual return of wealth may be said to pervade the whole town, increasing the fortunes of the principal adventurers, and contributing to the support of the majority of the inhabitants; almost every man in Liverpool is a merchant, and he who cannot send a bale will send a bandbox. It will therefore create little astonishment that the attractive African meteor has from time to time so dazzled their ideas that almost every order of people is interested in a Guinea cargo. (Pope-Hennessy, 1970, p. 155)

Leo Huberman (1968) quotes a Professor H. Merrivale, who delivered a series of lectures in 1840 at Oxford on the theme "Colonisation and Colonies" in which he asked two important questions and gave an equally important answer:

> What raised Liverpool and Manchester from provincial towns to gigantic cities? What maintains now their ever active industry and their rapid accumulation of wealth? . . . Their present opulence is as really owing to the toil and suffering of the Negro as if his hands had excavated their docks and fabricated their steam engines. (p. 167)

The importance of slavery and the plantation system for the United States as a whole, not merely the Southern slave states, is equally obvious (Bailey, 1990). The political structure created by the Constitutional Convention of 1787 reflected that importance. Slavery was incorporated into the basic structure of the new political system in a number of ways: The slave trade was protected until 1807, slaves were counted as three fifths of a human being for both taxation and representation, and a fugitive slave provision was incorporated.

These material acts were reflected in the ideological sphere and produced the ideological contradictions inherent in an economic system based on human slavery. In the first instance, this dependence on slavery posed a moral question. Equiano, an ex-slave and one of the leaders of the antislavery movement in 18th-century Britain, posed the problem: "Can any man be a Christian who asserts that one part of the human race were ordained to be in perpetual bondage to another?" (Fryer, 1984, p. 109). Interestingly enough, on the other side of the English Channel the French philosopher Montesquieu articulated the problem in similar terms when he wrote, "It is impossible for us to suppose these creatures to be men, because, allowing them to be men, a suspicion would follow that we ourselves are not Christians" (Drinnon, 1980, p. 138).

At the same time, capitalism in its struggle against the remnants of feudalism and mercantilism had evolved as an ideology alongside a political liberalism based on the individual as the key actor. Individual transactions in the free market were seen as the basis of economic activity and social progress; each individual was "free" to sell her or his labor to any would-be purchaser. People were to be "freed" from feudal ties to the land, and, of course, landowners would be "free" to displace labor no longer required to maximize profitable use of the land as a commodity. How, then, was it possible to create a new economic, political, and philosophical system dedicated to individualism, freedom, and profit on the backs of slaves?

The resolution of these problems was not the ending of slavery and of the slave trade until economic change and the resistance of the slaves made the alternative of free labor of the ex-slaves a satisfactory alternative. In a development very similar to that adopted earlier vis-à-vis the Irish Catholics whose land and freedom had been stolen by England, all of the victims of these processes, whether they were Irish or Africans, were defined as apelike, less than human, savage (see Hechter [1975], Rai [1993], and Rolston [1993] for discussion of the Irish dimension; see Rawick [1972] and Fryer [1984] for the African dimension). This "solution"—slavery—has had fundamental and continuing consequences. It facilitated a justification of barbaric practices in terms of the superior civilization of the British and other Europeans that was to be used subsequently to justify imperial conquest of Africa at the end of the 19th century.

At the time that slavery and the plantation economies were underwriting the development of capitalism in Britain and the United States, conditions of absolute misery were created for the mass of the population that was displaced from the land and was then exploited in the mills, mines, and factories. There was an ideological congruity between stereotypes of the white poor and the slaves. The poor were poor because they were lazy, they lived from hand to mouth, they seldom thought of the future; poverty was the necessary goad to their activity and to their children's activity in the labor market. Increasing their pay and removing the threat of hunger would only make things worse for them and for society as a whole. But, of course, the rich and the powerful were motivated by other considerations such as ambition and initiative, which required material incentives and rewards. These ideas of Thomas Malthus were by no means deviant at the time, nor, as we shall see, are they deviant in our own time. So, objectively and in terms of stereotypes, the poor in Britain were paying a high price for a production surplus that, alongside the surplus generated by the superexploitation of people of color, fueled the triumph of capitalism as a world system. The fact that there was this congruity in the ideology was, however, not the whole story. There was also the racist ideology that posited the particular inferiority of the Irish and of the peoples of the conquered periphery. The white and English poor were encouraged to adopt racism in order to have a feeling of superiority over someone else in a hierarchical society. But this construction of a racialized identity was not a reflection of a "natural" racism of the white, English working class.

Indeed, the history of class struggle is the history of attempts by major sections of the working class to develop their own consciousness and agenda. It is significant that at crucial points in this struggle they overthrew during brief periods of activism and creativity the exclusive definitions of "us" as the ignorance, the prejudices, the disunion and distrust that had kept them powerless. For example, John Foster (1974), in his study of the development of class consciousness among 19th-century workers, found militants in Oldham, Lancashire, very conscious of the need for solidarity, for an inclusive definition, as an alternative.

> In 1834 a mass meeting demanded the elimination of wage differentials and the levelling up of labourers' pay. The year before there had been a call for an end to coercion in Ireland. And throughout the period a predominantly English population was willing to accept Irishmen among its leaders. The very fact of class formation meant that the controlling spell of the ruling-class

had been broken, and with it, the subgroup system by which people accommodated "unfairness." (p. 185)

But within a decade of the defeat of these attempts to change society in the interests of a united working class, it became clear that state policy underpinned and reinforced the racist ideology that was being constructed to limit the consequences of the dislocations, tensions, and conflicts that accompanied the rise of the new order. State policy played a crucial part in the elimination of competition from Africans, Asians, and the other indigenous peoples encountered by white expansionism. The British government destroyed the textile industry in India and opened that enormous market to the domination of Lancashire textiles (Mukherjee, 1973). The slave trade, the plantation economies, and their ideological justifications were paralleled by conscious policies to separate physically in Britain the Irish and the English working class, and ideologically the white working class from the people of color on the periphery.

Within Britain's North American colonies, using both indentured white labor and black labor, either indentured or semi-enslaved, the need for separation and antagonism was made apparent by Bacon's Rebellion in Virginia in the mid-17th century. Bacon's Rebellion fundamentally threatened the status quo because it was a joint action by both racial groups. A way had to be found to maintain stability and order, to increase the supply of cheap, controllable plantation labor, and to avoid adding to the future numbers of yeoman farmers contesting for political power with the planter elite. The solution involved the enslavement of black labor and the non-enslavement of white labor. This strategy was bolstered by a series of concessions to white labor, which worked to divide the two groups further. Clearly, if no White could be a slave, and if all slaves were black, the objective conditions for racial separation were well established. Furthermore, laws were passed further providing for white supremacy. Thus, we see yet again the crucial role of state racism constructing and underpinning popular racism by providing material and psychic rewards for accepting a white identity, that is, a racialized identity in opposition to a more inclusive identity.

The ideology of racism was incredibly effective, even given the costs to the vast majority of the Southern population. So important was this separation of Whites from Blacks that George Fitzhugh, the slaveholding sociologist, could declare,

The poor (whites) constitute our militia and our police. They protect men in the possession of property, as in other countries; and they do much more, they secure men in the possession of a kind of property which they could not hold a day but for the supervision and protection of the poor. (Allen, 1975)

Thus, in the United States white supremacy was constructed and reinforced by race-based chattel slavery and a racialized definition of *us* as
opposed to *them,* which was an integral part of racist ideology (Drinnon,
1980; Ringer, 1983; Roediger, 1991; Saxton, 1991; Takaki, 1980). This was
underscored by the Naturalization Act of 1790, which established the requirements for citizenship, one of which was the necessity of being white. It
was not merely that one had to be white to be an American, but obviously to
be white was to be superior. The construction of a white identity provided
the basis for incorporation of European immigrants into the society. So the
Irish driven out of their own country by the consequences of Anglo-Saxon
imperialism arrive in another country largely controlled by Anglo-Saxon
elites but are able to avoid permanent suppression and inferiority by virtue
of being able to become white rather than remaining Irish and Celtic. Thus,
angry Irish miners in Pennsylvania denounced Daniel O'Connell, the Irish
Republican leader, for his call for Irish American opposition to slavery.
Despite their own exploitation and the attacks on them from nativist forces,
they declared that they would never accept Blacks as "brethren," for it was
only as Whites that they could gain acceptance and opportunity in the United
States.

Furthermore, acceptance and opportunity are of crucial importance in the
construction of "whiteness." Although the Irish suffered discrimination at
the hands of the "white, Anglo-Saxon Protestant" (WASP) elites, they had
the basis of gaining acceptance in U.S. society as Whites rather than as
Catholic Celts (Roediger, 1991). It is also conceptually important in challenging the "ethno-racial umbrella" thesis advanced by scholars such as
Glazer (1971), with the argument that ethnicity was "an umbrella term
subsuming all racial, religious and nationality groupings" to form a part of
a single family of social identities (Cornacchia & Nelson, 1992, p. 103).
Cornacchia and Nelson test the validity of this ethno-racial umbrella thesis
in contrast with the "black exceptionalism" thesis and conclude that it is the
latter that has greater validity: "The findings on the Black political experience demonstrate that it would be inappropriate to treat racial minorities as
merely ethnic groups competing in the interest group arena for entitlements
and preferments. The political system was nearly sealed shut to Blacks"
(Cornacchia & Nelson, 1992, p. 120).

The extension of democracy in the United States, particularly during the
Jacksonian era, was an extension of democracy—or at least of formal incorporation into the Republic as citizens—to white males. The outcome was the
creation of a "Herrnvolk democracy" or, in Roediger's terms, "Herrnvolk
Republicanism." This incorporation of Whites regardless of class played a
crucial role in ensuring the triumph of racism throughout the United States,

in the free states and in the slave states. Before the Civil War, poor Whites and the non-slaveholding yeomanry in the South, free soil farmers in the West, and artisans and the emerging working class—immigrant and native—in the North were all made citizens in the great white Republic and given an identity that was oppositional to people of color, slave or free.

Because "Herrnvolk Democracy" was not and could not be a reality in terms of "Democracy" despite its state constructed and supported "Herrnvolk" character, there remained a class tension within American society. This class tension became central at various points and remained more marginal at others in societal terms; for some working people it was more central to their identity than for others. The point is that it was part of an ongoing set of struggles and that the racially defined identity as Whites was not always hegemonic. As Herbert Aptheker has argued, the rank and file of the anti-slavery and abolitionist movements among Whites were made up largely of poor people:

> The hundreds of thousands of people who signed anti-slavery petitions were common people, the poor and the working class. The subscribers to the abolitionist newspapers had to struggle to assemble their pennies. . . . It was also common white people who took risks during this period. Those who saved Garrison from lynching were plain and ordinary people. (Aptheker, 1987)

There were, therefore, white people who acted on the basis of values that were alternative to those based on an identity as Whites. The triumph of the white identity, therefore, was not an inevitable consequence of natural or genetic forces but the outcome of unequal struggles.

In text we find that opposition to racism could and did go hand in hand in antislavery movements in Britain and the United States with attitudes and politics that opposed slavery without rejecting racism. Thus, the outcomes of the struggle against slavery, including the Civil War in the United States, did not lead to systems of racial justice or of class equality. For example, the ending of slavery in the British West Indies followed the rise of alternative centers of political/economic power. Fears of successful slave uprisings such as Haiti's, the increasing cost of suppressing such uprisings, and diminishing levels of profit overshadowed the moral crusade that had been waged against the evils of the slave trade and of slavery.

Emancipation, however, did not mean the dismantling of the plantation system and the transfer of land to the Afro-Caribbean peoples. Instead, barriers were placed in their way when they tried to obtain land. Indentured Asian labor was brought in until the 1920s, political control remained in

London, and new forms of superexploitation were devised. As a consequence of these actions, future class and racial relations in the Caribbean were shaped by imperialism for the benefit of the countries of the metropole. Similarly in the United States, the Civil War was fought by the leaders of the Union less to free the slaves than to extend the sway of the emergent industrial capitalists and serve the interests of their free soil allies. Emancipation in neither the Caribbean nor the United States required the overthrow of racialist attitudes or of racist structures, despite the commitment of antiracist Whites and free people of color and slaves struggling for freedom. Thus, in both cases, slavery died so that capitalism could continue to flourish, and with it, racism.

Racism in the Postslavery Period

Prejudices, disunion, and distrust were all characteristics of the response of the major part of the working class in both Britain and the United States to the triumph of capitalism. This response involved the acceptance of hierarchy itself and the situating of oneself and one's group into hierarchies based on skill, job status, ethnicity, gender, and race. One owed and was owed respect in relation to one's position along these scales. These divisions were reinforced by the distribution of material resources. State action directly and indirectly maintained this invidious social order and made possible the continued functioning of the system to control the production and distribution of the material resources. Politics based on an inclusive class consciousness had to confront and overcome these ideological and material reinforcements, including state repression, and it was not entirely surprising that such politics had an up-hill battle and were successful less frequently than they failed.

THE UNITED STATES

The development of class consciousness among the rapidly growing working class in the post-Civil War United States, was, as in Britain, fundamentally shaped and distorted by racism (Saxton, 1991). There was the presence of freed slaves and of other racially distinct colonized peoples within the metropole itself in large numbers. There was a massive immigration of European workers into the United States. Racism provided the ideological and material framework within which the millions of European immigrants who joined the labor force in the half century between 1865 and

1914 became "American." Then they and the indigenous white working class were given a racialized identity (or a racialized working-class identity) as an alternative to a working-class identity and this shaped their responses to being made wage-laborers.

The choice that presented itself throughout this period in U.S. history was between a politics based on an inclusive definition of "us" and one based on an exclusive racial definition. An inclusive definition and political strategy would have necessitated challenging the racialist ideology that had become a dominant characteristic of American identity in the antebellum period (Roediger, 1991). It would have required that workers recognize a common interest and need to cooperate to achieve common objectives. Although this was not the path chosen by most of the white working class and its organizations, there is evidence that there was consideration of such an option and evidence of attempts to develop such a politics. The Address of the National Labor Congress to the Workingmen of the United States in 1867, for example, declared that "unpalatable as the truth may be to many," Negroes were now in a new position in the United States, and the actions of white working men could "determine whether the freedman becomes an element of strength or an element of weakness" in the labor movement.

The solidarity option was not chosen. The exclusive racial definition of "us" was the dominant response. This divisive definition was based both on possession of craft skills and on racial prejudice. As Du Bois put it,

[the National Labor Union] began to fight for capital and interest and the right of the upper class of labor to share in the exploitation of common labor. The Negro as a common laborer belonged, therefore, not in but beneath the white American labor movement. Craft and race unions spread. The better-paid skilled and intelligent American labor formed itself into closed guilds and, in combination with capitalist guild-masters, extorted fair wages which could be raised by negotiation. (Du Bois, 1966, pp. 569-571)

The craft- and race-based unionization operated to retard the development of mass unionism until the Great Depression. It culminated in the formation of the CIO (Congress of Industrial Organizations) industrial unions of the late 1930s. Exclusiveness ensured the availability of large pools of workers willing to, or having no choice but to strike-break and thus weaken the effectiveness of the craft unions. These factors were reinforced by racial and ethnic divisions in the workplace and in housing, education, and social and political activities. This situation goes a long way toward explaining the present political weakness and lack of class consciousness of the American working class (Davis, 1986).

Matters were further complicated by white labor being encouraged to feel superior to non-Whites and thus become "White." Central Pacific Superintendent Charles Crocker, for example, pointed out the benefits to white labor from Chinese immigration:

> I believe that the effect of Chinese labor upon white labor has an elevating instead of degrading tendency. I think that every white man who is intelligent and able to work, who is more than a digger in a ditch . . . who has the capacity of being something else, can get to be something else by the presence of Chinese labor more than he could without it. . . . There is proof of that in the fact that after we got Chinamen to work, we took the more intelligent of the white laborers and made foremen of them. I know of several of them now who never expected, never had a dream that they were going to be anything but shovelers of dirt, hewers of wood and drawers of water, and they are now respectable farmers, owning farms. They got a start by controlling Chinese labor on our railroad. (Takaki, 1980, p. 238)

Not only could white male workers be elevated by the use of Chinese labor, and become "White" men, so could white women become "White" women. Takaki quotes an article by Abby Richardson in *Scribner's Monthly* titled "A Plea for Chinese Labor," in which she argued: "This is the age when much is expected of woman. She must be the ornament of society as well as the mistress of a well-ordered household." Thus, "Chinese labor could become a feature of both the factory and the home." Tensions of class conflict in white society could be resolved if Chinese migrant laborers became the "mudsills" of society, white men became "capitalists," and their wives "ornaments of society" (Takaki, 1980, p. 239).

These privileges, or more correctly for many white working-class men and women, these promises of privileges were only part of the process through which racism remained a dominant characteristic of the American ideology. Repression of those who challenged that response of the working class to their designated position in society also existed. There is a long history in the United States of legal and extralegal repression, ranging from the terrorism directed against Blacks and their white allies during reconstruction in the post-Civil War South, to the suppression of the Molly McGuires, the Industrial Workers of the World (IWW), to the judicial murders of Sacco and Vanzetti and then the Rosenbergs in this century.

Clearly, the threat posed by class-conscious interracial cooperation was perceived by the ruling class and its agents in control of the state. Repression was accompanied by propaganda campaigns against Populists efforts in the last two decades of the 19th century. There was a massive campaign appealing to white supremacist attitudes. The specter of black equality was used to divert the poor Whites away from any incipient class consciousness, toward a renewed racial consciousness. For example, the power of racial identity was tested in Lawrence County, Alabama, which represented Alabama's "strongest and most persistent opposition to the Democratic party" and in which "Free labor ideology and biracial class politics survived . . . because of the efforts of local black and white radical Republicans, who during congressional Reconstruction refused to be intimidated by Ku Klux Klan terror" (Horton, 1991, p. 65).

Horton (1991) identifies the campaign waged by the local, Democrat newspaper, the *Advertiser:*

> Because the Democratic party was threatened by the possible emergence of a biracial brotherhood of working men . . . the *Advertiser* resorted to a campaign of racial hatred that resembled its earlier pronouncements in support of the Klan. . . . To stir up racial discontent, the *Advertiser* on election day fell back on its tried and tested formula—race-baiting. The front page of the *Advertiser* was filled with reports of assaults by blacks on white women. "The Negroes . . . were getting very troublesome" in Mississippi. "Several Negro women of Tuscumbia" were reported to "have addressed a very insulting letter to several respectable white ladies." Jourd White (the editor) stated that they would "hug a barrel or look up a rope" as a just reward for the insult. The "white men of Lawrence County" were urged by White to "do" their "duty" to "protect the white race from this animalism. (pp. 76, 77)

Horton concludes that, "A strong tradition of free labor-oriented biracial politics coupled with worsening agricultural depression during the post-Reconstruction period could not overcome the dominance of racial politics even in a county where a legitimate space had been created for class politics" (p. 83).

The Southern state governments legitimated the process by establishing the Jim Crow system of de jure segregation, that is, of apartheid. The federal government accepted and legitimated the process through a number of Supreme Court decisions culminating in the 1896 *Plessy v. Ferguson* decision, which established the "separate but equal" principle. This decision justified segregation in all aspects of life in the South. The federal government's acceptance of the disenfranchisement of the Southern black population, of the lynch terror that took hundreds of black lives a year, and of the total denial of Blacks' citizenship rights were crucial developments. So was Northern capitalist support. This took the form of not recruiting Southern black labor into the growing industrial proletariat and by largely excluding the Northern black population as well. Capitalist reinforcement of racial hatred also meant recruiting Blacks solely as strikebreakers. This ensured the maintenance of the controlled labor force necessary for the Southern share-crop system that produced the cotton that was still so crucial to the economy of the United States. This also ensured the exclusion of black labor from the national industrial proletariat just like it had been excluded from the previous fundamental determinant of American life, the frontier. Now when Blacks entered the labor force, they would be entering turf considered by Whites as White.

In addition to the psychological privileges that poor Whites obtained from the Jim Crow system (being told that they were superior to all African Americans regardless of their own class position), they received some material privileges. These privileges were unequally distributed within the white working class and were tenuously held. There was the ever-present threat of cheap substitute black labor if Whites stepped out of line. The price white labor paid in the South for its superior position included wages significantly lower than those in other regions, lower levels of public services than in other regions, and the contempt of their ruling class "white allies" who looked upon them in much the same way as they did the Blacks. A politics characterized by the absence of issues and the absence of opportu-nities for poor Whites to obtain benefits, even by the standards of the rest of the country, became normal. Poor Whites, in effect, gave up their own suffrage through the denial of suffrage to African Americans as part of the price paid to become "White."

Faced with the political culture of racism, the white working class failed to create its own culture to challenge the class-based ethos or to defend and maintain the attempts to do so that were made during this period. Thus, the white working class was unable to meet the growing attacks on its interests that the rise of monopoly capital represented. The growing concentration of capital and centralization of control brought with it increased exploitation of the population by suppressing wages and benefits. It made possible the process of "de-skilling" and the degradation of labor associated with "Sci-entific Management" (Braverman, 1974). The skilled/unskilled hierarchy was reinforced in ethnic and racial terms, and the craft-based unions were unable to defeat the power of the monopoly capitalists and their political allies. Rather than reconsider its basic assumptions, the American Federation of Labor (AFL) became more and more exclusionist as it faced the compe-tition of cheaper labor. This pattern was similar to that which characterized British trade unions in the same period. In 1898 an article in the AFL's official organ, the *American Federationist,* declared that Blacks were unfit for union membership because they were "of abandoned and reckless disposition," lacking "those peculiarities of temperament such as patriotism, sympathy, sacrifice, etc., which are peculiar to most of the Caucasian race." The AFL therefore recommended deportation of Blacks to Liberia or Cuba. Samuel Gompers went further in a speech in 1905 when he declared that "the Caucasians are not going to let their standard of living be destroyed by negroes, Chinamen, Japs, or any others" (quoted in Saxton, 1970, p. 115).

White opposition to such attitudes came from movements that posited a class, rather than a sectional or racial, analysis of society. The IWW, for example, took a principled inclusive position and was consequently the target of repressive action by state and capital. The threat that such a position would challenge the commonsense popular racism that was being pushed by capital and the state and would offer an alternative identity for the new immigrants to that of "White American" was a serious one. This elicited a mixture of propaganda and repression, with the additional weight of science thrown in for good measure. As science and technology became more central to the economy, scientists and engineers became more important as authority figures (Noble, 1977).

For example, the expanding field of psychology became an especially important ally of the capitalists, who in their role as philanthropists provided the resources for the scientists. Edward Thorndike received $325,000 from the Carnegie Foundation from 1918 to 1934 and was the author of one of the basic textbooks used until the 1950s in major American universities. He and his colleagues, Terman and Goddard, adapted Binet's intelligence test for American use, propagandized the theories of genetically inherited intelligence, and offered scientific "proof" of the superiority of some races (the Nordic and Teutonic) and the inferiority of others. Coincidentally, the "inferiors" were not only the victims of the "white man's burden" overseas, and were the nonwhite superexploited races within the United States itself; they were also the recent immigrant employees of the philanthropists, such as the Italians, the Poles, the Slavs, and others. Science simply documented that the class hierarchy was as it should be. If the United States was the land of opportunity, those at the top got there because of their intelligence and hard work. Those at the bottom deserved to be there.

The scientifically objective data produced by such experts as Thorndike were used to justify the racist 1921 and 1924 Immigration Acts that kept out further immigrants from Southern and Eastern Europe. The demands for such control on immigration from the AFL and from nativist groups such as the Immigration Restriction League had all failed until after World War I. Why? Although sections of the working class supported such restriction, it was not in response to their wishes that restriction was adopted. World War I had stopped the flow of immigrant workers from Europe. There was a continuing, and indeed increasing, need for workers in the United States, first to supply the British and French war efforts and then its own. This need was met by recruiting black workers from the South. Racialist attitudes and—crucially—the construction of institutional racism by the local state, ensured that there would be antagonism between white workers and their new African American colleagues. Racist practices ensured that the latter would be concentrated in particular low-level jobs and in particular ghetto residential areas that were then systematically denied the level of public services to which they were entitled. Thus, the labor force would continue to be divided and controllable (Tuttle, 1977; Vittoz, 1978).

After the war, fear of the spread of Bolshevism made the prospect of recruiting labor from areas contaminated by its virus particularly unsatisfactory. Segregated reserves of black labor in the South made it unnecessary for capitalists and the state to take that risk. The racist culture provided the guarantee that lower levels of white immigrants and the new black industrial proletariat would be divided. The consequences for the white working class of adherence of most of its members to a system in which they were exploited as workers and were recipients of privileges, or the promise of privileges, as Whites can be seen in their political weakness, low level of unionization, high level of economic insecurity, and low level of state benefits. This situation was challenged by large sections of the working class during the Great Depression. How successful that challenge was to be and to what extent white workers would develop a class, rather than a racial, consciousness is the subject of the next section.

Racism, Welfare Capitalism, and the Authoritarian State

The development of welfare capitalism in the aftermath of the Great Depression and World War II has been one of the major developments of the contemporary period. It has been argued that capitalism has thus changed its nature. The state was now the protector of the weak and defenseless, the provider of a safety net to catch those who fell, for whatever reason, and the provider of services on the basis of need rather than the ability to pay. The corporations themselves were seen to have become "soulful," in Carl Kaysen's felicitous phrase. Power was seen to have become dispersed because of widespread stock ownership, the separation of ownership and control, and the responsiveness of the new managers in the postindustrial society to interests wider than the hitherto exclusive concern for profit maximization. There were no longer to be struggles over the distribution of scarce resources in an age of plenty and affluence. Class had become an irrelevant concept and, consequently, there was an end to ideology.

During this same period, there had been major changes in race relations. Civil rights legislation, executive action, judicial decisions, and political leadership had all been responsive to liberal ideology and political pressure from the civil rights movement. The state no longer endorsed racism, de jure segregation was overturned, and racial minorities could now compete and rise on the basis of their own worth. Although prejudice might still remain as a residual problem, racism was not—and could not be seen as—a structural characteristic of society in the United States.

Given the reality of capital's most recent counterattacks and revocations of most of these concessions over the past decades, it is, perhaps, hard to remember how taken-for-granted such fairy tales were in the dominant ideologies of American society from the end of the Great Depression to the present. The soulful corporation has turned out to be a transnational corporation moving production and jobs around the globe in search of ever-greater profits and using its ability to do so to force its remaining workforce in the metropole to accept an escalating series of "take-backs" as a condition of being allowed to continue to work. The state has turned out to be more committed to capitalism than to welfare, which is being eroded as a condition of keeping and attracting jobs. The ending of de jure segregation did not mean the end of racial polarization. But these challenges to the dominant ideology have not led to a reconsideration of the ideological assumptions of mainstream commentators. Far from it: It is either the genetic or cultural inferiority of the victims that accounts for continuing and increasing inequality. Indeed, it is the very welfare system itself that created a dependency culture in unemployment, homelessness, drug abuse, and so on (Gilder, 1982; Murray, 1986; for critique of these ideas see Boston, 1988; Reed, 1992). Racism, in both its material and ideological forms, continues to be a central characteristic of American society and has played a crucial role in capital's ability, along with the state's, to overturn what were supposed to have been fundamental changes in the nature of capitalism and in the nature and operations of the liberal democratic state.

The Modern Period

The Great Depression, the New Deal, World War II, and the working-class response to these events played a major role in extracting concessions from capital and in shaping the forms of the state. The federal government came to play the central role in subsidizing capital, in ensuring that a favorable investment climate existed within the United States and abroad, and in ensuring order and stability within the United States. Performing these tasks often brought the federal government into conflict with the states and with local authorities and into conflict with the belief in free enterprise, minimal government, and the inferiority of Blacks. For example, in order to ensure that black struggles in the postwar period did not continue the link with the Communist Party and with issues of class, it was necessary to combine repression of those wishing to continue that link, Du Bois and Robeson, for example, with sufficient concessions to ensure the triumph of Americanism, despite racism.

Such concessions required changes in the Jim Crow system of the South. De jure segregation was no longer necessary to maintain the Southern system of agriculture, which was being rapidly mechanized, in part supported by the policies of the New Deal. These policies served as a lightning rod for black demands and were a force of instability that the newer power centers in the South associated with industry and commerce and wished to defuse. Racial segregation was a contradiction for the United States in its efforts to shape the world order after World War II, a world in which two thirds of the people were not white and in which U.S. apartheid was available for the Soviets and other nationalist critics to challenge U.S. claims to moral leadership. Plus, incorporation of African Americans into the formal democracy would chan- nel the African American middle class into the system rather than run the danger of it becoming a counter-elite. This reasoning did not mean that the white leaders of the old order in the South would give up their power and privileges without a struggle. Also, poor Whites in the South were not going to give up power either, especially after being assured by word and deed by those with power in the South and in the nation as a whole that they too were superior to Blacks because they were white.

The federal government was, therefore, going to be in conflict with rural Southern elites as it attempted to overturn de jure segregation, with African Americans taking the lead and being beaten and killed as a necessary part of the campaign. The national administration had, at the same time, to deal with overt racial discrimination in the rest of the country where racial segregation was not legally required. Here, the federal government came into conflict with the principles of private property, which held that individuals could do whatever they wished to with their property, and could hire whom they wished, and rent to whom they wished. The level of struggle by African Americans and the imperatives of running the world required that overt racial discrimination be outlawed (see Kushnick, 1991; Marable, 1991).

The desegregation efforts of the federal government did not mean the end of institutional racism or the end of the role of the state in legitimating popular racism. Racism continued to be part of the normal operations of the state at every level. For example, one of the key engines of state intervention in support of the economy in the postwar years was support for suburbanization, which by 1965 had led to the construction of more than \$120 billion worth of owner-occupied housing—98% of which was owned and occupied by Whites. This was the result of official government policies administered through the lending decisions of the Veterans Administration and the Federal Housing Agency. State and local governments made similar decisions that led to the construction of what Arnold Hirsch has called Chicago's Second Ghetto (Hirsch, 1983). The racialized economic consequences of encouraging and financially subsidizing white flight to the suburbs included the loss of jobs, tax revenues, and affordable housing in the inner cities—which were becoming more black as African Americans were displaced from Southern sharecropping and came North looking for work. The decisions of the state at every level constructed the increasingly racialized ghettos with their underresourced education and health systems, appalling housing, and high levels of un- and underemployment. The construction of racialized criminal justice systems ensured the lack of police protection and a massively racialized disparity in imprisonment. These realities of state policy have to be set against statements in favor of tolerance and brotherhood and even against assertions of the decline of racism and the presumption that past civil rights legislation have fundamentally eliminated systematic racism in the United States.

Just as there is this contradiction between the ostensible purposes of the state in the field of race, so there is a similar contradiction in the state's relations with the white working class. An essential part of the construction of Pax Americana was the great or Keynesian accommodation that augmented the new era of welfare capitalism discussed above. Workers in the primary sector of the economy were allowed to enjoy high pay, job security, and a social wage. But the price they had to pay actually undermined their ability to protect these gains. The purge of the Left from the unions associated with the anti-Communist purges and the requirements of the Taft-Hartley Act was accompanied by the acceptance of the ideology and practice of the Cold War, of anti-Communism, of Military Keynesianism, and by the cessation of serious attempts to unionize the nonunion majority of the working class (see Bowles, Gordon, & Gintis, 1984; Davis & Huttenback, 1986).

The consequences of these concessions have proven devastating over the medium term for those workers who were to be the beneficiaries of this accommodation and devastating for those excluded. The purges of the unions had driven out those militants and activists who had wanted to challenge the structural racism within the workplace and within the unions themselves. It was these workers who wanted to create objective conditions of racial equality. The failure to continue unionizing drives, particularly in the South, created a potential region where capital could locate future investment and employ labor with a lower social wage. The lack of unionization created the basis upon which capital, the state, and the media could scapegoat organized labor as the cause of inflation and other ills of the society. The ensuing weakness of the working class made it even more difficult for members of that class to resist the transmission of the dominant racist ideology of white supremacy. The acceptance of Pax Americana helped capital and the state to define the national interest in terms most favorable to themselves.

This defining of interest included seeing any foreign government on the periphery that attempts to improve the living conditions of its people by taking control of its economy as an enemy of the United States and as part of the International Communist Conspiracy, of the Evil Empire. The consequence of such a hegemonic definition of the national interest has been political, military, covert, and economic interventions to overthrow such governments and to put and keep in power regimes that would allow transnational capital a free run in their countries, that would sell their people more cheaply than their neighbors and thus provide opportunities for the export of jobs from the metropole to the periphery (Sivanandan, 1990). The limitation of private sector unionization primarily to the major industrial sectors had another consequence—the expanding sectors of the economy (service, sales, and clerical) were not unionized and consequently were based on cheap labor. The weakening influence of organized labor, a political system that was coming to be more and more under the control of capital, and no meaningful alternatives offered by the Democratic Party has left large parts of the white working class alienated from the system and from the Democratic Party.

The essence of the Republican strategy since 1964 has been an appeal to the white South and to Whites in the rest of the country on the basis that the Democratic Party had been captured by Blacks and was no longer the White Man's Party. Race has become the best single predictor of voting behavior: For example, two thirds of all white voters voted for Reagan in 1984 and 60% voted for Bush in 1988. Manning Marable has calculated that overall white support in the South for Republican presidential candidates has been 70% and among white evangelical Christians, 80%. "Since the election of Ronald Reagan in 1980, in presidential contests the Republican Party operates almost like a white united front, dominated by the most racist, reactionary sectors of corporate and finance capital, and the most backward cultural and religious movements" (Marable, 1993, p. 76).

Racialized politics has made it possible for capital to use the electoral system to restructure the political economy, as done in Britain under Thatcher and Major, with large portions of those who will pay, and have paid, the highest price. For example, the median family income in the United States in 1993 in real terms was lower than it was in 1973, and it takes more family members working to earn that lower income. De-skilling, deindustrialization, decertification of trade unions, take-backs by capital from unionized workers, and cuts in the social wage have all been imposed during the decade since the first edition of this volume was published. During this period there has been an ideological assault on state and collective provision; on the supposed "dependency culture"; and on large sections of the reserve labor force, now called the "underclass." The level of state attacks on African American and Latino communities has increased massively during this period, and the level of imprisonment has escalated exponentially with the United States now the most imprisoned nation in the world. The United States is racialized to the extent that an African American male is more likely to be imprisoned than to be in higher education and is five times more likely to be imprisoned than is an African in South Africa (Mauer, 1990; Shine & Mauer, 1993).

The racial and gender divisions of the working class have weakened its ability to resist the dominant racialized and gendered ideology. This lack of working-class consciousness and autonomous culture severely weakens its ability to respond to these attacks on its living standards and hopes for the future. The increasing level of scapegoating of African Americans and women is an indication of the determination of those in power to stay in power and to use the system to their maximum advantage. Their ability to buy acquiescence through material concessions to white working-class men is becoming more and more limited and therefore they are relying more and more on scapegoating and division.

Until the working class creates its own identity and a racially inclusive consciousness and culture, it will continue to be unable to advance its own interests. The European American working class will have to reject the white part of that identity and the illusory privileges based on racism and sexism. The damage done is not only to people of color: European Americans are damaged as well. The dominant ideology of white racial supremacy has served, and continues to serve, the interests of capital and its political allies. Opposition has come from individuals and groups of whites, African Americans, Latinos, and others. This opposition to a racialized identity illustrates that it is possible to choose an alternative identity to that constructed and transmitted by agents of capital. Thus, it is possible for the individual effort and talent used in everyday struggles to survive and to resist class oppression, to be used to create a just and truly democratic society.

4

Race and Egalitarian Democracy

The Distributional Consequences
of Racial Conflict

PATRICK L. MASON

Racial categorizations and egalitarian democracy are antagonistic social constructions. The latter connotes egalitarian and participatory control over the institutions that shape one's life chances. The former is an inherently oppressive social construction; its sole purpose is to legitimize invidious distinctions with respect to access to power and income. Racial constructions are always commensurate with social exclusion. In a racialized society, one's racial identity becomes one element of the set of socially constructed codes used to preclude the construction of an egalitarian society.

AUTHOR'S NOTE: This chapter was originally presented as a paper at the January 1993 ASSA meetings, where John Willoughby and Robin Hahnel provided very insightful comments. Thanks to Bob Pollin for helpful criticism on the earliest draft of this chapter. The editorial comments of Benjamin Bowser greatly improved its readability. The usual disclaimers are applicable.

Political economists have long held that exclusionary social constructions, such as race, contribute to the reproduction of a society divided by class distinctions. Furthermore, this social division supports a power elite with hegemonic control over productive property and political institutions. That is to say, racism—the persistence of race as an invidious social construction—further strengthens the dominance of capital over labor.

This chapter presents a detailed analysis of the economic incentives for and consequences of racial conflict among workers. *Racial conflict* refers to the interracial struggle among workers for employment, earnings, occupational prestige, and desirable working conditions. Certainly, this is a significant narrowing of the scope of racial conflict as it is encountered in daily life. But, if the full scope of racial conflict—access to educational institutions, sex and marriage, residential segregation, the acquisition and disposition of political power, interracial violence, and so forth—is to be made intelligible, contained, and then obliterated, we must have a coherent analysis of the material incentives for persistent racial divisions among laboring groups in American society.

This chapter is not the first attempt at such an analysis. The economics of discrimination in the market for labor power has become the core element in a vast literature that seeks to answer an important question: Is persistent and systemic racial discrimination compatible with the operation of competitive markets in a capitalist economy? Economists have traditionally argued (Arrow, 1972; Becker, 1957) that a competitive capitalist economy is not consistent with persistent and systemic racial discrimination. If this is the case, then racial inequalities in economic outcomes are not the result of fundamental structural inequities in the economy. Instead racial inequalities are the result of racial differences in the quality and the quantity of worker skills (Smith & Welch, 1986), racial differences in propensities to quit (Bulow & Summers, 1986), racial differences in market functional values, attitudes, and behaviors (Loury, 1989), or "imperfections" in the competitive process.

In short, for orthodox economists, unequal treatment in the market for labor power is not a source of persistent and systemic racial conflict. Racial differences in earnings, employment, and occupational attainment reflect differences in individual marketable attributes. To the extent that racial conflict exists, eliminating such conflict requires eliminating individual prejudicial behavior and legal remediation in those exceptional cases where an individual organization or person does attempt to engage in discriminatory behavior. Gradual if not accommodating social reform, not fundamental structural change, is the order of the day. Alternatively, there is statistical evidence that fails to affirm these orthodox theories (Cain, 1986; Donohue & Heckman, 1992; Heywood, 1987).

Acting on Martin Luther King's insight that "racism, militarism, and economic exploitation" are the great and interrelated problems of American society, heterodox economists have taken a different approach. For example, labor market segmentation theorists argue that interracial wage discrimination persists because of racial differences in intersectoral mobility between primary and secondary sectors of the economy and because of mobility differences within the primary sector. However, within the secondary sector African American and white workers receive identical treatment (Gordon, Edwards, & Reich, 1982, pp. 206-210; Jeffries & Stanback, 1984, p. 121).

Racial differences in occupational mobility facilitate a divide-and-conquer strategy by managers against their workers (Reich, 1981b). Wage and employment discrimination creates divisions among workers, which lowers their bargaining power relative to the firm's owners and managers. This reduced bargaining power then leads to lower wages and working conditions for all workers—relative to the nondiscrimination levels of wages and working conditions.

The heterodox analysis links the persistence of racial conflict to the profitability of capital and managerial decision making. Indeed, Shulman (1984) has argued that increases in joblessness tend to increase the economic incentives for discrimination. The elimination of racial conflict in employment, earnings, and occupational attainment, which is a catalytic agent for racial conflict beyond the work site, requires changing the hearts and minds of individuals, legal remediation where necessary, and changing the ownership structure and managerial organization of economic institutions. The heterodox approach is not without problems. Rhonda Williams (1987) has argued that this approach "is essentially a paternalistic discourse wherein deceived (with respects to the subtleties of class relations) white workers partake in their own subordination, although they have everything to gain from the eradication of black-white earnings inequality" (p. 6).

Williams raises an important point. The economic processes and conditions of our daily existence guide our understanding of the manner in which society is constructed. They also guide our understanding of the dynamics of power and self-interest. Why, then, are interracial coalitions to overcome racial conflict and to increase the well-being of all workers at the workplace and beyond historically scarce, difficult to form, and often unlikely to be maintained?

This chapter draws on the insights of the recently developed job competition analysis of discrimination to construct a detailed answer to Williams's question.

Methodology

A *successive approximations* approach is employed to make clear the interactions among racial conflict, the distribution of income, and the democratic process (at work and in society at large). Successive approximations is a pedagogical device for presenting complex theoretical arguments in "layers," whereby each layer moves the discussion forward from abstract theory to observed reality. Hence, the first approximation initiates the analysis at the highest level of theoretical abstraction. Initially, firms and jobs are assumed to be homogeneous and, except for racial distinctions, workers are also assumed homogeneous. Clearly, these are rigid assumptions that do not describe any real-world capitalist economy. But, if one is able to show that even in a world of economically homogeneous workers, firms, and jobs there are material incentives for racial discrimination, then one has also simultaneously demonstrated that discrimination may not simply be the result of prejudicial beliefs. Instead, the material incentives for discrimination originate from the very nature of capital as a social relationship. In other words, the incentives for racial discrimination in the market for labor power (and thereby racial conflict in the larger society) may arise from the very nature of the economic system itself as well as the shortcomings of particular individuals.

Under these artificially stringent conditions, two propositions regarding the racial and class distributional consequences of racial conflict are derived. The first proposition argues that racial conflict in the workplace produces economic harm for laborers as a class. Proposition 2 states that class coalitions among workers have a potentially higher long-term payoff, but short-term incentives encourage racial coalitions among workers.

In the following sections, the approximations technique is used to test the strength of these propositions by progressively increasing the "realism" of the analysis. Approximation 2 discusses the historical economics of whiteness as a social construct using workplace and social segmentation. Although this section continues using the assumption of homogeneous business firms, it adds the important modification that jobs within a firm may differ and drops the assumption of economically homogeneous workers.

Approximation 3 relaxes the assumption of homogeneous business firms and extends the analysis to a discussion of the interrelations among the competition of firms, the reproduction of racial conflict, and worker well-being. Then there is a discussion of the role of social managers in rationalizing and managing the economic system to maintain capital and the social order. This final section utilizes the preceding analysis to sketch criteria for a racially democratic and egalitarian economy.

FIRST APPROXIMATION:
RACE AND THE RESERVE ARMY OF UNEMPLOYED

Let us begin with some facts. First, if ownership and control over capital defines class position, then the United States is a society of deep class divisions. Nearly four fifths of the nation's productive property is controlled by just 10% of the nation's families (Smith, 1986). The economic elite has a near monopoly of the means of production, whereas the primary income earning asset of most families is the family's supply of labor power (Kennickell & Shack-Marquez, 1992; Smith, 1986). Second, the American political and economic elite is racially homogenous (white), whereas the American nation is decisively and increasingly multiracial (Whites, African Americans, indigenous peoples, Asian Americans, Latinos) (Fullerton, 1989). Third, in a capitalist economy, the reserve army of unemployed will exist with or without racial conflict. The reserve army of unemployed is a regulator of the general wage, the intensity of labor, the length of the workday, and the quality of working conditions (Green, 1991a, 1991b). Fourth, the competitive process can sustain persistent noncompensating intra- and interindustry wage differentials within and between occupations (Botwinick, 1993; Mason, 1993, 1995; Williams & Kenison, in press).

Clearly, the United States is a racialized capitalist state, whose race-class social matrix does not permit an easy separation of racial and class conflict. Nevertheless, race and class are historically and analytically separate and irreducible categories. The accumulation of (white-owned and -controlled) capital reproduces a multiracial reserve army of unemployed that encourages a fierce interracial battle for the more desirable employment opportunities. Both dominant group workers (Whites) and subordinate group workers (indigenous peoples and workers of African, Asian, Mexican, Caribbean, and Central and South American origin) face an identical economic elite, white capital.

The class struggle between labor and capital over wages, employment, working conditions, the intensity of labor, and the expansion of workplace democracy generates competition among workers for comparatively greater access to the more desirable employment opportunities. Full-time employees confront reserve army participants as unwanted low-wage competitors; at the same time, in a racialized society, white capital recognizes that subordinate laborers are easily forced into the least desirable (more difficult to fill) low-wage occupations. And, subordinate labor experiences white capital as exploiters of their labor power and as racial antagonists, whereas white workers are often experienced as the foot soldiers of white racial supremacy.

Economic growth and the accompanying expansion of capitalist social relations is a racialized process. It reproduces: (a) a weakened and divided working class, and, hence, a group of workers less able to gain wage increases or improved working conditions; and (b) material incentives for exclusionary behavior. Accordingly, the persistence of racial conflict is consistent with an increased rate of exploitation and thereby the reproduction of the racial struggle is commensurate with the economic forces of accumulation and competition. All other things held constant, racial conflict at this level of theoretical abstraction can lower worker solidarity and thereby lower the general wage rate and increase the size of the reserve army. The consequence will be an increase in the intensity of work, or the length of the effective workday, or directly lowering the costs of labor compensation, or lowering the circulating capital expenditures that would normally be used for maintaining working conditions at a socially optimal level (Marx & Engels, 1972, p. 354).

The reproduction of racial conflict may be beneficial to capital. Yet the resulting increase in the profitability of capital may not necessarily lead to an identical increase in the rate of accumulation. First, it is doubtful that an increase in the intensity of labor can occur without an increase in the use of supervisors (Gordon, 1990). Hence, some of the increased profit resulting from racial conflict will be diverted to pay for supervisory labor—that is, nonproductive labor—and would be therefore unavailable for accumulation. Second, the amount of profit available for accumulation will be reduced further by any increase in capitalist consumption expenditures. Third, some of the increased profitability may be used to increase money wages of racially privileged workers. Finally, of course, the increased profits may be used for additional fixed capital investment (either domestic or offshore).

Let $I = I(i, d, j, c)$ represent an index of worker sovereignty and security, which is a function of work intensity per unit labor time (i), the extent of workplace democracy (d), the exposure to joblessness (j), and the relative pleasantness of working conditions (c). By construction, an increase in the pace or difficulty of work lowers worker sovereignty ($\delta I / \delta i < 0$); an increase in workers' voice in the firm's activities raises the index ($\delta I / \delta d > 0$); an increase in the exposure to joblessness reduces worker security ($\delta I / \delta j < 0$); and an increase in the pleasantness of working conditions raises the index ($\delta I / \delta c > 0$).

Workers' quality of life depends on both money wages and the extent of control workers have over their lives. For example, if money wages remain constant but workplace democracy decreases, work intensity increases, working conditions become more onerous, or the exposure to joblessness rises, then workers have surely suffered a decline in their quality of life. For the analysis below, it is important to know how a particular action influences the quality of workers' lives and their monetary income.

Therefore, we will employ the concept of social sustainable wages (Githinji & Perrings, 1993). Socially sustainable wages in period t (SW_t) are constructed as

[4.1] $SW_t = W_t*(I_t/I_0)$,

where W_t is the money wage rate during period t and I_0 is the base period index of worker sovereignty and security. If $SW_t > SW_{t-1}$, workers are "better off" today. On the other hand, if $SW_t = SW_{t-1}$ but $W_t > W_{t-1}$ and $I_t < I_{t-1}$, then workers have exchanged some of their economic sovereignty and security for higher money wages and they are no better off (as a class).

The short-term effect of changes in either the intensity or extent of racial conflict on the reserve army rate depends on whether these changes raise or lower effective demand (level of current output and employment). The longer-term effect depends on whether these changes alter the rate of economic growth. Increases in capitalist consumption, the money wages of racially dominant workers, and the pay of supervisory workers may help prop up effective demand even as lower money wages of subordinate workers reduce effective demand. Additional fixed capital expenditures may raise the rate of growth (while providing additional short-term support for effective demand) even as changes in either the intensity or extent of racial conflict may undermine the prevailing social structure of accumulation. As a simplifying hypothesis, assume that both the short- and long-term reserve army rates are invariant to changes in racial conflict; even as the composition of the reserve army is very much related to the extent of racial conflict.

Proposition One (P1): At a minimum, an increase in racial conflict reduces the aggregate wage rate (both money and sustainable), alters the racial composition of the reserve army, and raises the rate and mass of surplus value.

Racially differential outcomes regarding reserve army status can sustain persistent racial conflict. Consider the following example, where the subscript "W" refers to white workers, whereas the subscript "A" refers to African American, Latino, indigenous, and Asian American workers; $Y \equiv$ mean income, $Tr \equiv$ level of transfer payments, $L \equiv$ the labor force, and the subscripts "0" and "1" reference the ex ante and ex post state of racial conflict, respectively, and the subscripts "E" and "R" reference employed and reserve army status, respectively.

$$Y_{W0} = (W_{W0} / I_{W0})*(L_{W0,E}/L_{W0}) + \text{Tr}*(L_{W0,R}/L_{W0})$$
$$= \text{initial white income;}$$

$$Y_{W1} = W_{W1}*(I_{W1}/I_{W0})*(L_{W1,E}/L_{W1}) + \text{Tr}*(L_{W1,R}/L_{W1})$$
$$= \text{subsequent white income;}$$

$$Y_{A0} = (W_{A0}/I_{A0})*(L_{A0,E}/L_{A0}) + \text{Tr}*(L_{A0,R}/L_{A0})$$
$$= \text{initial subordinate worker income;}$$

$$Y_{A1} = W_{A1}*(I_{A1}/I_{A0})*(L_{A1,E}/L_{A1}) + \text{Tr}*(L_{A1,R}/L_{A1})$$
$$= \text{subsequent subordinant worker income;}$$

$$Y_0 = (L_{A0}/L_0)*Y_{A0} + (L_{W0}/L_0)*Y_{W0}$$
$$= \text{initial income of all workers;}$$

$$Y_1 = (L_{A1}/L_1)*Y_{A1} + (L_{W1}/L_1)*Y_{W1}$$
$$= \text{subsequent income of all workers.}$$

If racial conflict lowers the average socially sustainable wage, then $Y_0 > Y_1$ and therefore $(L_{A0}/L_0)*Y_{A0} - (L_{A1}/L_1)*Y_{A1} > (L_{W1}/L_1)*Y_{W1} - (L_{W0}/L_0)*Y_{W0}$. That is to say, the change in subordinant worker economic well-being exceeds the change in white economic well-being. This result suggests that the economic imperative for working-class solidarity becomes complex. Assume that privileged workers are a constant fraction of the workforce, that is, $L_{W1}/L_1 = L_{W0}/L_0$, and that the sustainable wages of privileged workers are constant with respect to changes in the extent of racial conflict. For example, the percentage increase (decrease) in the money wage of privileged workers is matched by an equal percentage decrease (increase) in the sovereignty and security index of privileged workers. To the extent that racial conflict alters the composition of the reserve army in favor of privileged workers, privileged workers will gain from racial conflict, that is, $(L_{W1}/L_1)*Y_{W1} - (L_{W0}/L_0)*Y_{W0} > 0$, and subordinate workers will lose, that is, $(L_{A0}/L_0)*Y_{A0} - (L_{A1}/L_1)*Y_{A1} > 0$.

Corollary to P1: At a minimum, persistent racial conflict among workers requires that at least one group of workers must experience some money "gain" from racial conflict relative to other workers.

The possibility of money gains by privileged workers from racial conflict does not imply the absence of compelling economic incentives for interracial coalitions to end racial conflict. Although we are currently operating at an extraordinary level of abstraction by essentially ignoring productive differences in workers, the organization of work within and between firms, the technical compositions of capitals, the role of the state, and the impact of historical-economic institutions—a multiracial working-class coalition for full employment, higher and equal money wages, better working conditions, greater workplace democracy, lower intensity of work, and an end to racial conflict at the workplace and beyond can make all workers better off.

Proposition 2 (P2): Multiracial coalitions have a potentially superior return, but the immediate material incentives are more conducive to "race first" organizing.

The second proposition is informative of the inherent difficulty of forming multiracial coalitions. The coalitional outcome is an analytical possibility that is far from immediately obvious to individual workers. Even if it is recognized by a critical mass of workers, it is an outcome that may require an organization or movement capable of crippling racialized competitive exclusion among workers. On the other hand, the reproduction of the reserve army and the interracial war for income positions does produce immediate material motivation for subordinant group individuals (African Americans, Latinos, indigenous peoples, Asian Americans) to understand the racially divisive outcome as a system of white privilege. In the same way, individual white workers may have every material incentive to view their employment and remuneration as justly deserved. Moreover, a "race first" noncoalitional outcome does not require either class organization or a structural transformation of the status quo—racialized competitive exclusion.

SECOND APPROXIMATION:
RACE AND SEGREGATION

Economic agents (the owners of firms, managers, workers, and organizations) are not the ahistorical and nonsocial entities of orthodox economic analysis. The economy is an interdependent collection of evolving historical-social processes with continuous feedbacks among the requirements for accumulation, the outcomes of market processes, the social consciousness of individuals, and the institutional requirements for preserving domestic tranquility.

"Whiteness," a necessary social construct for preserving the status quo, is both antiegalitarian and antidemocratic. Race has enormous material consequences for each person's life chances, yet individuals are barred from choosing their racial category. To say that race is a social construction is not to deny that there are phenotypical differences among individuals. Nor does the use of this concept deny that there are enormous differences in cultural affectations. But the manner in which a particular society privileges some people with certain phenotypical features against others with different phenotypical features produces the conflicting social construction of race.

It is immediately obvious then that racial categories are established on the basis of long-term conflict in the distribution of power and privilege. To be "black" means nothing more or less than not being "privileged." The essence of whiteness is to have preferential access to economic, social, and political opportunity (Bell, 1992; Cruse, 1988).

Historically, it is clear that "whiteness" was created as an exclusionary mechanism (Roediger, 1991). It is also clear that to be "privileged" is to be a part of a social group whose elites possess coercive power and have the material incentives to enforce principles of exclusion. As a rule, subordinant group workers have been forced into American society as suppliers of cheap resources. For example, the relationship between Whites and indigenous peoples was governed by the desire of the "founding fathers" forcibly to expropriate the lands of indigenous peoples (Takaki, 1990, 1993). Likewise, the white-African relationship was governed by the forcible expropriation of African labor to meet the enormous requirements for the production of cotton, sugar, and tobacco (Takaki, 1990, 1993; Williams, 1964). The conditions under which slavery was abolished and indigenous peoples herded into reservations forced African Americans, indigenous peoples, and other subordinant group workers to enter the labor process as a racialized reserve army. Once African American and other subordinant workers were forced into these positions, the dynamics of the accumulation, competition, and institutionalized racial conflict reproduced the racial pattern of employment.

With the historic identity issue outlined, in this next approximation will be an examination of how segmentation processes, workplace and social, affect the propositions regarding racial conflict in the market for labor power. With respect to workplace segmentation, it is now well understood that the hierarchial nature of capitalist organizations and the struggle between labor and capital over the production and appropriation of surplus value sustains a segmented labor process (Gordon et al., 1982). Given the segmented and hierarchial nature of work, the aggregate reserve army represents a collection of occupational reserve armies (Friedman, 1984; Mason, 1993). Further, the potential labor supply for any tier of the occupational hierarchy includes the following components: all full-time workers that are currently employed at that tier, plus a fraction of workers from lower tiers of the occupational hierarchy, plus a fraction of the general reserve army—certainly all persons who are involuntary part-time employees for a given occupational tier plus some of the reserve army members who currently have no employment at all. What is true of the economy in aggregate—a surplus of available workers—becomes the generalized characteristic of each occupation in particular (Mason, 1993). The reproduction of occupational reserve armies carries with it the possibility that jobs are not allocated solely on the basis of alleged productive attributes of individual workers. In this case, jobs may be allocated on the basis of non-productivity-related attributes without harming the firm's competitive posture in the output market.

The reproduction of the reserve army, capital's monopolization of productive assets, and the fact that jobs can be partially distributed on bases other than the supposed productive attributes of individual workers is encouraged by social segmentation of labor. Workers create formal organizations (unions) and informal organizations (job networks) to redress the inherent imbalance of power that exists between individual workers and individual firms, as well as the imbalance of power between labor as a social aggregate and the controllers of capital as a social aggregate. Furthermore, worker organization is both multileveled and unevenly developed across racial, ethnic—and gender—lines.

Worker organization may be developed at the level of the family, community/group, firm, state, or international in scope (Craig, Rubery, Tarling, & Wilkinson, 1985). These organizations are both empowering and exclusive. They increase the power of workers within the organization relative to capital while simultaneously increasing the power of workers within the organization relative to other workers excluded from the organization.

Job networks (Grint, 1991, pp. 236-273; Montgomery, 1992; Yans-McLaughlin, 1990) are an important source of worker organization and information that connects households to the market for labor power. These networks facilitate individual employment procurement, access to training, and ascension to the managerial class. Given unequal structures of labor remuneration, otherwise identical individuals will fare differently in the market for labor power if their respective job networks possess differential job information and job power.

The dialectical character of worker organizations blurs the analytical boundaries between nonmarket social reproduction and the processes regarding the distribution, utilization, and remuneration of labor power. That is, outcomes in the market for labor power and social segmentation among workers are mutually reinforcing.

The hierarchial distribution of jobs, the continuous reproduction of occupational reserve armies, and the social segmentation of labor coalesce to create the space for the distribution of jobs on the bases of the alleged productive potential and the ascriptive characteristics of workers. In short, hierarchy, occupational reserve armies, and social segmentation are the institutional mechanisms that facilitate the interracial allocation of labor in economies characterized by individual capital's continuous drive to decrease unit cost and to raise profit.

This more complex analysis of markets permits a more complex understanding of racial conflict, even as our analysis reinforces P1 and P2. *We can now understand racial conflict as altering the composition of the general reserve army, as well as the composition of occupational reserve armies, through its racially differential effects on direct occupational mobility and access to on-the-job training.* Yet there is nothing in this more complex analysis that alters the initial analysis of the distributive consequences of racial conflict. Racial conflict (a) lowers the sustainable wage rate and reduces working-class sovereignty, even as it may conceivably increase the money wage for a segment of privileged workers; (b) skews reserve army membership away from privileged workers and toward subordinant group workers; (c) skews on-the-job training away from subordinant group workers and toward privileged workers; and (d) increases the upward (downward) occupational mobility of privileged (subordinant) workers relative to subordinant (privileged) group workers.

The more complex analysis also highlights the additional complexity of forming multiracial coalitions. It remains true at the most abstract level of analysis that multiracial worker coalitions have substantial material interests in struggling for an economic agenda that eliminates racialized competitive exclusion. It is even more apparent at this lower level of abstraction that the material differences in hiring, training, and promotion, as well as the process of social segmentation among workers, will continue differentially to inform workers' understanding of the relative gains and losses from racial struggle for egalitarian access to income opportunities.

The basic propositions of racial conflict remain intact. The segmentation and division of workers at the workplace is mutually complementary to the social segregation of workers along racial lines. The social and workplace segregation of workers is incorporated into political struggles that are divided on racialized class lines. Moreover, given that both public and private sector managers are necessarily products of workplaces, neighborhoods, and political organizations that are segmented by both class and race—where our notions of race are endowed with something substantially more than descriptive content—it is the exceptional[1] manager who makes nonracialized, nonelitist decisions regarding the allocation and remuneration of labor power (Brimmer, 1985; Jones, 1986; Kirschenman & Neckerman, 1991; Riach & Rich, 1991, 1992).

THIRD APPROXIMATION: EMPLOYMENT SEGREGATION
AND WAGE INEQUALITY

Racialized employment competition and racialized class conflict reproduce preferences for discrimination. Race becomes a coalescing cultural
agent (Darity, 1989) for currently employed "insiders" to protect their
positions from "outsiders." Race also becomes a marker of low-wage workers. The interaction between racial conflict and the formation of inter- and
intra-industry wage differentials permits additional development of the basic
propositions of racial conflict.

Botwinick (1993) provides a classical Marxian theory of wage differentials, innovatively deriving the limits of the wage differentiation process
from the labor theory of value. In his approach, firms have differential
sources of pressure to constrain potential wage and security demands. These
differential sources of pressure to constrain laborers' demands are related to
the technical structure of firms. But, the actual ability of firms to constrain
workers' demands is inversely related to the bargaining power of workers.

According to Botwinick, variables related to the inter- and intra-industry
competitive structure of firms include capital intensity, size of the firm,
location of regulating firms, special conditions of production, value of fixed
capital investment, and the cost differentials between regulating and sub-
dominant firms. The competitive structure of firms provides technical limits
(potential sources of pressure to constrain wages) to wage increases between
and within industries. In addition, the nature and extent of worker organization across firms determines the capacity of workers to push wages toward
these limits and to control working conditions. Therefore, it is likely that
economically identical workers will receive differential compensation and
labor under differential degrees of worker sovereignty where wages and worker
sovereignty depend on labor power quality, the industry, firm, and strategic
location of the job, as well as the organizational capacity of workers.
Employment segregation and wage discrimination, then, are not in theory or
practice separable phenomena.

By Botwinick's analysis, the upper bound on the wage rate of regulating
capitals (w_R) is determined by a complex combination of structural limits to
wage differentials (S), labor power quality (E), working conditions and
workplace democracy (D), market stability (Y) variables, and the bargaining
power of labor (BP). This relationship is expressed in Equation 4.2 below.

Equation 4.3 concretizes the notion that worker sovereignty is related to
worker strength. In particular, it is hypothesized that job desirability is
positively related to bargaining power.

In turn, Equation 4.4 relates the bargaining power of labor to the extent and quality of labor organization, where one measure of the extent of labor organization is the percentage of workers organized (U) and where the quality of worker unity is related in part to interracial wage and employment ratios, R_w and R_q, respectively, as suggested by Reich (1981b).

[4.2] $w_R = F^1(S, E, D, Y, BP)$,

[4.3] $D = F^2(BP, Z_1)$,

[4.4] $BP = F^3(U, R_q, R_w, Z_2)$,

where Z_1 and Z_2 may contain elements of S, E, and Y.

Premium wages are paid for undesirable jobs (jobs with poor working conditions) only if labor has forced capital to increase the pecuniary returns to work. Disagreeable working conditions will not lead to higher monetary wages, but rather will provide additional proxies for the degree of dominance of capital over labor. If other factors are unchanged, poor working conditions are associated with low pay.

The wage rate is determined by the amount of socially necessary labor time required to produce a family's consumption bundle. Therefore, increases (decreases) in the quality of labor power required to produce the output of regulating capitals will raise (lower) the wage rate. Similarly, demand pressures (Y) will tend to raise (lower) the wage rate at capitals growing above (below) their long-term planned rate of growth.

For a given occupation, the wage premium may be determined by

[4.5] $\mu = w - w_{min}$,

where w_{min} represents the minimum wage rate for the occupation.

We have argued that race is an inherently invidious and exclusionary concept. Within this framework, ascriptive characteristics serve as labor allocation devices for scarce employment opportunities. As a historically related phenomenon, this principle of exclusion will vary across societies.

Equation 4.6 summarizes the principle of exclusion:

[4.6] $R_q = H(\mu, D, U, Z_3)$

where Z_3 may contain elements of S, E, and Y. Subordinant workers' (i.e., African American) employment relative to dominant workers' (white) employment (R_q) is hypothesized as negatively correlated with the wage differential (μ). R_q increases as the extent of (industrial) organization increases and as the level of racism within the organization declines. Similarly, the working conditions and workplace democracy vector (D) captures the often observed phenomenon that as working conditions worsen, the exclusion of subordinant workers decreases. Finally, Z_3 captures the effects of state policy, community pressures, interracial wage differences, and other exogenous variables.

Equations 4.2 through 4.6 reveal the interconnections between wage differentials, worker sovereignty, the interracial distribution of employment, and the competitive structure of capitals. Equations 4.2, 4.4, and 4.5 yield the "class struggle" locus in Figure 4.1. The "class struggle" locus reveals the relationship between the interracial employment level and the wage differential. The "racial exclusion" locus, given by Equations 4.5 and 4.6, exhibits a negative relationship between the size of the wage differential and the interracial employment ratio. Finally, the "dirty work"[2] locus, derived from Equations 4.3 and 4.4, captures the relationship between the interracial employment ratio and the quality of working conditions (worker sovereignty and security).

At $R_h > R*$, capital has an incentive to reduce subordinant worker employment ($R_h > \theta$) and the wage differential consistent with the interracial struggle among workers for the available job opportunities (μ_{RE}) is less than the potential wage differential (μ_{CS}). As workers attempt to increase wages, capital forms a coalition with dominant workers to push $R_h \rightarrow R*$. Simultaneously, the reduction in worker bargaining power leads to a decrease in worker sovereignty as $D_h \rightarrow D*$. In the end, the white worker "gain," due to the change in the composition of employment, is matched by a decline in the wage rate and a deterioration of worker sovereignty.

At $R_l < \theta < R*$, $\mu_{RE} > \mu_{CS}$ white workers will exit for greener pastures. Initially, when $R_q < \theta$, capital also has an incentive to "darken" its labor force so as to reduce worker solidarity. Hence, money wages and working conditions will decline. But, as R_l exceeds θ in its approach to $R*$, worker bargaining power improves due to the relatively greater exit opportunities of white workers; money wages and worker sovereignty stage a moderate comeback relative to their initial decline as $\theta < R_l \rightarrow R*$.

As the analysis has moved from the most abstract understanding of racial conflict as a labor allocation device for determining service in the reserve army to the more concrete understanding of racial conflict as a device for determining access to high wage jobs, P1 and P2 have remained in force. Moreover, it is now apparent that racial conflict is a multidimensional process whose elements are continuously reproduced and move in

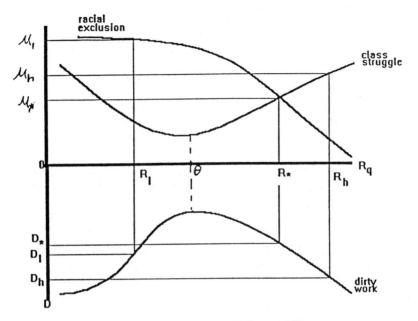

Figure 4.1. Race, Working Conditions, and Differential Wages

historically contingent directions in response to the initiatives of labor and capital.

Racial Conflict and Social Managers

The class struggle between labor and capital and the racial struggle between dominant and subordinate groups is mediated by armies of private and social managers. Indeed, the prevalence of managers has become so extensive that Darity (1983) has formed an analysis of capitalism based on the impact of managers.

It is inadequate to conceive of the United States as a "capitalist society" any longer. Instead, it is increasingly a "managerial society" where control over knowledge and information, that is, over ideas rather than finance, has become a fundamental source of power. . . The new age witnesses professionalization of careers involving supervision and management of human lives.

The coming of managerial society has been achieved by the rise of a managerial class which consists primarily of the social managers, the manufacturers or producers of public policy. Their vehicle for autonomous action—independent of the control of capital—has been the central government.

[I]t is useful to recognize three great social classes in modern America—managerial, capitalist, and working class. From the perspectives of the managers, both capital and the working class must be contained for the social good. Of course, the managers themselves necessarily define the social good. Idealization of "pluralist democracy" represents the essence of managerial thinking on conflict containment. (Darity, 1983, pp. 62-65)

In Darity's view, managers are "social structure neutral." The reason for managers' existence is as social intermediaries between the reproductive requirements of capital and the humanitarian demands of labor and between the competing interests of dominant and subordinate racial groups. Hence, social managers may agree on the ultimate objectives of managerial policy, which is to produce a society characterized by monopolistic control and ownership of productive property and managed change of the racial order. What managers disagree on is the optimal policy mix to accomplish that agenda. Managers are concerned with social structure stability rather than social structure transformation.

Black social managers—the self-proclaimed "talented tenth," voice of the downtrodden, and perennial special assistants to the dominant social managers—are the intermediaries between the African American working class and the racially privileged managerial and capitalist classes. By contrast, white social managers—the executive partners of the managerial class—are the intermediaries between the racially privileged social classes (labor and capital) as well as the intermediaries among racially privileged and subordinant social classes.

At this more concrete level of analysis, one sees again why the interracial terms of exchange may create the material impression of individual white worker gain from racism, even though systemic class analysis suggests the possibility of pan-racial working-class gain from coalitional efforts to eliminate racial privilege in economic processes. Roughly 5% to 7% of African Americans are members of either the managerial or capitalist class; both groups are characterized by relative smallness in their control over resources, and black capitalists are numerically small as well. Latinos, the next largest of traditionally excluded groups, possess a class distribution similar to African Americans. On the other hand, Asian and Native Americans are quite small numerically and in their combined control over political and economic resources (Waldinger, Aldrich, & Ward, 1990). Whites have a virtual monopoly over social management institutions and assets, as well as a virtual monopoly over private sector managerial decision making. Given the tremendous interracial disparity in access to managerial and capitalist power, "whiteness" is a source of absolute advantage in the interracial competition for power, control, and income.

Constructing a Racially Democratic and Egalitarian Economy

What are the options? The propositions regarding racial conflict and the analysis that supports them are guides to the requirements for constructing a racially democratic and egalitarian economy. At its core, the criteria for a racially democratic and egalitarian economy must create greater material incentives for racial cooperation and fewer incentives for racial conflict. Based on the preceding analysis, the following items are an outline of a broad agenda for achieving a racially democratic and egalitarian economy. The requirements are

   i. Employment as a right
   ii. Reorient objectives of production units:
      a. substitute a living wage for profit maximization;
      b. substitute the social good for private appropriation of profit.
   iii. Reconstruct ownership and organization of production units
      a. substitute worker/community democracy for elite hierarchy.
   iv. Aggressively incorporate racial democracy agenda into evaluation criteria of private and social managers.
   v. Expand the opportunities for self-employment by democratizing access to credit/financial resources:
      a. self-employment through worker and financial cooperatives;
      b. traditional self-employment.
   vi. Aggressive marketing of information by the state:
      a. free computer access to all government information;
      b. state financed radio and television stations whose sole purpose is to broadcast a continuing series of informational seminars on technology, government issues, educational retooling workshops, and so on.

We initially argued that at the most abstract level of analysis, racial conflict functions as a sorting mechanism for access to employment. Securing employment as a right for adults willing and able to work eliminates this source of racial conflict.

However, the right to employment does not address organizational hierarchy and its role in perpetuating racially differential occupational mobility and access to on-the-job training. Criteria iii through v above address these concerns. Expanding the opportunities for both traditional self-employment and self-employment within a democratic framework enhances the possibility that workers can exit discriminatory employment situations and thereby enhances worker power within production units. In addition, subordinant workers are better able to accumulate managerial training and expertise. Similarly, evaluating and rewarding managers (in part) according to their efforts at achieving the firm's racial democracy objectives substantially increases the possibility that managers will internalize racial democracy as a fundamental goal of the organization. Of course, it is ultimately desirable to have workers in direct control of a democratically oriented enterprise; hence, Criterion iii.

Criterion ii is concerned with a production unit's fundamental reason for existence. We have demonstrated that capitalist firms have a material incentive to encourage racial inequality (because it lowers wages and reduces working conditions, that is, increases profit) and that production for profit perpetuates a racial spoils system because of the relative scarcity of high-wage employment opportunities. Altering the firm's operational objectives may alleviate the racial spoils system. Finally, social managers must be "de-powered." This can be accomplished by a continuous and rapid decentralization of information.

Is this agenda possible? In the short term, no. This is a long-term agenda, concerned with creating a vision and a set of goals that are antithetical to the economic policies currently fashionable within the two-party framework. Indeed, as this chapter goes to press, even mildly reformist and formerly presumed safe policies such as affirmative action are being attacked. There are even signals from the Supreme Court that hard-won voting rights (for African Americans and Latinos) are under attack. In a very real sense, recent (1968-1994) political changes in the United States are frighteningly remindful of the rise of Jim Crow (1877-1896). Just as the 20-year period following the First Reconstruction established a racial agenda that required nearly a century to overcome, it seems that the all-too-limited Second Reconstruction—that is, the civil rights movement from 1954-1968—is falling victim to a racial order that will necessitate protracted struggle. But, if the analysis is correct—that egalitarian democracy and racially managerial capitalism are mutually inconsistent—then we should not flinch at the difficulty of the task that lies before us.

Notes

1. The manner in which race is socially constructed has become an implied locus of understanding regarding the most basic modes of expression and communications. For example, to be "middle class" or exhibit "middle-class behavior/values" is synonymous with being "white." Hence, in those circumstances where middle-class dress, behavior, values, attitudes, hairdos, and so on are deemed necessary prerequisites, "nonwhiteness" becomes an opportunity tax (and "whiteness" becomes an opportunity subsidy). For verification of these assertions, see Kirschenman and Neckerman (1991).

Goldfield (1990) examines a similar theme. He argues that white supremacy is the main explanation for the peculiar historical development of American politics, relative to the more class conscious politics of other industrially mature nations.

2. Stanback (1980) and Baron (1976) have argued for a relationship between the interracial employment ratio and the quality of working conditions. They contend that there is a relatively greater demand for subordinant workers in "dirty jobs."

5

Race for the Globe

U.S. Foreign Policy and Racial Interests

GERALD HORNE

The United States of America has a more racially diverse population than any other leading industrial nation, such as Japan or Germany. This population diversity can be a source of enrichment, strength, and innovation, or of conflict and national weakness that splinters governance and "balkanizes" the culture. One area in which the advantages and disadvantages of the nation's racial and cultural diversity can be seen is the conduct of U.S. foreign policy. Whether racial diversity has strengthened or weakened the nation is dependent on "whose ox is being gored" and whose interests are being served. This is not to suggest that racial concerns are the sole factors in advancing U.S. foreign policy. The economy plays an important and closely related role (Wilkins, 1964). However, the questions to be considered in this chapter are (a) to what extent has the conduct of U.S. foreign policy been shaped by domestic racial stratification; and (b) to what extent has the conduct of U.S. foreign policy served the conflicting interests of people of color and nonelite white Americans?

The answers to the central questions of this chapter are more obvious from the historical records than one might think. Foreign economic and political issues were responsible for the founding of the United States and for its racial dilemma. Foreign policy is not something external to the internal affairs of this nation. Quite the opposite, it is intrinsic to this nation's very existence and racial cultural diversity. The formation of this nation was itself a direct product of historic conflict with forces external to North America. Throughout the late 18th and 19th centuries, the United States, like any other developing nation, had to be acutely aware of developing designs and plans in foreign nations more powerful than itself.

The economic development of the nation was assisted immeasurably by an early foreign policy that linked economic growth with participation in the African slave trade. W.E.B. Du Bois, Eric Williams, and Walter Rodney have each pointed out that this foreign policy decision was instrumental in forming the foundation of modern capitalism on a global scale (Du Bois, 1973; Rodney, 1972; Williams, 1944).

In the past, scholars have ignored the influence of domestic racial differences and conflicting interests on U.S. foreign policy. Domestic affairs was conveniently separated from international affairs. Fortunately, some scholars are coming to recognize that to ignore domestic race and ethnicity when considering the formulation and orientation of U.S. foreign policy is a grave error. Gabriel Almond (1951), Louis Gerson (1964), and George W. Shepherd, Jr. (1970) were the first to point this out; then other important works followed (e.g., Schmidt, 1971; Weston, 1972). For a review of this early literature, see Bowser (1987). To consider race and ethnicity simultaneously in the formulation of U.S. foreign policy is to shed new light on one of the most pressing concerns of any nation; that is, how will it get along with neighbors, near and far, and how are its relations with neighbors affected by internal relations among citizens with diverse cultures and nationalities?

U.S. Foreign Policy: In Whose Interest?

No national government wants to admit that its foreign policy is designed to benefit first and foremost the ruling elite of the nation. To study racial and ethnic issues in foreign policy is to raise the question of in whose interest is the nation's foreign policy conducted? The masking of elite interests often takes the form of suggesting that foreign policy is designed to serve some amorphous "national interest."

A historic example of such a conflict was whether or not this nation would choose to honor international conventions against the slave trade that benefited a minority of property owners and disadvantaged nearly everyone else. Foreign policy in the 18th and 19th centuries was written for European American slaveowners (Blackett, 1983). It should be noted, however, that the European American population was not monolithic in support of the slave trade. For various reasons—religious, economic, and political to cite a few—European American dissenters hotly opposed this commerce in human flesh and paid dearly for their support (Aptheker, 1992). Some did so on the basis that it violated the basic tenets of Christianity. Others, particularly those in the European American working class, felt that the slave trade and slavery inevitably debased the notion of work itself, not to mention wages. Still others, particularly in the North of the nation, felt that the slave trade gave the South an unfair advantage in the ongoing jockeying for sectional hegemony. Inability to grapple effectively with these tensions ineluctably led to the U.S. Civil War.

Likewise, a tariff aimed at certain exports such as slavery could be seen as a measure bolstering Northern commercial interests, whereas Southern slaveowners' interests were tied more directly to English commercial interests, which would be hurt by such a tariff. In the same way, after the Civil War many European American workers in California objected violently to the immigration of Chinese to this nation on the premise that the Chinese were being used to undercut "white" wages and working conditions. On the other hand, many California employers supported this immigration and not because of altruism. This latter case points to a recurring problem of class differences in the conduct of U.S. foreign policy. Employers and other elites have been the driving force in the formulation of U.S. foreign policy, often at the expense of the nonelite European American majority, who have not consistently affirmed their own interests. As we will see, the major effect of racism on white Americans historically and into the present is that it obscures their economic class interests and predisposes white Americans to support interests that are harmful to their own.

Open and vigorous debate of these raw class and economic interests rarely takes place in any nation on a wide-scale basis. At times, debates between and among competing elites (as we currently have between liberals and conservatives) substitutes for a more widespread discourse on economic class interests. Historically, lack of real debate regarding the interests that founded this nation was combined with colonial foreign policy concerns that were racially coded—to maintain slavery and the expropriation of land from the indigenous peoples in the face of intermittent objection from London.

This history helped to ensure that race and ethnicity would be central in the later formulation of U.S. foreign policy.

An Example:
Slavery and U.S. Foreign Policy

Merton Dillon is the latest scholar to recognize the importance of race in the construction of U.S. foreign policy (Dillon, 1990). From the beginning of the presence of Africans on these shores, prevailing English American elites doubted seriously if African Americans could be relied on in times of invasion and national emergency. They were worried that because of the atrocities that were visited upon them, peoples of African descent would make common cause with the perceived and actual enemies of European American elites in London, Madrid, Paris, Port Au Prince, Mexico City, and elsewhere. Furthermore, there was fear that Blacks would form alliances with sovereign Native American nations. These concerns and fears were not far-fetched. Runaway slaves allied themselves in Florida with the Seminole Indians in an ongoing war against federal troops (Katz, 1986).

As demonstrated by Bacon's Rebellion in Virginia in the 1660s, there was also a fear that Blacks would ally with poor Whites. This alliance almost led to the overthrow of the colonial elite. Elite fears of such an alliance helped to hasten their moving to intensify the status of Blacks as slaves and to accelerate the distancing of Blacks from poor Whites (Sobel, 1987, pp. 44-45, 257). This could very well be deemed the decisive turning point in the history of North America: Opening the gap—and keeping it open—between poor Blacks and Whites that developed because of and then as a result of the racial slave codes and the ideology of racism.

U.S. SLAVERY AND FRANCE

Foreign reactions to U.S. slavery also highlight the strategic need to separate domestic race relations from elite-defined U.S. foreign policy, and to the all-important goal of making certain that the black and white nonelite majority perceived no common interests. In dealing with the European American elite, Paris saw fit to take a different attitude from what their American counterparts would have liked toward the African presence in North America (De Conde, 1978). The appearance of a more enlightened attitude toward African Americans not only allowed Paris to seize the moral high ground in its relations with Washington, it was a major point of political leverage that the French have used in Washington.

Similarly, Paris's defeat in 1763 in the so-called French and Indian War could be deemed a setback for African Americans, who had to endure the weakening of a real but unsteady ally and a victory for English colonial elites, most of whom were slaveowners. With the French out of the way, the American elite now had one less contender to confront in their effort to seize control of the entire North American continent from its indigenous peoples—and later Mexicans—in order to populate the nation with Africans for profits from slavery. Was the defeat of the French also a victory as well for nonelite European Americans? To the extent that they now could participate in the expropriation of Indian lands, the answer was yes. But because not all nonelite Whites were participants in this process, it is difficult to say that they all gained from the defeat of the French. An example of a group that "benefited" from the French defeat and highlighted nonelite racial advantage in the United States is the "Acadians," who fled persecution in Canada for Louisiana (where they have been referred to as "Cajuns"). Once in Louisiana, they were able to enjoy color privilege, gain property, and some were able to participate in the enslavement of Africans as a way to gain wealth far beyond what a farmer could imagine.

Although France's defeat in 1763 had weakened its presence in the Western Hemisphere, neither its influence nor its legacy had been eliminated. It is not unfair to suggest that the victory of the colonists would have been much more difficult if it was not for the aid of Paris, which still wanted to settle scores with its British antagonist. The world was turned upside down at Yorktown as the British were forced to retreat and concede defeat to colonial upstarts. However, after the French Revolution and its promise of liberty, equality, and fraternity, the slaveowners who had come to wield heavy influence in the new government feared that this subversive message of liberty would be heard by their slaves. It is not difficult to imagine that the movement from the decentralization of the Articles of Confederation to the centralization of the U.S. Constitution was assisted by Southern white fears that they might need help from beyond their state borders in the face of the presumed threat from France. Worse still, it was feared that their slaves would be sufficiently inspired to challenge the status quo and find a common alliance with nonelite whites.

The concern of slaveowners reached a crescendo in 1798 when it seemed that another war with France was unavoidable. There was fear that Blacks from the West Indies—allied with French troops—would land on these shores, ally with Southern slaves, and wreak havoc initially in the Southern states and ultimately in the rest of the nation. This hysteria generated massive violations of civil liberties: Southern planters were so paranoid about external aid to slaves that they moved to erode the civil liberties of anyone who sought to speak out against this institution. This paranoia often was directed at non-slave-owning Whites who often saw no need to support the "peculiar institution."

But some of the paranoid planters did have real enemies. When Gabriel Prosser sought to revolt against slavery in Virginia in 1800, he apparently believed that the undeclared naval war between France and the United States would mean that the attention of slaveowners would be sufficiently diverted to provide his forces with a distinct advantage. No doubt there were influential forces in Paris who did not view U.S. slavery benignly (Aptheker, 1963; Degler, 1974; Tatum, 1934). The connection between race and U.S. foreign policy was very real.

U.S. SLAVERY AND GREAT BRITAIN

One can view the victory over London by the colonists in the Revolutionary War of 1776 in a similar vein as the victory over France (Quarles, 1961; Walker, 1976). Like Paris, London was an objective ally of slaves against slaveowning elites, despite the fact that London countenanced slavery itself. To the extent that London resisted the ambitions of its colonial slaveowning elites to seize more and more Indian lands, Britain was standing in the way of the expansion of a brutal slavery in North America. Nevertheless, many Blacks stood with the Yankees against the British Redcoats and against their own long-term interests during the American Revolutionary War. However, a number of others did not.

The story of Lord Dunsmore, the last royal governor of Virginia, and the effort of London to entice Native Americans and slaves to their side is now well known. London itself was already familiar with the past efforts of Madrid to play upon the contradictions between slaves and the Indians on the one hand and European American elites on the other. The leadership of the rebellious colonies, notably in slaveholding and anti-British colonial Virginia, were understandably concerned that their effort to oust British rule would be made more difficult because of the presence of rebellious Africans and Indians. Slaveowners were concerned that their contentious property, African slaves, would seize the opportunity presented by revolutionary dislocation to align with London or at least to rise up against slavery itself. Then slaveowners would have been forced to conduct a two-front war against slaves internally and British Redcoats externally. Preventing such a development became a major foreign policy concern of European American elites during the American Revolutionary War.

In November 1775, Lord Dunsmore proclaimed freedom for all adult male slaves who would flee their masters and come under his protection (Quarles, 1961). It is difficult to pinpoint with precision the number of Africans who responded to his appeal. However, it is apparent that like others before and since who have confronted European American elites, Lord Dunsmore recognized that there were sharp and antagonistic divisions among those who would eventually be called "Americans" and that these divisions could be manipulated profitably. Recognition of this central fact also propelled the abolitionist movement toward ending slavery. Wisely, U.S. elites sought to ease racial oppression by eventually ending slavery rather than maintaining practices that could be manipulated by foreign foes. But in 1776 London was not able to prevail despite their foe's formidable weakness. In the race to control North America, London was not able to play successfully on race. Yet it was very apparent that race was at the heart of the earliest foreign policy challenge confronted by the nation that became the United States of America.

U.S. SLAVERY AND HAITI

The unease among European American elites about the explosive connection between race and foreign policy was galvanized further by the Haitian Revolution beginning in 1791. There was the fear that Southern slaves might be sufficiently inspired to seek to emulate the audacity of their Caribbean brethren. There was the fear that a newly independent Haitian government might seek to aid Southern slaves. The very appearance of a Haitian ambassador in Washington in itself would have served to undermine an ideological edifice that proclaimed the inherent and inevitable subordination and inferiority of peoples of African descent. This helps to explain why diplomatic recognition of Haiti was not extended by Washington until the U.S. Civil War (Hunt, 1988).

U.S. SLAVERY AND SPAIN

When Spain transferred its sizeable territory of Louisiana to France in 1800, Southern slaveowners worried that their slaves would see this as a boon to their cause insofar as Paris was viewed as the seat of the global movement toward liberty. As it turned out, Southern planting interests benefited in the short term from the defeat of French colonialism in Haiti; this defeat was a major factor in facilitating the acquisition by the United States of the vast Louisiana Territory as France moved to liquidate some of its external holdings. This may have been a foreign policy victory for the property rulers of the United States, but to the extent that it facilitated the extension of slavery and spurred the continuation of a soon-to-be illegal slave trade from Africa, it must be viewed as a defeat for Africans in the United States. On the other hand, citizenship in this nation was given as part of "white male privilege." Otherwise poor European immigrants could now participate in the continuing ousting of Native Americans from the land and become prosperous farmers as a result.

A foreign policy based on maintaining slavery may help to explain why so many Blacks flocked so eagerly to the British banner during the War of 1812. They were not alone. Native Americans began to recognize that they had a better chance of surviving if Europeans based in London rather than Washington had a foothold in North America. Creeks and Choctaws stood ready to fight alongside the British; Spain was ready to dispatch black Cuban troops, and this sent a frisson of apprehension cascading throughout the slaveowning class. They feared retribution. They feared being slaughtered by vengeful former and current African slaves (Remini, 1977). Whites in general who backed their government in Washington feared that vengeful Blacks would not make distinctions between those who owned slaves and those who did not.

The prospect of what a military defeat in 1812 might have brought should have given elite and nonelite Whites reason to reconsider slavery. But again, events evolved in a manner beneficial, at least in the short term, to the interests of the planter class. Slavery was spared. In fact, the defeat of Britain in the War of 1812 set the stage for the further expansion of slavery into Florida. Washington did not easily forget the specter of the black Cuban threat; Spain ceded West Florida to the United States in 1819. This was another profound defeat for African Americans. Though Britain remained in Canada, the evacuation of Spain meant the erosion of a possibility of Blacks playing upon conflicts among European American elites and their European counterparts.

AFRICA

On February 3, 1816, Paul Cuffee, an African American and self-made wealthy merchant, sailed into Freetown harbor in Sierra Leone with 38 of his black compatriots from the United States. The effort of this influential African American and others of like mind to emigrate not just to Africa, but as well to territory where London wielded more influence than Washington, was suggestive of the nature of racial difference and U.S. foreign policy. The antislavery movement was stronger across the Atlantic, as was evidenced by the abolishment of slavery in British colonies decades before the ratification of the Thirteenth Amendment to the U.S. Constitution barring slavery and involuntary servitude in the United States.

Ultimately, some European American elites found it desirable to support the repatriation of Africans with an emphasis on those who were "free." These nonslave Blacks were deemed to be a nuisance: Their very existence stood as a living refutation of the notion that Africans were bound to be slaves (Berlin, 1975; Franklin, 1969). They were viewed as being favorable to the idea of slave revolts, and as inclined toward working actively to foment revolt. Thus, the American Colonization Society was organized. Before the South's defeat in the U.S. Civil War, the Society helped to transport thousands to West Africa in order to form the new state of Liberia. The capital, Monrovia, with its obvious homage to former U.S. President Monroe, stood as a living symbol of one of the more visible aspects of U.S. foreign policy toward Africa.

The earliest U.S. foreign policy toward Africa was nothing more than a way to get rid of African Americans whose very presence and intent was to disrupt domestic slavery. There were few territorial ambitions. European American elites were much more concerned about the development of nation-states in the Western Hemisphere. The British move to abolish slavery in nearby Jamaica was more news that the master class wanted to keep away from its slaves. There was also concern about the antislavery attitudes of those involved in the liberation of Latin America and South America. Notably, the U.S. master class was highly suspicious of the South American liberator Simon Bolivar, and concerned that his devotion to white supremacy was not as fervent as their own.

By the early 1840s, European American elites succeeded in founding a national state whose central economy and main source of wealth was based on African slavery. They had defended the new state against more powerful foreign governments, and expanded its territory, increased the number of slaves, and increased the wealth that slavery generated. Potential alliances among African Americans, Native Americans, and foreign governments against European American elite interests were also defeated. But two far more important things were accomplished. First, domestic affairs, in particular race relations, was successfully separated from U.S. foreign policy. In the American mind, domestic race relations and foreign policy became two mutually exclusive and unrelated affairs. Second, potential popular alliances among African Americans, Native Americans, and the majority of nonelite European Americans were also defeated. This was done by dividing people who held their labor in common into separate and unequal races where perceived physical differences became stratified castes. Any European could be "white," and to be "white" was privileged with personal freedom, the right to own property (Indian lands) and slaves (Africans), and fundamentally the right to vote. To be "black" was to be a slave, to have no personal liberties that white men had to respect, and to be property. White racial privilege aligned nonelite Whites' sense of their long- and short-term interests with those of elite Whites, and was categorically separated from the interests of "Blacks" and other outsiders.

Aggression Against
Other Neighbors

Still, there was a Latin American "threat" closer to the hearts and borders of the slaveowners. This was Mexico. The ouster of Spanish colonialism from Mexico City in some ways mirrored the North American colonists' defeat of the British in 1776. The revolution in Mexico led in turn to the revolt of European American settlers in Texas. The successful effort by renegade U.S. colonists in Texas to oust the rule of Mexico City and then to affiliate with the United States was yet another victory for the slaveholding class and a defeat for slaves and indigenous peoples. As in Britain, the antislavery movement was much stronger and more influential in Mexico City than in Washington. Once more, in a pattern that was becoming repetitive, a European American victory was at the same time an African American and Native American defeat. For "white privileged" working-class European Americans, new lands meant that they could share in part of the booty—land stolen from Indians, opened to be worked by African slaves. But the expansion of slavery into Texas also meant that wage levels would be further depressed for most Whites who did not own property and who were unable to escape wage labor. This also brought the day closer when hundreds of thousands of nonelite Whites would have to fight and die in a Civil War between Southern slave and Northern industrial elite interests to determine whose way of generating wealth would dominate the nation's future.

The defeat of Mexico divided families and peoples on both sides of the newly carved border between Mexico and the United States. It also added a new angle to the question of ethnicity and U.S. foreign policy by making Mexicans in the newly acquired territories citizens of the United States. Were they a race, an ethnic group, were they "white"—what were they? And just as Washington had to be concerned that the indigenous peoples and Blacks would align with actual and imaginary foes of Washington, now there had to be concern that the people who were to become Chicanos would act in a similar fashion (Acuna, 1981).

Like so many of Washington's other fears about foreign interference in the institution of slavery, the fear of Chicano alliances with foreign powers was not altogether misguided. The fact is that runaway slaves from Texas and other parts of the South often found a haven in Mexico, just as runaway slaves from other parts of the United States often followed the North Star to Canada (Rippy, 1931). For example, in 1850 an ethnic group known as "Mascogas," who were runaway slaves and free Blacks from Texas, left the United States and fled south to a town in the border state of Coahuila, Mexico. They were allied closely to the Florida Seminoles, who had found their presence in the slave South under constant attack since the departure of Spain from West Florida in 1819. In return for sanctuary, these people of color vowed to patrol the border on behalf of the Mexican government after it lost more than half of its territory to Washington during the 1846-1848 war. And, as so often happened during the antebellum era, Mexico found that it could find common ground with Africans and Indians.

During the entire antebellum period, African Americans found that their interests dovetailed with those of Great Britain and Mexico in that they were all apprehensive about the aggressive intentions of the planter class that dominated the government in Washington. This government not only had seized territory in North America from other nations, including sovereign Indian nations; it had gone further to stock this land with African slaves. This hunger for land and slaves undergirded an aggressive U.S. foreign policy that was grounded in white supremacy. This white supremacy led directly to the genocide and impoverishment of the indigenous and the enslavement of Africans. It was virtually impossible to say that U.S. foreign policy was designed to serve the interests of African Americans, Indians, or Mexicans. It was quite easy to say that U.S. foreign policy was designed to serve the interests of a lily-white slaveowning elite and was not in the interest of nonelite Whites. By the majority of Whites not having a sense of their own interests and by adopting elite interests as their own, they fought and died in wars of aggression, participated in onerous and dangerous slave patrols, and paid taxes to support a repressive government.

Though Washington was worried about Africans collaborating with London and Mexico City, Latin America had a more legitimate fear concerning the plan of Southern planters to seize Cuba, much of Central America, and—perhaps—the entire Western Hemisphere on behalf of slavery (May, 1973). Fundamentally, the barbarous nature of slavery was driving a U.S. foreign policy that was not only becoming more aggressive over time, it was also becoming apparent that Southern-inspired aggression was propelling the young republic into repeated confrontations with a formidable array of foreign foes. Conservative interests in London viewed the upstart United

States as a threat to its sizeable interests in the Caribbean. If Washington could seize land from Mexico right next door, then why not from London thousands of miles away? Meanwhile, progressive and anticolonial forces in London could hardly be sympathetic to Washington with its toleration of slavery and continued slave trade.

London also had reason to fear U.S. aggression toward Canada, which was still a British colony. But even anticolonial forces in Canada who were hostile to British hegemony found it difficult to find common ground with Washington. It was well known since the War of 1812 that the United States wanted Canadian territory. Britain, Spain, Canada, Mexico, Cuba, and all of Central America, like African Americans, were quite wary of the slaveowning elite in the United States and their negative influence on the trajectory of U.S. foreign policy. The aggressive international position of the United States in the mid-19th century was largely due to a desire to expand slavery. Repressing Blacks, battering Indians, and seizing the land of Mexicans was one thing. But continuing to confront European powers like Britain and Spain was quite another. It was also clear that until slavery was abolished in the United States there was potential for collaboration among antislavery foreign governments and disaffected Africans, angry Indians, and working-class Whites who feared that they were simply cannon fodder in the planter class's wars of aggression.

The U.S. Civil War
and Reconstruction

From the point of view of abolitionists, slavery had to be abolished, in part to curb the land-hunger of the Southern elite, who were not adverse to plunging the entire nation into war, and other foreign adventures to satisfy their own narrow interests. With the onset of the Civil War in 1861, the U.S. government and its antislavery allies could more fruitfully exploit a potentially positive relationship with antislavery and anticolonial forces in London. These forces hindered the attempt by the Confederates to curry favor with the British government. Sovereign Indian nations fought for both sides. Yet in outlining the many reasons why the South lost the Civil War, high on the list would have to be the difficulty the Confederacy faced in developing a foreign policy that could attract international support. The vaunted ability of the planter class to make its own interests the interests of the entire European American elite finally dissolved during the Civil War. Similarly, it was becoming increasingly difficult for nonelite Whites to accept the notion that their interests were being served by a slave system that dragged wages down to the level of impoverishment. Why should they fight and die to preserve such a system? But another powerful and countervailing tendency was also prevalent: the uncanny ability of nonelite Whites to pursue policies contrary to their own interests. This was seen in the rampant "Copperhead" pro-slavery sentiment in Northern cities like New York City that erupted in an antiblack pogrom that plunged this metropolis into turmoil during the height of the Civil War.

But finally during the Civil War, forward-looking Northern commercial interests asserted their own interests forcefully and this led, inevitably, to the dissolution of slavery. The ability of the U.S. government to repress the rebellion of the slaveowners was aided immeasurably by its development of a foreign policy that could attract more international adherents precisely because of the perception that Washington finally was joining the modern world by turning away from slavery. Nonetheless, those Blacks and others who felt that the defeat of the Confederacy would signal a rosy dawn for a pacific, antiracist, and less aggressive U.S. foreign policy were disappointed by the effort of the administration of President U. S. Grant to annex Santo Domingo. To many, this did not seem any different from the racially tinged foreign policy of old that aimed to annex Cuba. Confirming this suspicion was yet another proposal flowing from the Grant White House to annex a troubled Cuba, now in the throes of insurrection against Spanish domination. To many, it seemed that the perceived racial bias of U.S. foreign policy, which was presumed to be driven by a slaveowning elite, would continue to persist despite the defeat of the Confederacy (Crapol, 1992). Racism continued to be a part of U.S. foreign policy because although the slave system was defeated, its central ideology of white supremacy was not.

Race and U.S. Foreign Policy
to World War I

The defeat of the Southern plantation elite by Northern industrial interests did not end the need for "white unity." Racism was now clearly an important factor for elite power maintenance. It is absurd to expect that Washington would use racism at home and avoid projecting it abroad. Washington ignored the Fifteenth Amendment to the U.S. Constitution and ignored the new Southern elite's deprivation of the right of black males to vote by means of the "Jim Crow" codes by the turn of the century. African American interest in pushing Washington in an antiracist direction globally was silenced. But it was not just the deprivation of black civil rights that hindered the development of a U.S. foreign policy free of racial taint. The need to keep white and black interests separate and in conflict played an equal part. The nascent U.S. labor movement accelerated its self-defeating practice of opposing and racially segregating itself from nonwhite labor and allying itself along racial lines with capitalist interests. White labor supported the anti-Chinese campaign to repeal the 1868 Burlingame Treaty with China, an agreement that allowed for unrestricted immigration and movement between the two nations. Ultimately, the nativist forces triumphed when Congress passed the Chinese Exclusion Act of 1882. U.S. business interests had come to see immigration as a new way to build a large labor force and more effectively occupy land seized from the indigenous. However, though U.S. immigration policy kept Chinese workers out, white supremacy was evident in that the immigration of people of primarily northern European descent continued.

This anti-Asian sentiment provided a further boost to a racially discriminatory orientation of U.S. foreign policy. Asians were now added to the list of Africans, Indians, and Mexicans who were victims of U.S. foreign policy. There was an additional development in this period: With slavery and the plantation economy finally defeated, the emerging industrial economies not only had a tremendous appetite for labor, but control of foreign natural resources was an essential key to expanding their power and wealth. The Congress of Berlin in 1884-1885 signaled a new scramble for Africa by the major colonial powers of Britain and France, now joined by a newly united Germany and by Italy. This new development in the evolution of colonialism gave a boost to the ideology of racism that was necessary for integrating European immigrants into white unity, as leading nations deemed it the "white man's burden" to "civilize" the supposedly untutored "natives" of Africa. This racial paternalism masked the fact that elite interests were served in white racial unity and that European national elites lusted for the raw materials, cheap labor, and captive markets of Africa and Asia.

At first, the United States was not a major competitor. But the United States still managed to obtain territory that either contained darker peoples or was controlled by them. In 1867, Alaska was "purchased" from a Russia undergoing a turmoil of its own over serfdom—another system of forced labor—that had some of the earmarks of U.S. chattel slavery (Kolchin, 1987). Like the seizure of Mexican territory, the acquisition of Alaska brought into the nation a large number of indigenous peoples whose unsatisfied land claims against the U.S. government were to agitate domestic politics for some time to come. By the same token, the ouster of the Hawaiian royal family approximately 25 years later was spearheaded by U.S. agribusiness interests and demonstrated that Washington was not adverse to old-style colonialism, and direct seizure of territory and the suppression of legitimate domestic rebellion.

The latter part of the 19th century witnessed the rise of social Darwinism, eugenics, and other notions that substantiated the proposition that certain peoples were inferior and others were superior. This was interpreted to suggest that nations like the United States should take up the "white man's burden" and bring enlightenment to the benighted colored hordes. These theories also carried negative implications for Italian Americans, Jewish Americans, Slavic Americans, and others not sufficiently "lucky" to hail from northwestern Europe. It was at this point—in 1898—that the war between Spain and the United States erupted. As a result of this conflict, Washington was finally able to oust Madrid from its position of dominance in Havana and Manila.

Many Filipinos felt that the ouster of Spain should have led to their independence, and when this did not occur a bitter guerilla war ensued that, in many ways, was a precursor to the U.S. war in Vietnam decades later. Just as in the Indo-Chinese war, there were allegations that racial animus helped to explain the ferocity of the U.S. military response in the Philippines.

Some felt that the establishment of U.S. sovereignty over the Philippines was a paternalistic taking on of the "white man's burden." But notably Southern Congressmen objected to bringing more darker peoples under the U.S. umbrella. African Americans and many Whites as well were ambivalent about this conflict. Increasingly, the American working class, regardless of racial or ethnic origin, argued that creating more low-wage competition abroad was not the ideal way to preserve their jobs. They were of the opinion that it was worthwhile to help Cubans and Filipinos fight a despotic Spanish regime, but others were of the opinion that a U.S. government that could countenance the lynching of Blacks at home could hardly be relied on as a liberator abroad.

This war was not the only foreign conflict involving the United States that had racial implications. In California, the movement to exclude Asians, notably Japanese and Chinese, continued. These racially biased anti-immigrant maneuvers were highly revealing. With its defeat of Russia in 1905, Japan was viewed by many African Americans and other peoples of color as striking a blow for colored peoples everywhere. Then Washington's negotiations with Tokyo over the plight of Japanese immigrating to the United States led to a "gentleman's agreement" that somewhat eased discrimination against Japanese Americans. The point was not lost on African Americans—a powerful Japan meant an eased plight for Japanese Americans. Would a powerful Africa mean an eased plight for African Americans? Likewise, African Americans had learned from the experience of Italian Americans with Washington. When some Italians were lynched in Louisiana in the 1890s, the intervention of the government in Rome forced Washington to grant assurances that such a practice would not continue. Despite the supposed all-embracing cloak of "white privilege," nonelite Whites were beginning to understand that a country that countenanced lynching of Africans could easily countenance lynching of themselves. Jewish Americans were forced to absorb the same lesson a few years later when one of their own—Leo Frank, a plant manager in Georgia—was lynched after he was falsely accused of sexually violating and murdering a Christian woman. But unlike Italian Americans, Jewish Americans had no "big brother" abroad to rely on; so this outrage impelled many in their community to give increasing support to a developing African American movement for equality on the premise that reduction of racism generally would ultimately be to their benefit.

African Americans, too, had no patron abroad; this perception fueled the Pan-African Movement, a movement symbolized in the figure of the preeminent black intellectual and leader W.E.B. Du Bois, in which Pan-Africanists argued for the commonalities of African peoples throughout the world and, further, that a liberated Africa would be a plus for African Americans. In a real sense, Pan-Africanism resembled the then contemporary movements that had led directly to the formation of powerful states in Italy and Germany. Moreover, if Africa were not liberated, if it continued to languish under colonial domination, it would continue to be an object of allure for the major powers, plunging them into conflict as they scrambled for hegemony over territory and raw materials. This was the argument used by Du Bois to explain the coming of World War I. Germany felt that its economic preeminence should have guaranteed it a larger colonial rule, and war became the only route to bring about the desired result.

Race and U.S. Foreign Policy to World War II

Germany's colonial ambitions were thwarted on the battlefield, but the question of race continued to percolate unabated abroad and in the United States. At Versailles, Japan sharply raised the question of establishing racial equality as a prime principle of international discourse and the postwar settlement. Once again, African Americans, Native Americans, and other racial minorities found that they were in objective alliance with a major power, akin to what had transpired more than a century earlier when London was resisting the expansion of slavery in North America. This effort by Tokyo was not greeted with praise in Washington, however. After all, President Woodrow Wilson, a Democrat with deep roots in Virginia, had allowed the spread of Jim Crow to Washington, D.C., after assuming office in 1912. As was to happen with the Genocide Convention and other international instruments after World War II, there was an earlier fear within the European American elite that international law could be used as a battering ram to knock down the walls of Jim Crow in the United States. Tokyo's initiative was not supported by Washington and was defeated. Yet the introduction of the question of racial equality into the rarified realm of international diplomacy was a further example of how global politics was impinging increasingly on the unpleasant domestic reality of racism in the United States.

It was understandable why Washington resisted the Japanese initiative formally to make race an international issue. There were those who charged that the U.S. military occupation of Haiti, its predominance in Panama and Cuba, and its bullying of Nicaragua were inconsistent with the principle of racial equality. Marcus Garvey, the Jamaican who immigrated to the United States and ignited one of the largest mass movements ever among African Americans, extended this critique of U.S. foreign policy to Africa itself.

One of the major forces shaping race relations in the United States after World War I and, therefore, shaping U.S. foreign policy, have been noted by the historian John Higham (1955). World War I involved severe conflict between and among various European ethnic groups (e.g., French vs. German, Hungarian vs. English, etc.). There were immigrants from all of these countries in the United States and therefore the potential for these European conflicts also to occur in the United States. In effect, "white" racial unity under the notion of Americanism could be undermined by ethnic nationalism. Again, it seemed that the ethnic diversity of the United States was not a strength but a dire weakness that could cause strain in the nation and stand beyond elite control. The response was to intensify the Americanization of these immigrants through public education. As Higham details, the decline of the so-called hyphenated American—the German-American, the Italian-American, and so on—was accelerated, resulting in the faster incorporation of these immigrants among "white" Americans. The Americanization process was symbolized in U.S. manufacturing plants when workers wearing their foreign national dress passed behind a partition and emerged on the other side dressed as prototypical "Americans." This tendency was showed concretely with the decline of the foreign language press and the general decline of bilingualism among immigrant European Americans.

To be sure, the decline of the "hyphenated American" was an uneven process. Certainly, Jewish Americans at this point were not being accepted enthusiastically into the hallowed halls of whiteness. Social Darwinist ideas were still in ascendance that mandated that Jews and Italians might be higher in the pecking order than Africans or Mexicans or even Asians, but they were certainly inferior to Americans from northwestern Europe. Still, the decline of the "hyphenated American" in the 1920s occurred, coincidentally enough, as racism accelerated, notably with the rise of the second Ku Klux Klan. The rise in racism complicated the effort of racial minorities in the United States to seek allies among nonelite Whites; there was the lengthening historic pattern for nonelite Whites of all ethnic national backgrounds continuing to ally themselves against their darker brethren in the working and lower classes and continuing to stand with the European American elite whether that was in their interest or not.

Tension among African American interests, nonelite native and immigrant European American interests, and the interests of elites who dominated this nation's government and economy were apparent in the reactions to the formation of the Union of the Soviet Socialist Republics (USSR). Black intellectuals like W.E.B. Du Bois had been pro-socialist, as were many in the largely immigrant-dominated union movement in the United States even before the Bolshevik Revolution of 1917. With the advent of the USSR and its policies of assisting Africa in ousting European colonialism and of supporting the international union movement, Moscow was able to gain even more adherents in the United States, especially among labor and black intellectuals. Because Washington, like most major powers, viewed the development of a socialist USSR as a threat to capitalism, this tendency among black intellectuals such as Paul Robeson, Langston Hughes, and Louise Patterson was viewed with particular alarm. Likewise, white radicals in the labor movement, such as William Z. Foster, adopted a similar pro-Soviet policy. This pro-Sovietism led to the formation of the U.S. Communist Party, which had within its ranks from the beginning black and white radicals who were willing to work together against elite American capitalist interests.

The existence of distinct racial and ethnic interests in the United States and their potential impact on the course of U.S. foreign policy was further revealed dramatically in the 1930s after Italy invaded Ethiopia. In Harlem, Italian Americans and African Americans lived closely together; the Italians backed Rome, whereas many Blacks stood firm with the regime of Haile Selassie. Both sought to influence the conduct of U.S. foreign policy in a direction viewed as favorable to their own interests. The question was: Was there a larger U.S. interest outside or beyond the interests of Italian and African Americans? Probably not. But as history showed only a decade later, it was in the interest of the United States to resist the onslaught of fascism. If it were not halted in Ethiopia, it would have to be halted later at a much greater cost to the United States. And that is precisely what happened. Overall, U.S. interest would have been better served if the voices of African Americans in Harlem had been heeded. But they was not. Washington did not move to isolate Rome or to assist the embattled Ethiopian regime.

The existence of a large black population in the United States complicated the efforts of Washington during the 1930s to align with Britain and France against Germany and Italy, just as it had in the prior century during slavery. Part of the explanation is that in large American cities like New York there were large "West Indian" communities. It was very difficult for Jamaicans and Trinidadians to accept the idea that London was the symbol of the "free world" against tyranny, when that very same Britain held their nations and, indeed, much of Africa in colonial bondage. Furthermore, the memory of World War I was all too clear; the notion of imperialist powers squabbling for hegemony in the Caribbean and Africa was part of that memory. It was difficult for many Blacks and other progressives to draw a sharp distinction between London on the one hand and Germany on the other.

The Cold War:
Race and Domestic Civil Rights

After the United States entered the Second World War in December 1941, despite any misgivings about the European colonial powers' intent, many Blacks fought valiantly against fascism. However, the nascent Nation of Islam refused to do so; and other Blacks wondered why they should be fighting for liberation abroad when they were third-class citizens at home. On the other hand, many Jewish Americans viewed the war as a holy crusade against Hitler's fascism, which had vowed to eliminate them from the face of the earth. Like many others, Jewish Americans had to wonder if countenancing racism at home against peoples of color helped to pave the way for racism abroad against Jews, Slavs, "Gypsies," and others deemed inferior by the so-called master race in Germany.

In any event, World War II and the Cold War that followed had profound and significant impacts on race relations in the United States and, consequently, on the course of U.S. foreign policy. World War II revealed once more that bias against Blacks helped to create resistance within the gates. Both German and Japanese propaganda targeted Blacks, raising the anomalous issue of their fighting to defend a nation that treated them in a prejudicial manner. Jim Crow in the United States had to be eroded after the war, partly as a result of the realization that racism had become an issue of national security in Cold War politics. In addition, many Africans fought in World War II against fascism and like their African American veteran counterparts, they were loath to accept the status quo on returning home. Anticolonial struggles erupted throughout the African continent, just as anti-Jim Crow struggles were erupting in the United States. These struggles created a synergy that was to result ultimately in the dissolution of the European colonial system and the diminishing of Jim Crow in the United States.

Similarly, the impact of the Holocaust on the United States was essential in explaining the postwar erosion of Jim Crow. The attempt to exterminate the Jewish population showed how bigotry could evolve if left unchecked. To a degree, World War II resulted in discrediting the idea of overt racial bigotry; within this window of opportunity evolved the civil rights movement to erode Jim Crow. In turn, this erosion of Jim Crow had the collateral impact of lessening discrimination against Jewish Americans, Italian Americans, and others who had also faced bigotry in this nation. Negative quotas limiting their admission to certain elite schools were eroded; and some country clubs opened their doors to those who had been previously excluded.

All of these changes and challenges took place in the context of Cold War tensions between Moscow and Washington. How could Washington purport to be the paragon of human rights virtue when darker citizens in this country were treated so harshly? It was difficult for Washington to win "hearts and minds" in a world where darker nations were coming to independence, when darker U.S. citizens were subjected to atrocious treatment. Moreover, the emissaries of these darker nations who traveled to the United States were at times treated as badly as darker U.S. citizens. This did not predispose Africans and Asians to align with the United States during the Cold War, and this factor created further impetus for the need to end Jim Crow. It is difficult to understand what is called the American civil rights movement absent a consideration of the Cold War.

The Cold War:
Pretext for Conforming to Elite Interests

The Cold War and its domestic handmaiden, the Red Scare, had sizeable impact on African Americans and the potential for defining and acting on black-white common interests. Along with the erosion of Jim Crow, the Cold War and the Red Scare involved the marginalizing of black radical activists and intellectuals like Du Bois, Robeson, Ben Davis, and Claudia Jones. It also involved the isolation and marginalizing of numerous white radicals who had become antiracists—consistent and early critics of Jim Crow. By definition, radicals were anyone—regardless of ideology—who questioned the elite underlying interests in the conduct of U.S. foreign policy or the conflicting class basis of "white" racial unity. These figures were all harsh critics of U.S. foreign policy and, unlike most in this nation, had a worldview that involved an interest in international affairs. They were also leaders who understood in whose interest white unity was maintained and who could define common ground apart from elite interests. With these voices silenced, the ability of Afro-Americans and of other Americans in general to take independent and critical stances on both domestic issues as well as U.S. foreign policy was hampered.

Radical organizations generally, be they led by African Americans or not, were marginalized during the Cold War era by being derided as "pro-Soviet" and as unpatriotic. For example, although Blacks like Du Bois and Robeson adamantly opposed the war in Korea and U.S. policy toward China, the largest mass organization among Blacks, the National Association for the Advancement of Colored People (NAACP), took an opposite tack despite its earlier critical stance toward racism in U.S. foreign policy. NAACP leadership was persuaded by the idea that Washington would be able to solve or address pressing domestic concerns like racism, while spending tax dollars on military adventures abroad that many deemed to be racist. Similarly, other critics had argued that the atomic bombing of Hiroshima, which concluded World War II and inaugurated the Cold War, was also racially motivated.

Other mainstream civil rights figures either remained silent or stood with Washington in the 1960s in its attempt to halt the development of socialism in Cuba and Vietnam and to blunt the rise of anti-imperialist regimes in the Congo, Ghana, and elsewhere in Africa. The rationale of the mainstream figures was that domestic civil rights concessions would not flow if positions were taken on international questions that were contrary to those taken by U.S. elites. The problem, of course, was that tax dollars going to fight wars abroad drained the treasury and hindered the effort to fight poverty at home, then and now.

It was clear with the onset of the Cold War and the increase in anticommunist sentiment that failing to genuflect at the altar of a "bipartisan foreign policy" was not viewed as the smartest way to advance a domestic agenda. Civil right alliances with elite interests were not the only strategic problems the Cold War presented. The civil rights coalition began to unravel due to conflicting domestic-international interests. For example, the war of aggression fought by Israel against the Arab states in 1967, the so-called Six Day War, caused further tension between the civil rights leaders and U.S. Jewish and foreign policy makers who were supportive of Tel Aviv. The Student Non-Violent Coordinating Committee (SNCC) opposed U.S. support for Israel in this conflict, which complicated the relations of the movement with both President Lyndon Baines Johnson and some Jewish supporters of civil rights. Such tensions and pressures caused many Blacks, in particular, to retreat further from foreign policy views that were deemed to be beyond the domestic mainstream.

This is further evidence of how the Cold War was used to drive a wedge between the historic connection between U.S. domestic and foreign affairs. The covert assistance of Washington in the overthrow of the Allende regime in Chile in 1973 was not supported by mainstream civil rights and labor organizations, nor did they back this venture. Civil rights and labor leaders had no position even when U.S. foreign policy seemed to be directed disproportionately at what was being called the "Third World," such as wars in Vietnam, covert action in Cuba and Chile, and the CIA's murder of Patrice Lumumba in the Congo. By this point, these leaders and organizations had developed a sort of agnosticism toward U.S. foreign policy. Even working-class Whites who were not part of established labor such as AFL-CIO had no position on U.S. foreign interference. It was only "radicals" who linked race and U.S. foreign policy, but they had no access to mass opinion.

It is no coincidence that working-class Whites were the most significant victims of the war in Vietnam. Then the collapse of the Berlin Wall simply created the "freedom" for more of their employers to deprive white Americans of jobs by moving those jobs to Asia and Eastern Europe. Yet the AFL-CIO remained one of the cardinal supporters of a foreign policy that was steadily undermining its own interests. Again this revealed the uncanny ability of nonelite Whites to pursue policies inimical to their own interests under the guise of "national interests." Sadly, a number of African Americans also tailed after them in this folly.

Fear of Communism?

Why were elite interests in the United States so concerned about "the spread of international communism" in the first place? And was it a real threat to all Americans regardless of class and race? Some argued that U.S. policy strategists legitimately felt that this nation could be overrun by Moscow and Peking and that this justified a rigid anticommunism that could rationalize Washington backing the most wretched dictators and the most odious racism worldwide. There is another line of inquiry that has not been adequately explored when considering the grip of anticommunism: the growth of socialism, to many in elite U.S. circles, meant the further expropriation of private property already controlled by transnational corporations, as happened in Cuba after 1959. If one did not own substantial wealth and property, socialism posed no particular threat. Ever since the expropriation of the plantation owners' slaves and property in 1865, the question of nationalization of property has been a sensitive issue in the United States. It is a question that is closely related to the equally sensitive question of race. Certainly, to gain a better understanding of the basis of U.S. foreign policy in the Cold War and, more specifically, the basis of anticommunism, more scrutiny has to be placed on the issue of property relations.

One has to begin to consider such matters if one is to begin to understand why Washington was so exercised by alleged security threats presented by tiny nations like Grenada—whose entire adult population could fit comfortably within Yankee Stadium in the Bronx. There was a fear expressed by U.S. elites that the Grenadian Revolution in 1979 presented a clear and present danger to the security of this nation. This fear contributed to the U.S. invasion of this island nation in 1983, as the Pentagon scored a major victory over a handful of Grenadian soldiers assisted by Cuban construction workers.

The Dismantling of Apartheid

Of course, there were exceptions to the idea that many Blacks and the working class generally adopted a posture of agnosticism toward U.S. foreign policy. The National Conference of Black Lawyers and members of the Congressional Black Caucus like George Crockett of Detroit and Ronald V. Dellums of Berkeley were not hesitant to criticize what they perceived to be the racist aspects of U.S. foreign policy, as did the Coalition of Black Trade Unionists. But they could be dismissed as "radicals," outside the mainstream, meddling in global issues and not paying sufficient attention to the pressing domestic concerns of their constituents. Nevertheless, throughout the 1970s and 1980s a number of organizations based in working-class communities raised thousands of dollars for liberation movements in southern Africa.

Though many did not foresee that the fall of the Berlin Wall may have had its most lasting impact by facilitating the fleeing of jobs to Eastern Europe and other newly discovered low-wage havens, many did recognize that these same corporations utilized South Africa as a bastion of cheap labor. Auto production was being accelerated in Port Elizabeth, South Africa, as it was being reduced in Detroit; this harmed the interests of workers of whatever race or ethnicity. Indeed, the anti-apartheid movement stands out like a beacon as one of the few foreign policy victories participated in by nonelite Whites, Blacks, and people of goodwill of various backgrounds.

Epilogue

But the question that was asked at the beginning of this chapter remains: Cui bono, who benefits? Some would say that cheaper gasoline prices were the result of the Gulf War and this was a boon to all. In that sense, the booty that some nonelite Whites had been able to garner in the 19th century from wars on Mexico and sovereign Native American nations had now been extended more broadly: this is now a true democratization for African Americans, Latinos, Asian Americans, and Indians as well. The entire country can now benefit from this booty of lower gas prices at the pump. However, just as in the 19th century when Britain, Spain, Canada, and other nations were beginning to wonder if they were safe from an aggressive U.S. foreign policy, signs were already developing as 1995 dawned that allies in Tokyo, Paris, and London—not to mention Beijing, Teheran, and Havana—are also having serious doubts about the direction of current U.S. foreign policy.

Erosion of internationalism among U.S. citizens of all hues meant that criticism and opposition to wars in Panama and Iraq were insufficient to make a sizeable dent in Washington's policy. Also, the erosion of black and nonelite white internationalism has led to a rise of various forms of ethnic nationalism and chauvinism among the various ethnic and racial groups in the United States. In New York City, headlines about "Black-Jewish tensions" are no longer extraordinary. In Miami, relations among Cuban Americans, Jewish Americans, and African Americans are similarly tense. In Los Angeles, the civil disturbances of 1992 targeted Korean American merchants in a manner deemed sufficiently serious to bring high-level protests and delegations from Seoul. The end of the Cold War might have brought the "end of history" but it did not bring to a conclusion the torturous history of race and foreign policy.

It appears that race and U.S. foreign policy will be taking a new twist as the 21st century dawns. It seems that some would like to substitute Tokyo or perhaps Beijing for Moscow as the foreign enemy of choice. To the extent that this maneuver triumphs, the connection between race and foreign policy could become even more explosive than it has been up to this point. Just as some saw a link between support for racism at home and support for apartheid in South Africa, it is evident that increased U.S. attention on Asia could cause anti-Asian American sentiment to increase, particularly in states like California. This is far from being an inevitable development. After all, the fact that Washington was obligated to impose sanctions on apartheid, despite the presence in the White House of a president entirely unsympathetic to this legislative goal, demonstrates that U.S. support for racism abroad can be successfully called into question.

As ever, a key determinant of how this process will unfold will be the attitudes of European Americans, particularly the majority who are not elites. Will the historic pattern of their acting against their own interests be repeated? This time the stakes are higher than ever with the ever-present thermonuclear threat and the formidable economies of Japan and China. Will they come to see cross-cutting cultural and racial interests within their overall class interests and act on these interests as opposed to the traditional pattern of viewing themselves as elites want them to see themselves? Unfortunately, there is little evidence to suggest they will. Some have suggested that there is only one other direction that they can go and that is toward racial, ethnic, and religious chauvinism as is evidenced by strife in the Balkans, Chechnya, Algeria, Burundi, and elsewhere. But there is and has always been a more positive alternative since before the founding of this republic, and that is a true racial and economic democracy. But this will require collectively defining and then acting on interests that benefit all alike.

Still, it must be repeated that unpredictability—as the passage of stringent anti-apartheid legislation in the United States in 1986 reveals—remains the prime constant of history itself. Nonetheless, the cleansing of U.S. foreign policy of racist influences remains an ongoing project of the highest priority.

6

If We Live in a "Post" Era, Is There a Post-Racism?

WALTER W. STAFFORD

Advanced market nations and, in particular, the United States are
undergoing a crisis of identity. For nearly a half century their international and domestic arrangements were defined by the Cold War with the
Soviet Union. Even before the collapse of the Soviet Union in 1989, the
cohesiveness of U.S. domestic arrangements had become strained and international relations troubled. Military spending drained the domestic economy,
leaving social problems to fester. Corporate restructuring of industries led to
massive layoffs, the gap between the rich and the poor widened, incarceration
increased, and racial tensions intensified.

Though George Bush declared a "New World Order" following the demise
of the Soviet Union and the defeat of Iraq, other observers were more
cautious. Far from a stable New World Order, national and international
relations have become more unstable. Old and new enmities have surfaced
in racial and ethnic nationalism, leading to genocide in Eastern Europe and
Africa. Riots in the United States confirmed that despite its economic and

military power, even it was not immune to the post-Cold War fragmentation. Then George Bush's defeat in the 1992 elections confirmed the vicissitudes of the New World Order. Suffering around the world has shown that the New World Order has deteriorated into a "New World Disorder."

Rather than construct meta-theories and grand political pronouncements about contemporary events, a growing number of analysts argue that neither international nor domestic changes have a clear direction. We now live in an amorphous frame of time: a "post" history where both our knowledge of the past and our confidence about the future have been shaken. So shaken, in fact, that those who appreciate the complexity of the events, but have no solution, have chosen to be silent or to adopt a stance of liberal "ironizing" (Rorty, 1989).

Post has been prefixed to prior historical stages to reflect this uncertainty. It is an explicit acknowledgment that the evolutionary theories about societies are inadequate guides for interpreting contemporary events. "Post" analyses often implode old canons and disciplinary boundaries, creating new areas for study that look for novel ways to describe the present and construct paths to the future (Rosenau, 1992).

The WE/Other:
Pretense and Paradox

This chapter examines the "post" period from the perspective of groups of color and the institutional protection of white privilege. It is shaped by three questions: First, if there is a post-history is there also a post-racism? Second, how does racism shape the institutional transformation of groups of color and Whites in the post era? Third, how have considerations of race shaped scenarios articulated by white analysts for the post era?

Underlying each of the questions is the assumption that Alexis de Tocqueville made in the 1840s. De Tocqueville (1969) predicted that

> the most formidable of all the ills that threaten the future of the Union arises from the presence of a black population upon its territory; and in contemplating the cause of the present embarrassments, or the future dangers of the United States, the observer is invariably led to this as a primary fact. (p. 340)

I take de Tocqueville's prediction to mean that any imagination for the future in the United States has to deal with racism, particularly that against Blacks. I also argue that any post scenario has to consider how Whites intend to respond to challenges to their privileges from the emerging nations of color.

I have contrasted the tensions of maintaining white privilege around the frameworks of WE and Other, the Pretense and the Paradox. The WE represents the white population, particularly the white male populations in the advanced capitalist, Judeo-Christian North Atlantic nations who constitute about 5% of the world's population.

The WE is not monolithic. Indeed, there are wide economic, cultural, and religious differences among the white populations. The similarities among the WE, particularly the nations of the North Atlantic community, have been their enslavement and colonization of people of color and their refinement of the institutions of capitalism. As late as the outbreak of World War II, nearly 710 billion human beings, more than one third of the world's population, were under European colonial rule, mostly from the North Atlantic countries (Ansprenger, 1989). Colonial exploitation fueled the engines of capitalism and helped reduce domestic class differences among Whites by tying the "progress" of the white working class to the external expansion and control over the resources of nations of color.

The Others are the formerly colonized and enslaved nations. They are people and nations of color and of Islam (Ani, 1994; Miles, 1989; Said, 1978; Sharbari, 1990). Islam, or the "green peril," is of particular concern to many of the analysts and leaders in the West, as well as to some developing nations whose structures depend on Western assistance (Hadar, 1993). Muslims are the majority in 45 countries, and Islam has one billion adherents spread across the globe. The wide appeal of Islam, including its growing number of Blacks in the United States, has led to a new crusade against its followers by some American analysts and politicians (Miller, 1993). For them, Islam, or more precisely "radical" Islam, has replaced communism as the universal threat to the United States and the West. Many of the states that the United States has described as "rogue" nations are predominately Islamic.

Others are situated in racial enclaves within the boundaries of the WE and on the periphery in the old colonies. They are not homogeneous. Their common denominator is their economic and military dependency on the WE, growing out of colonization. Many intellectuals and analysts in the West also insist that the Other continue to be culturally dependent (Sharbari, 1990).

In this chapter I argue that if we are in a "post" era, the possibilities for altering the exploitation of Others and improving the conditions for the white working class remain constrained by the leaders and analysts who shape policy and information for the WE, especially the United States. Amin (1992) observes that Western political thinking asks one question, "How can one manage that which is intolerable?" Whether in the United States where some analysts view Blacks as an "underclass" and a "despised foreign presence"

(Kaus, 1992) or in Central America where indigenous populations were eliminated with American assistance, many American analysts continually portray the Other as "wretched" groups who threaten the stability of Western privileges (Connelly & Kennedy, 1994).

On the eve of the 21st century, the West, notably the United States, still finds intolerable the Other's ideas for governance. It often assumes that during its long history, hegemony, the desire for sovereignty by the colonized were supplanted. As the growth of nationalism attests, this is not true. Traditions are not forgotten, and they take on renewed importance during the struggle with the colonizer. Chatterjee (1993) documents how Indians, in their strategies to remove the British from their country, developed an imagined community—a civil society based on Indian traditions that the British could not penetrate. Chatterjee maintains that an anticolonial nationalism created its own domain of sovereignty within colonial society well before it began its political battle with the British imperial power. Ultimately, the imagined communities served as the foundations for the nationalist challenge to the colonist and provided a framework for postcolonialist reconstruction. Chatterjee's observations are applicable to struggles against domination in South Africa, Cuba, Vietnam, and the Southern civil rights struggle in the United States.

The Pretense of Superiority

The pretense is the past and present rationalization of deserved dominance by the WE. It is the belief growing out of the Enlightenment that the West is the purveyor and framer of all rational ways of perceiving history and institutions. Robert Solomon (1993) calls this belief the "transcendental pretense": "the self-congratulatory pretense that we—the white middle classes of European descent—were the representatives of all humanity, and as human nature is one, so its history must be one as well" (p. xiv).

Although the Enlightenment offered, among other things, the promise of victories of tolerance over racism and of rationality over culture, it has always been a project to be completed. The pretense of the progenitors of the Enlightenment was that as representatives of all humanity, they could universally determine all rational and irrational actions and behavior. Because progress—one of the central tenets affirmed by the Enlightenment—only occurred in the history of the WE, the WE must be the interpreters of progress for the world (Nisbet, 1980). By such self-affirmations of superiority, the irrationality of racism and the subjugation of the Other have been rationalized as a manifestation of the WE's superior reasoning by political leaders, clergy, and academicians.

In the United States, which prides itself on being the practical synthesizer and the principal exporter of the Enlightenment ideals (Gay, 1969), reason and rationality have been prerogatives of Whites who were sanctioned as "WE The People" in the U.S. Constitution. The leaders who shaped the American nation/state believed that Providence itself would use America for the "illumination" and "emancipation" of all mankind (Freuer, 1990; Weinberg, 1935). The "All Other persons" in the Constitution were initially slaves but became all Other people of color. The beliefs of the Other—Native Americans, Blacks, Chinese, Latinos—were stigmatized as irrational and deviant.

The self-affirmation of Americans and Western Europeans as the rational interpreters of progress has been promoted through ideas and concepts of modernity and modernization. *Modernity* has as many definitions as authors. In general it describes the epoch that follows the Middle Ages or feudalism. Enlightenment philosophers championed reason as the source of progress in knowledge and in society, as well as the privileged locus of truth and the foundation of systematic knowledge. Reason was deemed sufficient to discover the theoretical and practical norms upon which systems of thought and action could be built and society could be restructured. The "moral" sciences of sociology, education, and psychology embodied the new emphasis on reason and produced "knowledge" that was used to discipline the colonial and industrial orders and to refine the administrative techniques of dominance (Foucault, 1977).

The dynamics by which modernity produced a new industrial and colonial world are often used to describe "modernization." Based on their North Atlantic and colonial experiences, Western academics claimed that they could translate a set of rules for making Others and their institutions like themselves. Modernization required changes in markets, culture, and behavior, and most notably in group loyalties. Individualism is considered essential for the progress toward secular, rational urban organizations. Lerner (1958) boasted in the 1950s that the West would transform the Arab world through "a rationalist and positivist spirit against which Islam is absolutely defenseless" (p. 45). Lerner admitted that modernization was only Westernization. He avoided specific mention of Westernization to cover his political intentions.

Lerner, like many of the modernization theorists, was wrong. Many tenets of modernization are rejected by the Islamic world even as it develops capitalist markets and integrates advances in technology and science. For example, Western popular culture is still condemned in much of the Islamic world, even going so far in Iran and Algeria as to ban satellite television.

However, science and technology are accepted, but they are subordinated to Islamic belief and values to avoid excessive dependence on them (Esposito, 1992).

The debate about modernization is not a mere academic exercise, but part of the broader issues of how the West, notably the United States, seeks to control and influence ideas of governance, rights, and the use of resources. The premises of modernization are elastic. They can fit most economic, cultural, and military frameworks where decisions are made about relationships with groups and nations outside of the WE.

In the Gulf War—the first postmodern war—the media in the United States uniformly described Iraq as a deviant nation that violated the principles of modernization and international law by invading Kuwait. By contrast, the United States was a rational and benign military force engaged in a "just war." Little mention was given in the press that the British had created the artificial boundaries between Iraq and Kuwait in 1922. Instead, as the rational arbiter of universal reason, the United States dismissed appeals for dialogue about the boundaries and dismissed criticisms about its military actions from countries outside of the North Atlantic community. Economic sanctions, a standard procedure in international conflicts, were deemed unacceptable for Iraq. In retaliation for Iraq's transgression, the United States unleashed one of history's most concentrated bombings. Aware that it had been responsible for history's most intensive bombing of civilians in World War II, including the use of the atomic bomb, the Pentagon described the explosives as "smart" bombs that had been developed to avoid civilians. Civilian casualties in Iraq were either denied or labeled "collateral damage." Critics of the bombing were labeled "irrational" or anti-Western.

The success of the pretense of superior rationality and the deception of the public in the Gulf War was widely celebrated by many conservative and liberal analysts and opinion makers. Echoing Henry Cabot Lodge (Shalom, 1993), who acknowledged at the turn of the century that if justice required the consent of the governed, America's record of expansion would be criminal, Charles Krauthammer (1991), a leading conservative columnist, admits that the cloak of the universal pretense during the Gulf War was used to convince the American public that they were supporting the policies of the world community. Krauthammer maintains that deceit was necessary to provide a cover against any enemy, such as Iraq, that might "demystify" the pretense.

Conservatives—and many liberals—also celebrated their success in convincing the public to accept the demonization of Iraq and Islamic religion. A measure of the success of their propaganda was the American attitude toward Iraqi civilians. Although Americans pride themselves on their humanitarian and altruistic values, when asked in a national survey if the United States should stop the bombing of Baghdad if civilians were being killed, only 20% of the respondents answered "yes" (ABC/*Washington Post,* 1991).

Ultimately, it is estimated that in 43 days nearly 100,000 Iraqi citizens died, either from the bombing or from other war-related causes (Peters, 1992). A Harvard University study estimated that infant and child mortality doubled, either directly or from diseases caused by damage to Iraq's water supply and infrastructure (Harvard School of Public Health, 1991). It turned out that only 10% of the bombs were "smart" and that of the 88,000 tons of munitions dropped on the country, 70% missed their targets (Burkhalter, 1992).

The Gulf War anesthetized the American public to "postmodern" wars against the Other, notably Muslims. The horrors of the Gulf War were followed by the horrors of "ethnic cleansing" of Bosnian Muslims by Serbians. Although the mass removals and murders of Muslims were front-page news throughout the middle 1990s, there was no mass uproar in the United States or the North Atlantic states for intervention, as was orchestrated by the media to "save" Kuwait from Iraq (Mestrovic, 1994).

The Paradoxes Created
by the Pretense

The success of the pretense and the rationalization of racism against the Other creates multiple paradoxes for democracy. The rationalization of racism depends on deceiving the public through an elaborate network of institutions that perpetuate myths about the inferiority of the Other and the superiority of the WE. Officials and academics have to constantly create artificial truths and manufacture consent through the state and the media (Herman & Chomsky, 1988). The dangers to democracy are evident. The more that consent is manufactured through propaganda, the greater the propensity for despotism.

In the Gulf War, the rationalization of racism relied on a complex network of institutions to deceive the white public, especially poorly educated Whites, who often opposed the war. Television, the source of news and information for this group, demonized Islam and provided continuous coverage of flaring bombs over Iraq accompanied by instantaneous "expert" commentary by white males on the action and technology. Debate and clarity about the war were stifled. Some journalists complained that they were reduced to secretaries (Burkhalter, 1992).

The "deception" and spectacle confirmed de Tocqueville's prophecy made in the 1830s of how future despotism might manifest itself in the United

States. Oppression, de Tocqueville argued, would be led by officials who acted like schoolmasters. Although the schoolmaster's authority would resemble parental authority, in reality, it would be used to keep the public in perpetual childhood. Citizens would be able to enjoy themselves as long as they thought of nothing but enjoyment (de Tocqueville, 1969).

The pretense creates even greater paradoxes for the Other. Like Whites, those who constitute Others are susceptible to the deceptions of the pretense and soft despotism. However, because they are viewed as irrational and are usually economically dependent, the paradoxes are even more exaggerated.

Two paradoxes illuminate the situation of Others. The first relates to what some Blacks have referred to as "double consciousness." This double consciousness, as W.E.B. Du Bois, Richard Wright, and Fanon have noted, provides an objective and "frightening" perspective of two worlds in which choices are often paradoxically agonizing (Du Bois, 1903/1969; Fanon, 1963).

The double consciousness was manifested by groups of color in the Gulf War. Groups of color revealed a kindred spirit of pain with Iraqi civilians; however, they also had a keen awareness of the advantages and the benefits that might accrue to them by identifying with the United States. This was not a new paradox for Blacks. It occurred in each of the world and regional conflicts, especially those wars against nations of color. The Gulf War, however, sharpened the dilemmas. The Chief of Staff, General Colin Powell, was Black; more than half of the total troops in the Gulf were people of color; and 60% of the women were also people of color (African American Leadership Summit, 1991). In 1990, General Powell praised the high registration of Black soldiers as a means of upward mobility, even though President Bush had just vetoed the Civil Rights Act that would have restored the antidiscrimination laws overturned by the Supreme Court the year before. Surveys, however, showed that the majority of Blacks opposed the war. Despite the pride in General Powell's accomplishments, black elected officials, activists, and the clergy spoke out openly against the war. And as stories unfolded that a disproportionate share of the reserves called for the Gulf War were black and Latino, their anger intensified.

The politics at home carried over to the battlefield. Black and Latino soldiers were often at odds with their white colleagues, who viewed them and the Iraqis with disdain. Indeed, white soldiers appropriated American racism to Saudi Arabia, designating the Iraqis as "sand niggers" (Peters, 1992). One way many black troops resolved the paradox was by joining Islam. Thousands of U.S. soldiers converted to Islam: Estimates are that more than 5,000 soldiers converted to the faith—most of them were Blacks (Noakes, 1991).

At the end of the Gulf War, Blacks sought recognition for their valor and the indignities they had experienced, as they had in previous wars. Advocates for black males cited the high proportion of black males in the Gulf as evidence of why the nation should address their economic and social problems at home. In Senate testimony they asked Congress to develop a national policy for the "Preservation of Black Males" (Committee on Banking, Housing, and Urban Affairs, 1991). And black businessmen complained to black Congressional representatives that they were being excluded from the lucrative contracts to rebuild Kuwait.

The second paradox relates to the appeals Others make for change. Appeals for fairness and justice by Others are often conditioned on the ideas of rights developed by the West. However, both the appeals for justice and for fairness are often rejected by the West, as are the expansion of human rights to protect Others against Western economic exploitation and cultural dominance.

Attempts by Others within the United States or in the former colonial states to create alternative visions for cultural and economic self-determination are met with resistance and often derision. White and some black analysts in the United States continually chastise Blacks for abandoning the "dream" of Martin Luther King, for rejecting "integration," and for embracing Afrocentrism. Yet internationally the United States refused until 1994 to ratify the 1966 United Nation's Covenants on Political and Civil Rights and it did not ratify the 1965 International Convention on the Elimination of All Forms of Racial Discrimination until 1995.

Rather than dignify the expanded visions of economic and cultural rights supported by many non-Western states, the United States has insisted on its universalist view of modernization. President Clinton elaborated the United States's contemporary vision of post-Cold War modernization in a speech to the United Nations Assembly in 1993. In the speech he said that the economic and technological unification of the world was being undermined by ethnic and religious tensions and that traditional nation-states could not easily accommodate the conflicts. He pointed to the United States as a country rooted in respect for all the world's religions and cultures and argued that expanding the community of *market democracies* (emphasis added) advanced the goals of the first Universal Declaration of Human Rights.

Despite Clinton's claims about the values of American market democracy and its respect for cultures, his administration limited discussion on human rights at home. When the Clinton administration developed the nation's first review of human rights under agreement of articles in the International Covenant on Civil and Political Rights, few of the major civil and human rights groups had a significant role in shaping the document. Moreover, none of the nation's major newspapers or periodicals carried stories about the review, despite its historical importance.

The Criteria for Inclusion in the Discussions of the "Post" Periods

President Clinton's vision of market democracies paving the way to global human rights is a clear articulation of how the United States imagines relationships with non-Western nations and domestic groups of color in the post-Cold War era. The policy framework, which is a continuation of the old ideas of modernization, conditions political participation on the promotion of capitalist markets and a narrow conception of human rights.

Western intellectuals and analysts of both liberal and conservative persuasions have also argued that capitalist markets and Western models of governance and rights should be the principal conditions for participation in the "post" dialogue. Although liberals often seek to reduce the differences between the WE and the Other in their discussions, they still maintain that Western institutions should guide the changes. Giddens (1990), one of the most incisive interpreters of the post transition, defends his limitation of the post dialogue to those nations that historically had systematic capitalist production and nation states. Habermas (1992), one of the most celebrated thinkers of the late 20th century, limits his analysis of the post period to Western Europeans who share democratic forms of government and occidental forms of life. Rorty (1989), widely described as a leading public intellectual, maintains that Western thinkers have provided all of the conceptual forms of government that will ever be needed.

Conservatives do not even entertain the possibilities of reducing the barriers between the WE and the Other. Some—such as Bloom (1987)—argue that racism is dead, except for among some poorly educated Whites, so there is no need for the dialogue. Other conservatives argue that the Other is irreconcilably disorganized and backward. They call for recolonization or new imperialism. Freuer (1989), for example, argues that the United States should accept its imperialist responsibilities because they elevated the moral and intellectual stature of the groups it colonized. A third group of conservatives stops short of promoting recolonization. However, they argue that most non-Western ideas add little to the dialogue about the post era. Fukuyama (1992) argues that democracy in its capitalist form represents the last and final form of government. He offers little hope that non-Western nations will or can devise systems based on their own cultures. Drucker (1993) maintains that Third World nations and leaders, especially those of color, have few ideas to offer for the post period. Drucker notes,

> If anything has been totally disproven, it is the promises of Third World leaders of the fifties and sixties—Nehru in India, Mao in China, Castro in Cuba, Tito in Yugoslavia, the apostles of "Negritude" in Africa, or Neo-Marxists like Che Guevara. They promised that the Third World would find new and different answers and would, in fact create a new order. The Third World has not delivered on these promises made in its name. *The challenges, the opportunities, the problems of post-capitalist society and post capitalist plight can only be dealt with where they originated.* (emphasis added) (Drucker 1993, p. 15).

The limited invitations to groups of color, especially those who live within the United States, are made by white liberals. Rorty (1989) wants a broader dialogue about the future, yet his invitation is primarily to artists, poets, and writers who are "storytellers." Although inviting groups of color to participate as "storytellers," Rorty urges them to resist the urge to join together based on their past oppression, because this unity could lead to the creation of a new universal pretense. Rorty's advice has been echoed in various forms by Blacks and Latinos. Orlando Patterson, a black sociologist, has encouraged Blacks to abandon their search for the past and to take pride in being the only group that reconstructed itself within a nation without an individual history of its own (Patterson, 1972).

Limiting Imagination:
The Continuation of Weber's Iron Cage

Few scholars have developed a more descriptive framework for examining the barriers of achieving Enlightenment ideals than Max Weber (Bernstein, 1992; MacIntyre, 1981). For Weber (1958), capitalism and bureaucratic organization created an iron cage that limited individual imagination and undermined the Enlightenment ideals. Market behavior became pervasive in all aspects of personal and organizational life, and reason was reduced to instrumental rationality: where the means and the ends were the same and all action could be reduced to costs-benefits.

Weber's conception of an iron cage is particularly useful when examining white privilege and groups of color. Weber, who was particularly critical of capitalism in the United States, only presented one side of the cage, that which constrained individuals. Takaki (1979) has taken the concept further and argued that the iron cage was also used as a means of organizing and socializing white Americans into bureaucratic capitalism and the WE. First, it served as an organizational framework for controlling and rationalizing the emotions of Western Europeans as they settled the United States; second, the iron cage became a framework for channeling and socializing white workers into the factories of capitalist expansion. The institutions, agencies, and organizations within the cage transformed European "outsiders" into "white" Americans who gradually had access to business and state benefits. Finally, the cage served as an organizational fulcrum for military and market expansion in the Far East.

The transformation of white Americans in the iron cage sustained their privileges by (a) constructing a rationalization of those outside the institutional cage—the Other—as childlike, inferior, and irrational; (b) reifying the transcendental pretense in academic discourse that the WE had superior knowledge about the Other; (c) maintaining the pretense that those outside the cage should perceive of themselves as designated by those within it; (d) reducing discussions of change and treatment of the Other to costs and benefits rather than on Enlightenment principles (in affirmative action law, racial discrimination now has to be proven by "business necessity"); and (e) claiming access to all knowledge of Others, including the spiritual domains of their civil societies.

In theoretical and practical terms, the iron cage transformed an agrarian nation of European settlers into organizations/bureaucracies essential for the expansion of American capitalism. The principal beneficiaries of this expansion were the WE/Whites. Those outside the cage—Native Americans, Blacks, Chinese, Mexicans, Puerto Ricans—were segmented into noncompetitive jobs and industries.

State agencies have had three disciplinary functions in sustaining the iron cage. First, the managers and professionals in state agencies reproduced the inequities of the market in their policies and practices. The state agencies responsible for socialization were often handmaidens to the interests of capitalists. Social welfare and socialization often served the interests of capital. Second, state agencies took the lead in independently establishing and supporting racist policies to control the Other. State agencies in the United States vacillated between policies of genocide and assimilation, ultimately settling into de Tocqueville's conception of "soft despotism." Under soft despotism, as previously noted, major segments of the population are kept uninformed, enjoying themselves in childlike conditions. Soft despotism, however, goes far beyond keeping groups childlike. It also requires the establishment of predetermined societal roles based on racial/cultural traits. Intelligence tests have been used since the early 1900s as rationalizations for predetermining the exclusion of groups of color from mainstream institutions. Third, the United States has taken on qualities of a garrison state. In 1994, the United States had 519 people in prison or jail for every 100,000 people. Only Russia imprisons a larger percentage of its population. The United States is the only Western nation that still uses capital punishment. A disproportionate share of the inmates are native Blacks and Latinos and immigrants from the old colonies.

Putting Race in the
Post Dialogue and Trends

Despite the major theoretical developments on institutional racism and internal colonialism developed by analysts in the 1960s and 1970s, there has not been a consistent body of thought integrating these concepts into a "post"-civil rights framework that parallels those of white North Atlantic analysts or the analysts shaping the postcolonialist dialogue. Many of the white social scientists rejected these concepts, promoting instead the assimilationist concepts of "race relations," America's domestic version of modernization for Others. They were supported in many cases by Blacks and Latinos, notably those who saw their communities as sites of disorganized "underclasses."

Because of the dominance of "race relations" ideas, few analysts in the United States have addressed the question of whether the historical transformations of the WE/Other in the iron cage will remain the patterns for the post market and state (Baron, 1985), and there has been limited discussion of how race and racism influence the purported "breaks" in history.

The most extensive work on post periods and race has been by writers and analysts born or living outside the United States, dealing with postcolonialism (a partial list includes Appiah, 1992; Bhabba, 1992; Gilroy, 1993; Hall, 1976; Said, 1978). However, because they are often dealing with the reshaping of imagined communities in former colonies or with the circulation of immigrants in the West, their contributions do not always fit the unique racial problems of the United States.

In the following section, I have situated race with the "breaks" identified by analysts in the literature on postindustrialism/postcapitalism, postmodernity, and the post welfare state.

Postindustrialism/
Postcapitalism

The debate about postindustrialism/postcapitalism has been highlighted by hundreds of books and articles on "breaks" in the structural rearrangement of industries, labor, and markets in Western capitalism. These breaks have been induced by changes in technology, production, and military commitments even though the dates are often disputed. The first purported break in the structural relationships was postindustrialism, which started in the 1950s. The second break was postcapitalism or "disorganized" capitalism, which started 20 years later (Lash & Urry, 1987). The third break was purported to be the end of the Cold War and the rearrangement of the military-industrial complex.

POSTINDUSTRIALISM

Postindustrialism was highlighted by a shift in the industrial composition of the economy from manufacturing to services, especially producer services (law, finance, business services, advertising). The industrial shift was accompanied by advances in technology, a weakening of union membership, and a migration of workers from the North to the South. The industrial, technological, and social contours of postindustrialism were shaped by the Cold War and the military-industrial complex. During the Cold War, the federal government financed the industrial transformation and urged cultural conformity of the workforce as a bulwark against communism. The federal government also incorporated and promoted business ideas of efficiency, cost-benefit analysis, and output. This instrumental language, or what Lyotard (1984) refers to as "performativity," was outlined in Executive Orders by President Johnson for the federal government and was prominently used in the Vietnam War, when enemy deaths were calculated as "kill ratios."

The transformation to postindustrialism provided few improvements for groups of color. Most groups remained segmented in low-wage manufacturing or the public sector. Some gradual inroads were made into the private sector as a result of the passage of the 1964 Civil Rights Act. Yet even then, Blacks and Latinos remained employed in peripheral clerical and operational jobs in low-wage industries.

POSTCAPITALISM

Postcapitalism was marked by greater fragmentation of markets and industries. The defining moment for this stage was the oil crisis in 1973 and the emergence of new cartels among the old colonies. The United States and Western Europe entered a "new relationship" with the Arab states, the Other, that sat on vast oil reserves.

The oil crisis created new domestic problems, as well. High unemployment and high inflation—stagflation—reshaped the U.S. economy. Productivity and real incomes declined, and the white workforce that had conformed and expected loyalty from corporate owners watched as corporations stepped up their search for new locations, new markets, and new workers outside of the nation's borders. The new phase of globalization was highlighted by greater international competition and a decline of union membership.

In postcapitalism, the transnational corporation operating beyond the boundaries of a nation-state became a major concern of global bodies, notably the United Nations. Improved technology helped facilitate instantaneous exchange of finances and information beyond state control. Workers of all races found themselves in a new and weakened bargaining relationship with corporate powers. Possessing neither the instruments of finance nor the control of information, they usually could only watch as companies fled. By the 1980s, corporate announcements of flight were front-page news in the international newspapers. This time, corporate leaders noted that they had no intention of returning. Moreover, they announced their intention to reduce their workforces, even if profits increased.

There is no doubt that postcapitalism weakened white male privilege more than at any time since the Depression (Block, 1990). Michael Harrington, the noted socialist, prophesied in the 1980s that the loss of jobs for white males and their growing poverty would create explosive political problems in the following decades. Harrington argued that the caricature of working-class white males as Archie Bunkers with a narrow and racist view of the world was a disservice to them and to those concerned with poverty. He also argued that the elite were using the ignorance about white men to manipulate them against Blacks and women.

Harrington's prophecy was confirmed in later studies and the 1994 Congressional elections. Studies in the 1990s by the Congressional Budget Office (CBO) (Congressional Budget Office, 1993) and the Bureau of Labor Statistics revealed that proportionately more white males than females lost their jobs in the restructuring that occurred in the transitions of the 1980s.

As harsh as the new workplace was for white males in the era of postcapitalism, the conditions for Blacks and Latinos were even harsher. Unemployed black and Latino males were unemployed longer and they were forced to take jobs at significantly lower salaries once they obtained new employment. Corporate restructuring of management led to disproportionate layoffs for those Blacks who had just begun to make inroads into the private sector.

THE POST-COLD WAR

The third break was purported to start with the end of the Cold War. American capitalism has always had a military arm. This arm grew longer after World War II, especially in the 1980s when the Pentagon accelerated its investment in aerospace, communications, and high-tech industries (Markusen, 1989). Although some analysts argued that the United States's military engagements overextended the nation and eroded its domestic economy, others, notably Nau (1990), maintained that the overextension helped expand American capitalism and American "values." Nau's position is supported by Layne and Schwartz (1993), who examined Security Council documents from the 1950s and found that the Soviet threat was often a pretext for American business expansion.

Military spending was the United States's version of an industrial policy. The defense industry employed large segments of the workforce, including some of the nation's best scientists and technicians (estimates by the Club of Rome are that at the height of the armaments race, half of the world's engineers were employed in military activities). University connections rationalized the military-industrial complex and the created cultural products (comics, movies) and sports events that promoted weaponry and nationalism. Technology helped nurture an adult paramilitary culture that included replicas of Vietnamese villages where weekend warriors could kill the "Cong" (Gibson, 1994).

The end of the Cold War was viewed by liberals and radicals as an opportunity to reduce the size of the military-industrial complex. Combined with declining real incomes and a deterioration of the nation's infrastructure, it appeared that the moment could be seized to shift military investment to domestic problems. Certainly, American workers needed to review other alternatives. By 1990, real wages had continued to decline for the past 20 years and more Americans lived in poverty than at any time since the 1960s. Income inequality was the highest in 45 years. The lowest fifth of the population received only 4.4% of the aggregate income, whereas 44.6% went to the highest fifth (Dembo & Morehouse, 1994).

A major shift in economic priorities was slowed, however, by the inability of groups of color and the white working class to define a common agenda for the economy. Paul Kennedy, in The Rise and Fall of Great Powers (1987), argued that although most powers declined because of the overextension of their military resources, the decline the United States had been spared because of its weak history of class politics and the political inactivity of large segments of the minority populations.

The inability of the white working class and groups of color to provide a united front against the pretenses of the Cold War would lead to a deterioration of both of their lifestyles. By the 1990s, the Cold War business expansions had reshaped the face of global capitalism and transformed the lives of

American workers. Robert Reich (1991), the Secretary of Labor under President Clinton, argued that it was nostalgic to believe that global corporations would sink their roots into the community any longer. Even as profits of the global industries increased, layoffs mounted. One study estimated that 90 million jobs in the U.S. labor force of 124 million were potentially vulnerable to replacements by machines (Rifkin, 1995). The prospects of full-time, steady employment seemed a promise of the past. By the early 1990s, workers' attachments to their jobs had eroded and layoffs had lost their stigmatization.

The uncertainty for white workers has made the future for most Blacks and Latinos even more problematic. Despite 30 years of affirmative action, Blacks and Latinos remain segmented in low-wage jobs and industries with limited opportunities for becoming part of the "symbolic workforce." A host of studies, including the Glass Ceiling Report, mandated by the 1991 Civil Rights Act, revealed that the upward mobility of groups of color remains limited. Moreover, political support of affirmative action has waned. President Clinton waited until half of his term had passed to appoint a Director of the Equal Employment Opportunity Commission (EEOC), and he equivocated on how he would deal with the subject when the Supreme Court restricted the ability of minorities and women to claim employment discrimination. By 1995, EEOC had a backlog of 100,000 discrimination cases.

POSTMODERNISM:
UNIVERSALISM AND VICTIMS

The debate about whether the United States and the West are in a postmodern period often centers around the theorists and observers who argue that the contemporary economic and cultural changes are "tensions in the modern period" and those who maintain that they are "breaks." Habermas (1992), Giddens (1990), Norris (1992), and Smith (1993), among others, argue that the West is in a period of radical modernization. Habermas in particular has argued for a continuation of the Enlightenment's universal ideals and the completion of the Enlightenment projects. He acknowledges that the Enlightenment's ideals have been undermined by modernity and false prophets. He is especially critical of American neo-conservatives who promote the ideals of the Enlightenment to promote cultural conformity and rationalization of inequality (Habermas, 1992). Habermas claims that modernity also has unlimited potential. He supports continued efforts to find space for rational communication among groups, drawing on their lifeworlds or traditions. Other radical modernists (Norris, 1992; Smith, 1993) argue that the principles of the Enlightenment should be upheld so that oppressed groups can unite against the inequities and ravages of capitalism.

Postmodernists represented by a host of social scientists and literary critics, most notably Lyotard, Foucault, and Baudrillard, argue against the continuation of the Enlightenment projects. The untold suffering that occurred during the modern era, including slavery, the holocaust, colonization, and sexism, should not be continued. Universalism, for the postmodernists, remains dangerous because groups without a critical perspective of their suffering can be manipulated in the name of larger causes of humanity or economic efficiency. Some postmodernists also argue that Habermas's concern about increasing rational communication is only an attempt to reinstitute the culture of white males. I added racism, slavery, and colonization: In reality, they are often omitted in discussions of postmodernity.

Lyotard (1984), who defines postmodernity as "incredulity against the modern," rejects the Newtonian perspective of totalization and meta-narratives in favor of understanding society as represented by multiple particles and narratives. According to Lyotard and other postmodernists, we can no longer rely on the old theories and paradigms and, especially, the grand meta-theories that claim universal applicability to explain contemporary changes. Meta-theories, including Marxism, have lost much of their explanatory powers. Marxism has been too closely associated with the Enlightenment heritage, and its class analyses have minimized the interests of Blacks, Latinos, gays, and lesbians. Marxian politics are also eschewed, particularly the idea that a revolutionary vanguard can embody the interests of the entire working class (Smith, 1993).

According to postmodernists, the meta-narratives of the past have now been dispersed and fragmented into multiple narratives and language games (Lyotard, 1984). The weakening of the bonds to jobs, combined with greater aesthetic experimentation and the proliferation of commodified symbols, have reshaped the cultural and architectural landscape (Audirac & Sgernyen, 1994).

The postmodernists take a particularly strong stance against the promotion of instrumental rationality as the pretense of reason. For postmodernists, and for philosophers and social scientists who do not share their perspectives, instrumental rationality remains a dangerous strategy of dominance (Barrett, 1979; Taylor, 1991). Technology with all its benefits also has increased the prospects of governmental and business organization reducing clients and workers to cost-benefit models. Social welfare and educational systems are increasingly discussed in terms of business rules of input-output and outcome measures. Western governments now treat education starting at the earliest grades as a productive asset and commodity to be measured by costs.

The concerns about instrumental rationality and its prospects for dominance raise troubling issues for the relationship of the WE and Other. Yet despite the prospective dangers, few of the discussants in the post dialogue have examined, as I noted earlier, how groups of color will be affected. Robert Young (1990), in *White Mythologies,* is one of the few. Young argues that postmodernism is Europe's cultural awareness that it is no longer the unquestioned and dominant center of the world. Other analysts, however, notably the editors of *Past the Last Post* (Adam & Tiffin, 1991), argue that postmodernism is a determined attempt of the Euro-American Western hegemony to retain its global centrality. They also argue that postmodernism represents a neo-universalism to which "marginal" cultures may aspire and from which products can be appropriated and sanctioned.

Perhaps, in part because postmodernism represents a new centrality of the United States-North Atlantic communities, there are few attempts to associate race with the breaks in history. This is ironic, for when one examines the various dates cited by analysts of the transition from the modern to the postmodern, racial issues have often shaped the major events of the period. For example, Harvey (1990) dates the transition to postmodernity to the leveling of the Puitt Igo public housing project in St. Louis in 1973. Although he discusses the fact that the Puitt Igo project represented a symbolic end to grand schemes of housing the working class, he does not mention that the housing project was predominately black.

If one takes Harvey's suggestion that 1973 represented the break in the modern period, the relationship of race to postmodernity becomes clearer. By 1973, the nation had not only given up on the idea of public housing, which it considered "too black," but it was in full retreat from the ideas of the Great Society and the civil rights victories (Baron, 1985). Moreover, in 1973, black poverty, unemployment, and incarceration began to accelerate.

The 1970s also marked the beginning of a major demographic transition. For most of the modern era, the voluntary flow of immigrants of color to the United States had been limited. However, as a result of the 1965 Immigration Act, the numbers of individuals and families from Asia, Latin America, and the Caribbean began to increase dramatically in American cities.

Race was also a major consideration in the new "identity" politics of postmodernism. Spurred on by the civil rights movement, women, gays, Latinos, Asians, and the handicapped demanded the same rights as those gained by Blacks in the 1960s. White ethnics also became more assertive.

The explosion of different political groups marked the beginning of "identity politics" and the cultural rehabilitation of "ethnic memory" (Berman, 1982). The new politics was neither conservative or radical; rather it became a safe haven for old and new cultures, defying the modernist idea that rationality would triumph over culture (di Leonardo, 1994). There was a Christian culture, a Jewish culture, a Latino culture, and the cultures of gender. In the "identity" political arena, race often became only one of many competing "oppressions." Race also became more complex as individuals attempted to eliminate oppression within the group (black gays, black lesbians). Some analysts argue that postmodernism and its politics are merely a retreat from racism.

The explosion of identity cultures combined with their increasing commodification (every group had its own music, clothes, etc.) became an increasing concern or worry among conservative and radical modernists. The conservatives feared that the fragmented identity cultures would undermine capitalism's stability. Neo-conservatives like Daniel Bell (1976), who celebrated the mass commodification of the United States in the 1950s, saw the new cultural forms as hedonistic and as revolts against everyday life. Radicals, however, feared that the postmodernist identity politics would keep groups from examining and organizing against capitalism.

In an effort to promote cultural conformity and social control, the conservatives and neo-conservatives increased their attacks on "identity" groups and their cultural styles and products. Blacks, who were the leaders in shaping the cultural products that altered the modern cultural landscape, were blamed for a variety of "cultural ills." These included corrupting the ideals of the young white radicals of the 1960s, thus promoting a rebellion against the modern, and turning new immigrants away from American culture in the 1980s and 1990s (Portes & Zhou, 1994; Schlesinger, 1992). The conservatives' arguments against Blacks were nuanced for the era. Though blaming Blacks for undermining the cultural stability of society, the neo-conservatives urged capitalists and state officials to ignore Blacks' pleas for justice.

Not all of the criticisms about Blacks' role in the postmodernist cultural changes came from Whites. There were sharp disagreements in the black community about the new cultural styles and products and whether, as Cornell West suggests, its manifestations were nihilistic. Yet for some, especially the youth, the narratives and lyrics of "rap" and similar "musical" genres were "revolutionary," other Blacks argued that they were miscegenistic and threats to the Blacks' culture (Wallace, 1992). Many adults, often led by black intellectuals, ministers, and former civil rights leaders, also argued that the commodification and diffusion of black revolutionary and spiritual symbols (e.g., Rap music is produced by Time/Warner Corporation, Kente cloth is used indiscriminately, spirituals are commercialized, Malcolm X logos are part of white fashion) represent falsely encoded representations of black traditions. The critics argue that commodified resistance, bereft of political consciousness and political action, fosters rather than weakens dominance.

The tensions within the black community about whether some commodifed cultural products represent a false encoding of black culture is in a larger sense an argument about how Blacks and groups of color view themselves in the transition between the modern and postmodern. Said (1993) has noted that many of the artists and intellectuals outside the North Atlantic community are still concerned with the direction of *modernity* within their regions (his emphasis). Their debate about what is modern and postmodern, he notes, is joined with how they are to modernize given the cataclysmic upheavals in the world.

For the groups of color, notably Blacks, *within* the North Atlantic community, the debate is less clear about the specifics of where they stand in the modern and postmodern. Those Blacks who use the terminology of the "discourse" often obfuscate its meaning with little reference to the dynamics of power and change in capitalism. Moreover, some of the black intellectuals are often used by the media and white intellectuals to disparage black nationalists whose narratives some Whites find offensive. For many Blacks, even if they are not clear about the modern-postmodern "discourse," their feelings about the modern are nevertheless clear. For them, the modern is exhausted and it has exhausted them. Their sentiments are captured in an editorial in the *City Sun,* a black newspaper in New York City:

> History is replete with examples of the only thing we need to know: We pay with our lives as victims of this system, and we pay with our lives to reform or rehabilitate our victimizers. . . . Let white America take on the task of redeeming and humanizing itself; we already gave at the office. (p. 8).

Post-Cold War Governance: The Role of the State

Postmodernist cultural fragmentation has coincided with attempts by oppressed groups and nations to renegotiate their relationships with the state. Old and new cultural groups are demanding recognition and inclusion of their traditions in the decisions of the state. The demands for state renegotiations have spawned two arguments. On one side are analysts and leaders who argue that 20th-century concepts of governance are exhausted. Zukier (1994) argues that the Western 20th century ended with the eruption of new ethnic and religious conflicts in Sarajevo. Analysts representing the Club of Rome (King & Schneider, 1991) maintain that traditional structures, governments, and institutions can no longer manage the problems that have emerged since the end of the Cold War. Huntington (1993) hypothesizes that nation-states will remain the most powerful actors in world affairs, but conflicts will occur between nations and groups of different civilizations.

On the other side are Western leaders and analysts who have articulated a Pax Americana view of governance. They do not disagree that ethnic, racial, and cultural tensions have undermined the capacity of nation-states to govern. However, they argue that they have a solution. That solution or vision, as I noted earlier, was elaborated in President Clinton's speech to the United Nations (1993). In that speech, Clinton argued that the best post-Cold War governance systems should be guided by market democracies. President Clinton's speech was devoid of any reference to or discussion about cultural recognition, equality, or equity.

Those who argue that governance systems are exhausted allow for the imaginations of racial and cultural groups to construct new state arrangements and new or revitalized civil societies. Those who advocate market democracies minimize the state and its possibilities for addressing historical or contemporary social and cultural grievances or imaginations.

The vision of a market democracy in the United States has been promoted as an alternative to the welfare state by conservatives and neo-conservatives against the welfare state since the early 1970s (Coser & Howe, 1976). Senator Moynihan has claimed that "just as unemployment was the defining issue of industrialism, dependency is becoming the defining issue of post-industrial society." The attack on welfare and dependency has been predicated on the idea that there is unlimited growth potential for marketable goods and services that would be unleashed once the state is pushed back into its proper, minimal terrain (Cohen & Arato, 1994).

Nine points summarize the conservative and neo-conservative's post-Cold War vision:

1. Incorporate values and techniques from business to reshape and manage the state.
2. Insist that state actions account for performance and costs.
3. Reduce the costs of welfare entitlement.
4. Promote privatization as a basic necessity for efficient markets.
5. Reduce government by describing public sectors as inefficient and anti-entrepreneurial.

6. Promote individualism as an essential asset in the changing markets.
7. Reduce the demand for "rights," particularly affirmative action.
8. Demand that the poor increase their responsibility to the state, rather than the state be responsible to them.
9. Revitalize the military and paramilitary forces to fight simultaneous wars against "Others" abroad and in the United States.

These nine points were incorporated into the Republican Party's Contract With America when they swept the House and Senate in 1994. The neo-liberal wing of the Democratic Party, the Democratic Leadership Council, offered similar alternatives.

The post-Cold War welfare state and market democracy confirm many of the observations of Habermas and Lyotard. Habermas has described the process by which market interests dominate the norms of clients as "colonization of the lifeworld." He argues that the traditional ways of communications of groups—that is, their lifeworlds—are undermined by the organizations that steer the economy. The private and public spheres of groups dependent on benefits become subordinated to the imperatives of the economic system because these groups are unable to subordinate administrative and economic dictates to those of their norms and cultures (Fraser, 1989). Colonization is hastened because technicians and officials guiding the economy and the state minimize ideas from representatives of the lifeworld. Such ideas are viewed as an unnecessary strain on efficient management (Habermas, 1992; Wolin, 1992). Once "colonization" occurs, the performance standards of individuals, families, and workers can be facilitated.

The colonization of traditional lifeworlds, or more precisely the undermining of the cultures of groups of color and the poor within the United States, provides a host of paradoxes. First, market democracy and the minimal state perpetuate antidemocratic trends. It is a pervasive form of colonization that rationalizes exclusion. In the postmodernist identity politics, however, there are few efforts by groups to confront the system. Though many women's groups have taken up the banner of maintaining the welfare state, there is a wide cultural gap between the leaders, who are usually white, and poor women of color, who constitute nearly 60% of the clients. Second, the limited dialogue between politicians and officials with Others usually takes places in the language of efficiencies and costs to the market. The paradox is that if Others embrace the dialogue, they sanction the procedures of colonization. If they do not engage in the dialogue, technicians determine the outcomes.

The ultimate problem for Others within the United States and for those subjected to similar dictates by international lending organizations, is that they have no alternative to market democracy without political movements. Although there are numerous resistance movements in many developing countries, within the United States there has not been a sustained movement for equity during the "post"-modern or "post" welfare state era. One of the more paradoxical trends of the post era has been the refinement of new techniques of colonialism and dominance even as postmodern narratives have exploded.

Conclusion

In answering the question of how racism affects Whites and whether there is a difference in the modern and the "post" eras, it is useful to return to Alexis de Tocqueville and Max Weber. De Tocqueville argued that race was intertwined with the American imagination of the future. He also predicted that a new form of despotism could arise in the United States in the future. The new despotism would be unlike anything in prior history and would be directed by officials who acted like schoolmasters and used their authority to keep the public in perpetual childhood. Weber issued similar warnings. He argued that the iron cage of bureaucratic rationalization would undermine any search for the ideals of the Enlightenment. Weber also argued that capitalism in the United States had been reduced to a sport.

De Tocqueville and Weber were prescient. Race continues to shape and influence most scenarios of a post era. Imaginative solutions for limiting its consequences are constrained by (a) the rationalizing away of racial and class inequalities by politicians, economic leaders, and academicians; (b) the reduction of reasoning about problems of race to instrumental discussions of costs and benefits to the economy; and (c) the abandonment of emancipatory ideals by many intellectuals and the public in general in favor of the "fun and games" of the consumer society. The first and second points confirm the continuation of the iron cage. The third confirms de Tocqueville's observations about the childlike qualities of the American public.

Tragically, neither the modernist perspectives on race nor the various post scenarios articulate frameworks that allow Whites to imagine benefits for themselves beyond the iron cage or allow groups of color to have their imagined communities recognized.

The modernist perspectives argued that Blacks and groups of color were inferior. Groups of color were told that they needed to assimilate and go through the designated steps of capitalist modernization to be recognized by Whites. Lower-income Whites were told to conform to the cultural ideals of

American institutions and to refrain from challenging racial inequality. Today's conservative modernists, or what Habermas calls "young conservatives," claim that racism is dead, so there is no necessity to deal with race or recognize alternative visions of community or human rights by groups of color. Any failure on the part of groups of color, they maintain, results from deficits in their character, genes, and behavior. They also argue that state benefits for groups of color and working-class Whites should be steered through the business sector and measured in terms of their relationship to profits.

Radical modernists paint a scenario in which the ideals of the Enlightenment can still be used to implode the differences between the We and the Other. However, they give limited recognition to the governance frameworks of groups of color. For the radical modernists, the elimination of class inequalities takes priority over racial inequalities. Thus, they usually reject the idea that the rules and procedures of capitalism can be used to steer the lives of social welfare and educational systems. The radical modernists usually support the rights of individuals, but they equivocate on the broader concepts of human rights, which recognize cultural and economic rights.

Postmodernists, especially those who are left of center, do not present elaborate alternative visions of change for fear of reconstructing grand theories. Thus, though they reject the conservative modernists' ideas about instrumental reasoning as another form of domination, they do not offer institutional alternatives. Postmodernists also provide few perspectives on reductions of the inequalities of the We and the Other. Although their frameworks provide groups of color with the greatest latitude to express their "voice" and articulate their ideas on community, they do not provide specific frameworks on racial inequality. Postmodernists tend to parallel racism with the oppression of other groups and seem to hope that racism can be overcome as groups constitute and reconstitute their cultural identities. Unfortunately, the serious racial issues of the modern era are often lost in the postmodernist dialogue and "identity" politics, leading some analysts to argue that postmodernist ideas represent a retreat from racism and rights.

All of this suggests that the Western analysts, especially those in the United States, stand at an impasse. They recognize that the old ways of thinking are bankrupt, but they are unwilling to change institutions. As Heller (1995) notes: "the waves of the real, not just fictitious, grand narratives are gone, but their results became our tradition" (p. 15).

The reluctance to change the institutional order, particularly when it comes to groups of color or the Other, is not limited by political identity, as the Gulf War proved. Yet the impasse deserves serious thinking about a new order that recognizes the cultures and interests of groups and nations that were oppressed by the modern. As Mestrovic (1994) notes:

> If Western Enlightenment narratives are no longer viable because they promote oppression . . . and if anti-Enlightenment phenomena such as nationalism and cultural identity as well as cultural relativism are going to grow stronger . . . then present-day or future intellectuals will have to make a serious and sobering search for non-modernist bases for social order.

We should seriously turn our attention to the search for a new social and economic order that recognizes the cultural contributions of all groups.

7

The Managing Diversity Movement

Origins, Status, and Challenges

OCTAVE BAKER

In the 1980s, "managing diversity" became one of the most popular management concepts among human resource professionals, business leaders, and academicians concerned with workplace issues. As testament to this increased interest in diversity, several major studies documented the changing nature of the workforce and the challenges posed to U.S. businesses by these changes (Bolick & Nestleroth, 1989; Johnston, Packer, & Jaffee, 1987). In addition, an increasing number of books, articles in newspapers and magazines, and conferences focused on helping organizations understand, manage, and capitalize on the trend toward more diversity in the workplace.

Although the managing diversity movement grew out of affirmative action (A.A.) and equal employment opportunity (E.E.O.) policies, it represents a significantly different perspective on issues pertaining to equity in the workplace. In contrast to these more traditional approaches, the diversity movement emphasizes that white America has a long-term self-interest in promoting and fostering a healthy diversity in the workplace. Whereas A.A. and E.E.O. focused on eliminating racism, prejudice, and discrimination primarily for the benefit of the protected classes, the diversity movement stresses the benefits to white America that derive from valuing and effectively managing a heterogeneous workforce and the costs to them of not doing so. Instead of emphasizing moral and legal imperatives, the proponents of diversity argue that the management of diversity is an important business issue affecting white America and its corporations in their struggle to gain and maintain competitive advantage in a changing domestic and global marketplace.

This chapter examines the origins of the managing diversity movement and explores key aspects of this movement. The first part of the chapter provides an overview of the movement's origins in the civil rights movement and in affirmative action. The second part examines more recent developments that have highlighted the issue of diversity in the workplace. The third section documents the corporate response to diversity. The fourth section discusses the implications of the diversity movement and offers recommendations on how it can more adequately address key issues of racial and economic inequality.

Origins of Managing Diversity

The managing diversity movement emerged in the 1980s as a new framework for human resource management. But the movement has its historical origins in the civil rights movement of the 1960s, which sought to promote equal opportunity and put an end to discrimination. More specifically, the managing diversity movement can be traced back to the passage of the Civil Rights Act of 1964 and to various executive orders issued to implement it. In addition, the movement's origins can be traced back to the various race relations training programs created after the Civil Rights Act and to the affirmative action programs designed to help organizations comply with federal equal employment guidelines.

The Civil Rights Act of 1964 banned discrimination in housing, education, transportation, and employment based on race, religion, national origin, or gender (Coffey, 1987). Specifically, it

- prohibited the exclusion from public facilities on the basis of race, color, religion, or national origin
- prohibited exclusion and discrimination in the workplace

- provided for the protection of minority group members in using public facilities, attending public schools, registering to vote, and participating in programs receiving federal assistance

The passage of the Civil Rights Act was followed by other efforts of the federal government and private employees to establish affirmative action programs. These programs generally attempted to achieve ethnic and gender balance in organizations by expanding recruiting and by training and placing minorities and women where they were underrepresented. The program was established in 1965 by Executive Order 11246, issued by President Johnson, to require goals and timetables for the hiring of women and minorities as a condition for getting federal contracts. Affirmative action was strengthened in 1971 when the Supreme Court ruled that plaintiffs did not need to show unequal treatment, but instead could use disparate impact as evidence of employment discrimination (Jackson & Associates, 1992).

As a result of these efforts to ensure equity in the workplace, many private sector companies and public agencies began to hire race relations consultants and to conduct training to ensure nondiscrimination and equal treatment. Most of these training programs were designed to help ease the organizations' compliance with federal equal opportunity guidelines and, at the same time, to maintain productivity and harmony in the integrated workplace. The focus was on such issues as how to assess hiring patterns to determine whether they were unfairly exclusionary, how to implement and administer equal employment opportunity and affirmative action programs, and how to supervise minorities. Whether explicit or not, the basic goal of these training and consulting activities was to encourage white males to share power with minorities and women in the mainstream institutions of the United States (Coffey, 1987).

By the late 1970s, race relations training and other programs to ensure equal employment opportunity and affirmative action were institutionalized in the federal agencies, educational institutions, and large employers in the private sector. These programs had been fairly successful in eliminating formal barriers to and discrimination against women and minorities and in integrating them into key sectors of the economy. At the same time, however, these programs began to generate more resistance and the feeling they did not live up to expectations.

Much of the resistance to affirmative action came from white males, who hold most of the decision-making positions in corporate America. Many white males believed that their self-interests and dominance were threatened by the increased competition for jobs, education, and housing from white women and people of color. Their resentment and anxiety were expressed in arguments that affirmative action was in conflict with the corporate meritocracy, that companies were hiring unqualified women and minorities in order to meet affirmative action quotas, and that affirmative action meant a general lowering of standards. These beliefs were further reinforced by uncertain economic conditions and by conservative politicians who capitalized on them to get elected. By the beginning of the 1980s, and with the election of Ronald Reagan, affirmative action had generally taken on a negative connotation and stigma in the perceptions of not only white males but also other Americans.

Additional dissatisfactions with affirmative action were voiced by some people of color who had benefited from these programs (Jackson & Associates, 1992). They believed that affirmative action had fallen short of expectations in breaking down the barriers to equal opportunity. Although affirmative action had considerable success in integrating women and people of color into many organizations, it had not been as successful in ensuring the promotion and retention of these groups. The perception was that many organizations had not addressed the root causes of resistance to people of color and women in organizations and had not created hospitable organizational climates in which no one is advantaged or disadvantaged.

During this time, the rise of the "new minorities" began to dilute the nation's focus on race, which had been a driving force behind affirmative action. For a complex set of reasons (Ladner & Stafford, 1981), the concept of being a minority in U.S. society during the late 1960s and the 1970s assumed a more inclusive interpretation beyond the nonwhite, powerless, and oppressed groups traditionally considered to be minorities. American society began defining minority status in broad political and economic terms to include women, white ethnics, gays, the elderly, and the disabled. As a result, by the end of the 1970s, federal civil rights efforts had in fact shifted from race to gender, age, and handicap status as the primary issues of concern.

In the 1980s, the managing diversity movement emerged, in part, as a response to the perceived limitations of affirmative action and the rise of the new minorities. The concept of managing diversity was consistent with the backlash against affirmative action in the 1980s because it was a broad, appealing, and inclusive concept. It appealed to many white males in corporate America because it explicitly included them in its discourse. By emphasizing superior business performance as a reason for diversity, diversity advocates moved beyond the moral imperatives of affirmative action. Moreover, by emphasizing skills and abilities, diversity advocates defused the charge leveled against affirmative action—that it meant a lowering of standards (Morrison, 1992).

The concept of managing diversity also responded to concerns of women and people of color about the limitations of affirmative action. Although managing diversity grew out of and incorporates key elements of affirmative action, it takes a different perspective on issues in the heterogeneous workplace. It addresses concerns of women and people of color over low promotion rates and inhospitable organizational climates by expanding the scope of earlier affirmative action programs (Jackson & Associates, 1992). This is accomplished in two ways. First, diversity advocates encourage not only racial and gender balance in hiring, but also in promotions, transfers, and working conditions throughout the organization. Second, diversity advocates seek to create organizational climates and cultures where gender, racial, and other kinds of diversity are not merely tolerated but also appreciated, nourished, and supported as valuable organizational resources.

The managing diversity concept was also consistent with the new political realities established by the rise of the "new minorities" in the 1960s and 1970s. Most advocates of diversity tend to use an expanded concept of diversity that includes these new minorities. For example, Roosevelt Thomas (1991), a leading diversity proponent, views diversity as "going beyond race and gender" to include "age, personal and corporate background, education, function, personality, lifestyle, sexual preference, geographic origin, tenure with the organization, exempt or non-exempt status, and management and non-management" (pp. 10-11). This inclusive interpretation of diversity includes white males. Thus, Thomas and some other advocates of diversity appear to be moving beyond what they may perceive to be an outdated focus on race and gender to a more inclusive concept of diversity. The use of a more expanded definition of diversity serves to distinguish managing diversity from the stigmatized concept of affirmative action, thus making it more palatable and appealing to mainstream America.

The managing diversity concept was also more appealing to mainstream America because it de-emphasized the role and significance of race and racism in the workplace. The de-emphasizing of race and racism was consistent with trends in U.S. society, as already discussed, to focus more attention on issues of gender, age, sexual orientation, and disabled status in the workplace and to minimize the significance of race. This de-emphasis on race and racism is reflected in several discursive practices used by proponents of diversity. The first practice is simply not to mention race or racism in the discourse on diversity. Instead, the focus is on concepts such as valuing differences and the minimizing of discrimination, prejudice, and stereotypes directed against individuals based on their culture, ethnicity, age, gender, disabled status, or lifestyle. A second discursive practice that de-emphasizes race and racism is to analogize racism to and lump it with a laundry list of other "isms" or forms of oppression such as sexism, ageism, and ethnocentrism that still plague the workplace and prevent individuals from managing diversity effectively. When the "isms" are lumped together, oppression may appear to be a uniform problem, and, thus, the unique significance of racism in U.S. society is obscured (Grillo & Wildman, 1991). A third discursive practice that minimizes the significance of racism is to focus exclusively on the negative attitudes, beliefs, and behaviors of *individuals* instead of on institutional or systemic practices and procedures that perpetuate racial domination and subordination.

Recent Developments

The increased concern in the 1980s with workforce diversity also coincided with a number of changes projected in the economic and organizational environment affecting American business. These changes in the business environment that highlight the importance of diversity include (a) demographic changes projected in the composition of the workforce and of the population as a whole and (b) new competitive pressures on U.S. business due to the shift to a service economy and the globalization of the economy. These changes have been widely discussed by proponents of diversity in organizations and have been used by them to bolster their claims that diversity is an important business issue affecting competitiveness of U.S. business for the 1990s and beyond. They argue that, as a result of these economic and organizational changes, the ability to promote and foster a healthy diversity within the workplace is a critical factor in a company's competitive position.

The projected demographic changes in the workforce and in the general population received widespread attention among corporate planners and others as a result of influential reports such as *Workforce 2000* (Johnston & Packer, 1987) and *Opportunity 2000* (Bolick & Nestleroth, 1989). These reports intensified concern for the effective utilization of a workforce that was projected to be increasingly diverse.

The demographic changes projected for the 1990s in these reports included the following:

- Women and people of color will constitute 85% of the growth in the workforce.

- Asians, African Americans, and Latinos will constitute almost 30% of the workforce by the end of the decade.
- People of color will constitute 85% of the population growth in the United States in the next 20 years.
- White males will continue to be a minority in the workforce by the year 2000.
- Immigrants, most from Asia and Latin America, will represent an increasing portion of the labor force.
- The workforce will continue to mature, with those in the 35-54 age group increasing from 30% of the workforce in 1985 to 51% by the year 2000.
- The workforce will grow at a slower rate than at any time since the 1930s, creating a potential labor shortage.
- The average skill level of new entrants to the workforce will fall, whereas skill demands will rise.

The authors of *Workforce 2000* (Johnston & Packer, 1987) suggest that these demographic changes represent both a risk and an opportunity. The risk is that employers will be unable to maintain productivity with fewer, less skilled, and less traditional entrants to the labor market at a time when skill demands of jobs are rising and international competition is rising. The opportunity involves the prospect that employers, facing a labor shortage, will be more willing to offer jobs to historically disadvantaged groups and to invest more heavily in their training.

But the authors are not optimistic about this prospect. They suggest that employers may instead respond to the situation by (a) bidding up the wages of the relatively small group of young, white workers entering the labor force, (b) substituting capital for labor in the service sectors of the economy, and (c) moving jobs to other parts of the country or the world that are faster growing or more youthful. The authors also suggest that African Americans, particularly African American men, are those most likely to suffer if these strategies dominate.

Another change in the business environment that is pushing diversity to the foreground is the shift from a manufacturing-based economy to a service economy. In a service economy, transactions involve a person-to-person exchange between the provider of the service and the customer (Jackson & Associates, 1992). Thus, in such an economy, success depends on employees who can understand the perspectives and preferences of their customers and who can interact and communicate effectively with them. Because similarities between people facilitate understanding and communication, companies offering services in an increasingly diverse marketplace have an incentive to hire a diverse workforce that mirrors the diversity among their customers.

Consequently, employers find themselves with a diverse workforce and with the challenge of effectively managing this internal diversity.

Still another change supporting diversity is the globalization of the economy. This change increases the importance of diversity as a business issue in two ways. First, international expansion entails the need to capture shares of foreign markets. This need, in turn, may lead to alliances with non-U.S. firms. Such alliances, to be successful, require increased cross-cultural sensitivity and the need to develop organizational systems that transcend cultural boundaries and that enable organizations to utilize fully the talents of diverse employees. A second consequence of international expansion is increased competition for U.S. firms, which must now compete with firms from around the world whether or not they seek customers overseas. As a result of this increased competition, more emphasis is placed on getting close to the customer, enhancing the quality of products and services, and beating the competition through innovation. To achieve these goals, companies are increasing the use of work teams, forming strategic alliances, and attempting to maximize the contributions of all employees. Because the workforce will be more diverse, these challenges underscore the importance of addressing domestic diversity issues, including the challenge of managing differences in corporate cultures.

Proponents of diversity maintain that all these changes in the business environment underscore the importance of diversity as a key competitive issue for business in the 1990s and beyond. Citing demographic changes in society and in the workforce, for example, they argue that the most competitive companies will be those that are able to (a) recruit and retain talented employees from a diverse labor pool, (b) create a climate that allows everyone to contribute to his or her maximum potential, and (c) use their diverse workforce to take advantage of diversity in the marketplace.

Proponents of diversity maintain that these demographic changes in the workforce present organizations with powerful incentives to understand and promote diversity. Not only is the workforce becoming much more diverse, it is also growing at a slower rate. It is said that business leaders should be aware that there is a very real potential for a labor shortage, thus creating a seller's market for labor. As a result, organizations may experience considerable difficulty in meeting staffing needs. With people of color and women constituting the majority of new entrants to the workforce, it is argued, organizations that foster and promote diversity will be well positioned to attract the most talented and skilled employees essential to maintaining and increasing competitiveness.

In order to succeed in this new environment, business leaders are being urged to adapt their organizations to the new reality of diversity. Proponents of diversity argue that today's employees are less willing to compromise their cultural and gender identities in order to blend into the corporate mainstream. Rather, they are more likely to want to maintain and celebrate their differences and insist that these differences be understood, respected, and valued as an important organizational resource.

With these vast changes in the workforce, proponents of diversity are encouraging business leaders to build cohesive and productive workplaces where all employees can contribute to their maximum potential. The proponents believe that simply putting diverse individuals together without such efforts can in fact damage productivity through the misunderstandings, stress, conflicts, and turnover that may be present to some extent in a diverse workforce.

The argument, then, is that diversity needs to be *deliberatively* and effectively managed. Special efforts are needed in the diverse workplace to develop cooperative and committed employees who work together to ensure quality and customer satisfaction. There is an urgent need to develop a climate that fosters mutual respect, acceptance, and cooperation among a diverse workforce in order to maintain competitiveness.

It is argued that companies can expect to benefit from promoting diversity by tapping into its potential for developing an exciting, flexible, and innovative corporate environment through the synergistic bringing together of individuals with different cultural backgrounds and perspectives. Research is cited by proponents of diversity to argue that heterogeneous groups are more creative than homogeneous groups in decision making and problem solving by virtue of the variety of perspectives found in the heterogeneous groups (Cox & Blake, 1991). This sort of creativity will be increasingly valuable to organizations as the challenges facing them become more complex and need diverse perspectives for effective solutions.

It is also argued that companies can also expect to benefit from diversity efforts by cutting personnel costs, which have become a major expense for most organizations. The claim is that effective diversity practices and policies will reduce the number of expensive discrimination complaints and will cut costs involved in recruiting, training, and relocating and replacing employees from diverse backgrounds (Morrison, 1992). In fact, cost savings in recruitment, turnover, and absenteeism as a result of diversity efforts have been documented by Cox and Blake (1991).

In summary, the desire for competitive advantage appears to be the main driving force fueling corporate interest in diversity. Proponents view diversity as a new framework for recruiting, retaining, motivating, and developing a high-performing workforce from an increasingly diverse population. They want to maximize the advantages of a culturally diverse workforce and to minimize the potential problems associated with diversity. The advantages include both the creativity that results from the contributions of different talents and perspectives and the ability to compete effectively in the diverse marketplace.

The Corporate Response to Diversity

An increasing number of companies have instituted formal diversity programs in response to demographic changes in the workforce and because of their concern with managing diversity as a competitive issue. In the largest survey of its kind to date, Towers Perrin and The Hudson Institute (1990) joined forces to examine how companies are responding to the key demographic and labor force issues identified in the influential report, *Workforce 2000*. In particular, the study focused on employers' level of concern about such critical human resource issues as the projected labor shortage; the skills gap; and the increasing number of minorities, immigrants, and women in the workforce. The study also focused on how companies were preparing to deal with these potential threats to their long-term success.

Surveying senior human resource executives from a cross-section of American business, the report found that the workforce of the companies surveyed is already quite diverse. For example, women constituted one half of the workforce of the average company surveyed. Minorities represented up to 20% of the workforce at just under 60% of the surveyed companies and more than 26% of the employees at one fourth of the companies participating in the study.

Moreover, the report found that cultural and ethnic diversity in the workforce is a paramount concern of top management in the surveyed companies. Almost three quarters of the respondents reported some level of management focus on the hiring and promotion of minority employees. Almost 70% of respondents reported significant concern with the needs of female employees.

The report also found a significant level of senior management concern about competing in a seller's market for talent; 68% of the respondents noted that their senior management was concerned about impending shortfalls in the labor pool. For 36% of the respondents, this concern was strong enough to shape management decisions and corporate strategy. More than one half of the surveyed companies reported a shortage of qualified workers. Scientists and technical workers were the most elusive, with 70% of the companies reporting difficulty recruiting them.

Although the surveyed companies appeared to recognize and be concerned about crucial labor force issues, their readiness to take action to address these issues was mixed, at best. Although 55% of the companies were concerned about supervisors' abilities to manage a diverse workforce, only about one quarter of them were taking steps to train supervisors in managing diversity. Though 42% of the companies engaged in explicit minority recruiting, they paid less attention to programs to support new entrants once they were hired. For example, only 12% trained minorities for supervisory positions, and relatively few used support groups or mentor programs for minorities and women or provided language or immigration assistance.

The authors of the report suggest that this hesitancy to take concrete action on diversity issues in the workforce may be due to the perceived sensitivity of the issues and to factors in the organizational climate that make it difficult to address diversity issues adequately. One fourth of the surveyed companies, for example, reported that their corporate cultures were not open to diversity. In addition, 29% said discrimination was a problem, and fully 15% reported "overt harassment" of minorities as a concern.

Another study of multicultural diversity programs, conducted in 1992 by the American Management Association (1993), reported somewhat different findings regarding the prevalence of these programs than did the Towers Perrin study. Surprisingly, the American Management Association (AMA) study found that almost 46% of the respondents in the surveyed companies reported the existence of formal multicultural diversity programs. Perhaps the discrepancy between the two studies with regard to the prevalence of multicultural diversity programs is a result of the AMA study using fairly broad criteria in determining whether or not a company had implemented such a program. In the study, a wide variety of activities was included under the rubric of a formal multicultural diversity program, including personal and corporate action plans around diversity issues, mentoring programs, cultural awareness programs, language training, and even the administration of employee surveys. The discrepancy between the two studies could also be due to differences in the samples used. The AMA sample was probably not as representative of a cross-section of American businesses as the Towers Perrin study was because it was drawn from companies served by AMA as members or customers.

The AMA study also found that large companies are more likely than smaller companies to sponsor diversity programs. Almost 65% of companies with 2,500 or more employees had diversity programs, compared with 47% of smaller companies. The authors of the report attribute part of the difference to the fact that large companies have more formal human resource programs of all kinds. They also suggest that the actual need for such programs is greater in larger firms. For example, their survey showed that the barriers to minority promotability are significantly higher in companies with 500 or more employees, thus suggesting a greater need for diversity programs in these companies.

Actual and projected changes in workforce demographics were the most important reasons given by companies participating in the AMA study for implementing these programs. Other less important reasons were government mandated programs, the shrinking labor pool, increased corporate competition, and the need for market share.

More recently, corporate America's response to diversity issues was explored by Louis Harris and Associates as part of a broad study to examine specific labor force issues and how companies were responding to them (Mirvis, 1993). Based on in-depth interviews with 406 human resource executives from companies associated with the Conference Board, the study found that almost two thirds of companies surveyed had diversity training programs for managers, and one half had statements from top management on the business need for diversity. Almost 40% reported having training programs for all employees; 31% had task forces in diversity; and 28% had minority mentoring programs. When asked about plans to offer such programs in the future, approximately one sixth to one quarter of the companies reported having plans to begin programs or to adopt other measures in the mid-1990s. Thus, four out of five of the companies surveyed either had programs in place to support the management of diversity or planned to implement such programs in the future.

When queried about which groups they expected would increase significantly in the workplace, many respondents predicted a significant increase in the number of minority women and men and in white women. Surprisingly, 41% of the companies predicted no significant change in the composition of their workforce. In addition, one half of the companies did not project a decline in the proportion of white males in their workforce, although the proportion of white males in the general workforce is expected to decrease. The authors of the study attribute these seeming contradictions to (a) the inability to project workforce changes because of pressures from downsizing or (b) a "head in the sand" approach to how demographic trends will affect these companies.

The companies most likely to have implemented diversity programs were those characterized as having "cutting-edge" human resource philosophies. These cutting-edge companies are more likely to view diversity as a competitive opportunity; that is, they believe that learning to capitalize on diversity will increase the company's productivity and lead to a competitive advantage. Thus, they view the management of diversity as a major challenge, with the need for new programs and management styles. In contrast, companies with less progressive human resource philosophies believe that diversity is best handled as just part of good management, presumably needing no special programs or changes in management style, or these companies may view the management of diversity as an affirmative action issue or as one with no serious impact.

Implications and Recommendations

It is clear from studies on the corporate response to diversity that many companies are responding to the strong arguments in favor of valuing and managing diversity in the workplace. Hence, the evidence is convincing that the diversity movement is having a significant impact on the human resource policies and practices of corporate America. However, to maintain and expand its positive impact on corporate America, the diversity movement must successfully meet a number of significant challenges. These include the challenges of (a) conducting valid and useful research on diversity programs, (b) addressing effectively the issues of race and the impact of racism on corporate America, and (c) establishing a broader and more sophisticated conceptual framework for the analysis of diversity issues.

Conducting Research on Diversity Programs. From the studies reviewed earlier, it is obvious that more research is needed on the corporate response to diversity. Specifically, there is a need to conduct valid and useful research about (a) the prevalence and distribution of managing diversity programs, (b) the developmental process that chacterizes these programs, and (c) the effectiveness of these programs in achieving their goals.

As discussed earlier, several studies have documented the increasing number of companies that have instituted formal managing diversity programs in response to key demographic and labor force issues facing U.S. businesses. Because the results of these studies have differed widely, there is still no definitive information on the prevalence and distribution of managing diversity programs. Thus, more research is needed in this area in order to clarify the corporate response to workplace diversity. More specifically, what is needed are more comprehensive studies with larger and more carefully selected samples to provide more reliable data on the size, extent, and distribution of managing diversity programs in the corporate sector. Which industries or sectors of the economy are more likely to have adopted this approach to human resource management? What specific activities and practices are being pursued as part of these diversity programs? What geographical locations are more likely to adopt these programs? Are different kinds of companies more likely to adopt a particular approach to managing diversity? How long have these programs been in place? These are some of the questions that need to be addressed by future research to more adequately clarify and document the corporate response to diversity.

Furthermore, more in-depth research is needed to document the initiation and development of various managing diversity programs in order to shed light on the stages of development of these programs and develop guidelines for organizations that wish to establish similar programs. For example, case studies of various programs could address such questions as those listed below.

- What was the perceived need(s) that led to the initiation of the program?
- What groups in the organization acted as advocates or champions of the program during the initiation phase?
- How was the need for change framed and documented?
- What kind of diagnosis was conducted to assess diversity issues in the organization?
- How was the commitment of top management gained?
- What kind of resistance to the establishment of the program was encountered?
- To what extent was a strategy of planned organizational change used?
- Who was responsible for guiding and managing the change process?
- What were the short-term and the long-term goals of the diversity program?
- What benchmarks were used to measure progress?

Research is also needed to develop frameworks and models for evaluating the effectiveness of managing diversity efforts. With continued corporate downsizing and belt-tightening, many proponents of diversity are increasingly being asked to justify their efforts and to show that diversity programs are achieving the results expected of them. In particular, they are being asked by their corporate sponsors to provide evidence for their claims that diversity programs enhance competitiveness and productivity. Consequently, there is a need to develop methodologies and measures to evaluate the effectiveness of the programs, activities, and practices associated with diversity efforts. Such methodologies may include quantitative as well as qualitative methods of collecting data. The measures may include objective numbers or subjective impressions concerning the desired outcomes. Also, an evaluation of effectiveness would consider both desirable and undesirable unanticipated consequences that may result from program activities.

Finally, the question of who benefits from diversity programs and practices that have apparently been adopted by significant sectors of corporate America must be examined. As discussed earlier, many proponents of diversity originally projected a potential labor shortage due to a slowdown in the growth of the labor force. The assumption was that this potential labor shortage represented an opportunity to integrate disadvantaged youth into the economic mainstream because employers would be more willing to invest in the training and placement of these youth. Contrary to expectations, however, the labor shortage did not materialize. This is because labor shortage problems have been forestalled by the downsizing that has occurred on a massive scale in American organizations and that will continue in the 1990s (Marks, 1993). At the same time, people of color, particularly African Americans, are suffering from layoffs and unemployment at a disproportionate rate. In view of these trends, proponents of diversity need to reassess their earlier sanguine predictions regarding opportunities for people of color and the disadvantaged in corporate America. They need to address the question of who really benefits from the widespread diversity programs.

In all likelihood, they will find that the diversity movement has not led to an improvement in the situation of disadvantaged youth and most people of color. They will find that the relative rates of unemployment and earnings of these groups have not improved over the past decade and, indeed, have actually worsened. Further, they will find that because of segmented labor markets African Americans and Hispanics in particular are still overrepresented in declining occupations and are concentrated in a small number of central cities beset by problems. It is likely that the beneficiaries of managing diversity are primarily well-educated white women, people of color with skills that are in demand, and the "new minorities" consisting of white ethnic groups, gays, the elderly, and the disabled. Interestingly, there is also some evidence that African American women professionals have benefited from the managing diversity movement more than have African American men. According to an analysis by the *Wall Street Journal* (Gaither, 1994) of EEOC data, there are nearly twice as many African American women professionals in corporate America as African American male professionals.

Addressing the Issue of Race and the Impacts of Racism. As previously discussed, the managing diversity movement evolved from A.A. and E.E.O. policies to become one of the most popular management concepts in the 1980s. Although the managing diversity movement grew out of and incorporates key elements of affirmative action and equal opportunity employment, it goes beyond these traditional approaches to diversity by taking a broader perspective on the heterogenous workforce. A.A. and E.E.O. have traditionally focused on building a diverse workforce by combatting the effects of racism, prejudice, and discrimination. These approaches emphasized providing "equal opportunity" for designated protected classes and correcting the effects of past discrimination. They tended to downplay culture or gender differences because being different was often interpreted in the past as being inferior.

According to its proponents, the managing diversity approach goes beyond A.A. and E.E.O. by *recognizing* and *appreciating* differences and by stressing the positive advantage of a diverse workforce. Managing diversity encourages the view that individuals can have equal rights and still maintain their differences. Differences are to be appreciated, nurtured, and supported—not simply tolerated. Hence, managing diversity encourages individuals to (a) be aware of and understand differences and (b) openly discuss them, whether they are based on race, culture, gender, age, sexual orientation, or other characteristics.

The managing diversity perspective also differs significantly from A.A. and E.E.O. approaches in that it tends to obscure, minimize, and marginalize the importance of racism and its impact on the diverse workplace. As discussed earlier, this is done by (a) simply not mentioning race and racism; (b) analogizing racism to other "isms," either implicitly or explicitly; and (c) focusing on aspects of racism at the *individual* level of analysis rather than at the systemic or structural level of analysis.

These discursive practices reflect a broader trend in academia and in society to deny and play down the reality of racism. These trends among white scholars have been noted by Feagin (1992) and in white society by Essed (1991). From the dominant perspective, issues of race and racism have largely faded into the background. In the larger society, there is now more concern about issues related to the so-called underclass, reverse discrimination, drugs, and the like. In the field of diversity, issues around race and racism have been replaced by concerns with "differences," usually defined in terms of ethnicity, gender, age, sexual orientation, and religion.

Yet because white racism is still very much a reality in the United States, proponents of diversity need to make racism a central issue in their analysis of workplace issues and resist the practice of ignoring it altogether or making it part of a laundry list of "isms" or forms of oppression. In particular, they need to focus more on the impact of racism on the workplace and on its costs to American business.

Because proponents of diversity tend to minimize or evade the role of race and racism in the diverse workplace, the impact of racism is currently more implicit than explicit in the discussion of diversity. The implicit impact of racism is to make U.S. companies less competitive in the face of changes in the economic and social environment affecting U.S. business. Racism and other "isms" prevent U.S. firms from capitalizing on diversity and from being more competitive domestically and globally. Proponents of diversity need to be more explicit in their contentions that firms that fail to deal with racism in the workplace will be less competitive and productive. They need to make the case that the costs of racism and the failure to minimize its impact are part of the general costs of failing to manage diversity of all kinds. These costs are a decrease in productivity and competitiveness resulting from the following:

- Increased ethnic conflict, misunderstanding, stress, tension, and low morale
- Inability to attract and retain the most talented and skilled employees essential to maintaining and increasing competitiveness
- Increased inability to capitalize on the creativity and flexibility resulting from the contributions and different perspectives of a diverse workforce
- Increased costs from discrimination suits, turnover, and absenteeism
- Difficulties in understanding the preferences and consumer habits in an increasingly diverse domestic marketplace and in the global economy

Establishing a Conceptual Framework. In addition to the challenge of being more forthright and explicit about race and racism, proponents of diversity face the challenge of developing a more sophisticated conceptual framework that incorporates insights from social science research in an analysis of diversity issues and their solutions. Such a framework would go beyond the current focus of most advocates of diversity on individual attitudes, perceptions, and assumptions. Rather, the focus needs to be on situational, structural, and economic factors that work to perpetuate patterns of domination and subordination in society.

Pettigrew and Martin (1987), for example, document the informal situational barriers to full participation of minorities in the workplace. They describe the social psychological dynamics that are set in motion when a minority worker is the only minority in the work group (solo status) or is assumed to have been assigned the position because of affirmative action (token status). Reviewing a large body of social psychological research, they outline how "modern racial prejudice" profoundly affects the work situation of a minority worker in the token or solo role. Minorities in these roles are adversely affected by stressful hiring practices, exaggerated expectations, and extreme evaluations during the recruitment and entry stages of employment. In later stages of employment, tokens and solos are likely to suffer from lack of realistic and helpful feedback on their performance and an array of cognitive distortions on the part of the dominant group that leads to negative evaluations of minority workers.

The structural perspective on diversity issues is illustrated by Braddock and McPartland (1987), who view racial segregation as "deeply embedded in our major institutions" (p. 28). Their research on barriers to equal employment opportunity found that African Americans and Hispanics face special structural features that present employment difficulties at different stages of the occupational process. At the job candidate stage, they face exclusionary barriers due to the "segregated networks" used by employers for recruitment. At the entry stage, they face "statistical discrimination," where employers make decisions regarding their job skills and work attitudes based on their perception of group differences between Whites and minorities on these traits. Finally, at the promotion stage, they may face barriers due to "closed internal markets."

In addition to incorporating situational and structural perspectives in their analysis of diversity issues, advocates of diversity need to take into account the economic, political, and social context around particular employment settings and particular employers (Feagin, 1987). They need to explore how the current "free market" economic system perpetuates racial and other kinds of discrimination. In particular, more attention needs to be paid to the impact of the continuing downsizing of companies, the exportation of higher-paying manufacturing jobs, and the consequent disinvestment in the nation's productive capacity. These economic trends will clearly exacerbate the reality that not enough jobs with living wages are being created in the United States and make it more likely that workers of color and white workers will continue to be routinely pitted against each other for too few jobs. Such competition heightens racial and ethnic tension, substantially contributes to discrimination, and generally undermines the chances of achieving the broad goals of the managing diversity movement.

Finally, if the proponents of diversity truly wish to eradicate racism and the other "isms," they must be prepared to join with others in building active community-based movements for social change. They must keep in mind that "just as it is not possible to make and sustain major alterations in individuals' lives without altering the organizations and communities of which they are a part, it is not possible to make and sustain changes in organizational structures without altering the community context in which the organizations practice" (Chesler & Delgado, 1987, p. 201).

8

The Impact of Racism on Whites in Corporate America

JOHN P. FERNANDEZ

In corporate America, racist behaviors and attitudes have historically been beneficial to Whites. White men in particular have been able preferentially to hire and promote mainly people like themselves. The impact of racism on the corporate bottom line, however, is negative. A major *Fortune* 500 company has estimated, for instance, that conflicts caused by racism, sexism, and the like, have reduced its bottom line between $20 million and $40 million. For one thing, as a black, male, upper-level manager wrote: "Many Whites who think they are not prejudiced unconsciously engage in offensive acts and display attitudes that are not conducive to a productive working environment."

In addition to limiting corporate effectiveness and the bottom line, racism (or any other "ism") also limits the ability of companies to create jobs and advancement opportunities for both Whites and people of color. As we will see, racism greatly impacts the quality of life not only for working people of color but for Whites as well.

Today in the United States, changing demographics, increased social awareness, and Civil Rights legislation have begun to work changes in racist practices. But, if we are to understand racism in corporate America and its impact on Whites, white men especially, we must understand some basic things about human behavior, the definition of racism, and how people are socialized into being racist.

Some Realities

How can so destructive a force as racism continue to exist in the face of its negative consequences for society? G. Prezzolini (1967), an astute student of human behavior, observes that,

> People seldom believe what seems reasonable, nor do they always willingly accept what is expressed clearly, because logic and clarity have a weaker hold than imagination and mystery. Propositions that run counter to common morality do not create a desire for discussion or even contradiction but rather an urge to sidestep, ignore, or misinterpret. Life, which is full of such blindness to the most clearly expressed ideas, is ruled not by intellect but by desire and pride. Men want to live, not to understand; and they want to live their own way. If an idea seems to contradict what they want to believe, they refuse to accept it. If they really understand it, they either suppress it or avert their gaze in order not to see it. (p. 1)

Consistent with Prezzolini, R. W. White (1952) notes that "the constant play of impulse beneath and through the rational, conscious, goal-directed activities of everyday life" shows that "beneath the surface of awareness lies a zone of teeming emotion, urge, fantasy, from which spring the effective driving forces, as well as various disrupting agents in our behaviors" (p. 9).

We will see that it is such realities of human behavior as these that allow us to become racist, to justify our racism, and enable us to act in a racist manner without acknowledging our negative behavior.

In previous writings (Fernandez, 1986, 1991, 1993), I have argued that the question in all of this is not one of whether or not we are mentally healthy, but of the extent to which we are unhealthy. Levinson (1976)—who has written extensively on managerial psychology—would, I think, agree with this. His definition of mental illness allows for ups and downs in human nature. All of us, for example, have days when we are on an even keel and other days when we are not. When we are in emotional distress, we can be said to be temporarily mentally ill. The inherent negative impact of racism creates tremendous stress and conflicts, and it is clear that many employees, especially those with racist attitudes, are in states of constant stress that effectively renders them mentally ill.

Pettigrew (1981), speaking of what he called "positive mental health," offered a definition that would exclude all racist people. All of the six criteria he identifies for positive mental health are missing in racists:

> Six categories of human functioning [may be] suggested to define the concept of positive mental health: (1) the mentally healthy individual is self-aware, self-accepting, and enjoys a stable identity; (2) an individual's degree of development and actualization of his or her potential is also indicative of positive mental health; (3) so, too, is an individual's integration of the many *psychic functions;* (4) an individual's autonomy, relative independence from social pressures, and ability to act independently under internal controls are also important indicators; (5) the adequacy of an individual's perception of reality has also been advanced as a criterion by a number of writers; and, finally, (6) positive mental health requires the ability to master one's environment at a reasonable level of competency. (p. 108)

Our relative degrees of mental illness or mental healthiness have a great deal to do with our natural temperament. At birth some children are quiet and some are not; some are easygoing, others are not. "Each person from birth differs both in his particular combination of natural endowments and in the degree to which these permit him to contend with various aspects of life" (Levinson, 1976, p. 7). However, tendencies deriving from "natural endowments" may be either encouraged or discouraged by cultural conditioning: by parents, teachers, and other agents of socialization.

Critical for the understanding of personality, then, are those aspects of mental health that have to do with socialization. As Ruth Benedict, Margaret Mead, and others have shown, some societies instruct children, explicitly and implicitly, to forsake individual success and prominence in favor of pleasant group interaction. Cooperation, generosity, and avoidance of greed or selfishness are emphasized. As adults, children trained in these traditions avoid public distinction. By contrast, we in the United States "train [our] children instead to climb to the top" through what Mead's and Benedict's informants might consider "sharp practice, theft and the use of magic" (White, 1952, p. 13). The competitive American culture is a fertile ground in which to develop and maintain racist attitudes and behaviors.

Kenneth Keniston (1960) has noted that as adults we lose touch with our spontaneity; growing up means leaving "a world of directness, immediacy, diversity, wholeness, integral fantasy," in favor of "abstractions, distance, specialization, dissociated fantasy and conformity" (p. 172). This transition from childhood to adulthood feeds our propensity for becoming overtly and covertly racist through socialization. In short, the many psychological and sociological factors we have mentioned work to "allow" or "assist" us in becoming racist, but also in overcoming racism.

Racism Defined

Racism I define as cultural ideologies that depict Whites as inherently superior to people of color solely because of their race. Whites, especially white men, wield the power in societal institutions to develop, evolve, nurture, spread, impose, and enforce the very myths and stereotypes that are the foundations of racism, in the minds not only of Whites themselves but as well in the minds of many people of color. These myths and stereotypes serve to maintain and justify white, and especially white male, social, economic, and political dominance.

Racism is deeply rooted in the very structure and fabric of society. It is not solely a matter of personal attitudes, beliefs, or, as I suggested earlier, of "mental illness." Indeed, it can be argued that racist beliefs are but accessory expressions of institutionalized patterns of Whites' power and social control. Based on recorded statements from workshop participants since 1990, the following are testimonies to the dynamics of continuing racism in the workplace.

As a black, male craftsworker aptly wrote,

> Racism is a creature of habit and so intertwined with American society. Many people don't know or consciously realize they are officially members of a racist group.

And a white, female craftsworker concurred, saying,

> I don't think any amount of training and/or awareness groups will correct attitudes. I think it is a basic attitude built in by culture, society, area of country the person grew up in, family values and prejudices.

Underlying racism are power struggles between dominant Whites who seek to maintain their privileged positions in society, and people of color who are determined to change the status quo. Even while they control society's major institutions, Whites greatly fear the loss of their hegemony. This drives them, consciously or unconsciously, to nurture myths and stereotypes about people of color in order to preserve the status quo. It drives them to behavior, as described by Pettigrew (1981), opposite to that of a healthy person.

NEO-RACISM

As the consciousness of contemporary Americans has been raised, growing numbers of people have come to oppose overt racism, not by eliminating
the feelings so much as just modifying them to be more palatable to others—
and to themselves. Such modified forms of racism are in most cases subtler
and more sophisticated than their predecessors, but they are just as harmful,
not only to the oppressed but to the oppressors. I call this modified racism
neo-racism.

An example of neo-racism is the lack of corporate mobility for many
people of color. Our interviews suggest that neo-racism is a key factor in the
lack of mobility, but the dominant-group bureaucracy attributes lack of
mobility to lack of experience, lack of opportunities, lack of political skills,
or lack of cultural compatibility. They will say that people of color are not
the "right" ones for higher levels, that they need to polish their image,
improve their style, or "smooth out their rough edges."

Comments from participants of our corporate client staff trainings demonstrate that the less blatant neo-racism (and neo-sexism) of the 1980s and
1990s is harder to detect than the overt discrimination of the past, but just as
real:

> The problems are less visible today than they were 10-15 years ago but I
> believe they have just gone "underground."
> Hispanic, female, middle-level manager

> There is still discrimination, it is just "in the closet."
> American Indian, female, craftsworker

> We have forced verbal/physical signs of racism and sexism underground. We
> have not changed the attitudes, only prevented them from being obvious.
> Nothing else has really changed.
> White, female, lower-level manager

> Eliminating racism and sexism is a wonderful idea, but unfortunately, there
> are a few bigots and chauvinists who will not allow themselves to view each
> person as an individual. These people will continue to humiliate, debase, and
> ridicule others. Then we have the bigots and chauvinists who do a great job
> of masking their feelings and attitudes. Only a major slip will show their
> "true color." These people can be more dangerous than those who do not
> conceal their feelings.
> White, female, craftsworker

INSTITUTIONAL RACISM

Inertia, the reluctance to change, tends to pervade bureaucracies. Their rate of change is naturally slower than that of the individuals who make up the organizations or groups of individuals who maintain them. Bureaucracies tend to captivate these groups and use them in a way that defies individual influence: The bureaucracies become systems or entities apart from the people whom they nominally serve. Institutional racism is grounded in these systems.

Institutional beliefs are bureaucratic regulations, policies, and practices that in and of themselves exclude people who are different. Established in times in the United States when open discrimination was more acceptable, they provide a continuing mechanism for discrimination, even though they were never established to do so.

The corporate "old-boy" network graphically illustrates a discriminatory bureaucratic system of institutionalized racism that remains functional today. Historically, the old-boy network was used to find and select candidates for higher-level public and private jobs. Because the network in America was primarily white, middle-class, Protestant, and male when it was used as a recruitment tool and/or a source of talent for promotion, it naturally excluded people who did not fit those characteristics. Current old-boy networks remain widely functional at higher corporate management levels: Upper management remains predominantly white and male, even in companies with a good mix of people of color and women at lower levels.

Not only is neo-racism (and neo-sexism) difficult to perceive, but the following quotations demonstrate how institutional racism, though not even considered discrimination, is just as damaging to women and minorities as overt discrimination.

> They don't discriminate. They just keep on using the old-boy network for promotion candidates. It discriminates for them.
> White, male, middle-level manager

> Our company very seldom recruits at black colleges . . . this is institutional racism.
> Black, female, lower-level manager

> They have women's jobs, Black jobs, Hispanic jobs, Asian jobs, and Indian jobs. Ninety-nine percent are not mainstream jobs to help you advance your career. Then you have white male jobs. Ninety percent of them are the right

jobs to advance your career. I don't care what you call it—racism/sexism—it is unfair and it is discriminatory.

White, male, middle-level manager

Ironically, covert forms of neo-racism and institutional racism are no less destructive to the profitability of corporations than overt discrimination: Vast numbers of employees continue to be underpursued and underdeveloped because of their race.

Development of Racist Attitudes and Behaviors

Racism develops in and is nurtured by all of the societal institutions controlled by the dominant white male group. Babies begin their lives with a sense of kinship to all humans, regardless of skin color or other physical features. Most infants and very young children are open, loving, and comfortable with people who show them love, attention, and caring. However, children learn racist attitudes and behaviors at an early age. Families, schools, churches, government, the media, and other social groups and institutions socialize the population by communicating what is "good" behavior and what is "bad." They teach us what to expect of ourselves, our friends, and our families. They teach us how to relate to society.

As a result of their socialization, children learn how to be people of color or Whites. They acquire a sense of the worth of their social group and of themselves from their earliest contacts with other members of their family, their peers, and their teachers; from what they see in the movies, on television, and in advertisements; from what they read, from conversations they overhear, and from their daily observations.

A black, male, lower-level manager observed:

> Until white parents stop instilling in their children that they are superior and have more intelligence than black people, race/ethnic discrimination will always have a base at this company.

Numerous studies have explored the development of racist attitudes in white children at very early ages. One study found that very young children strongly prefer the color white over black and that their low regard for the color black is transferred to their perception of black people (Clark, 1981, pp. 309-310; Singh & Yancey, 1974).

Impact of Racism
and Sexism on Society

With such strong forces operating to socialize people, many believe that a racist society is a natural consequence of human behavior. A consistent message about race from church, family, peers, schools, government, newspapers, and television instills in people an unconscious or conscious ideology, a set of beliefs and attitudes that many accept implicitly as the natural state of the universe. Everyone has heard a family member, schoolmate, co-worker, friend, or political, social, or economic leader say, "Of course I have racist/sexist attitudes. Everyone has them. We cannot help it. We were brought up this way."

As unconscious ideology, racism has a debilitating effect on people's psychological and physical health. For example, the U.S. Commission on Mental Health declared 29 years ago that Americans' racist attitudes, which cause and perpetuate tension, are a compelling health hazard, severely crippling the growth and development of millions of citizens. The commission diagnosed racism as a form of schizophrenia, "in that there is a large group gap between what whites believe in and actually practice" (Katz, 1978, pp. 11-12).

A white-centered, superior attitude leaves the people holding it isolated, confused, and mentally underdeveloped. Racism produces false fears in Whites and allows these fears to control where they live, where they go to school, where they travel, where they work, with whom they socialize, where they play, and whom they love and marry. Whites develop unhealthy mechanisms, such as denial, false justification, projection, disassociation, and transference of blame, to deal with their fears about minorities. As Katz (1978) has written, "racism ha[s] deluded whites into a false sense of superiority that has left them in a pathological and schizophrenic state" (p. 15). Further, she adds, it has produced "miseducation about the realities of history, the contributions of Third-World people, and the role of minorities in present-day culture. In short, it has limited the growth potential of whites" (p. 15).

Many Americans believe that their country has almost completely shed its negative racist stereotypes and attitudes. But the reality is not that racist attitudes are no longer widespread among white Americans, but that society has been better socialized to avoid expressing many attitudes openly. It has found new stereotypes that are much more acceptable than the old ones: "We don't hire Blacks" has become "Blacks do not have the right qualifications."

The suppression and refinement of racial attitudes have given us hope of change, perhaps; but, as studies using sophisticated techniques to measure both attitudes and behavior have documented (Crosby, Bromley, & Saye, 1980), the behaviors exhibited toward people of color have not been modified to the extent that the change in language suggests.

Reviews of an array of "unobtrusive measure" studies—research that looked at people's behavior without their knowing it—showed significant amounts of racial bias in interpersonal behavior among black and white Americans. For example, Whites were consistently more inclined to help a person in need if that person were white rather than black. Moreover, given the opportunity to deliver an electric shock, white subjects tended to be more aggressive against Blacks than against Whites. Furthermore, aggression was more likely when the target was in no position to retaliate. (Because Whites are in the dominant position of power in this society, it follows that white aggression toward Blacks rather than black aggression toward Whites would be more frequent.) Finally, in spite of positive attitudinal statements made about a person, the underlying "affective tone" implied negative emotional content when the target person was black (Crosby et al., 1980).

Meanwhile, Thomas Pettigrew (1981), a leading psychologist on racial prejudices, has offered some relevant comments: "The emotions of racism are formed in childhood, while the beliefs that are used to justify them come later. Later in life, you may want to change your 'isms,' but it is far easier to change your intellectual beliefs than your deep feelings." What Pettigrew is saying is that Whites can change, for example, their belief that African Americans are intellectually inferior to Whites and come to perceive them as equals, but may still react with something between slight discomfort and violence should their child choose to marry one.

My training teams have observed our client staffs in trainings and noticed that racist people tend to be older, less educated, and more traditionally religious. We strongly suspect that they tend to have lower self-esteem and higher anxiety and to be more authoritarian, intolerant of ambiguity, and likely to conform to group pressures. But no age group, educational level, or religious group has a monopoly on racism.

In his monumental work, *An American Dilemma: The Negro Program and Modern Democracy,* Gunnar Myrdal (1944) pointed out the fundamental contradiction between America's cherished values of liberty, equality, justice, and equal opportunity and the degraded position of Blacks in American society. To paraphrase Myrdal, the American Negro problem is a problem in the heart of the American. It is there that the interracial tension has its focus. It is there that the decisive struggle goes on. The "American Dilemma" is the ever raging conflict. On one hand, the conflict is over the values preserved on the general plane, which we will call the "American Creed," where the

American thinks, talks, and acts under the influence of high national and Christian precepts. On the other hand, the conflict is over the values on specific planes of individual and group living. What dominates personal and local interests are economic, social, and sexual jealousies; considerations of community prestige and conformity; group prejudice against particular persons or types of people; and all sorts of miscellaneous wants, impulses, and habits (Myrdal, 1944).

The same contradiction Myrdal saw between American values and actions can be seen in the following remarks:

> I am married to a white woman and I still prefer this for myself. I am not opposed to my friends' mixed marriages. I do feel that I might have a difficult time of it if any of my three daughters were to enter a mixed marriage. I am quite comfortable working with other races and ethnic people and do not know of anyone on the job who has any problem with this either.
>   White, male, craftsworker

> I have no problems working in a pluralistic environment. I feel the diversity of a workforce adds to everyone's character. All races and all genders have competent, incompetent, ambitious, lazy, conscientious, and apathetic people. I do have a problem with hiring practices when they involve the hiring of an obviously less qualified individual.
>   White, male, craftsworker

And a black, female, craftsworker points out where she believes most Whites are "coming from":

> Racism/sexism still exist . . . the sorry thing is that the people who still practice this don't see themselves as in this category. They have been in this mold so long that they don't see where they are wrong and are unwilling to have anyone tell them they have a problem.

White Employees' Perceptions
of Problems in the Workplace

If we are to understand the negative impact of racism on Whites, it is necessary to reflect carefully on issues and concerns of white men in corporate America. As early as 1964, but especially in the past few years, THE central issue has been white males' fear for their position in society. Collectively, these impressions suggest that white men believe that *they* are the disadvantaged group; that they are stereotyped and faced with tremendous amounts of discrimination because of their whiteness and maleness. As a result, many white men have become angry, defensive, stressed, and generally unhappy with their lot. I believe that, in large part, their reactions are based in their own racism or the racism of their society, which has placed white men in their current position. In this section I will try to shed some light on the reality of the white male's situation in corporate America and on how it is influenced by white racism.

Given current trends, the white population in the United States will become a minority by the middle of the 21st century. Although the majority of the white population believes in equal opportunities and fairness, there are dangerous signals that as the minority population increases and more white people, especially white males, see themselves competing with people of color for schools, housing, and jobs, old hatreds and animosities will awaken. Put another way, the realization of this fact on the part of many Whites has brought out a range of reactions about the fate of Whites, including great concern that Whites will lose "their country" to these people of color unless they fight.

White Americans hold and express numerous stereotypes about people of color but generally say that they do not bring them into the workplace. This is a clear example of a "mental illness," of not being honest with oneself about (or unaware of) the impact of racism on one's behavior. Following are some comments that demonstrate the neurotic perceptions of some Whites who claimed not to bring their prejudices to work.

I don't believe in interracial marriage (God doesn't allow robins to mix with crows). Only animals that man has domesticated cross over the lines of their own kind.
    White, male, craftsworker

When I started here, I did not feel I was prejudiced. This company has made me that way. The Blacks tend to stick together and exclude Whites. The company promotes Blacks because of their color when many times they have no seniority, qualifications, or ability.
    White, female, lower-level manager

I'm quite mixed up on the issue of Whites marrying Blacks and vice versa. I don't really know if we should mix the races. Only God can say and I haven't met him as yet. When I see it, I don't feel that it's right.
    White, female, upper-level manager

Because most Whites deny that they have racist views, they do not see as much discrimination against people of color as those groups themselves do.

Instead, Whites tend to attribute the problems experienced by people of color to their own individual inadequacies.

It makes me very angry to encounter a racist person, but it also makes me angry to encounter someone who uses their color [to obtain consideration in the company].
    White, female, lower-level manager

I know there are some people who think because of their race or gender the company should hand them good jobs, qualified or not. I believe I should only advance my position when I earn it and not because I'm a female purple midget.
    White, female, clerical/technical

Let time take its course. Just to promote a person of color or a woman [if they haven't earned it] doesn't do them or us any good. I don't respect them. I lose respect for the company. In time, those that show potential will be promoted and moved up with respect.
    White, female, lower-level manager

Minorities are angry with the world and think that they deserve everything on a plate and not to have to work for it. People with foreign accents should try to speak English at all times, because this is the U.S. language. In doing this, they would just improve their English every day.
    White, female, middle management

Employees in the work environment who are under qualified and do not perform an adequate job still maintain their status as employees. Why? Because maybe they represent a minority?
    White, male, clerical/technical

Many white workers, especially white men, believe that what they face now in the U.S. workplace is reverse discrimination. They believe that qualified white men are losing out to unqualified women and minorities.

Where's the white male organization? Oh no, that would be prejudiced. However, every other kind of person on the face of the earth has their own club. Talk about segregation! By the way, I'm a white female whose white male husband can't get a job because he's the wrong color. I guess white children don't need to be supported as much as children of color.
    White, female, clerical/technical

I believe that a total reversal in discrimination has happened. A white male and black male with the same qualifications will not be judged equally because of the federal government. The company will choose the black male because they're afraid of being called a racist company.

White, male, clerical/technical

I personally have been turned down for jobs and promotions because I was not female or nonwhite. The explanation was "off the record" of course!

White, male, lower-level management

I am a white male. I am discriminated against because I'm not gay, I'm not a minority, I'm not a woman, I'm not handicapped, and I'm white; therefore I get no favoritism, only the opposite. Our company is so busy trying to be fair to those who say "you are neglecting me because I have this particular (whatever)" that they hold off the average white male, which is discrimination in reverse.

White, male, clerical/technical

We are all individuals regardless of our color or sex and we should all be treated the same, as far as promotions, raises, and opportunities go. If a white female and black or other minority were both qualified for a position, the minority would receive the position. Whatever happened to seniority?

White, male, clerical/technical

Co-Workers' Perceptions
of White Male Employees

Not surprisingly, minority workers and women see white men's position in the workplace from a very different perspective. Some stereotypes used by employees in our seminars to describe white people, especially white men, are *arrogant, crazy, ignorant, insensitive, out of control, spoiled,* and *selfish.* The more positive stereotypes are *privileged, shrewd, in control, dominant, powerful,* and *smart.* These stereotypes about white men derive, in part, from racism. White men have benefited from racism, but because of racism they also suffer from negative stereotypes, in a social sense more than an economic one.

The following are some employees' comments from our studies regarding their perceptions of white people, and especially white men, in the workplace.

The only problem white men face today is that they have been spoiled for too many years and are having a hard time adjusting to sharing. They've been raised to think they get the whole pie.
    White, female, clerical/technical

White males have created their own problems. Many white males are very prejudiced against people of color and make no bones about it. Higher management men do not like women or people of color running the company. This makes it very difficult to work with them.
    White, female, lower-level management

I generally think all Whites have no respect for Blacks, and I start with that notion. I respond to them from that point. I have to . . . demand respect.
    Black, female, clerical/technical

I get angry at white males. Not only do they think that they're better than colored men and women, they think that they're the next best things to perfect. They can do no wrong.
    Black, female, clerical/technical

I'm defensive and get mad at Whites when questioned about data that I have done a lot of investigation on. I feel, if (I was) white, there would not be a second thought as to whether I knew what I was talking about.
    Black, female, clerical

The white man protects the white man politically or whatever. No demotion would be made; lateral move, yes. But still he is being taken care of. The white man supposedly does not have faults. They do, but these are not brought out openly and rapidly as they would be with a minority.
    Hispanic, male, clerical/technical

I believe that I see Whites as "bull-shit artists." I see them make schedules that are not attainable, present them to the department, and when the schedules do not materialize, they are not penalized for them. But if someone who is not white does it, one has to explain why and the assignment will be given to someone else. I feel that Whites can do sub-par work, present it to their buddies, and their buddies (in general) will look the other way. I feel that my attitude about white work ethics is biased. But I see nothing to dispel the notion.
    Hispanic, male, lower-level manager

White males are still in control or in power positions. There appears to be a reluctance to share this control and become pluralistic. This creates anger and hostility against them.
    Black, male, middle-level manager

Traditionally, white men have had hardly any problems in the company. In the last few years it may have been a little more difficult to be promoted because of jobs being filled by people of color, but they still have enough pull from friends or family to reach executive positions.
    Hispanic, male, technical

There is evidence that at least some minority people are beginning to act out their hostile feelings toward white people, even those white people who themselves have no problems with people of color. A personal experience illustrates this: In April 1990, while running for exercise, I noticed a large excited group of black children aged 5 to 14. In the middle of the large group were two 13-year-old white girls who were being spit upon, punched, and kicked. I entered the crowd and told the black children to leave them alone. I was cursed and spit at but not hit. However, as the two white girls and I turned our backs to walk away, a fusillade of sticks, bottles, and small rocks hit us. I turned around and chased the black youths away. As they dispersed, I escorted the girls safely to their home.

What had the girls done to the black children? Nothing, except that they were white! If this was not an isolated incident, Whites are becoming targets, especially where their numbers put them in a minority.

Although people of color are generally not in positions of power to negatively affect white careers, the coming decades will certainly produce changes in American demographics and thus in power relations. As has been shown in Los Angeles County schools, minority students are taking out some of their anger on white children, who represent far less than a majority of the county school population. It is certainly reasonable to conclude that minority feelings must get in the way of working effectively with white people.

In fairness to white men, it must be said that many of them are not insensitive, racist, or cry babies. The second most frequent comment we received from white men in our seminars concerned their fear of unintentionally offending minorities or women. This fear can be as nonproductive as racist and sexist views, because it inhibits open, healthy communication among people. This in turn leads to misunderstanding and lower corporate efficiency, as the following comments illustrate.

> When I'm supposed to be sensitive to some groups like Blacks, I find myself ill-at-ease for fear of offending, and probably come off as cold or indifferent.
>   White, male, upper-level management

> While in a group such as this I am afraid of possibly saying something wrong that may offend somebody.
>   White, male, clerical/technical

Feel that I must be careful about inadvertently offending someone of another race or the opposite sex (walking on eggshells). Sometimes I assume the other person is prejudiced against me because of my sex or race. We don't communicate.

White, male, lower-level management

I worry that the other person automatically assumes that just because I am a white male I am prejudiced against them. Any statements made could be taken as prejudiced because the other person is very sensitive to the issue. Not sure how to "break the ice" sometimes.

White, male, middle-level

Fear of getting accused of picking on a minority person when I'm in the work environment. I was at a review, and the person who was giving the review was a minority person. I was giving good feedback about the document. I felt some frustration about it and said to myself it looks like I'm picking on them. But before the review, I had asked myself, was it because of the document or the man, and it was the document.

White, male, upper-level management

Are white men or the people of color accurate in their assessment? Are companies treating white men unfairly and giving the opportunities to unqualified women and people of color? Or do white men, harboring a sense of entitlement perhaps, in Machiavelli's terms "expect more than they deserve"? As the realities of white males in corporate America are considered, the reader should reflect on the earlier discussion of human nature to assess the extent to which racism may have created "mental illness in white males."

A Change in White Men's
Advancement Opportunities

Whenever I give a speech on mobility in corporations, I like to start out by asking, "Would you prefer to compete for a promotion with thirty-three people or one hundred people?" Most respondents say they would prefer to compete with 33 people rather than 100 because they would have a much better chance for promotion. To understand this simple point is to understand the problem white men face in their desire to move up the corporate ladder and the psychological turmoil that they increasingly experience as corporations move toward greater commitment to equal employment opportunity.

Until the Civil Rights Act of 1964, white men in corporations had to compete against only 33% of the adult population, for—according to the U.S. Census of 1970—that was the percentage of the adult U.S. population that was white men. But after 1964, white men, at least by law, had to compete on a more equitable basis with the other 67% as well—that is, with women and people of color. Essentially, this meant that white men who were average and below average in abilities began to have a more difficult time advancing, because now they were competing with the entire adult population, which included many people with credentials and abilities superior to theirs.

Despite this, however, white men who were above average—especially those who fit the image of the promotable manager—then and now have little trouble advancing in work. The most numerous and powerful decision makers were and are white men and even average white men still, in many cases, have an advantage over above average women and people of color.

Terry (1981) has pointed out that, although white male managers currently face greater competition for fewer jobs as a result of affirmative action policies, racism (and sexism) have sheltered them from the need to test their skills. The tacit discrimination practiced by upper-level management created the need for affirmative action, Terry explained. This discrimination leaves white men ill-equipped to deal with pluralistic competition once it is forced upon them (p. 143).

Greatly increased competition with larger numbers of people whom white men believe, at some level, to be inferior or deficient in some way naturally leads to severe psychological dislocation, and to cries of unfair treatment and reverse discrimination. Corporations should recognize this as a normal reaction of people who are at risk of being displaced from a privileged power position. It is especially painful because white men, always a minority of the population, have perceived themselves to be the majority. As a white lower-level manager said to me, "The company in effect has produced a new minority—the white male."

Let's use an analogy to put the problem white men face into perspective:

Suppose that you and your immediate friends had controlled this society for 500 years. During those years, you and your ancestors were brought up to believe that you were in control because you worked hard, had the necessary credentials, and had the right values and attitudes. You were also taught that those other people (not your friends) failed to make it into the power positions because they were essentially inferior, did not have the right skills, values, or attitudes—but not because of discrimination. Now, after 500 years, you and your friends are told by law that you must share your privileged position with large numbers of "inferior" people who greatly outnumber you.

Do you think you would willingly share your position and power? Would you immediately stop believing, after 500 years of racist socialization, that the others were inferior? Would you think that the law was fair?

The answer to each of these questions, of course, is no. Neither you nor I would willingly give up or share something that we had been conditioned for more than 500 years to believe was rightfully ours because we had the right values, intelligence, and work ethic. Neither do white men now. What we would do, given the above scenario, and what some white men have done, is to become fearful toward people and programs that challenge our privileged position. In addition, we would begin to develop, consciously or unconsciously, an array of strategies to defend the status quo (the one we are accustomed to).

Certain news media tell the populace about how terrible things are for white men, and how women and people of color have it made. Academics write books about the terrible consequences of the new meritocracy and how this has negatively affected corporate efficiency and productivity. By developing theories that blame the victims and encourage them to accept the blame for their oppression, white men can feel more comfortable that they indeed deserve their privileged positions. In this way, they can concentrate on maintaining their bastions of power and privilege and avoid looking at their own deficiencies.

Some white men exhibit a siege mentality. This insecurity seems due in large part to white male upbringing. One way and another, he has commonly been taught that he is a superior being and will never have to compete with people of color or women. Many white men are like fish out of water in today's emerging, more equitable, and diverse environment. They are trying to figure out what is happening. In the past they have benefited from racism, but today and in the future they are being forced to deal with the negative impacts racism has had and still has on their "mental health."

Enhancing Career Opportunities

The most important step that today's white man can take to enhance his career opportunities is to accept reality in order to better develop his strategies. If one insists on living in a world of illusion, one cannot cope effectively with the real world. I have listed below some of today's realities that white men must recognize and accept.

Reality No. 1: Corporate America Is Unfair to All

Corporate America is an unfair bureaucracy. It has never given promotions, jobs, rewards, or anything else strictly on the basis of merit, not even to white men. In addition, it does not offer unlimited opportunities, as most white men have been brought up to believe.

Reality No. 2: Image Is Vital to Success

The higher a white man goes in the corporate structure, the more likely he is to be discriminated against by the white men in power if he does not fit the image of the "promotable manager."

It is essential for white men to recognize not only on an intellectual level but on a gut level that there are many subjective reasons why people get ahead. Factors such as informal networks, political views, religious affiliations, and the like all contribute to career mobility. Again, white men, because the system is theirs and because they see many successful role models, often find it hard to see reality. As developers and "owners" of the system, most of them have totally bought into the rhetoric of meritocracy and as a result are having extreme difficulties with their perceived limited career opportunities.

Reality No. 3: Competition Is Keen

White men must recognize that most of them will not get the promotions or jobs they desire and not because of reverse discrimination, but simply because the selection pool has increased from 33 people to 100 people. Inevitably, the opportunities for the 33 people, especially those who are average or below average in ability, are greatly decreased.

Despite the prevalent belief among white men that they are members of a superior group, each race and gender has only a small percentage of outstanding individuals and a very large percentage of mediocre people. The vital question for white men, then, is this: Now that you are competing with a larger pool of people, who among you will lose out to the increased competition? And in the new global market place, the competition will continue to increase!

Reality No. 4: White Men Are Still Advantaged

But even so, in most cases, below average and average white men still retain significant advantages over women and people of color of the same ability. The same advantage applies to above average white men who compete with above average women and people of color. Much of the expressed antagonism toward affirmative action is based on the belief that standards are lowered by allowing "less qualified" minorities and women in entry positions ahead of "more qualified" white males. The historical fact is that minorities and women have had to be overqualified in order to obtain opportunities. An implication of the overqualification requirement is that, historically, white males have obtained positions with substantially weaker qualifications (Jones, 1981, p. 43).

Reality No. 5: The Concept of Reverse Discrimination Is Based on Nontruths

White men's sense of reverse discrimination is based largely on the nontruths they hear from their own corporations, from the media, and from educational institutions. Over the past 29 years, we have observed many white men who believe they are victims of reverse discrimination, because their companies and managers do not tell them the truth. Some are told that their careers are going nowhere, or that they did not get a promotion or a lateral job, because of women and minority quotas. In fact, none of the companies in our studies ever had quotas. They did have goals and timetables for management positions up through middle management, but the goals and timetables were minimal, and there was no penalty for failing to meet them. Most managers or occupational workers who believed they were discriminated against actually failed to be promoted because they lacked skills, ability, or potential, or because of some subjective evaluation on the part of their bosses or the company.

Companies also promise many more opportunities than they are able to deliver and have not developed ways of satisfying the high expectations of many workers. Because most white men believe they are being discriminated against, it is much simpler and easier to tell them that they are; that they are going nowhere not because of their own limitations but because of women and people of color. And white men, who tend to feel much more in-group loyalty to the company than do other groups, are less likely to take formal action against perceived discrimination than are women and people of color.

When the lack of mobility of white men is blamed on women and people of color, it should be a red flag. White male candidates should recognize that, by allowing their superiors to shift blame, they are allowing them to avoid discussing the employee's actual ability to do the job. Most superiors want to avoid uncomfortable situations, especially those related to giving employees bad news like why they are not getting a promotion. Therefore, superiors pick the easiest way out. White men can commiserate with one another about how terrible it is for them now because of reverse discrimination, but there is no commiserating when one white man tells another, "I am not supporting you for a promotion because you just don't have it. I don't like your style or your personality."

Corporations have done a disservice to white men by not explaining the truth about their opportunities. Our society, which is controlled by white men, has done the same. News media, books, and articles have often basically presented an image that all it takes to succeed is to be a woman or a person of color. The statistics, however, show just the opposite. The one factor that probably has caused more psychological trauma in white men than any other is the Reagan/Bush administrations' constant attack on equal employment opportunities and affirmative action. How can white men believe they are getting a fair shake when two U.S. presidents have said that they are being discriminated against?

In order to deal constructively with the potential for reverse discrimination, white men should insist on quarterly written performance evaluations. They should also seek yearly written performance evaluations with career plans and development plans as integral parts of the evaluation process. In my book *Racism and Sexism in Corporate Life* (1981), I discuss performance, potential, and career planning, and offer commonsense advice on how to ensure that one is getting at least an even chance of being treated fairly in these processes. *Survival in the Corporate Fishbowl* (Fernandez, 1987) describes other survival tactics. The advice I give is useful not only to white men but to anyone trying to have a successful career in the corporate world.

White men should ask for a breakdown of all promotions by race, gender, and level. They should demand to know specifically why they did not get a particular job. If they believe they are truly the better candidates and that they have been discriminated against, they should pursue the matter to higher levels. Sitting around complaining about reverse discrimination instead of insisting on the full story from the company is shortsighted and unproductive.

Reality No. 6: White Men Must Adjust to Diversity

White men who attempt to change their prejudices will have greater promotional opportunities than those who do not. Many people of color and women have been socialized somewhat differently from white men. They have diverse cultural backgrounds. In some cases, they have value systems and expectations different from those of the white men who currently dominate the U.S. workplace. The coming together of these people of diverse backgrounds, in some cases for the first time in the corporate setting, has created great tension for everyone.

Which group has the correct background, values, expectations, and so on is not the issue. Although each group has unique good and bad qualities, there are more similarities than differences among Americans because of the American socialization process. What is important for white men to understand, however, is that because of their historical power and dominant position, they have not had to adjust to others; others have always had to adjust to them. This imbalance is what will have to be corrected if America plans to be not only efficient in coming years but competitive as well.

Out of competitive necessity, the U.S. workplace will become increasingly heterogeneous. The employees who will have the greatest chances of making it will be those who can accept and feel comfortable working in the new workforce. White men who retain their prejudices will never be able to work effectively with truly heterogeneous work groups. As a result, they will never be able to help their organizations achieve the best results. On the other hand, white men who can operate effectively in the new heterogeneous environments will have a definite advantage.

Conclusion

As human beings we are always struggling to be mentally "healthy"; but this struggle becomes much more difficult when we have been socialized into being racist. Racism not only impacts those who are the subject of racism, but also those who are racist. As the United States has moved toward a more equitable society, many white men, because of their own racism or the effect of society's racism toward people of color, are exhibiting essentially neurotic behaviors, with which they not only hurt themselves mentally but also undermine their abilities to be successful in a more diverse United States and a more diversely competitive global market place.

9

Diversity

Curse or Blessing for
the Elimination of White Racism?

ROBERT W. TERRY

White racism. Remember that phrase? It is rarely, if ever, used today in public discussions and seminars. The alternative, correct, and very popular term is *diversity.* Oh yes, there are still groups doing training programs on racism. However, terminology has shifted: *Counterracism* has replaced *antiracism,* supposedly emphasizing what one is for rather than what one is against. Nevertheless, these efforts to focus on racism are few in contrast to the popular use of diversity and diversity training.

Is this diversity focus good news or bad for the elimination of white racism? Is white racism still really "the problem?" Have the times changed to such an extent that a different orientation and type of training is required? I am old enough now and have worked diligently in the antiracism field long enough (more than 25 years) to have experienced the changes in contemporary U.S. culture and in myself. Though I was restive about much of the training on white racism during the 1960s and the 1970s I am even more uncomfortable with diversity training in the 1980s and the 1990s. In this chapter I will explore my unease with both training approaches and offer an alternative.

One note before I begin: This chapter is not a theory paper, in contrast to most of what I write. It is a practical chapter, sorting out options and proposing alternative educational strategies. Throughout this chapter I will refer to another of my works, a recent book titled *Authentic Leadership: Courage in Action,* published in 1993. In that text you will find the theoretical thinking that informs my work.

White Racism/Diversity:
Reservations About Training

Both *diversity* and *racism* cry out for definition. During the 1970s and 1980s I spent much of my intellectual energy defining racism. *For Whites Only* (1970) was one result. *Diversity,* too, means many things to many people. For some it is a cover for affirmative action. For others, it is good human relations that can release the creativity of a culturally rich workforce. Still others consider it a pawn in a politically correct game, a legal requirement, good management, an organizational necessity to respond to a dramatically changing workforce, or simply a cultural reality. As the meanings multiply, confusion and ambivalence about the term arises. So where do we turn?

If *diversity,* at its most fundamental level, means *difference,* then diversity (cultural and otherwise) is a fact. People differ, individually and collectively, in all sorts of ways. This fact of diversity requires recognition. There are profound cultural and political differences that we ignore at our peril. In contrast, it is equally important to acknowledge that not all differences are good. Some cultural traditions legitimate oppression. *Diversity,* therefore, is a more inclusive term than *race,* but does not exclude race, even white racism.

THE PROBLEM WITH DIVERSITY TRAINING

The danger in diversity training is that it shields participants from the depths of the problem of racism, especially racism perpetuated by Whites. The peril is enhanced when diversity training discounts the seriousness of racism by assuming that power issues can be sidestepped. "Racism is not the focus," is the often heard reply. "Get the best from each other, regardless of who you are," is a more common refrain in organizations pushing diversity training. At best, power imbalances and institutionalized discrimination become sidebars to releasing human talent for organizational success.

This approach is what I call "technical diversity training." How much should I learn about another group? The answer appears to be, "Just enough to get the work done without offending anyone or getting sued." Even though there may be some minimum merit in this approach, it is certainly not adequate. This minimalist orientation sidesteps rather than confronts tough problems. It also tends to stigmatize any anger around the issue of racism because anger is often interpreted as an attitude problem that undermines team effectiveness.

Focusing solely on white racism, the diversity approach suggests, is too narrow, too alienating, and too burdensome, especially for Whites. Diversity, in contrast, flattens the playing field, bringing equals into a searching dialogue. It can reduce fear and ignorance among groups. As groups push past the safety envelope and open the mind for understanding deep diversity, they go way beyond racism. For superficial or profound reasons there appears to be a rush toward diversity training and away from white racism training.

Is it a blessing or a curse? As with most either/or propositions the answer is, "yes!" It is both a blessing AND a curse.

ADVANTAGES OF DIVERSITY TRAINING

Even so, and in spite of the dilemmas of diversity, such a focus does contribute insights. It confounds the assumption that all oppressed people are alike and thereby have little to learn about and from each other. In fact, at times it seems that hardly anybody knows hardly anything about other cultures, and that many groups may even be grossly ignorant of their own culture. Furthermore, diversity education can assist disparate groups to recognize common issues. People of color are not of one mind. Even thoughtful counter-racists who are African American may not understand the struggle of Native Americans with regard to racial labeling in sports teams and food products. Yet the same group of African Americans are incensed by a Confederate flag flying over the capital of Georgia. Thus, diversity education can invite and open a deeper dialogue into others' and one's own history and experience, which can set the basis for common action. Each is affirmed in its own history, mixed bag that it is, but no one has a perfectly laudatory history. A varied history is one thing all people have in common.

WHITE RACISM TRAINING—
PROBLEMS AND INSIGHTS

One of the most challenging, even daunting, tasks of the late 1960s on through the 1980s was to get Whites to own up to racism as a white problem and mobilize to work against it. *For Whites Only* sought to do this, as did works by Barndt (1972), Katz (1978), and McIntosh and Eliot (1988). It was demanding work to face our own racism personally and collectively. We, as Whites, were confronted by people of color, called racist, and asked to reflect on and admit our deep-seated racist beliefs, feelings, and actions. Even our inaction was labeled racist; a passive racist was still a racist. Racism seminars were hard hitting. We looked at oppression, institutional racism, and ethnocentrism. Political correctness was out. Serious searching in.

Many Whites, tired of hearing about white privilege, discounted the idea that only Whites could be racist and rejected a white racism approach. For them, the rush to diversity made sense. Who needed the bashing, the shame, the guilt? Diversity was easier. Other Whites who were less directly involved in the racism struggle had already begun to shift their focus to ecology, the Vietnam War, or other social issues.

Yet for some Whites these experiences of dealing with white racism transformed their lives. Life was viewed with new eyes, revealing startling facts about the United States and the world. White racism was the problem; Whites had special work to do with other Whites and people of color to eliminate white racism.

EXIT RACISM, ENTER DIVERSITY

The toughness of white racism training trailed off on a side spur in the 1980s. Power issues diffused, institutional racism took a rear seat. White racism got lost in the rush toward diversity training. Even though celebrating differences came to the forefront, racism smoldered and later exploded as pent-up hostility and despair as in the Los Angeles riots. On reflection, diversity was too easy, too superficial, too nice.

Yet a lot of the white racism training of the past two decades suggested difficulties. By focusing on Whites as the problem, blaming and bashing easily replaced inquiry. Some instructors assumed they themselves had nothing to learn. An unthoughtful phrase was targeted as racist and the user of the phrase, regardless of intention, squashed. Some Whites who were told they were the problem decided they were also the solution. The arrogance of racism was replaced with the arrogance of white salvation. In neither case was partnership across color lines encouraged. The chasm divided rather than narrowed.

Some Whites wanted to claim their own ethnic identity as worthy of attention; "I'm Irish," for example. The Irish would suggest they were oppressed in Boston. Instead of working with a shared oppression, however, the all-too-common reply by people of color and "new whites trainers" was, "That doesn't count—you're still white and privileged." Surely many allies for the struggle were lost. *Oppression/oppressor* framed the issue; up versus down was the metaphor. If the downs were to rise up, the ups would have to come down. Racism was "prejudice plus power": Whoever had the power was racist, whoever did not, was not. The focus on white racism tended to rest solely on a moral and, at times, self-righteous foundation. Trainers were often abusive and fear producing and perpetuated a victimizer/victim orientation. No self-interest arguments were offered or explored.

Peggy McIntosh's (1988) work on white privilege offered a thoughtful approach. The list of white privileges she developed still shocks many Whites who naively ignore the everyday advantages of being white in America. But where to go from privilege is the puzzle. Her argument rests on the power of moral outrage: see the privilege, be incensed, fight against it. But what about the self-interest of Whites to fight privilege? As a friend of mine once remarked, "I tried up, I tried down. I like up."

Why would Whites want to give up white privilege? Is a moral argument strong enough to mobilize most Whites? Many people of color believe, and I agree, that if the privileges are so great and so deeply ingrained, no sensible person would want to yield them to another group. Do Whites actually lose anything from white racism?

And so we have a dilemma. Diversity programs, at their best, encourage long-term inclusive inquiry into one another's histories, plus one's own past and present. They also hold out the promise of a future partnership across great divides. At their worst, they trivialize the tough issues of power in racism, especially white racism, and offer an apparent escape. Racism programs at their worst misuse power to address power issues, self-righteously blame and shame Whites, are narrowly focused, deepen splits between groups, enhance mistrust, and divide the world into ups versus downs. At their best, they challenge people (Whites especially) to engage in serious long-term struggle to come to grips with themselves, to carve out a new identity, to recognize privilege, to join in common self-interested action to eliminate racism. Is there a way to take the strengths of both approaches and weave them together into a new synthesis?

I have taken up this challenge and want to share an approach. In seminars that I run, I have been searching for content and methods to create a marriage of these two perspectives and training methods. The curriculum that I suggest points toward an amalgam of many events. I will focus on a 2-day event that actually took place in a town in Minnesota.

Diversity/Racism Education:
A Case in Point

I was asked to conduct a 2-day diversity seminar for a mostly white town in north central Minnesota. After meeting with Alison (a fictitious name) to get her view on what she wanted, I proposed and conducted what turned out to be one of my most effective events. Readers who do diversity training know that sometimes the spirit moves, creativity takes over, and a new design emerges. What originally could have been an ordinary event sparkled at points as I seemed to be in rhythm with the group of community leaders.

Thomasville, Minnesota (fictitious name) is a 20,000-person town. Predominantly white, it hosts a community college with a small black student population and an even smaller black faculty. Indian reservations are located nearby and offer a Native presence in the community. As with many such communities, the Chamber of Commerce, concerned with the business climate, wanted to give pivotal persons in the community a deeper understanding of diversity that might prevent embarrassing, harassing, even dangerous incidents from occurring.

For 2 days, 50 people, mostly white and mostly new to diversity training, set to work. I had never met any of them before except Alison. My objectives were many. In 2 days I wanted this group (a) to explore in some depth its history, (b) to understand how each person got power and privilege from some important aspect of her or his life, and (c) to form side-by-side partnerships across ethnic divides. I also wanted (d) to emphasize equally both what we have in common and our differences. I sought (e) to create a safe place for participants to examine their fears that block partnerships. Finally, I also wanted (f) to build the confidence of the group so it could make policies and take informed action on complicated diversity matters.

First Day. 8:30-9:15:
Introduction and Personal Story

Alison introduced me and I asked participants to introduce themselves at their tables. I shared my expectations for the 2 days and laid out the six objectives outlined above.

I told my story of how I came to work in the diversity field. The story centers on a challenge made by Doug Fitch in 1968. After reading a paper that I had written on black power, he pressed me to think about what it meant to be white. I had never thought about it. Only after a group of Whites convened in my home did I come to the conclusion that what it meant to be white was *not to have to think about it!* (Terry, 1993, pp. 176-178).

Note: Storytelling is extremely effective, especially at the beginning of a seminar series and especially for a white male educator. It personalizes; it alerts the audience to one's orientation; it creates bonding; it levels the field of inquiry (everyone has a personal story); and it forms an authentic conversation with the group. At the outset it models a safe place for serious investigation.

9:15-9:30: Participants' Questions and Concerns

I asked participants to share their questions and concerns about diversity. I wrote these down on a chart pad without editorial comment, and posted them. As questions were addressed, I checked them off the list.

9:30-11:00: Diversity and Metaphors

At the outset, I like to get participants thinking about their own thinking processes. We all look at life through lenses that shape what we see and how we evaluate what we see. Not only is diversity a fact; diversity of perspectives on racism is also a fact. The following is an exercise to sensitize participants to the importance of taken-for-granted perspectives regarding self and race. It also provides a way to illustrate that power abuse is at the heart of the divisions that separate us.

The Exercise:

I introduced the idea of a metaphor. I asked the group what a metaphor is and contrasted metaphor with simile. A metaphor directly compares two ideas or objects; a simile indirectly compares two items using *like* or *as* (e.g., "Life is a rose" vs. "Life is like a rose.")

I practiced a short metaphor activity with the whole group to get the participants used to metaphorical thinking. I asked the group what images came to mind when I said "marriage is warfare." Then I suggested "marriage is poetry." What images come to mind? The point was to see quickly how frameworks shape perception. After this short practice, I divided the group into six subgroups of 10 or fewer. Then I assigned six metaphors, one to each group. The metaphors were:

- Life is a gift.
- Life is a market.
- Life is a body.
- Life is a conflict between ups and downs.

- Life is a journey.
- Life is art.[1]

Each group was jump started with a couple of examples. If life is a gift, it is not always wanted. The outside wrapping does not always reveal what is on the inside. Sometimes the gift comes with strings, sometimes you cannot give it back, and so on.

I allowed 7 to 10 minutes for groups to brainstorm. I told them to make a list of 15 items. When completed, one person from each group read the list, beginning with the gift metaphor, followed by the other metaphors—market, body, ups and downs, journey, and ending with art. Then I asked each group a series of questions and had them provide answers as directed by their orienting metaphor. For example, if life is a gift, what is your opinion about the purpose of education? Answer: To let all the gifts of the children express themselves. What about educational programs for the severely gifted? Good idea or bad? Answer: Bad, it separates people by gifts and ignores the fact that everyone is gifted. After 10 or so questions, I turned to the group using the market metaphors. I read their list and asked them questions. For example,

- What is your opinion about competition?—Good.
- What is your opinion about limited government?—Good.
- Rationing—Bad.
- Pricing—Good.
- Deregulation—Good.
- Choice in schools—Good.
- Welfare—Bad.
- Affirmative action—Bad.
- Equal opportunity—Good.

I heard the lists, asked the questions, and then got the participants' metaphorical views. Sometimes I asked one group a question and then turned to another group to show how the answer would be different. Affirmative action to a market metaphor is bad, but to a body metaphor is good.

The point of all of this is to tease out how different metaphors shape our perceptions both of what is real and what we should do. I make sure that I examine two issues through each metaphor—the purpose of education and of racism. For education the answers go as follows:

- Gift—Acknowledge and release all talents.
- Market—Build capacities to compete.

- Body—Develop personal and social skills.
- Up versus Down—Create self-determining power bases to control the future of education for one's own group.
- Journey—Expose students to multicultural experiences.
- Art—Develop higher order thinking skills, including critical thinking, reflection on assumptions, and so on.

The key to this method rests in the examination of racism and diversity. The first step in diversity training is to explore diverse perspectives on racism itself. Without acknowledging difference in our midst, we have no foundation for probing deeply the tougher issues that arise later in the seminar. So what then are the different definitions of racism rooted in the six metaphors?

- Gift—Superiority/inferiority. "My gifts are better than your gifts."
- Market—Discrimination. Exclude people from the marketplace.
- Body—Social disease and sickness of one part of the body that infects the whole body.
- Up versus Down—Oppression by the Ups.
- Journey—Ethnocentrism.
- Art—Denial of deeper realities.

We took a break about halfway through this exercise to give the participants a breather. To bring it to conclusion, I had the participants move to that part of the room predesignated as Gift, Market, and so on, on the basis of (a) their personal metaphor and (b) the dominant metaphor of their community (they had to guess, of course). Because every metaphor reveals as well as conceals reality, participants discussed with their metaphorical partner what they liked about their metaphor and what it blocked them from understanding and appreciating. Then participants looked for someone who believed in a different metaphor and discussed the strengths and weaknesses of an alternative perspective.

Finally, I told them to go to the metaphor of the community in the predesignated parts of the room. I noticed where no one went. Usually very few people go to the up-versus-down metaphor, either personally or by community. Then I asked the group to reflect on what the community will deeply understand and what it will not understand based on which metaphors are heavily populated and which are not. Thus, by concentrating on diversity, I was able to make the general point that is often missing in diversity seminars—the attention to power and its abuse.

The purposes of this activity are fourfold: To understand the importance of perspective, to cut across race and gender lines (e.g., Blacks and Whites may go to the same metaphor), to challenge everyone to check the ethnocentrism of their own perspective, and to concentrate on a racism training course that focuses on power and its abuse. If you are going to try this exercise, it is incumbent upon the trainer to know the metaphors well. I recommend sorting out the material with a group of friends first.

11:00-12:00: The Action Wheel—
Knowing What Is Really Going On

With the metaphors as backdrop, I introduced the group to the organizing theory supporting my approach. I call it The Action Wheel. The next exercise is useful because one of the problems I find in diversity and racism work is misdiagnosis about what is really going on. There are innumerable proposals for action: The problem comes in trying to figure out where to concentrate energy and attention. The Wheel consists of seven parts: Existence, Resources, Structure, Power, Mission, Meaning, and Fulfillment. They are displayed on a diagnostic wheel as shown in Figure 9.1.

The terms of the Wheel are fairly obvious (from Terry, 1993, pp. 53-81):

- MEANING: That *for* which we act—Reasons why, principles, excuses, explanations, values, rationale, justification.
- MISSION: That *toward* which we act—Goals, desires, hopes, purposes, direction, objectives.
- POWER: That *by* which we act—Energy, motivation, morale, spirit, capacity, momentum, will, drive, impetus.
- STRUCTURE: That *through* which we act—Organization chart, processes, systems, rules, policies and procedures, laws, "hoops."
- RESOURCES: That *with* which we act—People, capital, information, land, ideas, equipment, buildings, materials.
- EXISTENCE: That *from* which we act—History, past, limits and possibilities, "baggage," collective memory.
- FULFILLMENT: That *into* which we act—The completed act, the action that happens.

I taught the Wheel similar to teaching the metaphors. I divided the group into six sections. This time each group received a part of the Wheel. Without telling the groups, I assigned the Gift group to Existence; the Market group to Resources; Body to Structure; Up/Down to Power; Journey to Mission; and Art to Meaning. I did not focus on Fulfillment because that term is the

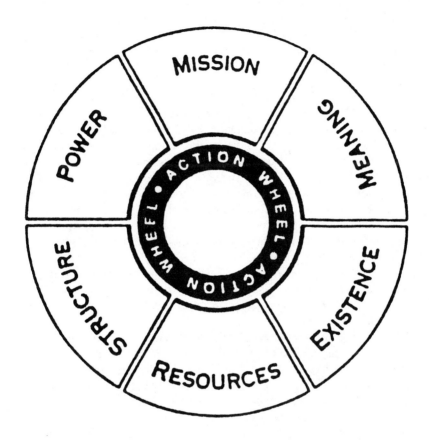

Figure 9.1. Diagnostic Wheel
SOURCE: The Terry Group, 871 Lennox Avenue, St. Paul, MN 55119

completed act, the hub around which the other parts turn. Each group thought about its word and came up with its own examples.

Three parts of the Wheel caused some confusion—Existence, Power, and Meaning. Existence concentrates on collective memory, history, environment—everything up to the present. It is the widest setting for action. Power is energy. I told the Power group to add *ing* to their words (e.g., planning, willing, helping, deciding, etc.). Meaning answers the question Why? If the Mission is to win, Meaning asks, "Why win?" Meaning also includes rationalizations as well as reasons. Likewise, Mission can point to the stated mission as well as a hidden agenda.

I invited the participants to do a quick exercise. I asked them to build a house. What would be their contribution to the house be? The answers presented Existence: the history of house building and past house building experiences; Resources: tools, materials; Structure: blueprints; Power: deciding, hammering, planning; Mission: to build a house; Meaning: rental property, family dwelling.

After some practice I asked the groups what metaphor linked to their part of the Wheel. They answered the way I had arranged and assigned the groups: Existence with Gift, and so on. Once the Diagnostic Wheel terms and relationships were understood, I shifted to the Action Wheel (see Figure 9.2).

The Action Wheel invites us to follow the arrows to figure out what is really going on. If the original diagnosis suggests Power, it is actually Mission or Meaning. Always go clockwise to frame the problem. Once framed, go counterclockwise to solve it. Leadership frames issues; management solves problems. First, locate the perceived issue or problem on the inner Diagnostic Wheel, then locate the real issue or problem on the outer Action Wheel.[2]

I encouraged two kinds of practice with the Wheel. First, one member in a group presented a problem to his or her small group and tried to frame it. I often coached if anyone got stuck. The second approach was directly related to diversity. I asked the whole group what they thought the problem of race was in their community.

Typically, the answer settled on Power, and Power was the metaphor with which they had the least skills and knowledge—and thus an occasion for insight. So the real issues were Mission and Meaning, because Power was the presenting problem. They asked themselves what kind of community they really wanted and what kind of diversity they really treasured. These became questions of Mission and Meaning triggered by Power.

Racism as oppression and ethnocentrism clearly expressed themselves as *the* community issues. We now established the basis for cultural education as action strategies.

Lunch

1:00-2:00: The Abilene Paradox

After an intellectually exhausting morning of metaphors and the Wheel, I changed pace. I wanted the group to understand and practice the differences between what a friend of mine calls "conference talk" and "kitchen table talk." The first is polite, noncommittal, and unrevealing; the second is honest and searching. To make this point, I showed the *Abilene Paradox,* a 30-minute

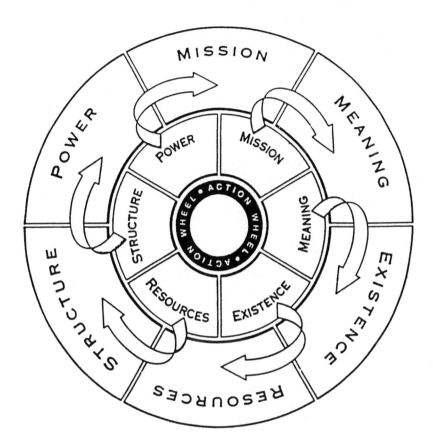

Figure 9.2. Action Wheel
SOURCE: The Terry Group, 871 Lennox Avenue, St. Paul, MN 55119

videotape based on Jerry Harvey's book, *The Abilene Paradox: The Management of Agreement* (1974).

Here is the basic storyline. A family is playing dominos in Coleman, Texas. There is no air conditioning and the temperature is over 100. The father suggests that the foursome go to Abilene after the game. The son-in-law asks the distance—106 miles—and whether the air conditioner in the Buick has been fixed. The answer is no. Everybody agrees to go. The next scene, detailing their return, exudes hostility. Finally, the son-in-law sarcastically comments on what a great trip it was. Everyone admits they did not want to go, even the father who suggested it. The question is: How could four rational people all go where no one wanted to go? And so Harvey asks the question: Do you think the family ever resolved its conflict? The answer is no, They were not in conflict. They were in agreement! The Abilene Paradox focuses people's lack of courage to tell the truth. Thus, they must guess where others want to go and play to those guesses rather than addressing their own deep beliefs.

After the videotape, I asked the group how many of them had been to Abilene. All hands raised. Then in small groups I asked them to share an Abilene trip they had made. Then I shifted to diversity. Where have we made Abilene trips on race, gender, and so on? Why do we go along? What do we fear? The point behind the film, of course, is that it takes courage to affirm core values, fight against racism, and tell the truth of your own perspective.

2:00-3:30: Courage Faces Upness

With power defined as the problem, and the up/down metaphor identifying upness as the trigger for down revolt, we were ready to confront the gains and losses of upness, especially in regard to white racism.

To set the context for this section I told the Parable of Ups and Downs. It goes as follows:

What makes an up an up and a down a down? An up can do more to a down than a down can do to an up. That is what keeps an up up and a down down. Ups tend to talk to each other and study the downs, asking the downs what is up, or what is coming down, for that matter.

The downs spend a lot of time taking the ups out to lunch and dinner to explain their downness. The ups listen attentively, often amazed about the lives of downs. They contrast one down's experience with another down's experience. At times they do not worry too much about what the downs are up to because the ups know that the downs never seem to get it together. If they did, the ups would have to shape up.

After a while, the downs weary of talking to the ups. They think, "If I have to explain my downness one more time to an up, I'll throw up." So downs form networks and support groups. This activity makes some ups nervous.

In order to cope with this rising up of downness, some ups hire downs, dress them up, and send them down to see what the downs are up to! The downs are often called human resources or affirmative action officers. This fact creates a serious problem for the down who is dressed up. That down does not know whether he or she is up or down and that is why downs in the middle often burn up.

Sometimes ups, to smarten up, ask downs to come into a program created by ups to explain and justify their downness. The ups call this "human relations training." Of course, ups never have to explain their upness; that is why they are ups.

There is good news and bad news in this parable. The good news is that there is no such thing as a perfect up or a perfect down. If people were perfect ups, they would not be able to stand up, they would be so heavily burdened with downess.

The bad news is that when ups are up, it often makes them stupid. I call this *dumb-upness*. Dumb-upness occurs because ups do not have to pay attention to downs. The only time ups worry about downs is when downs get uppity, at which time they are put down by the ups. The ups' perception is that downs are overly sensitive. It is never understood that the ups are "underly sensitive" (Terry, 1993, pp. 194-196).

At the conclusion of listening to the parable, the group engaged in four exercises.

First exercise: Each person identified his or her primary up categories—white, male, upper-middle class, straight, able-bodied, and so on.

Second exercise: Each person took one of these up categories and listed 10 advantages enjoyed just by being in that category.

Third exercise: Each listed five losses from being in that category.

Fourth exercise: Couples paired up and conversed. One person in the pair picked a down category, one an up. The down tried to convince the up to change. Why should ups change? What is in the short- and long-term self-interest of ups that would convince them to change their orientation and share power?

The idea for this part of the exercise actually came to me during the event itself. I liked it so much it now is a standard in what I do. One advantage that this activity has over typical white racism training is that everyone is an up on something and has something to learn. All of us are ups and downs on some significant issue. No longer do people of color instruct Whites with no learning on their own part. We are all learners called to confront our own dumb-upness.

3:30-4:00: Wrap Up the Day

I returned to the initial list of questions and concerns. For each one, I asked the group whether an answer had been provided by the day's work. I marked those questions still needing attention. Also, I praised the group for its hard work and asked each person to share one nugget for reflection.

Second Day

9:00-9:15: Welcome

In this particular event, the second day was separated from the first by a month, so I reviewed briefly what we had covered on the first day.

9:15-9:45: Teach the Wheel

In order to get the group to internalize some of the materials, I divided the group into trios and had them explain the Wheel to each other as if two of the three knew nothing. One person began the explanation, then after a few minutes I cut in and told the next person to continue the instruction. Not only did this solidify the learning, it made the Wheel a more integral part of their understanding.

There is another reason for encouraging the teaching exercise. Most people move to Structure and Resources to solve problems rather than focusing on the more difficult areas of Power, Mission, and Meaning. When people teach the Wheel, they tend to start at Structure and Resources. They define the terms and the Wheel structure. They forget to explain the reason and purpose of the Wheel. Teaching the Wheel drove this insight home.

9:45-12:00 (with a break):
Knowledge and Action—A Case Study

One of my goals for this group was to build its confidence in addressing tough issues. Community leaders *can* analyze and act knowledgeably on difficult issues of diversity.

To involve the participants in the really messy issues of race and gender, I christened them as decision makers of a local college. Then I made up various statistics—it is 90% white, 60/40 male/female, the faculty is 95% white and 80/20 male/female. The group's first task in small groups was to identify and put forward the most compelling reasons why the college needed a diversity mission and program.

After completion, I paired two small groups—one presented its ideas, the other critiqued and checked for authenticity of their claims. Then I reversed the task so each group gave and received feedback.

The second challenge called upon the groups to write a brief mission statement on diversity for the college. Each small group read its statement to the whole group. I then asked which metaphor seemed to be guiding the mission statement. Typically it was Body affirming diverse functions as healthy for the school and community. Little of the mission work was driven by Art and none by Up/Down.

Then the fun began. Into the groups I threw a series of real problems that might come up at their college. In fact, most of these problems are real and have occurred at a university in the Twin Cities.

Problem 1: An all-white fraternity has been found guilty of discriminating against Blacks, Hispanics, and Asians. What should the college do?

Problem 2: As a result of finding a local fraternity guilty of discrimination against people of color, a coalition of Blacks, Indians, and Asians want to establish their own fraternity. Should the college allow such a fraternity?

Problem 3: The Black, Hispanic, and Asian fraternity agrees to an open membership that could include Whites but wants to ensure that the officers are people of color only. Yes or no, and what is going on here?

Problem 4: A woman has been raped on campus. To protest and to organize women to stand in solidarity, a women's group requests a meeting site, a small budget for signs and supplies, and permission to demonstrate on campus. Will the college grant funds and space?

Problem 5: You learn the women plan to exclude men from the event. Is this allowable?

Problem 6: A men's group that has worked for years with other men to stop male rape and battery against women wants to join in the protest. Two thirds of the women say no, one third yes. What do you say?

Problem 7: A gay group wants to organize a pride day and wants college backing. Should the college give it to them?

Problem 8: A middle-class Hispanic family is uneasy about their daughter's experiences on campus. There have been no incidents reported to the college or the family by the daughter.

What should be done? Each problem was discussed thoroughly and we probed to find out what was happening in each situation.

As these examples illustrate, diversity is not easy. It is the struggle between the "one" and the "many." On what could we and should we agree and on what can and should we be different and still live together? Newspapers are filled with examples of clashes of values, each important in its own right but in conflict with another.

During the training, I did not look for agreement among the participants. Good people can and do differ. What I expected was clarity of thinking, understanding and appreciation of the difficulty of the events, and the necessity to step up to the issues. Also, I encouraged people to recognize that what other people say may at first strike one as odd but in the long term may offer deep insight.

Lunch

1:00-3:00: Facing Our Fears—The Pigs

In this portion of the seminar, participants were invited to struggle with their own authenticity. To place this struggle within reality and to gain wisdom about the world, I drew heavily from a wonderful little book by Charles Bates, *Pigs Eat Wolves* (1991). Bates employs the story of The Three Little Pigs to build a developmental continuum. Charles, who is a personal friend and mentor, does a magnificent interpretation of an everyday fairy tale to create a memorable examination of courage, fear, authenticity, and hope.

The experience consisted of reading parts of the story, doing exercises on each part, and in the process constructing a continuum of authenticity that links the Action Wheel, metaphors, and diversity to the quest for wisdom, maturity, and authenticity. As with my work, to get the full impact of this material one needs to go to the original text. I will present the bare bones of the connections that I drew in the seminar. The storyline and players are, I assume, known to you. What I want to outline are some of the key points about authenticity and "pig thinking" that go with the scheme that Charles unfolds (see Table 9.1).

As the storyline unfolded, I linked the Action Wheel and the metaphors to it.

Existence—Gift, Mother Pig
Resources—Market, First Pig
Structure—Body, Second Pig
Power—Up and Down, Third Pig
Mission—Journey, Turning Point
Meaning—Art, Apple Orchard
Fulfillment—Engagement
Fulfillment—Action, Pig eats Wolf

My basic method throughout this exercise was storytelling. As I read the story to the group, I paused and had them tell stories to each other. They told stories about being carefree and identified First, Second, and Third Pig experiences. I paused at the Third Pig. The Third Pig lives out of the Up/Down metaphor. He builds his house for protection. The good news is that he is safe; the bad news is that he is imprisoned. The Wolf is still at the door outside. I returned to the people of color wanting an exclusive fraternity,

TABLE 9.1 Pig Thinking

Players	Pig Thinking	Stages to Authenticity	Bates's Page Number
Three happy little pigs	Carefree	Unreflective and spontaneous	5
Mother Pig at home with little pigs/sent off	Instructions about life—fear the wolf	Be true to the past	9
First Pig/straw house	Arrogant, naive, narcissistic, weak and overconfident/ pig eaten	Pig thinks he is true to himself but there is no reflective self to be true to	19
Second Pig/ stick house	Conformist, other-directed, fit-in, do-right-thing pig/pig eaten	Seeks to be true to the world, yet doesn't understand the world	29
Third Pig/brick house	Confident, smart, creates a new self. Security in self and in group	True to reflective self	41
Turnip Patch/Third Pig	Tricks wolf, goes early	True to the world, learning how the world works	45
Apple Orchard	Third Pig faces directly. Sidetracks the wolf with the apple	Faces fear unprotected. Looks it in the face. Owns the wolf, not in the world but in one's self.	59
The Fair	Goes unaccompanied Test one's self on one's own.	Practices authenticity. Seeks to be true to self and the world.	67
At home again	Puts self in the butter churn. Rolls toward home. Wolf jumps away. Wolf up on the roof, down chimney, cooked. Pig eats wolf.	Becoming wise. Living in the truth. Beginning to understand the depths of a spiritual quest.	73

NOTE: Page numbers in *Pigs Eat Wolves,* by C. Bates, 1991. St. Paul, MN: Yes International.

which is Third Pig thinking. The basis of strength to deal with the wolves (Whites) is only a transitional step to full authenticity. Whites came to understand that they are the wolves in this part of the story. The restiveness of the Hispanic couple can also be clarified—the Wolf lurks, waiting to strike; the anticipation lodged in the collective memory.

The last exercise in the second day was a 2-hour block focusing on the Turnip Patch. Participants were asked to pair off. Each was invited to think of a small thing in life that angered them—people who are late, people who drop their clothes and never pick them up, that sort of thing. I stressed that I was looking for *little* things, not Bosnia! I asked them to share their stories with each other quickly.

Then we began the trip to the Turnip Patch. They helped each other understand that what one person is mad at has *nothing* to do with the world but is an unresolved conflict in his- or herself!

After the mouths closed, I gave a couple of illustrations. I talked to a man who said people who categorize people really make him mad. "Who does that," I asked. "Rich people," he quickly replied. A young woman was mad at people who were always late. As it turned out, she was mad at herself for not having the strength to leave.

This is a projection exercise. *There are no little angers.* Each is a window into one's self and one's relationship to the world. We project our fears onto others, claiming that *they* are the problem without also taking a look at what is inside us. The Wolf is our teacher, inviting us to maturity and wisdom. In order to get to that level, we have to sort out what is going on in the real world and what we are projecting onto that world.

I then invited discussions on the Willy Horton ads and the process of scapegoating. As I introduced the storytelling from Mother Pig through the Turnip Patch, I also suggested running diversity issues through the authenticity continuum. What were Mother Pig messages on race, gender, sexual orientation, and so on? What is a likely First Pig response to disability? I end with this summary statement. The secret to dealing with diversity is authenticity. When we are authentic, help is available—often from surprising sources. The goal of life is to live wisdom, to be authentic.

3:15-4:00

After a break, we returned to the participants' original questions. They admitted most were irrelevant, yet I took them all seriously. Although I did not do it this time, I usually ask participants to make up a new set of questions that draw on what they have learned in the 2 days. A very different list emerges— about courage, hope, openness, journey, development, and bonding.

The last exercise was action related. In groups of five, I asked participants what they were going to do. They wrote these down privately and then went public in their small group. The day ended with the entire group standing in a circle, each person sharing one action he or she planned to take to eliminate fear and oppression and to build authenticity and hope among diverse groups and themselves. It was a full, demanding, invigorating 2 days. I tried to build a synthesis, the best of diversity training tied to the best of white racism training.

Concluding Reflections

Obviously, there is no one best way to train or educate on diversity. The design I presented above is modified depending upon time and group. Although the exercises remain the same, the order may shift and certainly the examples change to match the group experience and interest.

If the group is very nervous about any diversity work, I usually begin with the Myers-Briggs Personality Type Indicator. It is fun, insightful, and highlights differences by type, not race. In one organization, I am taking everyone through Myers-Briggs to establish a base for more serious diversity work. In another organization, I took 1,000 through Myers-Briggs at one time—with an explicitly diversity focus. I also draw upon simulation games. Two old standbys that many of you most likely know about are Star Power (Shirts, 1975) and BaFá BaFá (Shirts, 1977).

No matter what particular exercises some are used to, critical constants persist. I firmly believe we get farther faster by a generic approach. If groups can first depersonalize the issue of racism by examining generic principles such as up/down relationships, it becomes easier and safer to personalize and own white racism in one's self as a white person. I can make more striking, hard-hitting points once the foundation is laid than by just moving headlong into the subject. The Up/Down Parable has proved to be a key tool. Everyone can relate to it. We are all both ups and downs.

Groups also have to experience hope. The situation *can* change and I as a participant can make a positive difference. We live between pain and promise. If all we experience and discuss is pain, there is little movement. Likewise, if all we attend to is a better tomorrow, there is little movement. The challenge is to create the context in which white racism is understood as a very serious problem and that as a White I lose from it. At the same time, I can do something about it and the situation can improve.

What about white-on-white training, popular in the 1970s? I did a lot of it. The argument for it at the time went like this: Whites were too frightened to talk openly with people of color present. We needed a safe zone for honest "kitchen table talk." We could only be in partnership with people of color if we knew who we were, what we stood for, and had sorted out our own feelings and beliefs honestly.

Surely there is a place for this kind of activity. However, I do not do it anymore. Given the approach I now take, it is actually better to have a diverse racial population in the room. There is comfort and closeness if everyone simultaneously sorts out his or her "upness," albeit on different dimensions. It frees up the conversation on race in particular later on.

In a different but related vein, I have been struck repeatedly by the separation of diversity training from leadership development and quality efforts. Diversity trainers do not talk to quality trainers and neither are in direct relationship with the process of executive development. The silo orientation to organizational learning denies in practice the underlying connection of all three activities.

How can we organizationally engage in continuous improvement to meet or exceed customer expectations and ignore the diversity of our customers? It makes no sense. Likewise, how can we increase sensitivity to diversity and ignore why diverse groups are together in the organization in the first place? And to mystify the problem even further, how can quality and diversity be pursued if executive education excludes both?

The generic principles—the metaphors, the Wheel, the Abilene Paradox— are directly germane to all three important issues in organizations today: diversity, quality, and leadership.

One image I use solidifies the deep union of these three organizational worries. It is the unity candle, used in many marriage ceremonies. The bride and the groom each lights his or her small candle. The two symbolically join together by simultaneously lighting the fat candle with their two skinny candles. Upon completion of the unifying act an odd event all too frequently happens—the bride and groom blow out their own candles! What a terrible symbol! A much more profound symbol would be for both partners to place their still lighted candles alongside the unity candle. This gesture tends to be more the practice today. Unity and diversity, the one and the many at the same time.

The struggle in every organization is reflected in this unity-diversity symbol. How much agreement, how much difference can and should an organization affirm and embody? Quality requires knowing and sensing a diverse customer base. Diversity requires unity if diverse peoples are to live and work together. And leadership lives at the intersection of quality and diversity, seeking to move an organization into what is authentic.

Thus, we conclude where we began—authenticity. The problem with traditional white racism training was its inauthenticity. It proposed to share power but all to often abused it. It proposed to unite people but all too often divided them. The same is true of diversity training. It proposes to understand differences but often masks power realities that separate us.

Authenticity requires both the understanding and the acceptance of differences and commonalities. It is a lifelong quest. Wisdom does not come easily. Wolves abound. Yet the very wolves that scare us can become our teachers and our partners. By having the courage to face our fears, we have the prospect of truly being a country and an organization unified without uniformity, serving all our customers well, and in the process exhibiting authentic leadership.

Notes

1. In *Authentic Leadership* (Terry, 1993, pp. 157-193), I not only deal with the metaphors but apply the metaphorical analysis explicitly to racism.
2. See *Authentic Leadership* (Terry, 1993, pp. 53-106) for a full discussion of the Wheel.

10

White Men's Roles
in Multicultural Coalitions

JAMES E. CROWFOOT
MARK A. CHESLER

In this chapter we discuss some of the potentials and pitfalls accompanying efforts to create and sustain multicultural coalitions. We focus on issues faced by white men in such situations because: (a) as power holders in most organizations and communities in this society, white men are important resources in multicultural living and working arrangements or social change efforts; (b) as repositories of historic racism, sexism, and class elitism, and the privileges accompanying dominant statuses, white men must learn and change in order to work effectively in multicultural settings; (c) in the current context of intellectual and political struggles around race and gender relations, new visions and practical options for white men (and for everyone else) are essential, and coalitions are one of these options; and (d) as two Progressive, upper-middle-class, middle-aged, white men working on these issues, we are in a position to speak of and to, and perhaps only of and to, white men and their/our concerns and hopes in this regard.

Our own learning about these matters is not complete by any means, but we share our current progress, partly in the hope of educating others and partly as a means of soliciting feedback. The issues to be discussed arouse strong reactions in us as well as in others. Many white men are unused to seeing whiteness and maleness addressed as group-level phenomena. But we are an identifiable and "nameable" social group, and a group with a great deal of power in race and gender relations. Though it is important to avoid stereotyping white males, it is also important to identify some of the characteristic ways in which we work and live, and especially how we interact with others.

White men with different kinds and levels of experience with multicultural interactions and coalitions will react variously to this material. Knowledge of this sort is created by experiential struggle with race and gender concerns, and differential involvement in such struggle leads to different perspectives. Based on the perspectives that often accompany different race and gender statuses, and different "positions" or "locations" in society's struggles with these issues, we also assume that white women and people of color will read and react quite differently from white men. We know most directly, and can write most clearly from, our own "reality" and that of white men similar to ourselves.

Our primary focus here is on issues of race in multicultural coalitions, but on occasion we address issues of class, gender, sexual orientation, religion, and status. All the dimensions of social diversity and social structure occur simultaneously and interact with one another. Moreover, they all have certain elements in common: the existence of domination and exclusion as well as privilege; historic difficulty in dealing with differences; the encouragement of internal divisions and internecine warfare; individual internalization of oppression; and often the semi-invisibility of oppression. Unless the existence and interactions of these varied dimensions are acknowledged, any single coalitional form will be rent with internal division or with the suppression of differences and thereby maintain oppression. The history and literature regarding intergroup coalitions in the United States, with few exceptions, concentrates on one of these dimensions—race—to the exclusion of others; and a focus on the binary aspects of race (e.g., Black-White only) distorts the multifaceted nature of group oppression and limits our view of positive options (Duster, 1993).

Why are multicultural coalitions important? We live in a society and in organizations marked by the dominance of white men and by the increasing diversity of populations and workforces containing both white women and people of color. In the context of historic patterns of stratification, segregation, and oppression, people of different races and genders (and classes and other statuses and ethnicities) are organized into adversarial struggles with one another and with our nation's legacy of domination and subordination, privilege and disadvantage.

In the decade of the 1990s, and beyond, we will see an increasingly global economy in which Whites are a minority, where increasing numbers of people of color and women are in the active workforce, where increasing numbers of people of color and women are in positions of moderate power in organizations and communities, where there are increasing gaps and tensions between the advantaged and the disadvantaged, and where there is increasing need for inter- as well as intra-national collaboration. For example, a report prepared for the U.S. Department of Labor states: "Over the next several years, almost a third of all new entrants into the labor force will be minorities—twice their current share" (Bolick & Nestleroth, 1989, p. 8; see also Johnston & Packer, 1987).

Many segments of the white American population continue to be committed to and to defend their positions of dominance, despite this evidence that our society is becoming more diverse and that previously excluded or dominated groups are challenging the status quo. In this period of transition, increasing acts of racism are all too common. The growing challenge we face is captured by Howard (1993):

> It is critical that we white Americans come to terms with our reality and our role. What does it mean for white people to be responsible and aware in a nation where we have been the dominant cultural and political force? What can be our unique contribution, and what are the issues we need to face? How do we help create a nation where all cultures are accorded dignity and the right to survive? (p. 37)

Neither revolutions by the oppressed, nor strategic planning by privileged groups, will be effective alone in dealing with these present and future issues. The quest for new economic, political, and cultural arrangements, let alone peace and justice, requires many groups to work together to overcome our heritage of division and dominance/subordination.

One model of how people may live and work together in the context of increasing diversity is the *Coalition.* Coalition refers to the organization of more than one party or unit, typically in (prior or current) conflict, working together to influence the actions of another party or social system. In this sense of the term a coalition is a temporary social system. A coalition works with, but does not eliminate or ignore, differences and conflicts of interests. Hence, it may disintegrate when certain specific (and perhaps localized) agendas are accomplished. This sort of coalition is a model of how to proceed, a model of a process for accomplishing certain tasks.

The process of maintaining a coalition also may be institutionalized in the structure of a new or ongoing economic or political organization, or a community decision-making apparatus. For instance, recent discussions of multicultural organizations and multicultural organizational development (Cox, 1991; Jackson & Holvino, 1988; Thomas, 1990) share some of the same principles found in discussions of more temporary multicultural coalitions for social change. The same is true for dispute resolution systems, which, if they are to be responsive to and effective in complex, multi-interest group disputes, must adopt many of the principles of the coalitional process discussed in this chapter. In fact, if conflicting parties who come to an agreement are not to lose their separate identities or agendas or constituencies, an effective settlement structure must create at least a temporary and issue-focused coalition (Crowfoot & Wondelleck, 1990). Thus, the coalition model has broad relevance and potential utility for many multicultural struggles, organizations, and situations.

Assumptions About Coalitions

What are some of the societal preconditions or assumptions underlying a theory of multicultural coalitions? First, we assume that our society is marked by economic and political stratifications based, at least in part, on racial, gender, class, and ethnic characteristics and statuses. Groups defined by these characteristics have different histories, cultures, power, and access to valued material and symbolic resources. It is natural, then, for contests and conflicts to occur over the allocation of these resources. A subordinate or challenging group that desires to protect and/or increase its share of societal resources (and/or create related social changes) often must find additional resources beyond its own group. These additional resources range from access to powerful establishment decision makers, to numbers of members, to information and skills needed to achieve change, to funds, to communication channels, to the power that requires response. Such resources all are potentially available in a coalition.

Second, interest groups that are stratified by social and economic status and access to key resources also are somewhat interdependent. Our society has not splintered apart in centripetal fashion, despite the fears of some spokespersons who resent the greater recognition, autonomy, and power of previously less visible and less powerful groups. If there was not a significant degree of interdependence and interaction, there would be little chance of multigroup conflict and contest. Moreover, particular groups do share some common or transcendent values and interests; and these commonalities, even when temporary and situationally specific, take us beyond simplistic conceptions of "identity politics" and fears of "balkanization." Coalitions that bring different groups together in (even a temporary) alliance are a positive response to both assimilation and balkanization, to the Scylla and Charybdis of U.S. racial relations. With each group insistent on retaining its own identity and agenda, yet agreeing to work together on some common agendas and to reduce coercion and violence toward the other, multicultural coalitions may help develop a realistic and practical model for how we may all learn to reduce exploitation and violence and to work together.

Thus, multicultural coalitions carry the positive potential of reeducating and rerelating Americans whose identities have been formed and socialized in separated communities, and whose relationships have been structured into superordination or subordination. Coalitions also may be arenas in which we can explore new relationships of greater equity and mutuality between groups and individuals, and where individualism can be honored in ways that recognize and cherish communal and group traditions and identities. The lessons learned from building multicultural coalitions may educate us to new relationships, organizations, and communities, and to the values, strategies, and programs of change needed to realize these possibilities. As Smith and Smith (1981) note,

> What I feel is radical is trying to make coalitions with people who are different from you . . . I feel it is radical to be dealing with race and sex and class and sexual identity all at one time. I think that is really radical because it has never been done before. (p. 126)

Some important new contributions to our knowledge of coalitions focused on social change come not only from racial studies, but from feminist theory. For instance, Alperin's (1990) focus on coalitions involving different race and gender groups is rooted in the ideas of other feminist analysts and activists (Bunch, 1990; Lourde, 1984; Reagon, 1983). She develops and advocates an interactive model to emphasize multiple types of racial, gender, class, and other forms of oppression, and how they are intertwined in the very foundations of the U.S. economic system. As she argues,

> (1) There are many types of oppression; (2) a single form of domination should not be considered a priori to be the driving force in all contexts, (3) the different types of oppression interact with each other in complex ways

and (4) eliminating a single form of oppression, even if it were the primary or original source of all other oppressions, would not automatically eliminate all other forms of oppression. (Alperin, 1990, p. 27)

DIFFERENT TYPES OF COALITIONS

Coalitions occur at different levels of social systems: (a) a *macro level* of political and economic systems and interactions; for example, in relations among nations, regions within nations, major social classes or ethnic groups, separate organizations, or major political parties; (b) a *micro level* of interpersonal relationships; for example, among two or several individuals, either alone or within a family or small group or work team; and (c) a *mezzo level* of organizational or community functioning; for example, among different political interest groups within a city, separate departments of a public agency or a business, or different racial groups within a company, school, or local church. Here, we address problems and issues in coalitions primarily at the mezzo level of organizations and communities because this level is critical for success at the other levels. We will focus on the internal processes or dynamics of coalitions—their "rules of engagement"—rather than on their strategic actions for change.

Coalitions between people of color and affluent white groups with liberal ideologies represent the classic case in writings on the U.S. experience. Most literature on racial coalitions deals with these formations, their successes and failures, and their promises and hopes. For instance, numerous case studies of school desegregation efforts have indicated attempts to create interracial coalitions between racial minorities and middle-class and/or affluent liberal white groups, including the NAACP, LDF, MALDEF, ACLU, Urban League, League of Women Voters, Councils of Churches, and others (Burgess, 1978; U.S. Commission on Civil Rights, 1976). On the other hand, many elite and liberal efforts to reform or improve race relations in America thrust advances for people of color against the immediate interests of working-class and poor Whites: school desegregation, for example, desegregated mainly white working-class schools; affirmative action mostly opened working-class Whites' jobs to minority entry; and funds to support new programs were taxed in such regressive fashion that they fell disproportionately on middle- and working-class Whites. Thus, these white groups "feel" the greatest threat from people of color, regardless of any view of them as parallel victims of class and race dominance (Hacker, 1992; Lynch, 1989).

Coalitions between people of color and working-class Whites are not so often discussed, but they occur with great frequency in little noticed daily events and activities. Certainly they involve many more people on both sides than do coalitions with white liberals or elites. For instance, Foner (1974) reports that Martin Luther King, Jr., sought to ally northern black and white laboring groups because of their common agenda in organizing the unemployed, expanding the war on poverty, and unionizing the largely minority groups of unorganized service workers. Such coalitions have so powerful a potential to create change that white elites have tried to prevent working-class alliances by manipulating racial perceptions and labels. Roediger (1991) argues, for instance, that early Irish immigrants were discriminated against, partly via the label "white nigger." Then, when these Irish began to create alliances with Blacks in the free labor debates and movement, they were relabeled as white and encouraged to join with other (immigrant) white laborers to resist the advance of free black labor. In a more current context, we have seen a Republican Party strategy to destroy the Democratic New Deal Alliance of working-class Blacks and Whites via the creation of new alliances between working-class Whites and affluent/elite Whites, partly on subtle or covert antiblack (and antiwelfare) terms. Despite these limitations, unions led by Whites have been the most reliable coalition allies of people of color, sometimes in direct support for the advance of people of color, and at other times indirectly, as in union advocacy of programs for white working-class people that also benefit black and Latino workers. Moreover, poor people of all races have benefited from labor-initiated/ supported social welfare programs, such as Head Start, welfare liberalization, vocational and career education, manpower retraining, and unemployment compensation.

Discussions of mezzo-level coalition dynamics between men and women, especially white men and white women, have occurred most often around the extent and conditions for males' effective participation (or lack thereof) in the women's movement (e.g., Hagan, 1992) and in intimate heterosexual relationships (e.g., Hagan, 1991; Rubin, 1983). In addition, reports of tensions and difficulties in interactions between white men and men of color, and men and women, have come from coalitions organized during the civil rights movement and the northern student movement (Carmichael & Hamilton, 1967; Evans, 1979; Flacks, 1971; Gitlin, 1987; Levy, 1968).

The realities of multicultural coalitions in the 1990s and beyond require new perspectives and analyses and new courses of action. White men must examine their personal and collective participation in societal systems of privilege and domination, and deal with the dilemmas and challenges arising from the impact of this social location on their ability to work with people of color and women—and vice versa.

The White Male Situation of Privilege

For white males, especially of middle- and upper-class status, a key characteristic of life in this society is a set of privileges that provides us with dominant positions, resources, and life opportunities. These privileged statuses are reflected in the ways we behave toward and interact with others—with other white men, with white women, and with people of color. Often these privilege-based behaviors and rewards are visible and known to us; then they typically are interpreted as the result of individually merited behavior or as part of a natural order of life's "givens." Often, however, they are invisible, not part of our consciousness, or vaguely understood but ignored. Perhaps, at some level of consciousness, it is true, as Hacker (1992) states, that, "All white Americans realize that their skin comprises an inestimable asset" (p. 60), but it is seldom acknowledged publicly. We often take these privileges and assets for granted because, as McIntosh (1989) notes, "whites are carefully taught not to recognize white privilege, as males are taught not to recognize male privilege" (p. 10). The very invisibility of these privileges (or our denial of them) lends them special power. If we were fully aware of our special privileges and their dominating effects, some of us would attempt to relinquish or temper them; of course, others of us would not.

McIntosh (1989) concentrates on a variety of everyday privileges she experiences as a white woman, whereas we concentrate on some of those that appear to accrue to white males operating in interaction or coalition with people of color and women. We do this not as an exercise in "mea culpa" or guilt expiation, nor as a "trashing" of white men. It is simply an effort to identify and analyze the issues we have seen and experienced in our own work (with ourselves and other white men) in multicultural coalitions. No doubt there are other examples; readers may add their own "favorites" to our list of white male privileges and dysfunctional behaviors.

EXERCISING OPTIONS

1. We have the option of not creating and/or of leaving interracial relations without affecting the privileges available to us personally and to white men in general.
2. We often fail to join with people of color and women to work for changes that will reduce oppression. Commitments to help others overcome "their inadequacies" are often offered as a substitute for "changing the system" or even our own behaviors.
3. We tend to interrupt others (more than others interrupt us).

4. We feel (and act) freer than others to deviate from group ground rules, expectations, and "appropriate" group behavior (e.g., sitting outside a circle, coming late to a meeting, announcing alternative pressing tasks, etc.).

5. We can hang out with other white men before and after group meetings and at breaks . . . and not be labeled "plotter," "in-groupy," or "separatist."

6. We can attend high-level meetings without colleagues suggesting (and whispering) that we got there because of affirmative action.

MAINTAINING THE WHITE
MALE POWER STRUCTURE

7. We have the freedom (and power) to select some members of oppressed groups we will listen to and others we will not. Thus, we sometimes select (and thereby legitimate) who will be the leaders of groups of people of color and of women.

8. We tend to maintain control of key group decisions in a coalition or work situation.

9. Those of us who are senior and of higher status often challenge and delegitimize (e.g., as "wimpy," "radical," "soft," or "naive") the perspectives of other or younger white men on matters of race and gender. Because we seldom confront our peers higher in the hierarchy/patriarchy when we are in a mixed group, and especially not on issues of racism and sexism, we avoid the potential consequences of being criticized or ostracized by powerful white men. White men also often avoid intervening in conversations or interactions to interrupt racist and sexist talk or behavior.

10. We accept and respond to the leadership of other white men more easily than the leadership efforts of women and people of color. One way this occurs is through the tendency to recognize and accept ideas/suggestions only from other white men, and to ignore inputs from women and people of color unless they have been affirmed by other white men.

11. White men in multiracial or multigender groups often are not open and disclosing about how power operates in traditional organizations and institutions. Instead, we are silent or defend directly or indirectly existing power structures and processes—and the myths about how fair and open they are. Sometimes we ourselves are unaware of the racism and sexism of these organizational dynamics, and at other times we avoid betrayal of our own group.

MAINTAINING EXCLUSION

12. We tend to tell (or signal) "in jokes" that only other white men can understand, and to speak in coded language (such as with sports, military, and culturally specific metaphors) that exclude others.

13. We tend to challenge or be bored by or "tune out" others' (perhaps non-linear rational) ways of knowing, thinking through a problem, influencing others or developing change priorities and strategies, as inappropriate and inferior. Sometimes we react negatively to different cultural tones or styles by labeling people (e.g., as "shrill," "overemotional," or "angry").

14. We conduct meetings in ways that are familiar and comfortable to us rather than seeking procedures that might be responsive to others' cultures and styles.

AVOIDING WHITE MALE VULNERABILITIES

15. There are certain issues (why we are so competitive), feelings (fear and anxiety), information (what breaks we got going up the ladder), and problems (inadequate skills and relationships) that we do not talk about in intergroup settings.

16. We often avoid saying "I don't know" or "I am confused" in front of other white men, or people of color and women, and thus do not have to treat others as equals or as equally vulnerable in the pursuit of information. We avoid sharing our feelings and ignore them or displace them onto issues or people who threaten us.

17. We usually can avoid being the only white male, or one of a minority of white males, in a diverse group.

18. We can afford to limit our efforts to talk with, seek out, and work with women and people of color to those with whom we agree or feel comfortable.

19. We rarely acknowledge, much less apologize for, behaviors that are racist or sexist, especially if they are done unintentionally.

20. We rarely talk about how we learned to be racist, sexist, and classist, nor about current norms and expectations from others and ourselves regarding their maintenance.

ACTIVELY DELEGITIMATING AND
DEMEANING PEOPLE OF COLOR AND WOMEN

21. When we hear about the painful experiences of women and people of color we often joke about, delegitimize, or trivialize these experiences, or offer uninvited suggestions about how to deal with them. We often tell people of color and women how they "should feel" about their experiences . . . and how they "should not feel."

22. We often tell "old boys club" war stories that implicitly recount the putting down of others . . . and by implication send a warning to people of color and women that they, too, can be put down.

23. We often ignore or do not listen carefully to women and men of color in group discussions and other interactions, and often do not ask for their inputs, ideas, insights, or experiences.

24. White men often avoid acknowledging the impact of oppression on people of color and women, and avoid taking responsibility for our own involvement in oppression (we argue that it started before we were born, that many of us are relatively unpowerful white men, or that women and people of color collude with oppressive norms).

25. White men often fail to select people of color and white women as leaders, and have a variety of difficulties supporting and following their leadership—including engaging in acts of sabotage that are generally unrecognized, and that when pointed out are denied.

These behaviors have certain common characteristics. They are rooted in the history of U.S. race and gender relations and, for most white men, represent unexamined, often unconscious and unintentional behavior. Even when identified for what they are and how they affect others, they continue to maintain and reproduce domination and oppression. They are taught to us, and learned by us, early in our lives, in families and schools, and are subsequently rewarded through prevailing cultural values and social structures. They represent behavior that we can get away with and are seldom held accountable for. They also represent behavior that women and people of color cannot count on being able to perform with the same effects. Such is the power of the white male culture and institutions that we inhabit, sustain, and benefit from.

They also are among the reasons why many people of color and women are understandably and realistically skeptical about participation in multicultural coalitions. At the same time, as Ruether (1992) argues, "The struggle against patriarchy cannot be won simply by a woman's movement. Patriarchy is itself the original men's movement, and the struggle to overthrow it must be a movement of men as well as women" (p. 17). Some white men, too, have tried to overcome the denial, hostility, guilt, and fear that attend these privileges and exploitative behaviors by becoming active participants in coalitions striving for a more just future. Howard (1993) echoes Ruether when he suggests, "The issue of racism and cultural diversity in the U.S. is a human problem, a struggle we are all in together. It cannot be solved by any one group. We have become embedded in the problem together, and we will have to deal with it together" (p. 40).

Incentives for White Men to
Join Multicultural Coalitions

Given the patterns of domination and privilege we have noted, why might white men join multicultural coalitions? What is in it for us? What are our possible incentives and motivations? Will these motivations merely generate minor adjustments in systems of inequality? Or can these incentives lead to fundamental changes in systems of power and culture, to transformations that will seriously challenge and reduce racism and sexism? Most important, what incentives and behavioral responses could lead to more effective white male participation in multicultural coalitions working for systemic change?

Thompson (1991) speculates on the potential benefits to white men of living in a multicultural society, and hence on what incentives exist for white men to change current race relations. He mentions access to the ideas and talents of others whose realities are different, relief from responsibility for the welfare of others who have been dependent subjects, freedom from the anxiety that the oppressed will rise up in anger against us, and freedom from crippling guilt regarding oppression. There obviously are many different perceptions of benefits for different white males who participate in multicultural coalitions or otherwise act for social justice. We must be careful about overgeneralizations and the tendency to stereotype both the characteristics and the incentives of white men, as prior inquiry has overgeneralized and stereotyped white women and people of color.

Using as a starting point Crain's (1968) discussion of why white community elites responded more or less positively to demands from racial pressure groups and interracial coalitions in the civil rights and school desegregation movements of the 1960s and 1970s, we can identify four major categories of incentives for white men to participate in contemporary multicultural coalitions. The left-hand column of Table 10.1 provides an overview of the four categories, each of which has some basis in self-interest: (1) enhancement of the welfare of a social unit (common good); (2) help for people of color and white women (charity); (3) enhancement of the welfare of the white male group (direct self-interest); and (4) meeting white males' unmet needs (growth). In the body of Table 10.1 we distinguish some of the different ways in which white men may respond to each of these incentives, by action that creates minor reform within a status quo system, and by action that is potentially liberative and transforming of the system of racism and sexism.

TABLE 10.1 Types of Incentives Leading to White Male Responses to Social Justice/Multicultural Work

| | Examples of Responses | |
Types of Incentives	Responses Oriented to Maintaining Status Quo Narrow Self-Interest	Responses Oriented to System Transformation Broad Self-Interest
1. Enhance unit welfare (Common good)	Make incremental adjustments while maintaining white male power	Improve unit, including redistribution of power and resources
	Maintain peace/order Reduce threat	Seek peace through justice
2. Help people of color and white women (Charity)	Paternalistic assistance which maintains subordinate status	Reparations and assistance which is empowering
3. Enhance white male group (Self-interest)	Learn new information and sensitivity while maintaining dominating behaviors	Change behavior to equitable sharing of resources and collaboration on tasks
4. Meet unmet individual white male needs (Self-growth)	Please the "other" by demonstrating that the other is special and an exception, without changing attitudes and behaviors	Change guilt and fear of "other" by making amends for hurtful behavior and doing things that do not engender retaliation but bring about transformation
	Maintain privileges	Reduce privileges

Efforts to advance the general welfare of a social unit can be seen as a commitment to prosperity or perhaps to productive efficiency ("bottom-line" language) in organizational or community performance and functioning. It clearly has a significant self-interest component, and often is the driving force behind senior management's or community leaders' stated commitment to racial change in the workplace or community. In work organizations, the market-based need to recruit and retain employees of color often is based on arguments that bringing together people who have different backgrounds and worldviews, and who can work together, will generate new and more interesting and effective ideas, access to markets, service to consumers, solutions to social ills, and the like (Cox, 1993; Fernandez, 1991; Jamieson & Mara, 1991; Loden & Rosener, 1991). In contrast, threats to peace and order, or to the good image of an organization, also often provoke a self-interest agenda in change in order to avoid negative consequences or challenges to the "common good." Thus, organizations may enter coalitions for multicultural change in order to avoid investigations by federal or state monitoring agencies; judicial or regulatory sanctions; mass employee defections; public embarrassment; market position loss; or impending strikes, boycotts, or protests. At the societal level, the motive may be to prevent, control, or co-opt negative sanctions or mass rebellion.

The second category of incentives for white male participation in multicultural coalitions involves advancing or protecting the well-being of people of color or women. In this case the focus of attention is the "other," the oppressed or disadvantaged groups and individuals. This commitment to redress wrongs, or to perform acts of charity, has rationales as diverse as noblesse oblige and egalitarian sharing of resources. The self-interest component of this motivation may be the hope that reduction in exploitation and oppression can make life better for people who, in turn, can contribute more effectively to the total society and to everyone's welfare, or to reduction in the costs of maintaining oppression (taxes that go to prison maintenance, welfare costs, police protection, etc.). It may also assuage guilt about privilege.

The third category of incentives for white male participation in multicultural coalitions focuses on the long-term well-being of white men as a group (or as a subunit in an organization). White male cadres increasingly are the targets of criticism and calls for change in the allocation of and access to resources. The lack of overt bonds of support among white men makes response to this situation especially difficult, as noted by Kupers (1993):

> There is less unity among men. This is not only because "men are the oppressors" though that is an issue men must eventually confront. It is more a matter of men's proclivity to compete for dominance. Men have trouble agreeing on anything because each would like to convince the others he has the sole correct answer to what ails us. (p. 140)

Thus, some organizations have created multicultural "study groups," interracial or race/gender workshops, or training sessions expressly for the purpose of (re)educating white males so they may relate with one another more successfully and perform better in a multicultural environment.

The fourth category of incentives for white men to participate in multicultural coalitions involves our own needs and desires in relation to our core selves. Some white men experience guilt and fear in individual or collective relations with white women and people of color; others experience isolation, lack of influence, or dissatisfaction with these relationships. Some white men also experience a sense of constriction and alienation from ourselves, which leads to awareness that we do not know parts of ourselves, or are unable to express and act upon those "hidden parts" or aspects that were repressed in the effort to perform well in the white male culture. To deal with these feelings and aspirations requires new conceptions of ourselves, as well as new behaviors and relationships with people of color and white women. Although many white male support groups exist in response to these needs, only occasionally do we encounter such groups or caucuses that explicitly place high priority on achieving change in the external social structures of racism and sexism.

These four varieties of incentives for joining multicultural coalitions are by no means mutually exclusive or independent of one another: They often overlap in particular circumstances. For instance, when white men seek to enhance an organization to which they belong by assimilating people of color, and the incentive of helping the "other" also is present, changes are not likely to occur in the organizational culture, distribution of power, or status of subordinate groups. Rather, attempts to reimpose the dominant white culture on people of color, under the guise of helping them, may simply lead to cultural confusion and resistance. At times, contradictory actions may be present: for example, responses to the incentive of organizational welfare that fail to redistribute power may be accompanied by other efforts to assist the "other" in ways that truly empower subordinate groups. Such contradictions and inconsistencies occur because of: (a) white males' different understandings of ourselves and our organizational motivations, and (b) different white males' differing commitments to altering institutional racism and sexism.

Recent (and ancient) history makes it clear that most white male participation in multicultural coalitions leads to maintenance of the basic power and cultural arrangements of existing social units—that is, the status quo. However, some white males and white male groups do focus on systemic transformation in cultures and power. How can we improve the chances of these transformative responses and involvements? What role can each white male reader play in the development of such theory and practice? What dilemmas or choices are involved in these roles?

Dilemmas Facing White Males
in Multicultural Coalitions . . .
and Some Guidelines

The everyday dilemmas discussed below are generic and apply to various partners in multicultural coalitions, but they apply quite differently to people of color and Whites, and to males and females. For instance, white men typically focus on ourselves as individuals and often fail to see our commonalities as a social group; we need to learn about the common styles and characteristics we share (as well as about our differences). By contrast, women of color often see themselves, and are treated by others, primarily as (members of) a group, and only sometimes do we (or they) elect to focus on their individualities and differences (Anzaldua, 1990). Moreover, Whites often see changes in race relations as matters of increased interpersonal understanding and prejudice reduction; people of color are more likely to emphasize changes in structures of power and resources (Blauner, 1972; Mohanty, 1989-1990). We can understand the very different experiences, orientations, and risks faced by people of different races and genders in these coalitions only by listening carefully to people from other groups. For instance, Reagon (1983), an African American woman, describes her involvement in multicultural coalitions:

> If you are really doing coalition work, most of the time you feel threatened to the core, and if you don't you're not really doing coalescing. The only reason you would consider trying to team up with somebody who could possibly kill you is because that's the only way you can figure you can stay alive. (p. 356)

We hope other writers will continue to address the issues faced by members of other groups and will, along with other white men, critique and extend the list of issues we present.

The particular dilemmas described below are organized in four major areas of coalition experience: (a) reasons for and forms of participation, (b) internal operations, (c) external relationships, and (d) demise of the coalition. In each instance we pose a question about appropriate behavior, or a dilemma, for white men. In some cases we provide alternative resolutions or guidelines. Each of these dilemmas requires reflective inquiry and action on the part of all people involved in multicultural coalitions, but especially on the part of white men.

SHOULD WHITE MALES PARTICIPATE?
IF YES, HOW?

1. Can or should white males participate in an interracial or multicultural coalition individually or as part of a white male group or subgroup? Kupers (1993) argues that, "Men must learn that connectedness with others can boost one's power, and that by working together we can be even more powerful, especially if we figure out ways to collaborate without constructing new hierarchies and rivalries" (p. 181). The emphasis on individualism (individual merit, achievement, responsibility, representation) among white males often leads to a denial of our group identity, our commonalities with other white men, our embeddedness in historic patterns and privileges of sexism and racism, and thus our collective responsibility for oppression and for change (Bennett, 1971; Carmichael & Hamilton, 1967). If white males participate without accountability to an organized constituency, how can we take responsibility for other white males in the coalition or for our peer group in general?

2. How can white males be aware of, and assert, our own needs and goals as part of the challenge to oppression? How can we show our understanding and commitment to changing patterns of racism, sexism, and classism, and at the same time seek what we want and need (e.g., respect, opportunities, a share in coalition decision making)? Will such needs be assessed thoughtfully by others, or as automatic evidence of white males' efforts to maintain current unjust privileges? If our own needs are not met, white men may sign on as passive followers of others' agendas or as imposers on others' behaviors: Both options fail to achieve new models of multiculturalism.

3. How do we white males handle our own needs for constant education and reeducation around issues of racism and sexism? How should the various stages of racial (and gender) awareness (Hardiman & Jackson, 1992) in white male coalition members be dealt with? Danzig (1966) argues that many Whites involved in collaborative or coalitional work with Blacks have felt that it is appropriate to be "color blind," to treat race as irrelevant and to "not see" a person's race. Hardiman and Jackson (1992) have argued that this is a relatively primitive stage of white racial awareness; more highly developed awareness includes color consciousness, with its clarity about differences and that equitable treatment is not necessarily the same treatment. White men must increase their own race and gender awareness in an educational or awareness-raising process in order to be effective coalition members. When undertaking these responsibilities, we must avoid the trap of playing off one another to "look good" or "look better than other white men" in the eyes of people of color (or of trying to "be black" by trashing other white men

[Carmichael & Hamilton, 1967]): to do so once again reproduces the culture of competitive individualism, avoids looking at ourselves by pointing fingers at others, and denies our collective white male responsibility for institutional racism and sexism. We need to support and cherish one another and our individual differences, and to avoid a stifling orthodoxy in this work.

In seeking our own growth, many white men place the burden of our education on women and people of color, on the assumption that they see (certain aspects of) us better than we see ourselves. But this is an unfair and onerous burden, one that increasingly is being rejected by coalition members. As Lorde (1984) argues,

> Women of today are still being called upon to stretch across the gap of male ignorance and to educate men as to our existence and our needs. This is an old and primary tool of all oppressors, to keep the oppressed occupied with the master's concerns. . . . This is a diversion of energies and a tragic repetition of racist patriarchal thought. (p. 113)

And Hagan (1991), though focusing on gender and not race, states a similar conclusion, but one that goes farther in placing responsibility for reeducation with men:

> avoid getting rooked into being the teacher or trainer: this is an inappropriate role for women and ultimately counterproductive. . . . Ultimately, to make authentic change, a man must take responsibility for his own education (just as whites must assume responsibility for learning antiracist behavior). (pp. 32-33)

4. White men doing multicultural work often want to gain the approval of and avoid rejection by the people of color and women with whom they work. Indeed, Hacker (1992) argues that "white liberals want to be liked by black people, as if having their goodwill is a seal of approval . . . (and be) counted on as friends and allies" (p. 55). How can we get our approval and rewards from the work itself, as well as from our white male companions, without requiring others to take care of us? In a similar vein, how can we respond to the "white bashing" or "male bashing" that sometimes occurs in mixed groups, especially when white men act out unintentional or unconscious racism or sexism? We know such things will occur; the question is how we and our coalition partners will handle them.

5. Are there some multiracial and multigender coalitions that white males cannot or should not be part of? In some situations, people of color and women pursue organizational or community goals that white males are

uneasy about. In other situations, people of color and women will not desire white male participation, for reasons of principle or strategy. For example, Crowfoot was part of a group of males who elected to work together in sponsoring public activities and operating a small organization to address the very different risks faced by people of different races and genders around issues of child abuse. Based on this work, he sought to write for a women's publication about childhood abuse, despite the policy of the publication to accept only articles written by women. When his inquiry and offer to write was ignored, he experienced doubts about continuing to support the publication, but came to accept the decision and recognize the legitimacy of women being separate in operating the publication and at the same time seeking male subscribers and funders. How can white males accept being excluded from such coalitions and still support their efforts from the outside? Can white males do this without being patronizing, denying feelings of exclusion, or alleging separatism? Is it possible for white males to be direct and honest about our reasons for wanting or not wanting to be part of some coalitions, including discussing our own goals, needs for safety, choices of strategies, and targets of change? Can white males who are engaged in multicultural coalitions challenge other white men to leave when they are behaving in repeatedly destructive ways?

WHAT ARE SOME KEY COALITION DYNAMICS . . . AND NEEDED ACTIONS?

6. Given typical patterns of white male domination in families, organizations, and communities, what should our roles be in a multicultural coalition? Should men be limited with regard to leadership, public visibility, strategy formulation, and the like? Several observers report that white members of interracial coalitions often have assumed the high status and dominant roles, thus reducing Blacks to the status of junior partners (Bonacich & Goodman, 1972; Braxton & Prichard, 1977; Burman, 1979; Foner, 1974; Marx & Useem, 1971; Wilcox, 1971). This is sure evidence of continuing racism and a recipe for co-optation and eventual difficulty. The obvious implication is for people of color and women in multicultural coalitions to "define the terms of engagement," lest they, too, "automatically operate under white assumptions, white definitions and white strategies." As Kupers (1993) sees this question,

> The challenge that confronts men is to find ways to be powerful without oppressing anyone, and in the process to redefine power, heroism and

masculinity. This is an immense challenge. And men will never meet it in isolation. We need new kinds of bonds among men and between men and women, straight and gay, if we are to construct, collectively, new forms of masculinity and new and better gender relations. (p. 183)

Clearly, Kupers's argument extends to new bonds among people of different races as well.

We suggest that white males adopt the role of a "powerful second banana" in such groups, in the sense of being responsive and supportive of the agenda and leadership of oppressed peoples, but at the same time strong advocates and negotiators for the coalition's public agenda and our own basic needs and priorities. Often this is difficult to do, both because of our personal styles and others' reactions to them. A good example of this role is reflected in a recent article eulogizing the late James Laue, written by Roger Wilkins (1993): Wilkins notes that in his work with Laue in the Community Relations Service, Laue would

lean into me with his little smile, and he would finish saying what he had to say, and smile at me and call me boss. And finally, one day after he had done this, I said, "Jim, why do you always call me boss?" He said, "I'm teaching boss . . . I'm teaching the white folks that a black guy ought to be your boss." (p. 5)

Chesler recently was part of a mixed-gender change team, and was constantly treated by other white men outside the team as the team leader, despite the reality that a white woman was the actual team leader. But Chesler's own style of getting out in front, of speaking quickly and forcefully, as well as other white males' inability or unwillingness to hear and acknowledge female leadership and a female leadership style, kept confusing the issue. Eventually, the issue was forced, although by no means fully resolved, by Chesler stating directly and frequently, and by indicating in public behavior, who the team leader was. In addition, as several authors have recommended (Bryant & Crowfoot, n.d.; Katz, 1978), team members held several feedback sessions where these issues were discussed and pursued among themselves.

7. How can the coalition be made a safe place for everyone? Given the level of distance, distrust, and competition within the white male group, as well as the competition and hostility that often exists among members of different races and genders, we can anticipate many problems in creating a safe and effective working environment within a coalition, just as we expect such difficulties in racially and gender mixed assembly lines, corporate or

public agency boardrooms, or college and public school classrooms (Feagin, 1991). White men generally do not know the conditions needed by white women and people of color in order to experience a modicum of safety in a multicultural setting. Thus, although the development of intragroup and intergroup working relationships are essential in a coalition, they cannot be built, as many white males have tried to do, on the basis of love and friendship (Bennett, 1971; Carmichael & Hamilton, 1967). They will be built, if at all, on the basis of proven behaviors of shared power, effective collaboration, accountability to shared goals, and actions for change that merit respect and greater trust. These are especially important criteria for people of color and women as they try to collaborate authentically with members of a social category that historically has exploited their extensions of friendship and love. It also is important for white men to overcome our training and predilection for domination and for avoiding sharing privileges and power, and to experience vulnerability to groups we have been socialized to control and defend ourselves against. In the process, white males may interact on a new basis among ourselves, creating increased mutual openness and vulnerability across the lines of class, status, age, sexual orientation, and ethnicity.

Arrangements need to be made whereby women and people of color can shape the coalition with a minimum of energy and negative fallout, perhaps by "caucusing" or meeting separately at times. The need for regular and legitimated separation among groups is articulated by Hagan (1991):

> I believe the cultivation of female power under male supremacy requires the practice of separation to a lesser or greater extent, depending upon the individual situation. Relief from constant exposure to men and male needs is necessary for a woman to perceive the depth of her innate female power. (p. 33)

White men, too, can benefit from separate meetings. While working within a multicultural coalition in a large bureaucratic public agency, Crowfoot had the experience of coalition members refusing to meet periodically in separate gender, race, and physical ability groupings. Although separate gatherings occurred informally, their formal absence denied some members' needs and reinforced a myth of "openness" promoted by the white male leadership. These norms and practices suppressed conflict and prevented each group from dealing fully with its unique perspectives and feelings. It is possible that members' needs to work together in a coalition made it risky for them to separate from one another even for a short time, but it also is possible that the needs of women and people of color to work on issues while safe from white male observation were thwarted by the lack of caucusing.

8. What differences in the dynamics of multicultural coalitions can be expected based on differences in the ratio of men and women and the ratio of people of color and white people? It is reasonable to expect that the race and gender of the majority of individuals in a coalition will influence how the coalition operates, but certainly organizations and constituencies with greater political or economic power also will have greater influence. Kanter (1977), among others, has explored this problem in corporate organizations, explicitly cataloguing the dangerous situation of lone or token members of oppressed groups in otherwise homogeneous situations. Whatever the race and gender sources of heaviest influence, but particularly when they are white and male, special efforts are required for the coalition not to adopt automatically these powerful groups' goals, strategic priorities, and operating styles.

9. What decision-making and implementation processes should be used? Most organizations dominated by white males rely on hierarchical authority, even though these arrangements may be undemocratic and have significant negative impacts on all people involved. At the same time, such decisional processes are familiar to almost everyone, and their use avoids the creation of new formats that might take a great deal of time and energy away from central coalition tasks. Crowfoot has experienced a consensus decision-making structure in a multicultural coalition that, although generally effective, reverted to a hierarchial arrangement when the group faced a crisis. Subsequent recriminations and guilt about power and control issues negatively affected the group. The experience demonstrated how deeply embedded and pervasive the tradition of hierarchial decision making is, even when people have good intentions and experience with other options. Walzer's (1971) notion of a caucusing process suggests a bargaining model within the coalition, and Crowfoot (1981) proposes several other models uniquely suited for social change-oriented organizations. Prior to actual decision making, Bonacich and Goodman (1972) suggest that discussions focus on implementation strategies as well as goals, because coalition partners may discover their differences only at this stage of action planning.

10. What multicultural rituals and/or celebrations need to be created? People of color who are uncomfortable adopting some white styles of relating and working within groups, as well as Whites who are offended by some Black or Latino styles (Blauner, 1987; Kochman, 1981), and women who are resistive to white male rational and linear working styles, all need to invent new patterns of work and play that are mutually appealing and that help to create a new multicultural culture. Otherwise, we are likely to end up

working on white males' turf in white males' ways, and to be limited by the constraints of the same dominant paradigm we are struggling to alter. We need to let go of "our way is the only way," learn other ways and support their adoption, and at the same time decide what elements of our culture we want to maintain and celebrate. Both Chesler and Crowfoot have been part of a small temporary organization that has some marked similarities to a multicultural coalition. We have seen that our style of conducting meetings and discussions often is neither effective nor comfortable for others. What appeared at first to be convenient ways of setting agendas, getting things done, responding to time pressures, keeping "on track," and exercising leadership, turned out to be expressions of white male norms. White women and people of color in the organization had different preferences and norms regarding the conduct of organizational business, including establishing time for the sharing of feelings and for personal "catch-up." A series of discussions and negotiations have resulted in concerted attention to these issues and efforts to construct meetings with an eye to various cultural styles.

11. How can white male coalition members make use of our special expertise on white maleness? Such expertise can help others understand how traditional organizations operate and how the coalition might plan and implement effective strategies for change. Information about the strengths, weaknesses, and vulnerabilities of white male-dominated power structures is vital for coalitions seeking to change these systems of privilege. However, sharing such information often makes white male coalition members defensive and uneasy, and perhaps guilty about telling "state secrets." Of course, other coalition members also have expertise about white maleness, and ways need to be found to join different perspectives and provide a broader and richer range of substantive and strategic analyses.

12. How might we deal with the feelings that are generated by coalition work . . . and learning? Regardless of the level of trust and safety that may seem to be attained in a multicultural coalition, threat and challenge remain. Even as we find pleasure and satisfaction in more equitable working relationships, white males in particular will face fear and anger as our own "knapsacks" (McIntosh, 1989) of prejudice and privilege are unpacked. We may experience embarrassment about our ignorance, fear of making a prejudiced comment or a mistake in racial courtesy, fear of being attacked, anger about being attacked, uncertainty and pain in recognizing unflattering aspects of ourselves. In the face of strong inquiry, challenge, or attack by people of color (three different forms of interaction that sometimes cannot be distinguished by whites), a typical white male stance is to sit back, maintain a (relatively) straight face and stiff upper lip, and "tough it out." People of color may anticipate a strong counterattack or an expression of

pain and anger. When they receive "nothing" they often assume that the white male feels impervious to challenge or cares nothing about the issues. The erroneous attributions on both sides (Kochman, 1981) often contribute to misunderstandings that are destructive to the coalition.

How can white men share our perceptions of coalition dynamics and the burdens and pains of our social roles with coalition partners—with other white men, white women, and people of color? Because it is crucial that all coalition members have some understanding of one another's experiences (Thompson, 1991), it is important for white men to share our own pain, both as oppressors and as occasionally oppressed members of this society (oppressed by class or religion or age or sexual orientation or ability and/or as children). However, it often is difficult for people of color and women to listen to what may be perceived as the "whining" of privileged group members, because they quite naturally may resent the notion that "everyone is oppressed" when their own oppression is so pervasive, so heavily institutionalized, and so often denied by white men. Thus, in the effort to reach mutual understanding and collaboration, we cannot expect much overt sympathy for our own pain, and have to demonstrate clear understanding and concern for the oppression experienced by people of color and women, without denying or equating our own experience to those of other groups.

WHAT SHOULD BE THE EXTERNAL RELATIONSHIPS OF WHITE MALES WHO ARE PART OF THE COALITION?

13. How should white men in a multicultural coalition deal with peers who are supportive of but outside the coalition? How can we inform, connect with, gain feedback and support from, and "bring along" this critical constituency in coalition agreements and actions? White men who are prepared to acknowledge collective responsibility for institutional racism and sexism, and who have a sense of accountability to a larger white male group, may create or join a peer support and resocialization group, and seek opportunities for formal reeducation and action regarding whiteness, masculinity, and economic privilege—for themselves and for other white men.

14. How can white male coalition members relate with other white men who are "perpetrators of oppression" or "bystanders," and who thus are the direct and indirect targets of the coalition's change efforts? How do we prevent the "trashing" and "bashing" of these white men? How can we approach them, in the face of our fears of being "trashed," disrespected, or excluded from important peer relationships? Rather than distancing ourselves from these white male peers, we need to acknowledge that at some

level "we are them" and "they are us." Meeting this challenge involves dealing with passive and active resistance (even attacks), influencing by-standers to become supporters, and not allowing targets to co-opt us or otherwise use us in ways that compromise the coalition's efforts. Co-optation is very delicate and often occurs at subtle levels we barely notice. In a wonderfully honest chapter, Alderfer (1982) discussed how he may have accepted the pressure of senior white male colleagues not to name in writing a respected peer whose work he felt was marred by inappropriate racial assumptions. He noted that requests for silence and to avoid embarrassing colleagues is a pressure that "is common for senior white men to exert on each other in racial matters" (p. 146). As we grapple with such peer pressures we also face a question of whether and how we will reach out to white men of different classes, religious traditions, sexual orientations, and the like.

15. We do not stop being members of the dominant group when we work in a multicultural coalition. If unmerited and accumulated privilege is at the heart of injustice in this society, and at the heart of being a white male (particularly a white male of upper-middle-class status), do we, and how do we, divest ourselves of some of these privileges? Must we commit "class suicide" (Freire, 1970), or are there other ways of working for justice and living well with these contradictions? Is the very notion of "living well" in the midst of oppression a key aspect of the ideology of oppressors? At the same time, continual immersion in guilt destroys hope, energy to work for change, and personal efficacy. What lifestyles, citizen roles, and roles of father, husband, friend, and lover are manifestations of wisdom on these matters?

WHAT ISSUES NEED ATTENTION
IN ENDING THE COALITION OR
IN FOLLOWING UP ITS WORK?

16. How does a coalition end? Not well, unless there is thoughtful planning. Coalitions that end with a whimper and that disappear into the dusk are usually read as failures. Coalitions that end in a planful way, with recognition and recounting of successes and failures, with feedback and analysis of progress, with multicultural rituals and celebrations of termina-tion, more often linger in our minds as fruitful and growth-producing experiences. Moreover, they are then more likely to linger in the public mind as successful models of work for change and as successful visions of future organizations and communities. Developing a multicultural coalition repre-sents a substantial investment in relationship and organization building.

Even if it was undertaken as a temporary partnership, the relationships that were built, and the values and skills that were developed, may be maintained in another coalition or in a more permanent effort for social change, organizational improvement, or multicultural organizational development.

Multicultural coalitions can be a powerful force for social change. They are not the only source, however. White men can act for change on our own. So can movements for social change led by people of color and white women. Such movements are essential sources of the ideas, visions, and values required to create and maintain more just structures and cultures. Efforts at coalition building must be careful not to detract from the need of these social movements to operate autonomously and powerfully; oppressed groups can seek ways to enhance their potential while helping create a truly multicultural society. Table 10.2 summarizes these critical dilemmas and questions.

Conclusions

Our argument has been that it is morally right, and in the self-interest of white males, to work for a just and multicultural society. The bases of this self-interest and moral priority may vary among us, as do our past experiences, awareness of privilege and exploitation, concerns for personal safety and survival, personal advantage, charity, moral integrity, system survival, and mutual gain. And the motives as well as the roles for change are different for white men of different classes, ethnicities, sexual orientations, and ages.

White men who wish to be involved in multicultural coalitions, including ourselves, have much to learn about our own whiteness, maleness, and other bases of privilege. We need to improve our understanding, our motivations, and our tactics for changing privilege and oppression. This involves deepening our cognitive and emotional understanding of our historic and current privileges and the ways in which we accept, deny, or otherwise deal with the privileges that we, and our ancestors and descendants, carry as a result of this status. It also means understanding better the negative consequences of the white patriarchy for ourselves as white men as well as for people of color and white women. Not all white people, and not all males, are alike in access to privilege and to the consequences of oppression. It is therefore important to explore the different meanings of maleness to men of different classes and sexual orientations, and the different meanings of whiteness to Whites of different ethnicities and classes. Divisions within the white male group obviously are easily exploited by enemies of a multicultural agenda, and we need to learn how to "unlearn" many of the values, attitudes, and behaviors associated with our status. At the same time, white male education and

TABLE 10.2 Dilemmas and Questions Surrounding White Male Participation in Multicultural Coalitions

---

How should white males participate?
- as individuals or as part of a white male group or subgroup
- acknowledging one's own oppression and asserting one's own goals
- which of us should be (and should not be) coalition members
- with needs for reeducation
- with needs for approval
- are there coalitions we should not be part of

What are key internal coalition dynamics?
- what roles for white males
- how to create safety for all
- what to expect from different racial and gender compositions
- what decision-making and implementation systems
- what multicultural rituals and celebrations
- how to use specialized white male expertise
- how might white men deal with our feelings

What should be external relationships with other white men?
- how can white men deal with supportive peers
- how can white men deal with oppressors and targets of change
- how deal with charges of reverse discrimination
- how deal with our institutional and personal privileges

What needs attention in ending the coalition?
- how can productive relationships and actions be continued
- how can temporary coalitions play a role in lasting organizational and community change
- how can images and models of success be promoted

---

exploration must include efforts to learn the histories, cultures, and future goals of people of color and of women.

Breaking the informal and often unstated bonds of the "white male club" invites conflict, rejection, and exclusion. Jobs may be lost, families alienated, friends distanced, competencies questioned, privileges lost, and maleness itself doubted. But part of the way this "club," like any institution, maintains its power over the behavior of white men (and others as well), is by the very mythology of its power and the caution and fear it engenders. Many white men will react negatively to white male actions for racial change, but many others will be glad to see new possibilities for their own and others' survival and growth. Often, we attribute to ourselves greater risk and less personal power than really exists and thereby render ourselves weaker and more passive. Risks that can be discussed with other white men and with coalition partners are risks that can be shared; risks that can be shared are risks that can be reduced via mutual support and collective action. Closely related to risk taking and status change, we need to learn how to develop positive forms of marginality (hooks, 1984, 1990; Mayo, 1982). Instead of revering our centrality in a system of injustice, and rather than withdrawing completely, we need to discover how to be "in" but not "of" such systems (Worden, Levin, & Chesler, 1976), and how to exert leverage from the margins of major institutions in ways that lead to personal and social change.

If we are to adopt new roles and values, we need to develop new sources of social support for our changed behaviors and our involvement in social change efforts. We need to operate alone less, and more often seek out and exchange support with men of diverse classes, races, and sexual orientations, and with women. Such exchanges need to include empathy and caring as well as honest feedback and skill sharing in the pursuit of new behaviors, attitudes, and values. As we develop new support relationships, our existing relationships with co-workers, family members, and friends will change; we need to be prepared for these changes and see them as some of the benefits of more just and fair ways of being and living. Indeed, these are among the key benefits for white male involvement in multicultural coalitions.

11

Afterthoughts and Reflections, From the First Edition

BENJAMIN P. BOWSER
RAYMOND G. HUNT

Writing these essays (see Bowser & Hunt, 1981) was difficult work. It required an inversion of one's customary focus of vision and way of thinking about racism, away from the nonwhite victims of it to its white carriers. No real tradition of prior research and thought was available to draw on, only hints and occasional afterthoughts in the mainstreams of race-related studies. Consequently, our authors were forced to explore unfamiliar terrain with relatively little guidance. Of the hundreds of writers who have produced thousands of books and articles on race in the past three decades, few have directly confronted the question: What effects does racism have on Whites? Of those few, four (Pettigrew, Chesler, Reich, and Terry) have contributed to this book. After thinking about the task we were proposing for them, several other prominent students of racism either declined to accept it, or, after a first cut at it, abandoned it, or else never were able to get beyond talking about non-Whites as objects of the effects of racism. Those individu-

230

als who persevered, and are represented in the book, honed their ideas at an intense 2-day symposium and then spent almost another year collecting their thoughts and reworking their chapters. What have we learned from their efforts? Two things, at least.

First, and most clearly, if black, brown, red, and yellow people are victims of racism, as of course they are, so in the end are Whites, even if some of them sometimes benefit from it, too. The other lesson from this book is less obvious, but possibly more important because of that. It is this: Any agenda for research or social action that takes as its goal effective and permanent change in the character of race relations in the United States must focus explicitly on white citizens. It must carefully take into account the causes of racism among them, the benefits and costs to them from it, and the societal constructions that help maintain it.

An essential reality of North American race relations is that its practitioners are white. Studying the victims of racism is obviously important, but limiting inquiry only to victims invariably leads only to proposing palliatives to soften abuses or comfort the oppressed. Such measures do little to alter permanently the determining circumstances of victimization. By examining the impacts of racism on Whites, however, we have an opportunity to comprehend why they persist in their racism and therefore have a better chance of doing something about it. In this chapter, then, we will reflect on the causes and motivations for racism among Whites; review again its effects on them; and consider some ideas for further research and social policy to eradicate racism.

I

Start with a basic question: Is racism primarily psychological, or organizational (i.e., social structural), or is it cultural? To answer this question, James Jones's definition of racism as a social process is a helpful beginning: "Racism results from the transformation of race prejudice and/or ethnocentrism through the exercise of power against a racial group with the intentional or unintentional support of the entire culture" (Jones, 1972, p. 172, cited in Jones, 1981, p. 28). Thus, as Jones says, racism is psychological and institutional and cultural. These are but different forms and levels of its manifestation. Racism, in other words, is multidimensional—individual, structural, and cultural. To describe it or combat it along any one dimension may not comprehend or reduce it on another. It spills over from any of these levels into the others. In his chapter, Pettigrew (1981) examined racism as a psychological and mental health problem of Whites. He concluded that prejudiced Whites are not necessarily mentally sicker than others, although they may not be as "healthy." Meanwhile, studies of Southerners in the 1960s found them to be more antiblack than Northerners, but not because of any known personality derangements or psychic distress. Their antiblack attitudes were evidently situational and cultural. In fact, the overall picture seems to be that for most white Americans racism does not have deep psychological footings. Joan Karp (1981) connects racism among Whites with personal trauma and childhood experiences of oppression: and Dennis (1981) describes some searing confrontations by Whites with racism. But Pettigrew (1981) estimates from survey data that approximately 60% of white Americans simply conform to whatever attitude is fashionable. They have no compelling need to accept or reject a racist view; in general their bigotry is due to conformity with external influences. What is more, another 20% of Americans are open-minded and unprejudiced. They not only have no need for racial prejudice, they reject it outright. Apparently only a fifth of all white Americans have a deep personal need for an identity based on racial superiority—certainly a large number that implies plenty of work for Karp's and others' counseling groups, but in the scheme of things, an encouraging number.

We may speculate, then, as Pettigrew (1981) suggests, that at any given time up to 80% of white Americans might participate in or favor actions for or against non-Whites. But only 20% would have a strong personal and psychological basis for their stance, either way. Racism thus may actually not be so compellingly rooted in White individual psychology as might have been guessed. For most white Americans, their prejudice is chiefly reflective of environmental influences—social structures and culture. Racist attitudes and beliefs may well be acquired in childhood—possibly in settings of personal oppression—but they are learned together with the discriminatory avoidance behaviors toward minorities so pointedly illustrated in Dennis's (1981) vignettes, and as a justification of those behaviors. In fact, runs one argument, racism at an individual level (prejudice) may represent mostly the post hoc rationalization of racist actions that are impelled primarily by sociocultural imperatives "helpfully" institutionalized as ideology.

There are, after all, no significant formal institutions in American life— not the government, not the national economy, not the church, and not education—that are not controlled by Whites. The way these institutions are run promotes and rewards racism in the lives of all those affected by them. This is institutional racism. Now, under a psychological theory of racism as prejudice, a reasonable person casually familiar with market economics might reasonably expect racism (or prejudice) to ebb whenever labor is in short supply and to flow under the competitive pressures of surplus; and that the more prosperous the economy, the greater will be nonwhite as well as white prosperity. The state of the U.S. economy during the decades of the 1960s and 1970s actually suggests some vindication of these surmises. But a straightforward theory of supply and demand may in fact be an uncertain guide to the economic dynamics of racism (Thurow, 1976). The causes and consequences of racism are complicated.

Michael Reich (1981a), for instance, shows that reductions in racial inequality are correlated with higher earnings for Whites (as well as for Blacks) and with unionization. It is also correlated with falling industrial profit rates. Where racial inequality increased, however, low- and middle-income Whites lost from it financially, while the upper 1% of white incomes increased and actually exceeded the losses to the white majority. Thus, the greater the extent of unionization and the more racially integrated is the union, the higher are white earnings and the lower are profits. The lower the percentage of the work force that is unionized, and the less integrated it is, the more depressed are white wages and the higher are profit margins. Clearly, then, there are strong economic reasons for Whites in the upper 1% of incomes to favor a status quo with a racist character. But there are also good economic reasons for white middle- and lower-income groups to do away with segregation in the workplace. Ironically, however, Kushnick (1981) cites numerous cases where the upper classes of industrial management in the United States and Britain, historically and in the present, have acted to maintain high profits and incomes while the middle and lower classes, partly due to racial fears of immediate loss, have rarely realized or acted in their own best interest. The failure of labor to unite internally and to unionize Blacks in the South was due to labor's shortsightedness regarding its own interest and its racist attitudes. To unionize in the South would have meant unionizing Blacks. The failure to do so provided industrial interests with a region of the country where they could escape union influence, depress all wages, and, of course, increase profits and upper-class incomes. In retrospect, racism plainly played an important part in the profitability of Northeastern and Midwestern industries. It helped to limit the range and impact of unionization; and it depressed the wages and benefits that Whites might have earned. Finally, white racism provided a safe haven for industrial flight. It is hardly coincidental that Northeastern and Midwestern cities, which are highly unionized and relatively union-integrated, have been hardest hit by industrial flight.

Reich (1981a) and Kushnick (1981) have each provided a picture of social institutions being directed, manipulated, and influenced to produce some given outcome. The particular modes of organization and functioning of an institution in themselves do not necessarily result in racism, however. To say that the social structure is literally the cause of racism is incorrect. It is correct, as we said in our introductory essay (Bowser, Hunt, & Pohl, 1981), that the phenomena of racism reside within an institutional order, and that power, privilege, and social control are the motivations behind racist actions. What is incorrect is to view the institutional order and social structure as one and the same with power, privilege, and social control. A social order acts out racism. It does this because it is influenced by economic and political interests that benefit from racism either as an intended condition or as an unintentional consequence of pursuing those interests. To say that institutional racism is a result of the highest 1% of Whites maintaining and pursuing their wealth and privilege is, of course, solidly Marxian. It is based on the argument that not all social classes influence the organization of government, business, and other institutions equally. The higher the class, the greater the influence. Marxists (and others) have attached great importance to this fact and have used it as an organizing principle in their analyses of social relations.

Historically, Great Britain has been characterized by rather clearly defined social classes. In the United States, on the other hand, social classes have always been ambiguous (see Boorstin, 1965) and certainly are as we approach the 21st century. Marxian arguments like Kushnick's (1981) hold that this is due to a failure of the working class to define its interests well. Perhaps—but the definition of *class* is pertinent, too. The fact that class is not well defined in the United States and yet the highest 1% of white Americans have vested interests in doing whatever they believe is necessary to manipulate institutions in order to preserve and protect their self-interest is not a contradiction. What we suspect is that we are not dealing with the same social classes that Marx saw in the 19th century, not even necessarily some kind of coherent Millsian power elite (Mills, 1956). Instead, what we may be dealing with are influential interest groupings whose memberships cut across political party memberships and traditional social "classes." The members of these groupings need not be, and often probably are not, conscious of one another. Moreover, this sharing of interests is mainly tacit. Hence, not all antiunion and antiblack sentiment among white workers need be the result of maliciously deliberate upper-class manipulation; and not everyone in the highest 1% of Whites need see their interest as the blind pursuit of profits and damn the social consequences. Some, albeit not all of them, believe the essential truth of Thurow's (1980) assertion, that "if we cannot learn to make, impose, and defend equity decisions, we are not going to solve any of our economic problems" (p. 194). Oliver Cox's (1948) theory of political classes might also be worth considering in this context.

Obviously we are not satisfied with the thesis that racism originates only out of upper-class interests or interest groups or the social institutions they spawn. At bottom, racism is a cultural phenomenon. Jones (1981) again is suggestive: Cultural racism, he points out, involves believing or accepting as plausible the idea that Whites are superior to Blacks or other racial group(s), and have as well the right to exploit and use them in whatever way they (Whites) see fit. Furthermore, persons and groups that are inferior can have no ideas, insights, identity, or culture worthy of respect or consideration. Russell Means (1980), a principal figure in the American Indian Movement, makes this vivid in his view of revolutionary Marxism.

> It is a materialist doctrine that despises the American Indian spiritual tradition, our cultures, our lifeways. Marx himself called us "pre-capitalists" and "primitive." . . . The only manner in which American Indian people could participate in a Marxist revolution would be to join the industrial system, to become factory workers, or "proletarians" as Marx called them. . . . So, in order for us to really join forces with Marxism, we American Indians would have to accept the national sacrifice of our homeland; we would have to commit cultural suicide and become industrialized and Europeanized. (p. 28)

Pettigrew (1981) has informed us that if we review survey reports from the past two decades (i.e., 1960s and 1970s) it becomes apparent that the percentage of Whites with blatant racist ideation has decreased dramatically. There is less opposition from Whites to public contact with Blacks. There is less of the traditional offensive stereotyping of Blacks, Asians, and others in the press and on television. Charley Chan and "Birmingham" now are infrequent images. Like structural racism, however, negative ideation now is subtler and more selective, but still effective in maintaining within both black and white minds the idea of white superiority and black inferiority. Current media expressions of Blacks, for example, still generally portray them as subordinates, and, if as superiors, then of little importance, and as forever humorous and laughable, if not ominous, and as nonthinking and ill-informed. We can argue about the extent to which the media represent and reflect our culture; but consider the role of cultural racism in the continuing debate over racial differences in intelligence (IQ). On attitude surveys, Whites have increasingly rejected attitudes that presume white superiority. To voice such attitudes now is inappropriate, unintelligent, and "racist." Yet behaviorally, Whites still express strong implicit reservations and fears about fundamental racial equality in intelligence and human worth.

A fundamental characteristic of (cultural) racism is that it undermines and distorts personal and organizational authenticity. Our efforts "to make sense out of our world and (to) act purposefully in that world" are undermined and distorted. The distortions are endless: One can "believe" in racial equality but still always find a reason why a Black, an Asian, a Chicano, an Indian, or a woman should not assume a position of real responsibility in one's organization. Or they may be seen as "acceptable" so long as they do what one presumes is best. Or if Blacks, Asians, or others oppose our will and design for a world order, it must be because they are unreasonable and/or influenced by communists. Dennis's (1981) white biographies document these cognitive and emotional distortions from cultural racism.

Cultural racism has been necessary to the acting out and reinforcement of racism in both social structures and individual behavior, because of the inception of racism as an ideology of white racial and cultural superiority in the 16th century. Over four centuries, ideology became reality. Only within this century has this reality been seriously challenged. It has been challenged but not yet broken. Racism generated through culture is self-generative and, consequently, hard to change. One can believe that real changes have occurred when, in fact, only appearances have altered.

After reviewing the chapters in this book (see Bowser & Hunt, 1981) and ruminating on the possible causes of white racism at personal, institutional, and cultural levels, we think the following picture emerges. White racism is a result of cultural conditioning that is reinforced by and in turn is reinforcing of specific interest group actions. Institutions are organized and, to a degree, manipulated by powerful actors in a political economy to provide a maximum of social control and selective privilege. Racism, thus, is an element of culture that conveniently lends itself to interest group struggles for social power. Success in gaining societal control and securing its benefits reinforces cultural racism by verifying the "truth" of white supremacy and buttresses its institutional bastions. Institutional racism finally compels personal racism. The thesis can be illustrated in the following model:

White Racism = [cultural racism $\longleftrightarrow$ (interest group action $\rightarrow$ institutional racism)] $\rightarrow$ Personal Racism.

Jones is right to point out that racism has personal, institutional, and cultural dimensions, and that any solution to it that addresses only one of these dimensions will tend to be ineffective because racism can then be reinstated by the other two. But, as a tridimensional phenomenon, racism has an inner structure. If we were somehow able to separate interest group manipulated institutions from their cultural hearts, racism would loose its ideological veil, appear as exactly what it is, and thereby loose legitimacy. Whites would not then be compelled by ostensibly legitimate pressures of social conformity to act out racism. Our model of the etiology of racism also tells us that even if we were to succeed in wiping out the personal bases of racism discussed by Karp (1981), or their expression at any rate, institutional racism would not thereby be diminished.

II

As an exploration of the conditions, causes, and consequences of racism among white Americans, this collection of essays (see Bowser & Hunt, 1981) has really only touched the surface. Even so, what we have found, or have been led to suspect, is plainly indicative of an unhappy state. If our authors are correct in their assessment, and in the main we think they are, then racism adversely affects the well-being of the great bulk of white Americans and still is a significant part of their personal identities. Racism may have provided a certain short-term differential status and material benefit to some Whites, but the hierarchical social reward structure it has helped sustain has worked to distort the perceptions of the long-term interest and even the more immediate needs of the white working and middle classes, if not of all Whites.

Intentionally or not, racism has served both to blunt and to divert the point of social reform in the United States. As a part of the North American culture, racism has provided Whites with visions of self-in-the-world based on beliefs of superiority and rightful control over non-Whites (Fredrickson, 1981). And it has affected our international relations in ways that other nations respond to with growing resistance as well as with resentment toward Americans. A high price has been and continues to be paid by white Americans for their racism. Let's briefly take stock of some components of this price that were identified in this short volume.

At the individual or psychological level, racism impairs the quality of life of Whites

- by isolating them from persons of color and dividing them from one another
- by promoting an ignorance and disdain of other races and cultures that becomes more dangerous as the world community grows closer and more interdependent
- by invasions of in-group behavior by the habits of out-group oppression
- by sometimes feeding or aggravating psychiatric disturbances
- by promoting misperceptions of overlapping interests with non-Whites and thereby losing opportunities for social progress

- by basing their orientations to reality on distorted views and allowing misinformation and false fears to control and limit their lives
- by the stunting of human potential caused by inauthentic personal and social relationships
- by "sociological ambivalence"—the moral and social confusion that distorts images of reality; causes uncertainty about one's feelings and beliefs about self, others, and world; and forces one to act cautiously and indecisively
- by personal and racial insecurity

Whites who are socialized with and believe in the idea of white supremacy, as Dennis observes, experience in these days of national and international racial turmoil "a mounting sense of suffocation, because Blacks refuse to recognize their place. . . . Any sense of 'progress' for Blacks gives Whites with racist feelings [the idea] that the world is becoming unhinged and that a new unbearable [one] is on the horizon" (Halsey, 1946, p. 41, cited in Dennis, 1981, p. 80). For one who believes in his or her superiority, changes that challenge this status as false are threatening and unnerving. Coupled with threats of a declining standard of living and U.S. resource dependency on non-Whites, this personal and racial insecurity fuels the fires of a new American and British political conservatism. Racial insecurity similarly encourages what Ladner and Stafford (1981) call "a new individualized type of politics that strains the system but invites new ideological dimensions of rights and freedoms" (p. 67). As one result, any perceived gains that racial minorities have made are presumably to be available to ethnic Whites as well as to women, gays, and others. On an institutional level racism not only distorts personal reality but organizational reality. Robert Terry (1981) shows this in his discussion of problems in organizational authenticity. More generally, racism lurks in social structures that functionally disadvantage minorities and nonminorities as well, although the latter in lesser degree than the former. Neubeck and Roach (1981), Reich (1981a), and White (1981) illustrate the phenomenon in different arenas. Moreover, in this era of equal opportunity and affirmative action, institutional structures deflect the thrusts of social reform to reduce their impact on society's core, forcing unequal sharing across segments of the white population of the burdens of zero-sum resource redistribution. The result is erosion of the standard of living of some Whites, while others profit, and a growing sense of insecurity and dissatisfaction with life's chances that breeds disaffection and disorder. Chesler (1981) notes, for example, that "most elite and liberal efforts to reform or to improve race relations in America thrust minority groups against the immediate interests of working-class and poor Whites" (p. 228). Working-class schools are desegregated, not middle-class suburban schools; there is real affirmative action for jobs mostly open to working-class Whites, not real affirmative action in senior management or the corporate board room; and funds to support new social programs are paid disproportionately by middle- and working-class Whites, not the wealthy or highly profitable corporations. Thus the areas of society in which change would have its greatest (and most needed) institutional effects are shielded, but areas where change has minimal systematic effect are made salient. This kind of sowing of the national wind may yet reap the whirlwind of rebellion.

Meanwhile, the assumption of white supremacy has corrupted U.S. world affairs, especially, of course, with Africans and Asians, and has never allowed American foreign policy experts to imagine that the increasing reliance of the United States on African, Middle Eastern, and Asian natural resources could ever be used effectively as a political instrument by non-Whites. Who would have thought that OPEC might successfully exploit the model of the Texas Railway Commission? "Racism [in the international community] derives its significance from the *differential power* among racial groups such that one group is capable of consistently dominating other groups, thereby reinforcing its beliefs in the inferiority of other groups," Philip White (1981, p. 179) comments. Domestic distortions about racial reality have been matched by international distortions about it. Racist distortions in U.S. foreign policy have encouraged an arrogance in assumptions about international order, stability, and the U.S. capacity to manipulate events—the Pax Americana. As within the United States changes of attitude and behavior among domestic minorities are viewed as threatening and suspicious, so such developments on the international scene as the Afro-Asian solidarity conferences are not welcomed and instead are viewed as threats to American security. As Russell Means (1980) has said: "It's the same song." The idea that Blacks in the United States, for example, have no social and political thoughts or ideas worth taking seriously, encourages the same view of Blacks (and others) overseas. It follows that revolutionary aspirations in Africa, Asia, and Latin America could not possibly have legitimate and indigenous bases; they could only be communist inspired. Thus, white Americans, unable to see a world free of racist distortion, are severely impaired in their ability to understand the causes of and to cope with foreign revolutionary change.

James Baldwin (1963) once said that America's survival in the world may depend on its ability to resolve its racial dilemma justly and correct its supremacist view of itself. Others, too, have made this point. It is an increasingly critical point as we enter the 1980s—what may be a watershed decade. This country is unlikely ever to be invaded and overrun by some nonwhite horde. But there is the possibility of its eventually being isolated from meaningful contact with much of the African, Asian, and Latin American worlds. The United States has had an uncanny knack of perceiving its security and interests in those parts of the world to be best served by reactionary, extreme right-wing, and often openly racist governments, which, however, manifestly cannot survive indefinitely. This is a dangerous condition; one must therefore be concerned about the impact of racism on the tone and character of the U.S. military posture toward the world community. Racism breeds distortions about self and reality, about control and security, and about threats to it. We must necessarily wonder, therefore, about connections between the psychology and ideology of racism and the U.S. nuclear posture. Does "the bomb" somehow represent an ultimate "proof" of white supremacy? Is it an ultimate means of maintaining supremacist control? Is it not a broad illusion to think that peace and national security can be maintained indefinitely by the threat of and readiness to wage nuclear war? And is it not an equally broad illusion to believe that American foreign and military policy are unconfounded by racist preconceptions?

III

Some time ago, W.E.B. Du Bois laid out plans for a hundred years of research on Blacks in order to correct white misconceptions. Rutledge Dennis (1981) points out in our anthology (see Bowser & Hunt, 1981) that what we really need is one hundred years of research on the character and reinforcement of racism by Whites. We understand this much less than we do the plight of Blacks and other minorities. We therefore began this endeavor with plans to devise recommendations for social policy and action, and also to suggest some directions that future research might take. Some of this we have done. Some more is in order.

In our introductory essay (Bowser et al., 1981) we observed that "constructive change has been impeded [in America] by a persistent failure to deal directly with the structural aspects of racism" (pp. 18-19). All signs point to the manner in which we have organized our social order as a key factor in presenting, fostering, and perpetuating racism in our society, both in its informal day-to-day life and more formally in its organizations and institutions. But when considering the structural nexus of racism, attention must focus on the conjunction of institutions and culture. Our social order is not simply flawed structurally, it is distorted by the pervading idea of racial supremacy. The blunt fact is that we don't understand the workings of this very well. Coming to grips with it is a major challenge, because it is important and also because it is difficult. Distancing oneself from one's own culture is hard to do. It is hard to be self-conscious about things that are premises of daily life and have long been taken for granted. This is why Whites so rarely think about being white. It is also why white America has had to depend so heavily on non-Whites, as in this book, to tell it about itself.

These facts limit the making and force of public policy. It is uncertain to what extent any government policy can address and effectively counteract practices having dimly seen cultural foundations, which government itself has more often than not been a party to reinforcing, albeit often unwittingly. But whatever the difficulty, there should be, in the words of President Reagan, a new beginning. The following are some thoughts about its directions.

1. We need more extensive multicultural education and exposure in the United States. The deficiencies in our knowledge of our own ethnic and racial concatenations, not to mention those involving foreign peoples, is a national disgrace that goes hand in hand with the low priority we put on foreign language training.

2. Corporate and governmental actions can have far-reaching social consequences. Many of these can be anticipated in advance. Responsible organizations seek to know the probable impact of their planned actions and give attention to mitigating their negative consequences and enhancing their advantages. This may mean making minor and sometimes major changes in plans before their implementation. The possible aggravation of racial and social class inequities, we think, should be factored into these calculations explicitly. What we have in mind is a "social impact" report analogous to survey-based environmental impact statements.

3. We need to limit and loosen the hold of powerful special interest groups on government in order to enhance democracy and reduce inequality in America. Limits on political campaign contributions are not enough. In fact, such stratagems largely miss the point. The point is power sharing and equalization. America needs a wider representation of citizen interests in its policy councils and in the management of its vital institutions. Movements toward industrial democracy in West Germany and Scandinavia illustrate promising models for nonindustrial as well as industrial sectors of American society. Without them, or something like them, we are left with no answer to the puzzle posed by one Joseph C. Bradford of Alexandria, Virginia. In a letter commenting on the article by Russell Means, from which we have quoted, Mr. Bradford said this:

I believe Russell Means has some very good ideas; but how does one sitting on Baltic Avenue convince those on Park Place that life's game of Monopoly is not the most expedient for the "human beings" of our world. (*Mother Jones,* February/March, 1981, p. 2)

4. The power of government to do good is limited. But so are its alternatives. Certainly we have learned from experience that laissez faire capitalism is not universally beneficent. Business values are business values. They are not of a piece with the Ten Commandments. Getting government off the backs of the people may be welcome. But there are some people on whose backs government needs to be. Only governments—the national government especially—have explicit responsibility for preserving and advancing the public interest. Only governments can be held directly accountable for stewardship of the nation's well-being. Only governments can make and enforce the hard equity decisions essential to that well-being over the long term. Government must, therefore, continue accepting this responsibility and seek not to shed it, but to find creative and effective ways of doing it, and doing it aggressively. No other institution of society can. The market place is no universal surrogate for Solomon; nor are individualism and materialism the only values worth respecting. And racism has never yielded to free enterprise.

There are also things people can do about racism, as individuals and in groups. Karp (1981) recommends antiracism support groups in which Whites cannot simply take for granted being white and must instead explore their own racial behavior and attitudes. Terry (1981) has analogous operations by which organizations can gain authenticity and move affirmatively against racism. Chesler (1981) recommends procedures for the formation of interracial and interclass coalitions that can attack racism on broad institutional fronts. Chesler's ideas have great appeal and potential; but once again a cautionary word from Russell Means. As before Means (1980) refers to revolutionary Marxism but makes a general point when he says:

Now let's suppose that in our resistance to extermination we begin to seek allies. . . . Let's suppose further that we were to take revolutionary Marxism at its word: that it intends nothing less than the complete overthrow of the European capitalist order which has presented this threat to our very existence. This would seem to be a natural alliance for American Indian people to enter into. After all, as the Marxists say, it is the capitalists who set us up to be a national sacrifice. This is true, as far as it goes.

But . . . the truth is very deceptive. Revolutionary Marxism is committed to even further perpetuation and perfection of the very industrial process which is destroying us all. It offers only to "redistribute" the results . . . the power relations within European society will have to be altered, but once again the effects upon American Indian peoples here and non-Europeans elsewhere will remain the same. It's the same old song. (p. 28)

Obviously the potential for cross-cultural coalitions is limited. Chesler knows this, of course.

IV

Critics of this book may say it is speculative and insufficiently empirical. We admit that in advance and claim the state of the art as our defense. Moreover, we challenge critics and supporters alike to begin more intensive research on the motivational basis of white racism and its impact on white Americans. In order to begin this research one must have ideas, hypotheses, even suppositions to examine. We trust we have provided some of these, at least for a beginning. But we have so little to work with that is firm. A new agenda for research on racism must involve thorough examination of the blind side of race relations scholarship—white racism's motivations and its impacts on Whites. For example, we need more research on the manifestations of racism in the significant institutions of American society—policing, for instance (see Locke & Walker, 1980)—and the ways it affects the quality of the lives of Whites and non-Whites alike. We need research on the particular ways that racist ideation distort self-concepts and images of social reality. And we need more process-oriented evaluations of the social impacts of specific actions by government or private agents (such as changes in welfare, or affirmative action programs) as ways of exploring further the nature and ramifications of white racism.

In an earlier draft of his chapter, James Jones had some critical observations about research in his field of social psychology. We close this reflection on the impact of racism on white Americans by reporting those observations.

In social psychology, the research literature on race generally has been one of three kinds. The first consists in studies of the racial prejudices of Whites and typically shows that Whites have negative and stereotypic attitudes toward Blacks, are less likely to help Blacks who are in trouble, behave more aggressively toward Blacks, and so forth. These studies have also documented some of the negative characteristics of Whites which are associated with antiblack prejudice.

A second kind of study has looked at Blacks and Whites in a comparative fashion. Ordinarily these comparisons are with regard to a variable or concept that has been developed within a majority cultural context and is linked to psychological attributes assumed to be indicative of positive functioning in this society (e.g., need for achievement, level of aspiration, locus of control, and so on). Typical studies show that Whites tend to perform better on virtually any criterion of performance. Having "demonstrated" these deficiencies of black people, much of this research then tends to consider genetic versus environmental explanations for the deficiencies and, in some cases, to propose remedies for them based, for instance, on principles of behaviorism and/or social engineering.

The third kind of study looks at black subjects and tries to determine what it is their deficiency is related to and ways in which it can be alleviated. These studies often follow from the second kind mentioned above. Their premise for studying black subjects is to show how Blacks "measure up" on attributes already normalized, theorized, and conceptualized from the perspective of the majority white culture. What does not exist in the literature is any serious attempt to develop principles of behavior and indicators of successful functioning that grow out of the experience of minority cultural groups. Whenever an attribute of black Americans rises to a level of stature commonly acknowledged as good, it is almost without fail, an attribute of the body. Black athletes run fast, hit hard, have good balance, can jump high and so forth (they can't, however, think so they can't play quarterback, or plan so they can't coach); entertainers can sing and dance; women models have long elegant legs and contemporary designer clothes look good on their bodies. So their attributes are presumed to be somehow genetic and the talents, "natural abilities." Since effort is rewarded more than ability in this society, the positive "natural" attributes ascribed to Blacks show up as second-class virtues. And, once again, a one dimensional evaluation distorts reality in a multicultural society.

As Russell Means says, "It's the same old song." We need a new song, a new research tradition, free of these cultural biases.

12

Conclusion to
the Second Edition

BENJAMIN P. BOWSER
RAYMOND G. HUNT

In our introduction to this edition, we argued that if there is to be real progress in race relations in the United States, the problem of racial inequality and dehumanization must come to be seen by European Americans as a problem for themselves. White Americans hold the keys to real long-term change. This was also our judgment in 1981, at the end of the first edition of *The Impacts of Racism on White Americans*. What is apparent after a decade and a half, and as this second edition stresses, is that the stakes are even higher today than we had imagined in 1981 that they would be. This nation's future in the world community, its relatively high standard of living, and its continued potential for generating creative solutions to human problems are all dependent upon European Americans facing the imperative of racial supremacy embedded in historic American culture and manifest in the institutional practices that perpetuate historic racial inequality. The authors in this book who work directly with European Americans on issues of race—Lillian Roybal Rose, John Fernandez, and Robert Terry—each tell us why it is essential that Whites take on the race problem as their own problem, not somebody else's—it is in their self-interest to do so.

This nation was founded on slavery and the taking of Native American lands, but there is an opportunity to create a future where the cultural diversity of the nation is not only acknowledged or even accepted, but is actively used as a strength and source of creativity and vitality (Fernandez, 1993). Without this crucial step, the fulfillment of the European Enlightenment movement that inspired democracy and freedom of speech, of the press, and of religion, must remain incomplete.

We can continue as we have, perceiving the race problem as the victim's problem and deficiency, using race as a covert caste system to negate competition and to maintain white unity across conflicting class interests. But this racism, we have seen, is a key reason for white Americans' inability and unwillingness to turn inward and see their real short- and long-term interests, and to realize that those interests are not in keeping with the current course of American events and media shaped public sentiments.

We are starving education, building more prisons than universities, alienating our youth, disinvesting from cities, allowing more and more citizens to go homeless and to starve on the streets, creating the conditions for rampant drug abuse, and witnessing the slow unraveling of civility because we value money, individualism, and the prospect of wealth and power more than we do each other. The inability and unwillingness of white Americans to deal with race has much to do with these realities and negative trends—realities and trends with which white Americans must live along with people of color.

The reader may protest that these are strong words and extreme conclusions. They are strong words, but they are not extreme conclusions. W.E.B. Du Bois noted that to study African American life is to study American life: What happens with African Americans, happens later with white Americans. In the 1960s, black parents protested poor education and the sudden appearance and spread of drug sales and use. A substantial part of the black working class was laid off as plants and factories that once were dependent on black labor moved to the suburbs, into the rural South, and overseas. The results were devastating. We can see the outcomes of this economic abandonment today in blighted streets, run-down buildings, failed up-lift programs, drug dealing gangs, violence, and the hopelessness and fear in the faces of youth in this nation's ghettoes and barrios.

The American nation did little in the 1960s as white Americans stood by, watched, and blamed it all on black cultural deprivation and inferiority (Ryan, 1976; Valentine, 1968). The irony is that now we hear in white working- and middle-class communities every one of the 1960s black complaints. And, if nothing is done to address racial inequality, the black present will become the white future.

Why? Simply because problems that are left unaddressed in the most vulnerable of communities sooner or later will show up in the larger and better-off communities; it is only a matter of time. America's future has always been evident first in black communities.

Why? Because of something that was made clear in the first edition of *Impacts* and is all the more evident in this second edition: Most European Americans truly believe that their racial interests as "white Americans" are more important than the larger and more important differences among themselves. Hence, for the sake of racial unity, European Americans will disregard real internal differences in power, interests, and vision. The implication of white unity is that powerful interests among Whites who benefit from the exploitation of people of color would never exploit fellow Whites in the same way. The implicit presumption is that whatever powerful interests gain, all other Whites also gain or at least have the prospect of gaining.

Of course, this is nonsense. Powerful interests who successfully exploit people of color will eventually exploit other Whites as well and in much the same way. This is why what happens among Blacks in one generation, happens among Whites in the next. So European Americans have reason to oppose racial exploitation, to be a part of an enlightened racial diversity, and of uniting with people of color with whom they have common visions, hopes, and conditions, to create a generally more equitable society. It is in their very best interest to do this, because their future depends upon it. Even absolute racial harmony would not itself mean an end to injustice.

Basic Motivations for
and Impacts of Racism

The basic anatomy of racism, what fuels it, what effects it has on white Americans, and what can be done about it, are outlined in Chapter 11—our concluding chapter from the first edition of *Impacts*. The core of what our authors presented 15 years ago is not only still timely, but is even more relevant today. If you have not already read it, you should do so. This second edition reiterates the main points made in 1981, and then builds upon and extends them here with new findings, insights, and prescriptions.

We know, for example, that racism has not gone away, as many 1990s conservatives would like to believe (Murray, 1986). Because racial segregation is no longer countenanced by law, and because overt individual racism in the South now is widely condemned, leads many to think that historic racism no longer exists. And they now see affirmative action and other attempts to remedy past discrimination and equalize opportunity as the new racism (Glazer, 1975).

What is missed in these beliefs and perceptions is that racism can be reconstructed across levels—individual, institutional, and cultural. To address racism at one level and not at the others will change only the way racism is expressed. It will not eliminate it.

The institutional racism that now produces racially segregated housing and schools, and racially segmented and unequal employment opportunity, has hardly been eliminated in the United States. In fact, very little long-term progress can be made to improve individual racism without reinforcement from institutions and culture. In order to have any real impact on racism, it is essential to go beyond such institutional redress as affirmative action. One must attack racism at its cultural level along with institutional remedies.

A Summing Up

As a conclusion to this book, we shall try to show where and how the findings and insights of this second edition have advanced what was presented in the first. We will add new prescriptions to our old list and discuss what can be done in the current national climate of conservatism and enthusiasm for rolling back the social progress of the previous three decades.

In keeping with the first part of the first edition's concluding chapter, we will review in order the subjects of Individual, Institutional, and Cultural Racism, and then take up Attempts to Address White Racism. We then will offer some Recommendations on these several subjects and end appropriately with A Look Ahead.

INDIVIDUAL RACISM

In the first edition of *Impacts,* Thomas Pettigrew (1981) presented evidence that not all white Americans were racist. Based on inferences from decades of survey data, he pointed out that approximately 20% of white survey respondents have consistently opposed racist propositions, whereas another 20% have consistently supported racism. The remaining 60% majority had no compelling internal motivation either to support or to reject the racialization of American society. They conform to whatever are the prevailing institutional and cultural practices. We have no reason to believe that this 50-year trend has changed in the past decade.

Pettigrew provided us with a first dimension of the organization of racism and its dynamic expression among Whites. In this new edition, Jones and Carter (Chapter 1, this volume) suggest a second dimension by answering questions posed in 1970 by Robert Terry: What does it mean to be white and how is this related to racism? Jones and Carter's answer is psychological. For European Americans whose white identity is assumed, unquestioned, and taken for granted, the historic cultural script of white supremacy and non-white inferiority is a central part of their individual self-identity.

Like anything that is unquestioned, deeply held, and is self-defining, this identity is vigorously defended; and it is in one's interest to see the mental script replicated in reality. Whites who have had no exposure as peers to people of color AND have never had the opportunity to wonder, question, or explore their racial and cultural identity are what Jones and Carter refer to as being in the Contact stage of white identity. They are Pettigrew's racist 20% of Whites.

The 60% who simply conform are more likely to fall within what Jones and Carter call the Disintegration and Reintegration stages of white identity. They, too, have absorbed the historic culture of white racism, but are in varying ways aware that something is inconsistent between what they have experienced and what they believe about race. Their encounters with people of color have not led them to question "whiteness"; but they have some doubts about what they have been told and what is idealized about others.

These are the Whites who expressed a mix of sympathetic insight and racial animosity in Blauner's *Black Lives, White Lives* (1989). They are easily influenced by stereotypes and shifting conventions in general opinion. They are confused about their racial identity and what it should mean with regard to expressed racial attitudes and behavior. And because they have no particular reason to sort out the confusion and address the contradictions, they do what anyone would do under the circumstances: try not to think about it, be "color blind," and disassociate themselves from whatever benefits they enjoy due to past racial exploitation. As a group largely defined by a conformist identity, this is the majority of white Americans who can support civil rights measures in one decade, be influenced by racial symbolism and innuendos in political campaigns, and then, in the next decade, be convinced that racism does not exist and that instead they are being discriminated against.

The 20% of Whites who are on the continuum from non- to antiracists are in the Pseudo-Independence, Immersion-Emersion, and Autonomy stages. These are people whose life experiences have led them to look inside themselves and begin questioning the racial supremacy assumptions of their cultural identity. Working with people of color as peers has led them to shatter racial stereotypes in historic scripts.

Lillian Roybal Rose's (see Chapter 2, this volume) seminars actually are attempts to move Whites from a lower stage of white racial identity to these higher stages. She provides insights from practice as to how such growth occurs, which is a point not addressed in Jones and Carter's chapter.

In order to begin the emancipatory process, it is necessary to face one's racial identity; it must be chosen and consciously constructed, not simply accepted as a given of one's childhood socialization. Part of this process is to accept the living history of one's family, which, for most, does not support the historic stereotypes about one's race. This is essential to developing real historic pride rather than maintaining notions of self based upon false racial supremacy. Only then can European Americans accept others who are culturally different.

The surprising insight in Roybal Rose's work is that internalized notions of racial supremacy are forms of self-oppression. They allow one to be easily manipulated by others who use appeals to racial unity, to have one's real self-interests obscured, and to be easily threatened by others who are different.

What this tells us is that European Americans are not one-dimensional in their racial identities and that there is an important psychological connection, conditioned by historic culture, between racial identity and where one stands on the racism to antiracism continuum. By better understanding their own historic backgrounds and by having primary experiences with people of color, European Americans' growth in racial identity is possible along with progression from individual racism to individual antiracism.

The implication of these insights is that it is important to make the distinction between "European" Americans and "white" Americans. European Americans are Americans from diverse European cultural backgrounds. There is diversity here, as well as a basis for common national identity. There is here a tremendous need to face, understand, and accept the past in order to develop real cultural pride and real historic identities.

In contrast to a genuine identity as "European" American, to be a "white" American is part of a fictional monocultural unity and racial nationalism that is based on myths of white supremacy. European Americans who have internalized a "white" identity are not only confused as to who they are in history and in the present, they are also compelled to act out individual racism as an important part of who they think they are. Being a "white" American is a unity that is absolutely essential to maintaining the power and privilege of a minority of European Americans, most often at the expense of the majority of Americans, regardless of color.

INSTITUTIONAL RACISM

In order to maintain individual racism there must be institutional reinforcement. What is new on this front? In the first edition of *Impacts,* Kushnick (1981) asserted that institutional racism is essential not only to exploiting people of color, it is essential to the continued exploitation of European Americans as well. Both are exploited by giving European Americans, "Whites," status over people of color. This creates a historic "racial" identity and a basis of unity that is essential to obscuring class dominance and exploitation of the European American national majority.

Racism was essential not only to the maintenance of the American economy through slavery, but it continues to be essential to the continued growth of American capitalism. The failure of European Americans to see how a "white" racial identity and racism are also used to exploit them is evident in the strategic failure of "white" labor to aggressively unionize Blacks in the South and people of color in urban centers. This racially limited view of their collective interests and mission left the South wide open for industry to flee unionized labor in Northern and Midwestern cities. It has also produced an urban history of racial conflict between "white" ethnics and Blacks over jobs and housing. The decline in the proportion of American labor that is unionized can be directly attributed to the racial exclusion attitudes of white union's rank and file. Kushnick also charged that the state (i.e., federal and state governments) played an active rather than a corrective role in maintaining the racial divisions necessary for American capital to maximize profits.

The events of the past 15 years not only support Kushnick's overview, but his comments on the role of the state in 1981 anticipated the current trend toward conservatism. In his revised chapter here, Kushnick (Chapter 3, this volume) expands his earlier analysis. Not only have jobs been moved out of U.S. urban industrial centers in the South, he notes that they have been moved overseas where U.S. corporations have been shifting American capital since World War II. They now are reaping higher profits than if they had continued to pay higher taxes, salaries, and benefits for U.S. workers.

European Americans have much in common with other racial groups in the progressive loss of jobs and a declining standard of living. But they have real conflicting interests with other "Whites" who benefit from their economic demise. Yet major news sources, public officials, and other public opinion makers focus on welfare recipients, crime, affirmative action, and family decline as THE sources of the declining standard of living among Americans and of rising white joblessness. Racial stereotypes such as the violent black man (Willy Horton), hordes of welfare-seeking Mexican im-migrants, and unqualified minorities getting "white" jobs and being admitted to colleges are being used effectively by politicians as appeals to "white" unity to roll back benign institutional attempts to address racial inequality. These are only distractions from the real agenda where the majority, regard-less of color, are more effectively oppressed.

In our 1981 edition, Michael Reich summarized the economics evidence in support of Kushnick's arguments and provided his own analysis of the matter. In a pure capitalist system, he suggested, there should be negative incentives for racial discrimination, because it reduces competition, leads to inefficiencies, and wastes human resources. What Reich found, however, was that the greater the disparity between white and black incomes, the higher were business profits. But the disparity among racial incomes was lowest in cities with high rates of racially integrated union labor. At the same time, it was in these locations that profits were the lowest.

Patrick Mason's (Chapter 4, this volume) analysis in this edition is complementary to Reich's. Mason's inferences from successive approxima-tion analyses suggest that, even without racial conflict, any conflict among workers has the effect of lowering general wages and increasing the number of people in a reserve labor force, that is, those who are willing to work for less than those who are currently employed. By posing a racial hierarchy in the workplace, more privileged (white) workers (not all white workers hold good jobs) get slightly higher incomes, and less privileged (black) workers get lower incomes; but overall, all workers' wages and benefits are reduced while profits are increased. Furthermore, the greater the need to constrain worker wages, to address racial conflict, and to increase production effi-ciency, the larger is the number of managers and supervisors needed. These additional middle-level employees reduce the employer profits that were gained from lack of unity among workers.

Together, the implications of Mason's analyses and their extension of Reich's analysis are to the effect that those who clearly benefit from and control profits are the *only* ones with a clear interest in a lack of unity among the majority of workers. They are also the only ones to benefit from having a large reserve labor force, that is, large numbers of people who are unem-ployed and underemployed. The minority of white workers at the top of a racialized labor hierarchy also benefit with higher wages and less competi-tion, but only as long as those who control their labor do not demand higher efficiency and higher profits.

Middle managers, who form the backbone of the American middle class, benefit as well, so long as there is need to control a large labor force and to minimize racial and other drains on overall performance and productivity.

But with the internationalization of U.S. capital, foreign labor can be found to work for much less, for longer hours, and often more efficiently. The effect is that there is no longer a need or place for large numbers of Blacks and other minorities in primary industries and factories; and the need for white labor is also reduced, as is the need for middle managers to supervise a large domestic labor force. Arguably, this is what is behind current U.S. deindustrialization, plant closings, the de-skilling of American labor, decertification of unions, take-backs by management from unionized workers, and cuts in health and other "safety net" benefits.

If Kushnick's and Mason's analyses are accurate, why are not the longer-term implications of overseas investment and domestic labor flight primary topics of public policy debate and common knowledge among Americans? Arguing conspiracies and the co-optation of the press is at best an inadequate answer to this question. Although the flight of jobs and investments from the United States has been reported and discussed, the problem of economic decline is somehow viewed as much less important than welfare reform, reducing government, and punishing criminals. At least a part of this problem in public priorities is that understanding trends in the U.S. economy requires one to appreciate the wider international picture. This is not a simple task and the "average" American, if he or she doesn't fear or become befuddled by matters foreign, has little interest in taking the time to understand them. It is part of a long American tradition of avoiding foreign entanglements.

Gerald Horne (Chapter 5, this volume), however, provides some insights into other facets of the apparent lack of public interest, knowledge, and concern about these important issues. One legacy of the Cold War, he suggests, was to encourage in the public's mind a separation of domestic from foreign affairs. After World War II, organizations such as The Foreign Affairs Council and individuals such as Paul Robeson and W.E.B. Du Bois consistently called attention to the connection between domestic racism and the exploitative conduct of U.S. foreign affairs. At the beginning of the Cold War, radical individuals and organizations were quieted and discredited as "pro-Soviet" and unpatriotic, especially during the McCarthy Red Scarce in the early 1950s.

In the decades that followed, both labor and civil rights organizations, by and large, avoided criticism of U.S. overseas activities in order to maintain a united front against Communism in return for domestic concessions. Consequently, the public has had little encouragement to consider the importance of connections between domestic and foreign affairs. Abetting this neglect was the decline over the past half century of the ethnic presses (and language bases) that before World War II helped to keep international awareness high among large numbers of working-class and other Americans who spoke European languages.

CULTURAL RACISM

Given that an effective antiracist movement in the United States must attack cultural and institutional racism simultaneously, can one learn anything about cultural racism from this book? In the first edition, Rutledge Dennis (1981) described the psychological fallout from racist socialization, and Robert Terry (1981) outlined how racism distorts American values. Theirs still are important statements.

In this second edition, Walter Stafford (Chapter 6, this volume) has added another perspective. He looks directly at how race is addressed in intellectual and cultural efforts to shape world societies for the next century. Specifically, how will cultural leaders continue to reconstruct out of diverse European American cultural identities a unified "whiteness" and project it into the next century? This is a formidable task, given the increasing proportion of Americans whose ancestry will be Asian, Latin American, and African.

Stafford's review of postmodernist and postindustrialist thinking reveals that people of color are missing from these analyses, both as subjects of discussion and as discussants. Race and racism are left out, solved, forgotten, done away with, and are not even elements in historic memory. Eighty-six percent of the world's population and 20% of the U.S. population are missing! The only explanation for this must be that Third World thinkers (including "minority" Americans) are dismissed or simply ignored because of the failure of democratic government to take root in their nations, and/or the failure of their worlds to generate affluence. Western (white) thinkers are assumed to have and to provide all the conceptual forms of government and economy that will ever be needed.

In effect, Stafford outlines the present and future conceptual forms in which racism will be manifest. The notion of race and stratification by race (racism) will continue as a major "pretense" in order to continue the distortion of essential class conflicts among European Americans. European thinkers assume that the West will continue to dominate the world community through economic interrelationships. But this cannot be done by force as it commonly was in past centuries. It will require domination of two other institution as well: the media and communications.

Stafford outlines the relationship between racism and the imperative of continued domination. He maintains that the more a societal consensus, as with white racism, is based on perception (pretense) rather than on fact or reality, the greater is the need to create additional artificial truths and to shape the perceptions, thoughts, and images of people throughout the world. We can see this today in the United States when powerful media distortions take on lives and mythologies of their own: reverse discrimination, political correctness, liberal-conservative (left-right), racial color blindness, the war against drugs, or benign neglect.

These distortions of fundamental realities are then acted upon as if they were real. But, in fact, a good public relations distortion has only one reality, and that is in the minds of the publics who believe it. In the case of "reverse discrimination," it does not matter that virtually all of the evidence on racial discrimination points in just the opposite direction.

The tragedy is not only that the use of "pretense" is for manipulating public opinion and covering up the gains of special interests at the expense of the majority of Whites and others. It is also that it is the beyond-race Western theorists and apologists, and not the antiracist and Third World scholars, who, as described by Max Weber's "iron cage," lack real historic identities and suffer from limited imaginations. The keys to the "cage" will be found in the subcultures of resistance to past eras that attempt to re-create rather than obscure community. The most successful resistance communities are fragmented, distant, and mentally inaccessible to media distortions.

The keys to open the "iron cage" exist among people of color and European Americans who have reached what the white racial identity theorist Helms describes as Autonomy in their sense of racial identity. They are no longer compelled by the pretenses of "white" racial unity and of racial superiority.

ATTEMPTS TO ADDRESS WHITE RACISM

Much of this book is based on psychological and historic evidence, but great insight into white racism and its effect on Whites comes from practice, from those who conduct human resource workshops and training. Lillian Roybal Rose is one practitioner in this field who brings from her experience insights into white racism. Octave Baker (Chapter 7, this volume) does, too. He provides a brief history of management training efforts that began in response to affirmative action and, over the years, have evolved into diversity training. The motivation for companies to pay good money for such training is not simply to reduce racial conflict in the workplace and to avoid law suits. Demographic changes strongly suggest that in coming years employers will have to rely increasingly upon a racially and culturally diverse workforce. They will have to hire and promote more women and minorities, not because of affirmative action, but because workers marginalized in the past will, in the next century, constitute higher percentages of the workforce in the United States; and larger proportions of American consumers will be women and minorities. There also is growing evidence that heterogeneous work groups are more creative in decision making and problem solving by virtue of the variety of perspectives they bring to the table.

John Fernandez's (Chapter 8, this volume) records of the comments of people who participated in his training seminars provide important on-site insights into how institutional racism is carried out in workplaces. "Neo-racist" discrimination is never direct or overt: Criteria for promotion and other acknowledgments are set in legally defensible and public processes; but they also are subjective enough and flexible enough to be manipulated by those in power in order to favor whomever they want and whatever decision they want. Examples of this are using "old boys" networks to promote inside candidates, limiting information about openings and decisions, writing job specifications around specifically favored individuals, and using seniority as a basis for promotion and lay-offs with no regard for the discrimination that kept minorities and women from accumulating seniority in the first place.

Fernandez notes that white men in lower organizational positions, who previously would have been automatically advanced, now feel that they are being discriminated against because they have to "compete" with women and minorities. Any instance where they fail to compete successfully is viewed by them as a case where a woman or a minority candidate's only advantage is special preference. The bottom line is that white men now have to compete (metaphorically) with 100 people instead of 33. What this means is that white men with average to below average ability now are having difficulty advancing against a larger number of people with superior credentials and abilities. And they resent it and the system of "preference" they believe to be its cause.

Robert Terry (Chapter 9, this volume) reports that, in his training groups, the reality of competition for Whites now is so immediate that focusing solely on white racism is too alienating. An advantage of diversity training is that it avoids the assumption that all oppressed people are alike and so cannot learn from one another. In order to cut through the emotions and defensiveness, Terry uses metaphors to help individuals in his groups identify issues and begin to make connections among them. In order to cut through racial "pretenses" and other distortions, Terry finds it necessary to get individuals and groups to process particular metaphors about meaning, mission, power, structure, resources, existence, and fulfillment. This depersonalizes the issue of racism and provides a process where "it is easier and safer to personalize and own white racism in one's self as a white person."

Terry agrees with Roybal Rose's point that European Americans can accept people of color only after they know who they are themselves and have honestly sorted out their own feelings and beliefs. Helm's Autonomy level of white racial identity, outlined by Jones and Carter, is what Roybal Rose is working toward, and it is what Terry regards as the basis of the personal authenticity that is crucial to a higher quality of life, regardless of one's material resources.

Finally, Crowfoot and Chesler (Chapter 10, this volume) go straight to the most resistant group of all those that trainers encounter: white men. They explore links between males' beliefs in paternity and dispositions toward racism and sexism. In the male role they find an implicit "license" to exploit and take advantage of what are thought to be weaknesses in others that cut across race, gender, and class. Coming to terms with this historically conditioned license to exploit is a particular challenge for white men, especially as the opportunities to exploit and to exercise automatic privilege over others diminish—as they must in the coming years—for the majority of White men.

Crowfoot and Chesler remind us that many of the reasons why working-class and poor white men resist efforts to up-lift Blacks and others has genuine merit. It was the schools, the housing, and the jobs that working- and lower-class Whites have traditionally enjoyed and considered their own that elite and liberal Whites have attempted to integrate. Virtually the entire physical burden of improving race relations has fallen on less privileged Whites. Upper- and upper-middle-class Whites have gotten away with token concessions.

Crowfoot and Chesler invite others, and not only social and behavioral scientists, to explore the different meanings of maleness for white men of different classes and the different social constructions of "whiteness" for European Americans of different ethnic backgrounds and classes. For very practical reasons—personal safety and survival, political stability, moral integrity, and mutual gain—most white men eventually are going to have to work with women and people of color as peers. Crowfoot and Chesler regard this as essentially a problem of coalition building that focuses on the potential contributions of white men, not only to social movements, but to improve workplace morale as well.

They list taken-for-granted and dysfunctional behaviors associated with white male's privileged status that raise conflict in groups. These are important points of reference because they provide white men with opportunities to see themselves as others experience them. Such an uncomplimentary image provides some men for the first time with an opportunity to see and address behaviors that not only make life miserable for others, but for themselves as well. This is new ground that advances the work of McIntosh (1995), who was one of the first to outline the features of everyday, taken-for-granted white privilege.

A LOOK AHEAD AND SOME RECOMMENDATIONS

In the first edition of *Impacts* we set out a series of social policy recommendations. Among other things, they were premised on a belief that any serious attempt to negate racism and reduce its impacts on Whites, and certainly on people of color, will require governments to pay closer attention to the long-term implications of corporate investment policies and practices, to limit the power and influence of special interests, and to define and more aggressively protect "the common good." In the past 15 years, however, the trend has been toward dismantling and restricting government rather than trying to make it more effective. Meanwhile, the negative effects of racism continue to erode the quality of life and the well-being of both Whites and people of color.

Many conservatives argue that our premise is dead wrong, that it is precisely because of "big" government that life in the United States has been degraded. Our response is that the "pretense" of this perspective becomes obvious when one considers how much larger is the size, scale, and centrality of all the private sector business organizations, especially corporations, in comparison with government. It is in the private sector where the majority of Americans are employed (and unemployed), where single corporations are larger in wealth and influence than most Western governments, and where investment decisions can make and break cities and states—to say nothing of political careers. National and international economic trends are made in corporate boardrooms, not in legislatures. It has gradually become the "subsidiary" role of government to react supportively to any private sector initiative and to accept responsibility for the social fallout of boardroom decisions with social services and law enforcement.

It is not pretense but an essential point of reality that only the top 1% of Americans have gained financially in recent years; and everyone, including the top 1%, has experienced a continued loss of personal security and optimism; heightened anxieties; and increasing alienation from society, government, and work along with a general decline in civility and public regard for one another. As a nation, we are going in the wrong direction, and there are no present indicators that a continued dismantling of government will reverse the negative trends.

The contributors to this second edition of *Impacts* have added much to our first edition list of "things that must be done" (see Bowser & Hunt, 1981, chap. 12). We offer such a list for directional guidance in the hope that we as a nation will realize how fundamental the perpetuation of racism is to the current national malaise, and that we will begin the hard work of up-rooting racism, institutionally and culturally, so that there can be a better future for us all.

For those accepting this challenge, some of the major points to be remembered from this second edition follow:

1. Psychological evidence regarding "white" racial identity indicates that the recognition of race and racial differences are essential to advancing personal identity and tolerance. To ignore race and to act as if one is color blind retards rather than advances personal growth (see Jones & Carter [Chapter 1], Roybal Rose [Chapter 2], and Terry [Chapter 9]).

2. The most progress in eliminating individual (personal) racism can be made by exposing its reinforcement by and support from covert institutional practices and cultural stereotyping in politics and the media (see Jones & Carter [Chapter 1], Kushnick [Chapter 3], Fernandez [Chapter 8], Terry [Chapter 9], and Crowfoot & Chesler [Chapter 10]).

3. The historic American "pretense" of white racial unity should not be confused with European ethnic identities. Pride, acceptance, and knowledge of one's European background are essential in order to be personally rooted in history rather than in pretense (see Stafford [Chapter 6], Roybal Rose [Chapter 2], and Terry [Chapter 9]). Pride in Italian ancestry, for example, does not require one to take pride in Columbus's "discovery" of America and then to feel a necessity to defend or ignore the subsequent genocide of Native American peoples and cultures. Italian ancestry is the real identity and Columbus's "discovery" is the pretense.

4. For European Americans, a continued belief in "white" racial supremacy (racism) requires internalization of oppression. In order to maintain the pretense, despite experiences and evidence to the contrary, it is necessary to distort reality, negate personal and group authenticity, and ultimately negate human growth. Some of these distortions are expressed in reverse discrimination against all Whites as a class of workers; in the idea that pain and oppression build character; in the belief that others' experiences somehow are always more important than one's own; and in thinking that there is a hierarchy of oppressions, that "my group is more oppressed than your group" (see Roybal Rose, Chapter 2).

5. Strategies must be sought to deracialize politics so that European Americans can face and then address conflicting economic class interests. Racism stands as a barrier to public recognition of the need for consideration of the

"common good" as a factor in economic decision making rather than simply for the profit of a few (see Kushnick [Chapter 3] and Horne [Chapter 5]).

6. Strategies must be sought to make the globalization of capital socially responsible. The manipulation of governments and impoverishment of the vast majority of people in both the metropolitan First Worlds and the Third Worlds is not in the long-term interests of either the business community or the general public, whether here or abroad (Kushnick [Chapter 3] and Mason [Chapter 4]).

7. It is necessary now for European Americans and people of color to come together in a common coalition in order to get economic concessions from globalizing American capital (Kushnick [Chapter 3], Mason [Chapter 4], and Horne [Chapter 5]).

8. Control of the state, through government immobilization, reduction in size, or by default (i.e., majority voter alienation) needs to be recognized as basic to continued state support of private sector disinvestment at home and reinvestment abroad (Kushnick [Chapter 3] and Horne [Chapter 5]).

9. The long-term implication of continued white racism is continued impoverishment for European Americans as well as African, Hispanic, and Native Americans. The only long-term advantage Whites will enjoy is that of not being quite as poor as people of color. To retain or improve one's standard of living in the long run will require negating covert racism and its distorting effects: having a level playing field where talent can rise regardless of race, gender, and social class (Kushnick, Chapter 3).

10. Given the absolute importance of employment to participation in society and to having a stake in its future, employment paying a living wage sufficient for quality food, shelter, clothing, and medical care needs to be recognized as a human right (Mason, Chapter 4).

11. One way to encourage domestic economic expansion and job production is to expand opportunities for self-employment by democratizing access to credit and financial resources (Mason, Chapter 4).

12. American businesses may find that they can keep jobs in the United States, be more efficient and productive, compete globally, and generate reasonable profits if they substitute elite hierarchical management with worker participation in workplace decision making (Mason, Chapter 4).

13. It is in the interest of all Americans to have greater international knowledge, exposure, and literacy as well as domestic multicultural education and exposure to cultures so that Americans can have a better sense of what is in the nation's national interest. In the absence of interested and knowledgeable publics, special interests define the national interest as their own and to the detriment of the majority (Horne, Chapter 5).

14. The most competitive companies in a nation with such cultural diversity as the United States will recruit and retain talented employees from a diverse labor pool; will create a climate that allows everyone to contribute to his or

her maximum potential; and will use their diverse workforce to take advantage of diversity in the marketplace (Baker, Chapter 7).

15. "White" men need to be told the truth about their own and other's job performance and opportunities. Despite their continued racial advantages, many are now having to compete for the first time against an expanded and diverse pool of talent. The average-to-poor performers need to know that they are average or poor performers and that this and not their race or affirmative action is the reason they are not being advanced (Fernandez [Chapter 8] and Stafford [Chapter 6]).

16. Training groups can help white Americans deal with racism. If groups can first depersonalize the issue of racism by examining generic principles, such as up/down relationships that we all have experienced, it is easier and safer to personalize and "own" white racism in one's self as a white person and to communicate with others about it.

17. In a diverse society, all groups, but particularly white men, can learn to define and then work toward a common good by building coalitions. All of us need to value our differences and value "connectedness with others" and perceive it as a social good that is the basis of community, rather than fragmentation and competition with sloped playing fields (Crowfoot & Chesler, Chapter 10).

18. In a diverse society, the public interests must be defined collectively and inclusively (Stafford, Chapter 6).

19. Men have a particular challenge to take responsibility for finding ways of contributing to community without controlling, oppressing, and competing (Crowfoot & Chesler, Chapter 10).

20. Decisions made through consensus will have greater value for the common good than decisions made in hierarchies where self-interest is the highest good (Crowfoot & Chesler, Chapter 10).

Into the Next Century

Americans, as we have said, stand at a crossroad in their nation's history. Much is at stake in the decisions that will be made and the directions taken in the coming years. The decline of affluence during the past two decades is slowly straining the pretense of American generosity and openness to each other and to the less fortunate. The nation is undergoing a trial of character. The approximately 20% of European Americans whose personal identity is constructed around racial supremacy fear the future, may wish to return to the past, and are intent on trying to convince the majority of their fellow "white" Americans that their problems are due to the poor, minorities, and the federal government.

"Conservatives" are succeeding in these efforts and, if they continue to succeed, the outcome is not likely to be simply a rolling back of the progress made over the past half century. Rather, it will prove necessary to move toward progressively more extreme measures with what Bertram Gross referred to as "friendly fascism" as a possible end point.

Why? Because putting the unemployed (the poor) on the streets to beg, doing away with affirmative action, and destroying the capacity of the federal government to serve "the common good" will not succeed in securing or producing American jobs. Nor will it limit the minority presence, rebuild community, produce happiness, make us secure from crime, reinvigorate "family values," or bring back the 1950s. Instead, our material and social conditions will continue to deteriorate; and that, in turn, will prompt calls for increasingly desperate measures and increasingly outrageous pretense, not at all unlike the progression toward fascism in Germany after World War I (Fritzsche, 1990). Why? Because the major institutions of society that will be shaping the American future are not being addressed or challenged, and so will continue to operate for the profit of a few, but with even less encumbrance from government or an informed citizenry.

The reactionary conservatism that now is trying to reshape government is, in a way, a desperate last-ditch effort to maintain the pretense and re-create the old days of unchallenged "white" domination. This reactionary agenda can only continue to shape government as long as a majority of Americans are alienated from the "system" and fail to vote. The last three presidents and most of the current senators and representatives were elected by distinctly less than a majority of the potential electorate (Chen, 1992). Hence, their incumbencies and powers can hardly be taken to represent a citizens' mandate for the public policy directions in which they are seeking to move the nation.

These themes and the contents of this book are not simply a variety of liberal posturing against conservatism. Nor is it intended to encourage an ideological struggle between American liberals and conservatives. Liberal government leaders were, in many cases, heading in essentially the same directions as those of the current Congress. It is our view that, on the whole, *neither* liberals nor conservatives today are leading us toward working together for a "common good" or to fulfill the promises that the American nation has to offer.

Conservatives will no doubt quickly dismiss this work because it is inconsistent with their views. Liberals will find the emphasis on Whites disturbing, and maybe too close to home. For their part, Marxists will applaud the inclusion of class as an analytic lever, but will be disappointed that Marxism is neither the basis of that analysis nor its concluding message.

Racial nationalists will decry the focus on Whites and the presumption that Whites can become nonracist. Empiricists will point out that much of what is advanced here has not been rigorously (statistically) demonstrated. In fact, ideologists of all persuasions probably will have difficulty with this book. It has not been our aim to satisfy any of them.

The approximately 20% of "white" Americans who are antiracist and who cannot be distracted or deterred by racist pretenses need now to come together with one another and with other antiracists to provide real, pragmatic alternatives to reactionary conservatism or ineffective liberalism. We hold to an optimistic belief (even if we do not always sound that way) that the majority of Americans may be confused about who they are and may continue to be manipulated by pretenses of racial unity and superiority, but, in fact, have no inner and compelling personal reason to affirm racism.

They would welcome a humane alternative that would bring us together as a nation in new communities with a future based in perceptions of a "common good" rather than the advantages or profits of a few. No impersonal social dynamics or natural laws will decide for us the direction we must take and what personal actions are required to motivate white Americans to negate racism and its short-term benefits. No one group has *the* answer.

The key to unlocking the "iron cage" that has held captive the real potential contribution of the United States to the world community and to history lies in authentic, culturally diverse Americans coming together and defining themselves as genuinely open communities and as a nation organized for their common interest.

References

ABC News/ *Washington Post* survey, February 20, 1991.

Acorn, D. A., Hamilton, D. L., & Sherman, S. J. (1988). Generalization of biased perception of groups based on illusory correlations. *Social Cognition, 6,* 345-372.

Acuna, R. (1981). *Occupied America: A history of Chicanos* (2nd ed.). New York: Harper & Row.

Adam, I., & Tiffin, H. (Eds.). (1991). *Past the last post.* Calgary: University of Calgary Press.

African American Leadership Summit. (1991). *On the Gulf War.* New York: Abyssinian Baptist Church.

Alderfer, C. (1982). Problems of changing white males' behavior and beliefs concerning race relations. In P. Goodman (Ed.), *Change in organizations* (pp. 122-165). San Francisco: Jossey-Bass.

Allen, T. (1975). They would have destroyed me: Slavery and the origins of racism. *Radical America, 9*(3), 41-63.

Allen, T. (1994). *The invention of the white race.* London: Verso.

Almond, G. (1951). *The American people and foreign policy.*

Alperin, D. (1990). Social diversity and the necessity of alliances: Developing a feminist perspective. In L. Albrecht & R. Bewer (Eds.), *Bridges of power.* Philadelphia: New Society Publishers.

264

American Management Association. (1993). *1993 AMA survey on managing cultural diversity*. New York: Author.

Amin, S. (1992). *Empire of chaos*. New York: Monthly Review Press.

Ani, M. (1994). *Yurugu: An African-centered critique of European cultural thought and behavior*. Trenton, NJ: Africa World Press.

Ansprenger, F. (1989). *The dissolution of the colonial empires*. New York: Routledge & Kegan Paul.

Anzaldua, G. (1990). Bridge, drawbridge, sandbar, or island. In L. Albrecht & R. Brewer (Eds.), *Bridges of power* (pp. 216-233). Philadelphia: New Society Publishers.

Apostle, R. A., et al. (1983). *The anatomy of racial attitudes*. Berkeley: University of California Press.

Appiah, K. (1992). *In my father's house*. New York: Oxford University Press.

Aptheker, H. (1963). *American Negro slave revolts*. New York: International Publishers.

Aptheker, H. (1987). Anti-racism in the U.S.: An introduction. *Sage Race Relations Abstracts, 12*(4), 3-32.

Aptheker, H. (1992). *Anti-racism in U.S. history: The first two hundred years*. Westport, CT: Praeger.

Arrow, K. (1972). Some mathematical models of race discrimination in the labor market. In A. Pascal (Ed.), *Racial discrimination in economic life* (pp. 187-203). Lexington, MA: Lexington Books.

Ashmore, R. D. (1976). Black and white in the 1970s. *Journal of Social Issues, 32*, 1-9.

Audirac, I., & Sgernyen, A. (1994). An evaluation of neo-traditional design's social prescription: Postmodern placebo or remedy for suburban malaise? *Journal of Planning, Education and Research, 13*, 161-174.

Bailey, R. (1990). The slavery trade and the development of capitalism in the United States: The textile industry in New England. *Social Science History, 14*(3), 373-414.

Baldwin, J. (1963). *The fire next time*. New York: Dell.

Banks, J. A. (1988). The stages of ethnicity: Implications for curriculum reform. In *Multiethnic education: Theory and practice* (2nd ed.) (pp. 193-202). Boston: Allyn & Bacon.

Barndt, J. (1972). *Liberating our white ghetto*. Minneapolis, MN: Augsburg Press.

Baron, H. (1976). *The demand for black labor*. Cambridge, MA: New England Press.

Baron, H. (1985). Racism transformed: The implications of the 1960s. *Review of Radical Political Economics, 17*, 10-33.

Barrett, W. (1979). *The illusion of technique*. Garden City, NY: Doubleday.

Bates, C. (1991). *Pigs eat wolves*. St. Paul, MN: Yes International Publishing.

Becker, G. S. (1957). *The economics of discrimination*. Chicago: University of Chicago Press.

Becker, G. S. (1971). *The economics of discrimination*. Chicago: University of Chicago Press.

Bell, D. (1976). *The coming crisis of postindustrial capitalism*. New York: Basic Books.

Bell, D. (1978). *The cultural contradictions of capitalism*. New York: Basic Books.

Bell, D. (1992). *Race, racism, and American law* (3rd ed.). Boston: Little, Brown.

Bennett, L. (1971, October). White hopes and other coalitions. *Ebony*, pp. 33-42.

Bennett, M. J. (1986). A developmental approach to training intercultural sensitivity. *The International Journal of Intercultural Relations, 10*(2).

Berlin, I. (1975). *Slaves without masters: The free Negro in the antebellum South*. New York: Pantheon.

Berman, M. (1982). *All that is solid melts into air*. New York: Simon & Schuster.

Bernstein, R. (1992). *The new constellation*. Cambridge: MIT Press.

Bhabba, H. (1992). Postcolonial authority and postmodern guilt. In L. Grossberg (Ed.), *Cultural studies*. New York: Routledge.

Blackett, R. J. (1983). *Building an antislavery wall: Black Americans in the Atlantic Abolitionist Movement.* New York: Cornell University Press.

Blalock, H. M., Jr. (1967). *Toward a theory of minority group relations.* New York: John Wiley.

Blauner, B. (1989). *Black lives, white lives: Three decades of race relations in America.* Berkeley: University of California Press.

Blauner, P. (1972). *Racial oppression in American.* New York: Harper & Row.

Block, C. J., Roberson, L., & Neuger, D. (1995). White racial identity theory: A framework for understanding reactions toward interracial situations on organizations. *Journal of Vocational Behavior, 46,* 71-88.

Block, F. (1990). *Postindustrial possibilities.* Berkeley: University of California Press.

Bloom, A. (1987). *The closing of the American mind.* New York: Simon & Schuster.

Bluestone, B. (1983). Deindustrialization and unemployment in America. *Review of Black Political Economy, 12*(3), 27-42.

Bobo, L., & Kluegel, J. (1993). Opposition to race targeting: Self-interest, stratification ideology, or racial attitudes. *American Sociological Review, 58*(4), 443-463.

Bolick, C., & Nestleroth, S. (1989). *Opportunity 2000: Creative affirmative action strategies for a changing workforce.* Indianapolis, IN: The Hudson Institute.

Bolton, C. C. (1994). *Poor whites of the ante-bellum South: Tenants and laborers in central North Carolina and northeast Mississippi.* Durham, NC: Duke University Press.

Bonacich, E., & Goodman, R. (1972). *Deadlock in school desegregation: A case study of Inglewood, California.* New York: Praeger.

Boorstin, D. J. (1965). *The Americans: The national experience.* New York: Vintage.

Boston, T. (1988). *Race, class, and conservatism.* Boston: Unwin Hyman.

Botwinick, H. (1993). *Persistent inequalities: Wage disparity under capitalist competition.* Princeton, NJ: Princeton University Press.

Bowles, S., Gordon, D., & Gintis, H. (1984). *Beyond the waste land.* Garden City, NY: Anchor Books.

Bowser, B. P. (1987). Race and U.S. foreign policy. *Sage Race Relations Abstracts, 12,* 1, 4-20.

Bowser, B. P., & Hunt, R. G. (Eds.). (1981). *Impacts of racism on white Americans.* Beverly Hills, CA: Sage.

Bowser, B. P., Hunt, R. G., & Pohl, D. C. (1981). Introduction. In B. P. Bowser & R. G. Hunt (Eds.), *Impacts of racism on white Americans* (1st ed.) (pp. 13-26). Beverly Hills, CA: Sage.

Braddock, H., & McPartland, J. M. (1987). How minorities continue to be excluded from equal employment opportunities: Research on labor market and institutional barriers. *Journal of Social Issues, 43*(1), 5-39.

Braverman, H. (1974). *Labor and monopoly capital.* New York: Monthly Review Press.

Braxton, T., & Prichard, K. (1977). The power erosion syndrome of the black principal. *Integrated Education, 15,* 9-14.

Brimmer, A. (1985). Black directors in the corporate boardroom. *Black Enterprise, 16*(5), 41.

Bryant, B., & Crowfoot, J. (n.d.). *Issues raised by affirmative action in an innovative organization.* Ann Arbor: University of Michigan, School of Natural Resources.

Bullock, P. (1966). *Equal opportunity in employment.* Los Angeles: UCLA, Institute of Industrial Relations.

Bulow, J., & Summers, L. (1986). A theory of dual labor markets with applications to industrial policy, discrimination, and Keynesian unemployment. *Journal of Labor Economics, 4*(3), 376-414.

Bunch, C. (1990). Making common cause: Diversity and coalitions. In L. Albrecht & R. Brewer (Eds.), *Bridges of power.* Philadelphia: New Society Publishers.

Burgess, B. (1978). *Good things can happen in your community: Your community organization and school desegregation.* Cleveland, OH: Federation For Community Planning.

Burkhalter, H. (1992). Moving human rights to center stage. *World Policy Journal, 1X*(3), 417-429.

Burman, S. (1979). The illusion of progress: Race and politics in Atlanta, Georgia. *Ethnic and Racial Studies, 2*(4), 441-454.

Cain, G. (1986). The economic analysis of labor market discrimination: A survey. In O. Ashenfelter & R. Layard (Eds.), *Handbook of labor economics* (pp. 693-785). Amsterdam: North Holland Press.

Campbell, A. (1971). *White attitudes toward black people.* Ann Arbor: University of Michigan.

Carmichael, S., & Hamilton, C. (1967). *Black power.* New York: Vintage.

Carter, R. T. (1990). The relationship between racism and racial identity among white Americans: An exploratory investigation. *Journal of Counseling and Development, 69,* 46-50.

Carter, R. T. (1995). *The influence of race and racial identity in psychotherapy: Toward a racially inclusive model.* New York: John Wiley.

Carter, R. T. (in press). Exploring the complexity of racial identity measures. In G. R. Sodowsky & J. Impara (Eds.), *Multicultural assessment.* Lincoln, NE: Buros Institute of Mental Measurement.

Carter, R. T., & Goodwin, A. L. (1994). Racial identity and education. In L. Darling-Hammond (Ed.), *Review of research in education* (Vol. 20, pp. 291-335). Washington, DC: American Educational Research Association.

Carter, R. T., & Helms, J. E. (1990). White racial identity attitudes and cultural values. In J. E. Helms (Ed.), *Black and white racial identity: Theory, research, and practice* (pp. 105-118). Westport, CT: Greenwood.

Carter, R. T., & Helms, J. E. (1992). The counseling process as defined by relationship types: A test of Helms' interactional model. *Journal of Multicultural Counseling and Development, 20,* 181-201.

Cecil-Fronsman, B. (1992). *Common whites: Class and culture in antebellum North Carolina.* Lexington: University Press of Kentucky.

Chatterjee, P. (1993). *The nation and its fragments.* Princeton, NJ: Princeton University Press.

Chen, K. (1992). *Political alienation and voter turnout in the United States, 1960-88.* San Francisco: Mellon University Press.

Chesler, M., & Delgado, H. (1987). Race relations training and organizational change. In J. W. Shaw, P. G. Nordlie, & R. M. Shapiro (Eds.), *Strategies for improving race relations* (pp. 182-203). Wolfsboro, NH: Manchester University Press.

Chesler, M. A. (1981). Creating and maintaining interracial coalitions. In B. P. Bowser & R. G. Hunt (Eds.), *Impacts of racism on white Americans* (1st ed., pp. 217-244). Beverly Hills, CA: Sage.

Chin, J. (1985). Divergent trends in white racial attitudes toward blacks. *International Journal of Sociology and Social Policy, 6*(1), 25-38.

Clancy, D., & Parker, W. M. (1988). Assessing white racial consciousness and perceived comfort with black individuals: A preliminary study. *Journal of Counseling and Development, 67,* 449-451.

Clark, N. (1981). *Racism and sexism in corporate life.* Lexington, MA: D. C. Heath.

Coffey, J. F. (1987). Race training in the United States. In J. W. Shaw, P. G. Nordlie, & R. M. Shapiro (Eds.), *Strategies for improving race relations* (pp. 114-130). Wolfsboro, NH: Manchester University Press.

Cohen, J., & Arato, A. (1994). *Civil society and political theory.* Cambridge: MIT Press.

Comer, J. P. (1972). *Beyond black and white.* New York: Quadrangle.

Committee on Banking, Housing, and Urban Affairs. (1993). *1991 Congressional Budget Office, displaced workers: Trends in the 1980s and implications for the future.* Washington, DC: Congressional Budget Office.

Condran, J. (1979). Changes in white attitudes toward Blacks: 1963-1977. *The Public Opinion Quarterly, 43*(4), 463-476.

Congressional Budget Office. (1993). *Displaced workers: Trends in the 1980s and implications for the future.* Washington: Author.

Connelly, M., & Kennedy, P. (1994). Must it be the rest against the West? *The Atlantic Monthly.*

Corbett, M. M., Helms, J. E., & Regan, A. M. (1992, August). *A measure of Helms's Immersion-Emersion stage of white racial identity development.* Paper presented at the 100th convention of the American Psychological Association, Washington, D.C.

Cornacchia, E. J., & Nelson, D. C. (1992). Historical differences in the political experiences of American blacks and white ethnics: Revisiting an unresolved controversy. *Ethnic and Racial Studies, 15*(1), 102-124.

Corzine, J., et al. (1988). The tenant labor market and lynching in the South: A test of the split market theory. *Sociological Inquiry, 58*(3), 261-268.

Coser, L., & Howe, I. (Eds.). (1976). *The new conservatives: A critique from the left.* New York: New American Library.

Cox, O. E. (1948). *Caste, class, and race.* New York: Monthly Review Press.

Cox, T. (1991). The multicultural organization. *Academy of Management Executive, 5*(2), 34-47.

Cox, T. (1993). *Cultural diversity in organizations: Theory, research, and practice.* San Francisco: Berret-Kohler.

Cox, T. H., & Blake, S. (1991). Managing cultural diversity: Implications for organizational competitiveness. *Academy of Management Executive, 5,* 45-54.

Craig, C., Rubery, J., Tarling, R., & Wilkinson, F. (1985). Economic, social, and political factors in the operation of the labour. In B. Roberts, R. Finnegan, & D. Gallie (Eds.), *New approaches to economic life, economic restructuring: Unemployment and the social division of labour* (pp. 105-123). Manchester, UK: Manchester University Press.

Crain, R. (1968). *The politics of school desegregation.* Chicago: Aldine.

Crapol, E. (Ed.). (1992). *Women and American foreign policy: Lobbyists, critics, and insiders.* Wilmington, DE: SR Books.

Crosby, J., Bromley, S., & Saye, L. (1980). Recent unobtrusive studies of black and white discrimination and prejudice: A literature review. *Psychological Bulletin, 87,* 546-563.

Crowfoot, J. (1981, March-April). Accommodating growth in democratically managed organizations. *Moving Food: A Trade Journal of the Cooperating Food Distribution System,* pp. 40-43.

Crowfoot, J., & Wondelleck, J. (1990). *Environmental disputes.* Washington, DC: Island Press.

Cruse, H. (1988). *Plural but equal: A critical study of blacks and minorities and America's plural society.* New York: William Morrow.

Cummings, S. (1980). White ethnics, racial prejudice, and labor market segmentation. *American Journal of Sociology, 85*(4), 938-950.

Danzig, D. (1966, September). In defense of black power. *Commentary,* pp. 41-46.

Danziger, S., Gottschalk, P., & Smolensky, E. (1989). How the rich have fared, 1973-1987. *The American Economic Review, 79*(2), 310-314.

Darity, W., Jr. (1983). Reaganomics and the black community. In S. Weintraub & M. Goodstein (Eds.), *Reaganomics in the stagflation economy* (pp. 59-77). Philadelphia: University of Pennsylvania Press.

Darity, W., Jr. (1989). What's left of the theory of discrimination. In S. Shulman & W. Darity (Eds.), *The question of discrimination: Racial inequality in the U.S. labor market* (pp. 335-374). Middletown, CT: Wesleyan University Press.

Davis, L. E., & Huttenback, R. A. (1986). *Mammon and the pursuit of empire: The political economy of British imperialism, 1860-1912.* Cambridge, UK: Cambridge University Press.

Davis, M. (1986). *Prisoners of the American dream.* London: Verso.

De Conde, A. (1978). *A history of American foreign policy* (3rd ed.). New York: Scribner.

de Tocqueville, A. (1969). *Democracy in America* (J. P. Mayer, Ed.). Garden City, NY: Doubleday.

DeFleur, M. L., & Westie, F. R. (1958). Verbal attitudes and overt acts: An experiment on the salience of attitude. *American Sociological Review, 23,* 667-673.

Degler, C. (1974). *The other South: Southern dissenters in the nineteenth century.* New York: Harper & Row.

Dembo, D., & Morehouse, W. (1994). *The underbelly of the U.S. economy: Joblessness and the pauperization of work in America.* Council on International and Public Affairs. New York: Apex Press.

Dennis, R. M. (1981). Socialization and racism. In B. P. Bowser & R. G. Hunt (Eds.), *Impacts of racism on white Americans* (1st ed.) (pp. 71-85). Beverly Hills, CA: Sage.

Devine, P. G. (1989). Stereotypes and prejudice: Their automatic and controlled components. *Journal of Personality and Social Psychology, 56,* 5-18.

Devine, P. G., Monteith, M. J., Zuwerink, J. R., & Elliot, A. J. (1991). Prejudice with and without compunction. *Journal of Personality and Social Psychology, 60,* 817-830.

di Leonardo, M. (1996, Winter). White ethnicities, identity politics, and baby bear's chair. *Social Text, 41,* 165-191.

Dillon, M. (1990). *Slavery attacked: Southern slaves and their allies, 1619-1865.* Baton Rouge: Louisiana State University Press.

Donohue, J., & Heckman, J. (1992). Continuous versus episodic change: The impact of civil rights policy on the economic status of blacks. *Journal of Economic Literature, 29*(4), 1603-1643.

Dovidio, J. F., Evans, N. E., & Tyler, R. B. (1986). Racial stereotypes: The contents of their cognitive representations. *Journal of Experimental Social Psychology, 22,* 22-37.

Dovidio, J. F., & Gaertner, S. L. (1986). Prejudice, discrimination, and racism: Historical trends and contemporary approaches. In J. P. Dovidio & S. L. Gaertner (Eds), *Prejudice, discrimination, and racism* (pp. 1-34). Orlando, FL: Academic Press.

Drinnon, R. (1980). *Facing west.* New York: Schocken.

Drucker, P. (1993). *Post-capitalist society.* New York: Harper Business.

Du Bois, W.E.B. (1903). *The souls of black folk.* New York: A. C. McClug.

Du Bois, W.E.B. (1966). *Black reconstruction in America.* London: Frank Cass.

Du Bois, W.E.B. (1969). *The souls of black folk.* New York: New American Library. [Original work published 1903]

Du Bois, W.E.B. (1973). *The suppression of the African slave trade to the United States of America, 1638-1870.* Millwood, NY: Kraus-Thomson.

Duster, T. (1993). The diversity of California at Berkeley. In B. Thompson & S. Tyagi (Eds.), *Beyond a dream deferred* (pp. 231-255). Minneapolis: University of Minnesota Press.

Edgar, D. (1981). Reagan's hidden agenda: Racism and the new American right. *Race and Class, 22*(3), 221-238.

Ehrlich, H. J. (1973). *The social psychology of prejudice: A systematic theoretical review and propositional inventory of the American social psychological study of prejudice.* New York: John Wiley.

Eisinger, P. K. (1976). *Patterns of interracial politics: Conflict and cooperation in the city.* New York: Academic Press.

Ellison, M. (1991). David Duke and the race for the governor's mansion. *Race and Class, 33*(2), 71-79.

Esposito, J. (1992). *The Islamic threat.* New York: Oxford University Press.

Essed, P. (1990). *Everyday racism: Reports from women of two cultures.* Claremont, CA: Hunter House.

Essed, P. (1991). *Understanding everyday racism: An interdisciplinary theory.* Newbury Park, CA: Sage.

Evans, S. (1979). *Personal politics: The roots of women's liberation in the civil rights' movement and the New Left.* New York: Vintage.

Fanon, F. (1963). *The wretched of the earth.* New York: Grove Weidenfeld.

Farley, R., & W. Frey. (1994). Changes in the segregation of whites from blacks during the 1980s: Small steps toward a more integrated society. *American Sociological Review, 51*(1), 23-45.

Feagin, J. (1991, February). The continuing significance of race: Anti-black discrimination in public places. *American Sociological Review, 56,* 101-116.

Feagin, J. (1992). Theory and research on racism [Review of the book *Understanding everyday racism: An interdisciplinary theory*]. *Contemporary Psychology, 37,* 9.

Feagin, J. R. (1987). Changing black Americans to fit a racist system. *Journal of Social Issues, 43*(1), 85-89.

Fernandez, J. (1981). *Racism and sexism in corporate life.* Lexington, MA: Lexington Books.

Fernandez, J. (1986). *Child care and corporate productivity: Resolving family and work conflicts.* Lexington, MA: Lexington Books.

Fernandez, J. (1987). *Survival in the corporate fishbowl: Making it into upper and middle management.* Lexington, MA: Lexington Books.

Fernandez, J. (1991). *Managing a diverse work force: Regaining the competitive edge.* Lexington, MA: Lexington Books.

Fernandez, J. (1993). *The diversity advantage: How American business can out-perform Japanese and European companies in the global marketplace.* New York: Lexington Books.

Flacks, R. (1971). *Youth and social change.* Chicago: Markham.

Foner, P. (1974). *Organized labor and the black worker, 1619-1973.* New York: Praeger.

Foster, J. (1974). Nineteenth-century towns: A class dimension. In M. W. Flinn & T. C. Smout (Eds.), *Essays in social history* (pp. 178-197). Oxford, UK: Clarendon.

Foucault, M. (1977). *Discipline & punish: The birth of the prison.* New York: Vintage Books.

Frankenberg, R. (1993). *White women, race matters—The social construction of whiteness.* Minneapolis: University of Minnesota Press.

Frankl, V. E. (1959). *Man's search for meaning.* New York: Washington Square Press.

Franklin, H. (1969). *American imperialism and the Philippine insurrection: Testimony taken from hearings on affairs in the Philippine Islands before the Senate Committee on the Philippines, 1902.* Boston: Little and Brown.

Fraser, N. (1989). *Unruly practices*. Minneapolis: University of Minnesota Press.

Fredrickson, G. M. (1981). *White supremacy: A comparative study of American and South African history*. New York: Oxford University Press.

Freire, P. (1970). *Pedagogy of the oppressed*. New York: Continuum.

Freuer, L. (1989). *Imperialism and the anti-imperialist mind*. New Brunswick, NJ: Transaction Publishers.

Friedman, S. (1984). Structure, process, and the labor market. In W. Darity, Jr. (Ed.), *Labor economics: Modern views* (pp. 175-218). Boston: Kluwer-Nijhoff.

Fritzsche, K. P. (1990). *Rehearsals for Fascism: Popularism and political mobilization in Weimar Germany*. New York: Oxford University Press.

Fryer, P. (1984). *Staying power*. London: Pluto.

Fukuyama, F. (1992). *The end of history and the last man*. New York: Free Press.

Fullerton, H. (1989, November). New labor force projections, spanning 1988-2000. *Monthly Labor Review*, pp. 6-74.

Gaither, D. J. (1994, March 8). The gender divide: Black women's gains in corporate America outstrip black men's. *Wall Street Journal*, pp. 1, 12.

Gay, P. (1969). *The enlightenment: An interpretation*. New York: Knopf.

Gelfand, D. E., & Lee, R. D. (Eds.). (1973). *Ethnic conflicts and power: A cross-national perspective*. New York: John Wiley.

Gerson, L. L. (1964). *The hyphenate in recent American politics and diplomacy*. Lawrence: University of Kansas Press.

Gibson, J. (1994). *Warriors dreams: Paramilitary culture in post-Vietnam America*. New York: Hill & Wang.

Giddens, A. (1990). *The consequences of modernity*. Stanford, CA: Stanford University Press.

Gilder, G. (1982). *Wealth and poverty*. New York: Bantam Books.

Gilroy, P. (1993). *The black Atlantic*. Cambridge, MA: Harvard University Press.

Ginthinji, M., & Perrings, C. (1993). Social and ecological sustainability in the use of biotic resources in sub-Saharan Africa. *Ambio, 22*(2-3), 110-116.

Gitlin, T. (1987). *The sixties: Years of rage, days of hope*. New York: Bantam Press.

Glazer, N. (1971). Blacks and white ethnics: The difference and the political difference it makes. *Social Problems, 18*, 444-461.

Glazer, N. (1975). *Affirmative discrimination: Ethnic inequality and public policy*. New York: Basic Books.

Goldfield, M. (1990). Class, race, and politics in the United States: White supremacy as the main explanation for the peculiarities of American politics from colonial times to the present. *Research in Political Economy, 12*, 83-127.

Goldsmith, W., & Blakely, E. (1992). *Separate societies: Poverty and inequality in U.S. cities*. Philadelphia: Temple University Press.

Gordon, D. (1990). Who bosses whom? The intensity of supervision and the discipline of labor. *American Economic Association Papers and Proceedings, 80*(2), 28-32.

Gordon, D., Edwards, R., & Reich, M. (1982). *Segmented work, divided workers: The historical transformation of labor in the United States*. New York: Cambridge University Press.

Grabb, E. G. (1980). Social class, authoritarianism, and racial contact: Recent trends. *Sociology and Social Research, 64*(2), 208-220.

Green, F. (1991a). The relationship of wages to the value of labour-power in Marx's labour market. *Cambridge Journal of Economics, 15*(2), 199-214.

Green, F. (1991b). The "reserve army": A survey of empirical applications. In P. Dunne (Ed.), *Quantitative Marxism* (pp. 123-140). Oxford, UK: Polity Press.

Grillo, T., & Wildman, S. M. (1991). Obscuring the importance of race: The implications of making comparisons between racism and sexism (or other -isms). *Duke Law Journal, 2,* 397-412.

Grint, K. (1991). *The sociology of work: An introduction.* Cambridge, UK: Polity Press.

Habermas, J. (1992). *The new conservatism.* Cambridge: MIT Press.

Hacker, A. (1992). *Two nations.* New York: Scribner-Macmillan.

Hadar, L. T (1993). What green peril. *Foreign Affairs, 72*(2), 62-72.

Hagan, K. (1991, November/December). Orchids in the attic. *MS.,* pp. 31-33.

Hagan, K. (Ed.). (1992). *Women respond to the men's movement.* San Francisco: Pandora.

Hall, S., & Jefferson, T. (Eds.). (1976). *Resistance through youth rituals: Youth subcultures in post-war Britain.* London: Macmillan.

Halsey, M. (1946). *Color blind.* New York: Simon & Schuster.

Hamilton, D., & Gifford, R. E. (1976). Illusory correlation or interpersonal perception: A cognitive basis of stereotypic judgments. *Journal of Experimental Social Psychology, 12,* 392-407.

Hamilton, D. L., Stroessner, S. J., & Driscoll, D. M. (1994). Social cognition and the study of stereotyping. In P. G. Devine, D. L. Hamilton, & T. M. Ostrom (Eds.), *Social cognition: Impact on social psychology* (pp. 291-321). San Diego, CA: Academic Press.

Hardiman, R., & Jackson, B. (1992). Racial identity development. *New Directions for Teaching and Learning, 52,* 21-37.

Harding, J., Prohansky, H., Kutner, B., & Chein, I. (Eds.). (1969). In G. Lindzey & E. Aronson (Eds.), *The handbook of social psychology* (Vol. 5, pp. 1-77). Reading, MA: Addison-Wesley.

Harvard School of Public Health. (1991). *Harvard study team report: Public health in Iraq after the Gulf War.* Cambridge, MA: Harvard University Press.

Harvey, D. (1990). *The condition of postmodernity.* Cambridge, UK: Blackwell.

Harvey, J. (1974). *The Abilene paradox: The management of agreement.* New York: AMA-COM, Organizational Dynamics.

Hechter, M. (1975). *Internal colonialism: The Celtic fringe in British national development, 1536-1966.* London: Routledge & Kegan Paul.

Heller, A. (1995). Where are we at home? *Thesis Eleven, 41,* 1-19.

Helms, J. E. (1984). Toward a theoretical explanation of the effects of race on counseling: A black/white interactional model. *The Counseling Psychologist, 12*(4), 153-165.

Helms, J. E. (Ed.). (1990). *Black and white racial identity: Theory, research, and practice.* New York: Greenwood.

Helms, J. E. (1992). *Race is a nice thing to have.* Topeka, KS: Content Communications.

Helms, J. E. (1994). Racial identity and "racial" constructs. In E. J. Tricket, R. Watts, & D. Birman (Eds.), *Human diversity* (pp. 285-311). San Francisco: Jossey-Bass.

Helms, J. E. (in press). Towards an approach for assessing racial identity. In G. R. Sodowsky & J. Impara (Eds.), *Multicultural assessment.* Lincoln, NE: Buros Institute of Mental Measurement.

Helms, J. E., & Carter, R. T. (1991). Relationships of white and black racial identity attitudes and demographic similarity to counselor preferences. *Journal of Counseling Psychology, 38*(4), 446-457.

Herman, E., & Chomsky, N. (1988). *Manufacturing consent.* New York: Pantheon.

Herring, M., & Forbes, J. (1994). The over-representation of a white minority: Detroit's at-large city council, 1961-1989. *Social Science Quarterly, 75*(2), 431-445.

Heywood, J. (1987). Wage discrimination and market structure. *Journal of Post-Keynesian Economics, 9*(4), 617-628.

Higham, J. (1955). *Strangers in the land: Patterns of American nativism, 1860-1925.* New Brunswick, NJ: Rutgers University Press.

Hirsch, A. (1983). *Making the second ghetto: Race and housing in Chicago.* New York: Cambridge University Press.

hooks, b. (1984). *Feminist theory: From margin to center.* Boston: South End.

hooks, b. (1990). *Yearning.* Boston: South End.

Horton, P. (1991). Testing the limits of class politics in postbellum Alabama: Agrarian radicalism in Lawrence County. *The Journal of Southern History, 57*(1), 63-84.

Hoult, T. F. (1975). *Social justice and its enemies.* New York: John Wiley.

Howard, G. (1993, September). Whites in multicultural education. *Phi Delta Kappan, 75,* 36-41.

Huberman, L. (1968). *Man's worldly goods.* New York: Monthly Review Press.

Huckfedt, R., & Kohfeld, C. W. (1989). *Race and the decline of class in American politics.* Urbana: University of Illinois Press.

Huddy, L., & Virtanen, S. (1995). Subgroup differentiation and subgroup bias among Latinos as a function of familiarity and positive distinctiveness. *Journal of Personality and Social Psychology, 68,* 97-108.

Hunt, A. (1988). *Haiti's influence on antebellum America: Slumbering volcano in the Caribbean.* Baton Rouge: Louisiana State University Press.

Huntington, S. (1993, Summer). The coming clash of civilizations. *Foreign Affairs,* pp. 22-49.

Jackins, H. (1978). *The human side of human beings* (2nd rev. ed.). Seattle: Rational Island Publishers.

Jackson, B., & Holvino, E. (1988). *Multicultural organizational development* (Working Paper #11). Ann Arbor, MI: Program on Conflict Management Alternatives.

Jackson, S., & Associates. (1992). *Diversity in the workplace: Human resource initiatives.* New York: Guilford.

Jamieson, D., & Mara, J. (1991). *Managing workforce 2000.* San Francisco: Jossey-Bass.

Jaynes, G. D., & Williams, R. M., Jr. (Eds.). (1989). *A common destiny: Blacks and American society.* Washington, DC: National Academy Press.

Jeffries, J., & Stanback, H. (1984). The employment and training policy for black America: Beyond placebo to progressive public policy. *The Review of Black Political Economy, 13*(1-2), 119-137.

Jensen, A. R. (1969). How much can we boost IQ and scholastic achievement? *Harvard Educational Review, 38,* 1-123.

Jensen, A. R. (1995). Psychological research and race differences. *American Psychologist, 50*(1), 41-42.

Jensen, A. R., & Johnson, F. W. (1994). Race and sex differences in head size and IQ. *Intelligence, 18,* 309-333.

Johnston, W., & Packer, A. (1987). *Workforce 2000: Executive summary.* Indianapolis, IN: The Hudson Institute.

Johnston, W. B., Packer, A., & Jaffee, M. P. (1987). *Workforce 2000.* Indianapolis, IN: The Hudson Institute.

Jones, E. (1986, May/June). Black managers: The dream deferred. *Harvard Business Review,* pp. 84-93.

Jones, J. M. (1972). *Prejudice and racism.* Reading, MA: Addison-Wesley.

Jones, J. M. (1981). The concept of racism and its changing reality. In B. P. Bowser & R. G. Hunt (Eds.), *Impacts of racism on white Americans* (1st ed.) (pp. 27-49). Newbury Park, CA: Sage.

Jones, J. M. (1992). Understanding the mental health consequences of race: Contributions of basic social psychological processes. In D. N. Ruble, P. R. Costanzo, & M. E. Oliveria (Eds.), *The social psychology of mental health: Basic mechanisms and applications* (pp. 199-239). New York: Guilford.

Kanter, R. (1977). *Men and women of the corporation.* New York: Basic Books.

Karlins, M., Coffman, T. L., & Walters, G. (1969). On the fading of social stereotypes: Studies in three generations of college students. *Journal of Personality and Social Psychology, 13,* 1-16.

Karp, J. B. (1981). The emotional impact and a model for changing racist attitudes. In B. P. Bowser & R. G. Hunt (Eds.), *Impacts of racism on white Americans* (1st ed., pp. 87-96). Beverly Hills, CA: Sage.

Katz, D., & Braly, K. (1933). Racial stereotypes in one hundred college students. *Journal of Abnormal and Social Psychology, 28,* 280-290.

Katz, I., & Hass, R. G. (1988). Racial ambivalence and American value conflict: Correlational and priming studies of dual cognitive structures. *Journal of Personality and Social Psychology, 55,* 893-905.

Katz, J. H. (1978). *White awareness: A handbook for anti-racism training.* Norman: University of Oklahoma Press.

Katz, P. A. (Ed.). (1976). *Toward the elimination of racism.* Elmsford, NY: Pergamon.

Katz, W. L. (1986). *Black Indians: A hidden heritage.* New York: Atheneum.

Kaus, M. (1992). *The end of equality.* New York: Basic Books.

Keniston, K. (1960). Alienation and the decline of utopia. *American Scholar, 29.*

Kennedy, P. (1987). *The rise and fall of great powers.* New York: Random House.

Kennickell, A., & Shack-Marquez, J. (1992). Changes in family finances from 1983 to 1989: Evidence from the survey of consumer finances. *Federal Reserve Bulletin, 78,* 1-18.

Kinder, D. (1986). The continuing American dilemma: White resistance to racial change 40 years after Myrdal. *Journal of Social Issues, 41*(2), 151-171.

Kinder, D. R., & Sears, D. O. (1981). Prejudice and politics: Symbolic racism versus racial threats to the good life. *Journal of Personality and Social Psychology, 40,* 414-431.

King, A., & Schneider, B. (1991). *The first global revolution: Report of the Club of Rome.* New York: Pantheon.

Kinloch, G. C. (1974). *The dynamics of race relations: A socio-economic analysis.* New York: McGraw-Hill.

Kirschenman, J., & Neckerman, K. (1991). "We'd love to hire them, but ...": The meaning of race for employers. In C. Jencks & P. Peterson (Eds.), *The urban underclass* (pp. 203-232). Washington, DC: The Brookings Institution.

Kluegel, J. R. (1990). Trends in whites' explanations of the black-white gap in socioeconomic status, 1977-1989. *American Sociological Review, 55,* 512-525.

Kluegel, J. R., & Smith, E. R. (1982). Whites' beliefs about black opportunity. *American Sociological Review, 47*(4), 518-532.

Kluegel, J. R., & Smith, E. R. (1983). Affirmative action attitudes: Effects of self-interest, racial affect, and stratification beliefs on whites' views. *Social Forces, 61*(3), 797-824.

Knowles, L. L., & Prewitt, K. (1969). *Institutional racism in America.* Englewood Cliffs, NJ: Prentice Hall.

Kochman, T. (1981). *Black and white: Styles in conflict, Chicago.* Chicago: University of Chicago Press.

Kolchin, P. (1987). *Unfree labor: American slavery and Russian serfdom.* Cambridge, MA: Belknap Press of Harvard University Press.

Krauthammer, C. (1991, March 22). Bless our pax Americana. *Washington Post,* Sec. A, p. 25.

Kupers, T. (1993). *Revisioning men's lives: Gender, intimacy, and power.* New York: Guilford.

Kushnick, L. (1991). Race, class and civil rights. In A. Zegeye, L. Harris, & J. Maxted (Eds.), *Exploitation and exclusion: Race and class in contemporary U.S. society* (pp. 158-159). Oxford: Hans Zell.

Kushnick, L. (1995). Racism and anti-racism in Western Europe. In B. P. Bowser (Ed.), *Racism and anti-racism in world perspectives* (pp. 181-202). Newbury Park, CA: Sage.

Kushnick, L. V. (1981). Racism and class consciousness in modern capitalism. In B. P. Bowser & R. G. Hunt (Eds.), *Impacts of racism on white Americans* (1st ed.) (pp. 191-216). Beverly Hills, CA: Sage.

Kutner, B., Wilkins, C., & Yarrow, P. R. (1952). Verbal attitudes and overt behavior. *Journal of Abnormal and Social Psychology, 47,* 549-562.

Lacy, D. (1972). *The white use of blacks in America.* New York: Atheneum.

Ladner, J. A., & Stafford, W. W. (1981). Diffusing race: Developments since the Kerner Report. In B. P. Bowser & R. G. Hunt (Eds.), *Impacts of racism on white Americans* (1st ed.) (pp. 51-69). Beverly Hills, CA: Sage.

Landrine, H. (1992). Clinical implications of cultural differences: The referential versus the indexical self. *Clinical Psychology Review, 12,* 401.

Landry, B. (1987). *The new black middle class.* Berkeley: University of California Press.

LaPierre, R. E. (1934). Attitudes vs. actions. *Social Forces, 13,* 230-237.

Lash, S., & Urry, J. (1987). *The end of organized capitalism.* Madison: University of Wisconsin Press.

Layne, C., & Schwartz, B. (1993). American hegemony: Without an enemy. *Foreign Policy, 92,* 5-23.

Lerner, D. (1958). *The passing of traditional society.* Glencoe, IL: Free Press.

Levin, J. (1975). *The functions of prejudice.* New York: Harper & Row.

Levinson, H. (1976). *Psychological man.* Cambridge, MA: Levinson Institute.

Levy, C. (1968). *Voluntary servitude: Whites in the Negro movement.* New York: Appleton-Century-Crofts.

Linville, P. W., & Jones, E. E. (1980). Polarized appraisals of outgroup members. *Journal of Personality and Social Psychology, 38,* 689-703.

Lipsky, S. (1987). *Internalized racism.* Seattle: Rational Island Publishers.

Locke, H. G., & Walker, S. E. (Eds.). (1980). Institutional racism in American policing: A special issue. *Social Development Issues, 4*(whole No. 1).

Loden, M., & Rosener, M. (1991). *Workforce America!* Homewood, IL: Business One Irwin.

Lorde, A. (1984). *Sister outsider.* Freedom, CA: Crossing Press.

Loury, G. (1989). Why do we care about group inequality? In S. Shulman & W. Darity (Eds.), *The question of discrimination: Racial inequality in the U.S. labor market* (pp. 268-292). Middletown, CT: Wesleyan University Press.

Lynch, F. (1989). *Invisible victims: White males and the crises of affirmative action.* New York: Greenwood Press.

Lyotard, J. (1984). *The postmodern condition.* Manchester, UK: Manchester University Press.

Maass, A., Milesi, A., Zabbini, S., & Stahlberg, D. (1995). Linguistic intergroup bias: Differential expectancies or in-group protection. *Journal of Personality and Social Psychology, 68,* 116-126.

MacIntyre, A. (1981). *After virtue.* Notre Dame, IN: University of Notre Dame Press.

Macrae, C. N., Bodenhausen, G. V., Milne, A. B., & Jetten, J. (1994). Out of mind but back in sight: Stereotypes on the rebound. *Journal of Personality and Social Psychology, 67,* 808-817.

Macrae, C. N., Milne, A. B., & Bodenhausen, G. V. (1994). Stereotypes as energy-saving devices: A peek inside the cognitive tool box. *Journal of Personality and Social Psychology, 66,* 37-47

Marable, M. (1991). *Race, reform, and rebellion* (2nd ed.). London: Macmillan.

Marable, M. (1993). Race and class in the US presidential election. *Race and Class, 34*(3), 75-85.

Marks, M. (1993). Restructuring and downsizing. In P. Mirvis (Ed.), *Building the competitive workforce: Investing in human capital for corporate success* (pp. 60-94). New York: John Wiley.

Markusen, A. (1989). Dismantling the cold war economy. *World Policy Journal, IX*(3), 389-401.

Marx, G., & Useem, M. (1971). Majority involvement in minority movements: Civil rights, abolition, untouchability. *Journal of Social Issues, 27,* 81-104.

Marx, K., & Engels, F. (1972). *Ireland and the Irish question: A collection of writings by Karl Marx and Frederick Engels.* New York: International Publishers.

Mason, P. (1993). Accumulation, segmentation, and the discriminatory process in the market for labor power. *Review of Radical Political Economics, 25*(2), 1-25.

Mason, P. (1995). Race, competition, and differential wages. *Cambridge Journal of Economics, 19*(4), 545-568.

Mauer, M. (1990). *Young black men and the criminal justice system: A growing national problem.* Washington, DC: The Sentencing Project.

May, R. (1973). *The Southern dream of a Caribbean empire, 1854-1861.* Baton Rouge: Louisiana State University Press.

Mayo, C. (1982). Training for positive marginality. In L. Bickman (Ed.), *Applied social psychology annual* (Vol. 3, pp. 57-74). Beverly Hills, CA: Sage.

McArthur, L. Z., & Friedman, S. A. (1980). Illusory correlation in impression formation: Variations in the shared distinctiveness effect as a function of the distinctive person's age, race, and sex. *Journal of Personality and Social Psychology, 38,* 615-624.

McCaine, J. (1986). *The relationships of conceptual systems to racial and gender identity, and the impact of reference group identity development on interpersonal styles of behavior and levels of anxiety.* Unpublished doctoral dissertation, University of Maryland, College Park.

McCorkle, M. (1991). Grant versus Helms: Toward the new progressive era? *Reconstruction, 1*(3), 18-24.

McIntosh, P. (1988). *White privilege and male privilege: A personal account of coming to see correspondences through work in women's studies* (Working Paper Number 189). Wellesley College.

McIntosh, P. (1989). *White privilege: Unpacking the invisible knapsack.*

McIntosh, P. (1989, July/August). White privilege: Unpacking the invisible knapsack. *Peace and Freedom,* pp. 10-12.

McIntosh, P. (1995). White privilege and male privilege: A personal account of coming to see correspondences through work in women's studies. In M. L. Andersen & P. H. Collins (Eds.), *Race, class, and gender: An anthology* (2nd ed.) (pp. 76-87). Belmont, CA: Wadsworth.

Means, R. (1980, December). Fighting words on the future of the Earth. *Mother Jones,* pp. 22-38.

Mestrovic, S. (1994). *The balkanization of the west.* New York: Routledge & Kegan Paul.

Miles, R. (1989). *Racism.* London: Routledge & Kegan Paul.

Miller, J. (1993). The challenge of radical Islam. *Foreign Affairs, 72*(2), 43-56.

Mills, C. W. (1956). *The power elite.* New York: Oxford University Press.

Mirvis, P. (Ed.). (1993). *Building the competitive workforce: Investing in human capital for corporate success.* New York: John Wiley.

Mohanty, C. (1989-1990, Winter). On race and voice: Challenges for liberal education in the 1990s. *Cultural Critique,* pp. 199-208.

Montgomery, J. (1992). Job search and network composition: Implications of the strength-of-weak-ties hypothesis. *American Sociological Review, 57*(5), 586-596.

Morrison, A. (1992). *The new leaders.* San Francisco: Jossey-Bass.

Moyers, B. (1993). *Healing and the mind.* Garden City, NY: Doubleday.

Moynihan, D. (1989). Toward a postindustrial social policy. *Public Interest,* pp. 16-27.

Mukherjee, R. (1973). *The rise and fall of the East India Company.* New York: Monthly Review Press.

Murray, C. (1986). *Losing ground: American social policy, 1950-1980.* New York: Basic Books.

Murray, C., & Hernstein, R. J. (1994). *The bell curve.* New York: Free Press.

Myrdal, G. (1944). *An American dilemma.* New York: Harper & Row.

Nau, H. R. (1990). *The myth of America's decline.* New York: Oxford University Press.

Neubeck, K. J., & Roach, J. L. (1981). Racism and poverty policies. In B. P. Bowser & R. G. Hunt (Eds.), *Impacts of racism on white Americans* (1st ed.) (pp. 153-164). Beverly Hills, CA: Sage.

Nisbet, R. (1980). *History of the idea of progress.* New York: Basic Books.

Njeri, I. (1989, December 28). Facing up to being white. *Los Angeles News,* Sect. E, pp. 1, 6.

Noakes, G. (1994, February/March). Muslims on U.S. military make advances. *The Washington Report on Middle-East Affairs,* p. 85.

Noble, D. (1977). *America by design.* Oxford, UK: Oxford University Press.

Noel, D. L. (Ed.). *The origins of American slavery and racism.* Columbus, OH: Charles E. Merrill.

Noel, J. G., Wann, D. L., & Branscombe, N. R. (1995). Peripheral in-group membership status and public negativity toward out-group. *Journal of Personality and Social Psychology, 68,* 127-137.

Norris, C. (1992). *Uncritical theory: Postmodernism, intellectuals, and the Gulf War.* London: Lawrence & Wishart.

Oliver, M. L., & Glick, M. A. (1982). An analysis of the new orthodoxy on black mobility. *Social Problems, 29*(5), 511-524.

Ottavi, T. M., Pope-Davis, D. P., & Dings, J. G. (1994). Relationship between white racial identity attitudes and self-reported multicultural competencies. *Journal of Counseling Psychology, 41,* 149-154.

Pascal, A. H. (Ed.). (1972). *Racial discrimination in economic life.* Lexington, MA: D. C. Heath.

Patterson, O. (1972). Toward a future that has no past-reflections on the fate of blacks in the Americas. *The Public Interest.*

Perry, W. G. (1968). *Forms of intellectual and ethical development in the college years.* New York: Harcourt Brace Jovanovich.

Peters, C. (1992). *Collateral damage: The new world order at home and abroad.* Boston: South End.

Pettigrew, T., & Martin, J. (1987). Shaping the organizational context for black American inclusion. *Journal of Social Issues, 43*(1), 41-78.

Pettigrew, T. F. (1973). Racism and the mental health of white Americans: A social psychological view. In C. V. Willie, B. M. Kramer, & B. S. Brown (Eds.), *Racism and mental health* (pp. 269-298). Pittsburgh, PA: University of Pittsburgh Press.

Pettigrew, T. F. (Ed.). (1975). *Racial discrimination in the United States.* New York: Harper & Row.

Pettigrew, T. F. (1981). The mental health impact. In B. P. Bowser & R. G. Hunt (Eds.), *Impacts of racism on white Americans* (1st ed.) (pp. 97-118). Beverly Hills, CA: Sage.

Pinderhughes, D. M. (1987). *Race and ethnicity in Chicago politics: A reexamination of pluralist theory.* Urbana: University of Illinois Press.

Pope-Davis, D. B., & Ottavi, T. M. (1992). The influence of white racial identity attitudes on racism among faculty members: A preliminary examination. *Journal of College Student Development, 33*(5), 389-394.

Pope-Davis, D. B., & Ottavi, T. M. (1994). The relationship between racism and racial identity among white Americans: A replication and extension. *Journal of Counseling and Development, 72,* 293-297.

Pope-Hennessy, J. (1970). *Sins of the fathers: The Atlantic slave traders, 1441-1807.* London: Sphere.

Portes, A., & Zhou, M. (1994). Should immigrants assimilate? *The Public Interest, 116,* 3-18.

Powledge, F. (1991). George Bush is whistling "Dixie." *The Nation, 253*(12), 446-449.

Prager, J. (1987). American political culture and the shifting meaning of race. *Ethnic and Racial Studies, 10*(1), 62-81.

Prezzolini, G. (1967). *Machiavelli.* New York: Farrar, Strauss & Giroux.

Quarles, B. (1961). *The Negro in the American revolution.* Chapel Hill: University of North Carolina Press.

Rai, M. (1993). Columbus in Ireland. *Race and Class, 34*(4), 25-34.

Rawick, G. P. (Ed.). (1972). *The American slave: A composite autobiography.* Westport, CT: Greenwood.

Reagon, B. (1983). Coalition politics: Turning the century. In B. Smith (Ed.), *Home girls: A black feminist anthology* (pp. 356-368). New York: Kitchen Table Press.

Reed, A. (1992). The underclass as myth and symbol: The poverty of discourse about poverty. *Radical America, 24*(1), 21-40.

Reich, M. (1981a). The economic impact in the postwar period. In B. P. Bowser & R. G. Hunt (Eds.), *Impacts of racism on white Americans* (1st ed.) (pp. 165-176). Beverly Hills, CA: Sage.

Reich, M. (1981b). *Racial inequality: A political economic analysis.* Princeton, NJ: Princeton University Press.

Reich, R. (1991). *The work of nations: Preparing ourselves for 21st century capitalism.* New York: Random House.

Remini, R. (1977). *Andrew Jackson and the course of American empire, 1767-1821.* New York: Harper & Row.

Reynolds, L. (1992). Retrospective on "race": The career of a concept. *Sociological Focus, 25*(1), 1-14.

Reynolds, M. D. (1973). *Economic theory and racial wage differentials.* Madison: University of Wisconsin, Institute for Research on Poverty.

Riach, P., & Rich, J. (1992). Measuring discrimination by direct experimental methods: Seeking gunsmoke. *Journal of Post Keynesian Economics, 14*(2), 143-150.

Riedsel, P. L. (1978). Comments on Szymanski's racism and sexism as functional substitutes in the labor market. *Sociological Quarterly 19*(2), 351-354.

Rifkin, J. (1995). *The end of work.* New York: Putnam.

Ringer, B. (1983). *We the people and others.* New York: Routledge & Kegan Paul.

Rippy, J. (1931). *The United States and Mexico.* New York: F. S. Crofts.

Rodney, W. (1972). *How Europe underdeveloped Africa.* London: Bogle-L'Ouverture.

Roediger, D. (1991). *The wages of whiteness: Race and the making of the American working class.* New York: Verso.

Rolston, B. (1993). The training ground: Ireland, conquest and colonisation. *Race and Class, 34*(4), 13-24.

Rorty, R. (1989). *Contingency, irony, and solidarity.* Cambridge: University Press.

Rose, D. D. (Ed.). (1992). *The emergence of David Duke and the politics of race.* Chapel Hill: University of North Carolina Press.

Rosenau, P. M. (1992). *Post-modernism and the social sciences.* Princeton, NJ: Princeton University Press.

Rothbart, M. (1976). Achieving racial equality: An analysis of resistance to social reform. In P. A. Katz (Ed.), *Towards the elimination of racism* (pp. 341-375). Elmsford, NY: Pergamon.

Rubin, L. (1983). *Intimate strangers: Men and women together.* New York: Harper & Row.

Ruether, R. (1992). Patriarchy and the men's movement. In K. Hagan (Ed.), *Women respond to the men's movement* (pp. 13-18). San Francisco: Pandora.

Ryan, J., & Sackrey, C. (1984). *Strangers in paradise: Academics from the working class.* Boston: South End.

Ryan, W. (1976). *Blaming the victim.* New York: Vintage.

Ryan, W. (1981). *Equality.* New York: Pantheon.

Saenger, G. (1965). *The social psychology of prejudice.* New York: Harper & Row.

Said, E. (1978). *Orientalism.* New York: Random House.

Said, E. (1993). *Culture and imperialism.* New York: Knopf.

Sampson, E. E. (1989). The challenge of social change for psychology: Globalization and psychology's theory of the person. *American Psychologist, 44*(6), 914-921.

Saxton, A. (1970). Race and the house of labor. In G. Nash & R. Weiss (Eds.), *The great fear: Race in the mind of Americans* (pp. 98-120). New York: Holt, Rinehart & Winston.

Saxton, A. (1991). *The rise and fall of the WHITE republic: Class politics and mass culture in nineteenth century America.* London: Verso.

Schlesinger, A. (1992). *The disuniting of America.* New York: Norton.

Schmidt, H. (1971). *The U.S. occupation of Haiti, 1915-1934.* New Brunswick. NJ: Rutgers University Press.

Schruijer, S. G., Blanz, M., Mummendey, A., Tedeschi, J., Banfai, B., Dittmar, H., Kleigaumhuter, P., Mahfoug, A., Mandrosz-Wroblewska, J., Molinari, P., & Pettilon, X. (1994). The group-serving bias in evaluating and explaining harmful behavior. *Journal of Social Psychology, 134,* 47-53.

Schumann, H., & Hatchett, S. (1974). *Black racial attitudes: Trends and complexities.* Ann Arbor: University of Michigan Press.

Schumann, H., Stech, C., & Bobo, L. (1985). *Racial attitudes in America: Trends and interpretations.* Cambridge, MA: Harvard University Press.

Sears, D. O. (1988). Symbolic racism. In P. A. Katz & D. A. Taylor (Eds.), *Eliminating racism: Profiles in controversy* (pp. 53-84). New York: Plenum.

Sears, D. O., & Kosterman, R. (1991, October). *Is it really racism? The origins and dynamics of symbolic racism.* Paper presented at the annual meetings of the Society for Experimental Social Psychology, Columbus, OH.

Shalom, S. (1993). *Imperial alibis.* Boston: South End.

Sharbari, H. (1990). The scholarly point of view: Politics, perspective, paradigm. In H. Sharbari (Ed.), *Theory, politics, and the Arab world* (p. 51). New York: Routledge & Kegan Paul.

Shepard, A. W., Jr. (1970). *The study of race in American foreign policy and international relations.* Denver: University of Denver Press.

Shepherd, G. W., Jr. (1970). *Racial influences in American foreign policy.* New York: Basic Books.

Sherover-Marcuse, E. (n.d.). *Liberation theory: Part I. Axioms and working assumptions about the perpetuation of social oppression.* Oakland, CA: Unlearning Racism Workshops.

Sherover-Marcuse, E. (1986). *Emancipation and Consciousness.* New York: Basil Blackwell.

Shine, C., & Mauer, M. (1993). *Does the punishment fit the crime? Drug users and drunk drivers, questions of race and class.* Washington, DC: The Sentencing Project.

Shirts, G. (1975). *Star Power simulation game.* Del Mar, CA: University Associates.

Shirts, G. (1977). *BaFá BaFá simulation game.* Del Mar, CA: Simile II.

Shulman, S. (1984). Competition and racial discrimination: The employment effect of Reagan's labor market policies. *Review of Radical Political Economics, 16*(4), 111-128.

Shweder, R., & Bourne, E. J. (1982). Does the concept of the person vary cross-culturally? In A. J. Marsella & G. M. White (Eds.), *Cultural conceptions of mental health and therapy* (pp. 97-137). London: Reidel.

Simpson, G. E., & Yinger, J. M. (1959). The sociology of race and ethnic relations. In R. K. Merton, L. Broom, & L. S. Coltrell, Jr. (Eds.), *Sociology today* (pp. 376-400). New York: Basic Books.

Simpson, G. E., & Yinger, J. M. (1965). *Racial and cultural minorities: An analysis of prejudice and discrimination* (3rd ed.). New York: Harper & Row.

Singh, S., & Yancey, A. (1974). Racial attitudes in white, first grade children. *Journal of Educational Research, 67,* 370-372.

Sivanandan, A. (1990). *A different hunger.* London: Pluto.

Smith, A. W. (1981). Racial tolerance as a function of group position. *American Sociological Review, 46*(5), 558-573.

Smith, B., & Smith, B. (1981). Across the kitchen table: A sister to sister dialogue. In C. Moraga & G. Anzaldua (Eds.), *This bridge called my back* (pp. 113-127). Watertown, NY: Persephone.

Smith, J. (1986). *The concentration of wealth in the United States: Trends in the distribution of wealth among American families.* Washington, DC: U.S. Congress, Joint Economic Committee.

Smith, J., & Welch, F. (1989). Black economic progress after Myrdal. *Journal of Economic Literature, 27*(2), 519-562.

Smith, T. (1993). Postmodernism: theory and politics. *Against the Current.*

Sniderman, P., Piazza, T., & Tetlock, P. E. (1991). The new racism. *American Journal of Political Science, 35*(2), 423-427.

Sniderman, P., & Tetlock, P. (1986). Symbolic racism: Problems of motive attribution in political analysis. *Journal of Social Issues, 42*(2), 129-150.

Sobel, M. (1987). *The world they made together: Black and white values in eighteenth century Virginia.* Princeton, NJ: Princeton University Press.

Solomon, R. (1993). *Bully culture.* Lanham: Littlefield Adams.

Sonenshein, R. J. (1993). *Politics in black and white: Race and power in Los Angeles.* Princeton, NJ: Princeton University Press.

Stanback, H. (1980). *Racism, black labor and the giant corporation.* Unpublished doctoral dissertation, University of Massachusetts, Amherst.

Stanfield, J. H. (1991). Racism in America and other race-centered nation-states: Synchronic considerations. *International Journal of Comparative Sociology, 32*(3-4), 243-261.

Steeh, C., & Schumann, H. (1992). Young white adults: Did racial attitudes change in the 1980s. *American Journal of Sociology, 98*(2), 340-367.

Steele, S. (1990). *The content of our character: A new vision of race in America.* New York: St. Martin's.

Szymanski, A. (1976). Racial discrimination and white gain. *American Sociological Review, 41,* 403-414.

Takaki, R. (1979). *Iron cages: Race and culture in 19th century America.* London: Athlone.

Takaki, R. (1990). *Iron cages: Race and culture in 19th century America.* Oxford, UK: Oxford University Press.

Takaki, R. (1993). *A different mirror: A history of multicultural America.* Boston: Little, Brown.

Takaki, R. T. (1980). *Iron cages: Race and culture in 19th century America.* London: Athlone.

Tatum, G. (1934). *Disloyalty in the confederacy.* Chapel Hill: University of North Carolina Press.

Taub, D. J., & McEwen, M. K. (1992). The relationship of racial identity attitudes to autonomy and mature interpersonal relationships in black and white undergraduate women. *Journal of College Student Development, 33*(5), 439-446.

Taylor, C. (1991). *The ethics of authenticity.* Cambridge, MA: Harvard University Press.

Terry, R. (1970). *For whites only.* Grand Rapids, MI: Erdmans.

Terry, R. (1993). *Authentic leadership: Courage in action.* San Francisco: Jossey-Bass.

Terry, R. W. (1981). The negative impact on white values. In B. P. Bowser & R. G. Hunt (Eds.), *Impacts of racism on white Americans* (1st ed.) (pp. 119-151). Newbury Park, CA: Sage.

Thomas, R. (1990, March-April). From affirmative action to affirming diversity. *Harvard Business Review, 2,* 107-117.

Thomas, R. (1991). *Beyond race and gender.* New York: AMACOM, American Management Association.

Thompson, C. (1991, Winter/Spring). Can white heterosexual men understand oppression? *Changing Men, 22,* 14-16.

Thurow, L. C. (1976). Equity concepts and the world of work. In A. D. Biderman & T. F. Drury (Eds.), *Measuring work quality for social reporting.* New York: John Wiley.

Thurow, L. C. (1980). *The zero-sum society.* New York: Basic Books.

Tokar, D. M., & Swanson, J. L. (1991). An investigation of the validity of Helm's (1984) model of white racial identity development. *Journal of Counseling Psychology, 38,* 296-301.

Towers Perrin & The Hudson Institute. (1990). *Workforce 2000.* New York: Author.

Tuch, S. (1988). Race differences in the antecedents of social distance attitudes. *Sociology and Social Research, 72*(3), 181-184.

Tuttle, W. (1977). *Race riot: Chicago in the red summer of 1919.* New York: Antheneum.

U.S. Commission on Civil Rights. (1976). *Fulfilling the letter and spirit of the law: Desegregation of the nation's public schools.* Washington, DC: Government Printing Office.

Valentine, C. A. (1968). *Culture and poverty: Critique and counter-proposals.* Chicago: University of Chicago Press.

Van den Berghe, P. (1967). *Race and racism: A comparative perspective.* New York: John Wiley.

Van den Berghe, P. (1972). (Ed.). *Intergroup relations: Sociological perspectives*. New York: Basic Books.

Vittoz, S. (1978). World War I and the political accommodation of transitional market forces: The case of immigration restrictions. *Politics and Society, 8,* 49-78.

Waldinger, R., Aldrich, H., Ward, R., & Associates. (1990). *Ethnic entrepreneurs: Immigrant business in industrial societies*. Newbury Park, CA: Sage.

Walker, J. (1976). *The black loyalists: The search for a promised land in Nova Scotia and Sierra Leone, 1783-1870*. New York: Africana Publishing.

Walzer, M. (1971). *Political action: A practical guide to movement politics*. Chicago: Quadrangle.

Wann, D. L., & Dolan, T. J. (1994). Spectators' evaluations of rival and fellow fans. *Psychological Record, 44,* 351-358.

Weber, M. (1958). *The Protestant ethic and the spirit of capitalism*. New York: Scribner.

Webster's Ninth New Collegiate Dictionary. (1990). New York: Merriam-Webster.

Weinberg, A. (1935). *Manifest destiny: A study of nationalist expansionism in American history*. Baltimore, MD: Johns Hopkins University Press.

Weinberg, M. (1990). *Racism in the United States: A comprehensive classified bibliography*. New York: Greenwood Press.

Wellman, D. T. (1977). *Portraits of white racism*. New York: Cambridge University Press.

Westie, F. R. (1964). Race and ethnic relations. In R.E.L. Faris (Ed.), *Handbook of modern sociology*. Skokie, IL: Rand McNally.

Weston, R. F. (1972). *Racism in U.S. imperialism: The influence of racial assumptions on American foreign policy, 1893-1946*. Columbia: University of South Carolina Press.

White, P. V. (1981). Race against time: The role of racism in U.S. foreign relations. In B. P. Bowser & R. G. Hunt (Eds.), *Impacts of racism on white Americans* (1st ed.) (pp. 177-189). Beverly Hills, CA: Sage.

White, R. W. (1952). *Lives in progress*. New York: Holt, Rinehart & Winston.

Wilcox, P. (1971). To negotiate or not to negotiate: Toward a definition of a black position. In W. Chalmers & G. Cormick (Eds.), *Racial conflict and negotiations* (pp. 23-70). Ann Arbor: University of Michigan & Wayne State University.

Wilder, D. A. (1986). Social categorization: Implications for creation and reduction of intergroup bias. In L. Berkowitz (Ed.), *Advances in experimental social psychology* (Vol. 13, pp. 291-355). New York: Academic Press.

Wilkins, M., & Hill, F. (1964). *American business abroad: Ford in six continents*. Detroit: Wayne State University Press.

Wilkins, R. (1993). My friend, Jim Laue. *ICAR Newsletter, 5*(6), 1, 5.

William, R., & Kenison, R. (in press). The way we were?: Discrimination, competition, and inter-industry wage differentials in 1970. *Review of Radical Political Economics*.

Williams, E. (1944). *Capitalism and slavery*. Chapel Hill: University of North Carolina Press.

Williams, E. (1964). *Capitalism and slavery*. London: Andre Deutsch.

Williams, E. (1967). *Capitalism and slavery*. London: Andre Deutsch.

Williams, R. (1987). Capital, competition, and discrimination: A reconsideration of racial earnings inequality. *Review of Radical Political Economics, 19*(2), 1-15.

Williams, R. L. (1975). The BITCH-100: A culture-specific test. *Journal of Afro-American Issues, 3,* 103-116.

Wilson, F. D. (1979). Patterns of white avoidance. *Annals of the American Academy of Political and Social Science, 441,* 132-141.

Wilson, W. J. (1973). *Power, racism, and privilege: Race relations in theoretical and sociohistorical perspective*. New York: Macmillan.

Wolin, R. (1992). *Introduction to Jurgen Habermas: The new conservatism.* Cambridge: MIT Press.

Wolpin, K. I. (1992). The determinants of black-white differences in early employment careers: Search, layoffs, quits, and endogenous wage growth. *Journal of Political Economy, 100*(3), 535-560.

Woodward, C. V. (1966). *The strange career of Jim Crow.* New York: Oxford University Press.

Worden, O., Levin, G., & Chesler, M. (1976). Racism, sexism and class elitism: Change agents' dilemmas in combatting oppression. In A. Sargent (Ed.), *Beyond sex roles* (pp. 451-469). Los Angeles, CA: West Publishing.

Yans-McLaughlin, V. (Ed.). (1990). *Immigration reconsidered: History, sociology, and politics.* New York: Oxford University Press.

Young, R. (1990). *White mythologies: Writing history and the West.* London: Routledge & Kegan Paul.

Ziglar, W. (1988). The decline of lynching in America. *International Social Science Review, 63*(1), 14-25.

Zukier, H. (1994). The twisted road to genocide: On the psychological development of evil during the holocaust. *Social Research, 61,* 423-457.

Name Index

Subject Index

Affirmative action, reaction to: 15; in
    management, 141-144
Apartheid, dismantling of: 110

Capitalism, development of: 52; welfare:
    62-63; unemployed, 72
Civil Rights Act of 1964: 140
Class struggle: 52, 72
Coalitions: principle of, 41-2; definition,
    204; types of, 207-209; incentives, 213
Communism, fear of: 109

Discrimination, cost of: xix; reverse, 176-177
Diversity, in management: 144-148;
    corporate response, 148-151

Diversity training: 150; problems with, 180;
    advantages of, 181

Economy, egalitarian: 85

Foreign policy, racial aggression: 97-99;
    U.S. Civil War, 99-100; to World
    War I, 100-103; to World War II,
    103-106
Foreign policy and domestic civil rights:
    106-107; elite interests, 107-109

Helm's White racial identity theory: 3-5;
    contact, 5; disintegration, 5;

291

About the Contributors

Octave Baker is Psychologist and Senior Partner with Communication Training Consultants (Sunnyvale, CA). His work focuses on organizational development, cross-cultural and diversity training, and research. He is also a member of the Engineering Management faculty at Santa Clara University and holds certificates from the Stanford Institute for Intercultural Communication and the Society for Intercultural Education, Training, and Research. He was formerly Professor at Saybrook Institute in San Francisco.

Benjamin P. Bowser is Professor of Sociology and Social Services at California State University at Hayward, and Associate Editor of *Sage Race Relations Abstracts* (London). His research, grants, and consulting have focused on AIDS prevention, organizational management, and race relations. He has authored 25 journal articles and book chapters, and is editor of *Black Male Adolescence* (1991), *Toward the Multicultural University* (1995), and *Racism and Anti-Racism in World Perspective* (1995).

Robert T. Carter is Associate Professor of Psychology and Education, Program in Counseling Psychology, Teachers College, Columbia University. He has published extensively on black and white racial identity development, cultural values, psychotherapy, and career development. He authored *The Influence of Race and Racial Identity in Psychotherapy* (1995).

Mark A. Chesler is Professor of Sociology at the University of Michigan and a core faculty member in the Program on Conflict Management Alternatives, and Executive Director of Community Resources Ltd. He is author and coauthor of 16 books, including *Childhood Cancer and Family* (1987), and more than 150 journal articles, book chapters, and technical reports.

James E. Crowfoot is President of Antioch College. He was Dean of the School of Natural Resources and Environment and Professor of Natural Resources and Urban and Regional Planning at the University of Michigan. From 1989 to 1994, he served as Director of the Pew Scholars Program in Conservation and the Environment, and in 1985 cofounded the University of Michigan Program in Conflict Management Alternatives.

John P. Fernandez is President of Advanced Research Management Consultants, a Philadelphia-based consulting firm specializing in human resource and marketing issues that provides services in survey and marketing research, and corporate training. He is the author of eight books; the latest is *The Diversity Advantage* (1993).

Gerald Horne is Professor of Black Studies and History at the University of California at Santa Barbara. During 1995 he was a Fulbright Scholar in the Department of History at the University of Zimbabwe, and he is the author of *Fire This Time: The Watts Uprising and the 1960s* (1995).

Raymond G. Hunt is Emeritus Professor, Department of Organization and Human Resources, School of Management, State University of New York at Buffalo, and currently Program Manager, Hungarian Quality Management Initiative, SUNY/Technical University of Budapest, Hungary. He is author and editor of six books and more than 100 articles in psychology, organizational science, and management.

James M. Jones is Professor of Psychology at the University of Delaware, and Director of the American Psychological Association Minority Fellowship Program. He is past Chair of the Society of Experimental Social Psychology and a member of the NIMH Behavioral Science Task Force. He has written numerous journal articles and book chapters, and his pioneer work, *Prejudice and Racism* (1972), is being revised.

Louis Kushnick is Senior Lecturer in American Studies at the University of Manchester (United Kingdom), editor of *Sage Race Relations Abstracts,* and Vice Chair of the Institute of Race Relations in London. He has published extensively on race and class in the United States and Great Britain.

Patrick L. Mason is an economist and Associate Professor of Black Studies in the Department of Africana Studies at Wayne State University. His journal articles have focused on labor economics, political economy, and African American families, and have appeared in the *Review of Black Political Economy, Cambridge Journal of Economics,* and *Review of Radical Political Economy.*

Lillian Roybal Rose conducts the Lillian Roybal Rose Seminars, based in Santa Cruz, California. She is an educator and consultant in the area of cross-cultural communications, and presents seminars and workshops nationally. Her seminars help people of all backgrounds to reclaim pride in their roots through exploring shared experiences.

Walter W. Stafford is Associate Professor of Public Policy and Urban Planning at the Robert F. Wagner School of Public Service, New York University. He has contributed to Herbert Gans's (Ed.) *Sociology in America* (1990), James Jennings's (Ed.) *Race, Politics, and Economic Development* (1992), and has written widely about racism, public policy, planning, and politics.

Robert W. Terry is President of The Terry Group, a consulting firm that provides speakers and trainers in leadership, diversity, and organizational excellence. For more than a decade he was Senior Fellow and Director of the Reflective Leadership Center at the Humphrey Institute of Public Affairs of the University of Minnesota. He is author of *For Whites Only* (1971) and *Authentic Leadership: Courage in Action* (1993).